T0366908

THE I TATTI
RENAISSANCE LIBRARY

James Hankins, General Editor

THE BATTLE OF LEPANTO

ITRL 61

THE BATTLE OF LEPANTO

EDITED AND TRANSLATED BY

ELIZABETH R. WRIGHT

SARAH SPENCE

AND

ANDREW LEMONS

THE I TATTI RENAISSANCE LIBRARY

HARVARD UNIVERSITY PRESS

CAMBRIDGE, MASSACHUSETTS

LONDON, ENGLAND

2014

Series design by Dean Bornstein

Library of Congress Cataloging-in-Publication Data

The Battle of Lepanto / edited and translated by Elizabeth R. Wright, Sarah
Spence, and Andrew Lemons.
pages cm. — (The I Tatti Renaissance Library ; ITRL 61)
Includes bibliographical references and index.
Latin on the verso, translation on the recto.
ISBN 978-0-674-72542-3 (alk. paper)
1. Lepanto, Battle of, Greece, 1571, in literature.   2. Italian poetry — 16th century
Translations into English.   3. Latin poetry — Translations into English.
4. Spanish poetry — 16th century Translations into English.
I. Wright, Elizabeth R., 1963– editor of compilation.   II. Spence, Sarah, 1954–
editor of compilation.   III. Lemons, Andrew, editor of compilation.
PQ4123.L46B38 2014
851′.408 — dc23   2013032965

Contents

࿓࿒࿓࿒

THE BATTLE OF LEPANTO

Introduction

꒰ঌৎ꒱

A Banner News Event of the Renaissance

This volume casts light on how neo-Latin poets responded to and participated in one of the most widely reported international events of the sixteenth century: the Battle of Lepanto. Incited by the crusading Pope Pius V and fears of the westward expansion of the Ottoman Empire, Spain, Venice, and the papacy set aside longstanding differences to form the Holy League Alliance in May of 1571. On October 7, 1571, this coalition of western powers achieved a decisive and unexpected victory over the Ottoman navy. As news spread of a galley battle whose scale and intensity stunned even the most seasoned war veterans, poets responded with a speed we associate today with journalists and bloggers. Literary scholars have explored how Lepanto shaped the literary sensibility of Miguel de Cervantes, who lost use of one hand in combat. Others have examined how poetry of Lepanto in the vernacular languages of Spain and Italy informed distinct national identities. But this volume draws attention to a counterbalancing phenomenon that has attracted far less scrutiny: the large number of poets from diverse social contexts and regions who chose Latin as their medium.[1]

To capture the diversity of the Latin responses, this volume features the work of twenty-one poets (three anonymous) from Italy and one from Spain. The Italian poets featured here come from every corner of the peninsula, from Liguria to the Veneto, Tuscany to Naples (See Appendix II). From the Hispanic world, we feature the two-book epic of one of the most intriguing figures in the history of Renaissance Latinity: Juan Latino. A black African former slave, Latino rose to prominence in Granada, where he taught Latin to students preparing for university studies. To complement scholarly investigations of Latino's importance in the African Diaspora, we feature his Lepanto epic here in the context of the international republic of Latin letters, which offered the freedman a safe haven from the era's growing color prejudice.

An astounding number of poets chose Europe's only international literary language when they responded to Lepanto. The responses took shape immediately, as writers provided Latin songs to accompany the celebratory processions and triumphal entries that followed the victory, and continued into the early seventeenth century. We concentrate here on the first wave of responses that took shape from the moment news of the battle reached the Holy League realms and extend to just beyond its first anniversary (October 1572). Many of these poems were anthologized in the spring of 1572 by Pietro Gherardi, a lawyer from Borgo San Sepolcro (d. 1580). Evidence suggests, however, that this was a second printing for most if not all of these poems: for instance, the long epyllion by Guglielmo Moizio appears in another 1572 printing prefaced by a dedicatory letter to Alessandro Farnese dated the Ides of November, 1571, just over one month after the battle. Poems not drawn from Gherardi's anthology are found either in other smaller collections published during the first year after the battle or, as is the case for two of the poems, in manuscript. Though in many cases information is scarce, we have determined that the different poets we feature ranged widely in geographic provenance and educational background; details about their lives are included in Appendix II. Textual and contextual evidence suggests that all the poets we feature composed their works based on first-line bulletins, letters, and eyewitness accounts. As such, this collection shows how neo-Latin poets not only responded to a breaking news story but also consciously claimed relevance in shaping the cultural memory of a major international news event.

Historical Context, Part 1: Precursors

Lepanto was the largest galley battle of the Renaissance and also the last major clash involving the Mediterranean's nimble but fragile warships.[2] It also ranks as one of the bloodiest single days in military history, with an estimated forty thousand fighters killed and another ten thousand wounded. This naval encounter culminated a half-century in which frequent conflicts between Muslim and Christian fleets intertwined with commerce and cross-cultural contacts. In terms of Christian-Muslim relations, Lepanto followed from a religious divide that had shaped events in the Mediterranean from the 1453 fall of Constantinople. After their 1522 capture of Rhodes, the Ottomans retained the offensive in the eastern Mediterranean, threatening Venetian commercial and cultural preeminence. Ottoman alliances with North African client states, in turn, undercut Habsburg Spain's imperial ambitions. Five military clashes that preceded Lepanto bear special mention: Preveza, Djerba, Malta, Granada, and Cyprus. Time and again, the poems we selected allude to them as precipitating events or precursors to Lepanto.[3]

Preveza, 1538: An earlier Holy League alliance — led by Giovanni Andrea Doria, the renowned Genoese seaman — suffered a decisive defeat at the hands of Ottoman and North African forces under Khaireddin Barbarossa. For the European allies, the setback sowed mutual distrust that lingered for decades.

Djerba, 1560: A disastrous setback for the Spanish fleet, the battle transpired off the coast of North Africa, where Ottoman and North African fleets under Piali Pasha and Turghud Reis routed a contingent under Giovanni Andrea Doria, grandnephew and heir to Andrea Doria.

The Siege of Malta, 1565: An Ottoman fleet under Piali Pasha and Mustafa Pasha besieged Malta in May 1565, whose overlords, the Knights of Saint John, had controlled Rhodes until it fell to the Ottomans in 1522. The defenders repelled Ottoman forces after prolonged and intense fighting that inflicted devastating losses on both sides.

Granada's Morisco revolt, or Second Revolt of the Alpujarras, 1568–70: Several thousand Moriscos of Granada — descendants of the Hispano-Muslims required to convert to Christianity after 1502 — took up arms to resist a series of royal decrees that curtailed their cultural and economic activities. Philip II's half brother, John of Austria, ultimately defeated the rebels by unleashing overwhelming firepower on their strongholds, after which he oversaw the collective expulsion of approximately eighty thousand Moriscos from Granada to other parts of Castile, making no distinction between the small number of rebels and the majority who remained loyal to the crown. The same infantry units and commanders who suppressed the revolt fought at Lepanto.

Cyprus, 1570–71: Breaking a peace treaty with Venice, an Ottoman invasion force landed on Cyprus in early 1570. Nicosia fell in September 1570, but Famagusta held out until August 1571, when the Venetian governor, Marco Antonio Bragadino, surrendered to Lala Mustafa. News of Bragadino's torture and execution reached the Holy League fleet just days before the battle.

Historical Context, Part 2: Lepanto in Brief

While still awaiting news about Famagusta, a large Holy League coalition fleet converged at the Sicilian port of Messina in August 1571. John of Austria was its commander in chief, Rome's Marco Antonio Colonna its second in command, and Sebastiano Venier led the Venetian contingent. As they converged, Ottoman forces under the command of Ali Pasha, the brother-in-law of Selim II, had begun to sail westward toward Lepanto. For more information on the protagonists, see Appendix I.

By mid-September, the Holy League fleet had reached Corfu. There, the gruesome details of how Famagusta's Venetian defenders perished gave new impetus to the coalition forces, momentarily allaying the notorious conflicts among the allies. Meanwhile, the Ottoman fleet had taken a position at the Gulf of Lepanto. Each side anticipated that they would confront a much smaller enemy fleet. On the morning of Sunday, October 7, a Holy League advance force caught sight of the Ottoman fleet. As they prepared to fire, the wind shifted in their favor; in retrospect, many poets and chroniclers would attribute the changeable fall weather to divine providence.

Fighting began with a cannonade from the Holy League vanguard. Six Venetian merchant ships (galleasses) had been retrofitted with heavy artillery never before used in Mediterranean galley warfare. Firepower notwithstanding, once galleys from the opposing sides rammed and boarded one another's ships, fighting resembled the brutal hand-to-hand combat of infantry warfare on land, with the added danger to soldiers of the narrow galley decks. After a half-day of intense fighting, the initial destruction wrought by the Venetians galleasses, plus the ability of Holy League ships to keep their line-abreast formation, proved decisive.[4]

One particular mystery relates to how the Ottoman admiral died. First-line Spanish reports state that Ali Pasha died in the bloody combat that unfolded after Spaniards under John of Austria boarded the *Sultana*, the Ottoman flagship. Some reports described how one of John's lieutenants cut Ali's throat, though others reported he was killed by a musket ball. What we do know is that Spaniards displayed his severed head on a pike as a trophy. Eyewitness accounts maintained that the gruesome sight sapped fighting strength among Ottoman forces. The one Holy League setback came on the right seaward flank. There, Uluj Ali, the corsair governor of Algiers, outmaneuvered Giovanni Andrea Doria and then attacked the Maltese contingent, after which he escaped with thirty galleys intact. Uluj Ali's escape notwithstanding, the Holy League forces hailed a great victory after a morning of combat, at which point the victors shifted their focus to seizing war spoils.[5]

News of the victory incited celebrations across Catholic Europe, fomenting hopes of a renewed crusade against Islam and even Protestantism. For the Spaniards, intimations of divine providence redoubled two months later with the birth of the royal heir, Prince Ferdinand (December 4, 1571), an event fervently awaited since the tragic, unexpected death of Philip's previous heir, Don Carlos, a half-decade earlier. The ailing Pius V issued directives designed to channel the profits from the spoils to crusading purposes, still hoping to retake Constantinople and Jerusalem.

Reality would prove more Machiavellian than miraculous. Winter storms, exhausted troops and rowers, as well as lingering mistrust among ostensible allies prevented the coalition fleet from liberating Cyprus or attacking Constantinople. Pius V died in May 1572. The Holy League's own death knell was the separate peace Venice negotiated with the Ottomans, signed in March of 1573. Given this nebulous outcome, historians continue to debate the long-range strategic impact of the Holy League victory.[6]

Yet, as the poems in this volume attest, Lepanto's cultural resonance in Catholic Europe was profound. The feared navies of the Ottoman sultan and his North African client states had lost seasoned commanders, valuable weaponry, and thousands of Christian galley slaves. Indeed, many passages in this anthology draw on the rhetoric of holy war to exalt this turn of events. But many of these poems also bear witness to the devastating human costs of modern weaponry and acknowledge Mediterranean cultural reference points that transcend the religious divide. For this reason, some points of caution are in order.

Religious Conflict and Cross-Cultural Contact in the Mare Nostrum

Though both coalition navies sailed into battle with orders from their rulers to crush the "infidel," affinities that connected diverse Mediterranean nations remained vital, whether acknowledged openly or not. The militant Catholics who had gained the upper hand in Spanish government notwithstanding, Iberia's rich and varied Hispano-Muslim heritage continued to inform daily life in myriad ways. For their part, Venetians had longstanding trade relations with the Ottomans, though the siege of Cyprus had temporarily frozen the open diplomacy. The Ottoman battle orders at Lepanto provide a particularly eloquent testimony of cross-cultural ties and boundary crossing in the Mediterranean. High-profile converts to Islam led contingents at Lepanto, including the former Dominican friar Kara Hodja and the Calabrian Uluj Ali. Their biographies exemplify what the noted Ottoman scholar Giancarlo Casale calls the "Rumi [Turkish] challenge" to European identity. Such "renegades" fighting against the Holy League fleet had prospered in the cosmopolitan, meritocratic Ottoman navy, attaining status and influence that would have been limited to aristocrats in their home countries.[7] In terms of Europe's humanist traditions, the dominant crusading rhetoric coexisted with more moderate voices, some of which proposed an ethnographic line of inquiry that associated early modern Turks with ancient Trojans; this line of thinking could undercut normative Islamophobia.[8]

A major challenge for studies of Lepanto emerges from the need to adequately consider Ottoman perspectives on the events. Far fewer Ottoman documents survive, in part because the losing side chose to rebuild the devastated navy rather than dwell on the disaster. Furthermore, officials at the Ottoman Porte destroyed letters and memoranda once they had been delivered and read. Only a small number of Turkish chronicles are available in translation.[9] We thus propose this selection of poems as one further step in the ongoing effort to gauge the international cultural impact of Lepanto, fully aware of the need for a wider dissemination of Ottoman sources and Muslim perspectives on the battle.

Literary Context: The Vergilian Tradition

The poems in this volume show poets grappling with the complexities of empire, trade, and cross-cultural exchange in their own time. In Vergil they had a model for more nuanced explorations of the human costs of war in the early modern era. All the poems selected demonstrate a profound engagement with the Vergilian corpus. Most are composed in dactylic hexameter, the meter of all of Vergil's works; the two that are in elegiac couplets are Vergilian in characterization and lexicon. The selection was determined to highlight the depth and variety of the poets who engaged Vergil in writing about Lepanto.[10]

The Gherardi volume alone contains hundreds of poems in Latin about the battle. These poems range from epyllia to short, occasional poems, composed to celebrate the heroes of the battle through often enigmatic references. Here we find a dense clustering of the topical with the mythological, as current events and their protagonists are presented in an atemporal celebratory context. The depth of the poets' familiarity with Vergil enabled them not only to quote extensively from the ancient poet but also to adapt his works to these new circumstances, as they displayed their skill at *imitatio*. The poems also make reference in an equally searching way to Ovid, Horace, and Lucan. All three are poets of the early empire, but each offers something different: Ovid's fascination with *eros* meant an ongoing engagement with Venus, who is seen as important to this battle because of the role played by her toponym Venice; Horace's prominence as occasional poet of imperial victory made him a logical choice; and Lucan's focus on civil war and its toll, often recorded in terms of severed body parts, offers a wealth of phrases and descriptions these poets thoughtfully draw on.

But Vergil remains the primary source, for reasons that are not altogether straightforward. In many of these poems Lepanto is presented as a second Actium. Its setting off the coast of Greece provided a clear parallel with the battle of 31 BCE, when Octavian vanquished Antony and Cleopatra to become the sole ruler of the Roman world. The event was recorded in the eighth book of the *Aeneid*, on the hero's shield, where it is preceded by a teleological history of Rome. As David Quint has argued, the battle came to be seen, through texts such as the *Aeneid*, as the victory of West over East. A chapbook published a year after Lepanto ("Discorso sopra due grandi e memorabili battaglie navali") presented the two naval battles side by side along the lines of Plutarch's *Parallel Lives*, where a long description of Actium is then followed by one of Lepanto. To the extent that the *Aeneid* overall tells of the victory of the West over the East — of Rome over Troy — Lepanto comes to represent a latter-day version of that event. Moreover, the intervening elevation of Vergil to the status of Christian prophet because of his predictions about the birth of a miraculous child in *Eclogue* 4 led sixteenth-century poets to view the events at Lepanto more as instances of divine fulfillment than of historical replay. Such a view was aided by historical coincidence: the name of the pope who formed the Holy League, Pius V, echoed *pius* Aeneas's defining trait; both Marco Antonio Colonna and John of Austria, two of the three admirals in the Holy League, claimed Augustan lineage. Perhaps most striking, Aeneas's own name provides the adjective most often used for the weapons, *aenea* (bronze); through this the arms and the man are joined.

Key phrases such as "stans celsa in puppi" (Moizio, XXI), "dona ferentem" (Taglietti, XVI), and "paulo maiora" (Odescalchi, XVII) recur verbatim, also assuming the same metrical position as in their Vergilian sources. More complex examples of imitation abound. The simile of Laocoön as a bull struck by an ax is employed by Ottaviano Manini (XVIII) to describe the death of the Ottoman admiral Ali Pasha. While the intent of the simile is virtually identical in both cases, the poet has marked his difference from Vergil by subtle variations in the language. Vergil's "qualis mugitus, fugit cum saucius aram / taurus et incertam excussit cervice securim" (*Aen.* 223–24) becomes "qualis ubi ante aras percussus colla securi / procubuit taurus, mugitibus aera complet" in Manini. Sometimes the depth of knowledge of Vergil is only the beginning: Nicolò Paladino (V) echoes Aeneas's first words ("quis ante ora patrum Troiae sub moenibus altis / contigit oppetere," *Aen.* 1.95–96) but changes them slightly: "queis ante ora virum tot millia contigit orbis / oppetere ad scopulos Ithacae inter stragis acervos," thereby referring to the location of the Battle of Lepanto, which took place close to the island of Ithaca, and also indicating that Vergil's line is itself drawn from a similar line spoken by Odysseus as he, like many at Lepanto, wishes he had died a more glorious death as he floats in the waters not far from Naupactus.

Some of the poems exploit Vergil as a propagandistic poet of empire; that propaganda is always Christianized. These poems make the case that Lepanto is the intended purpose or fulfillment of the promise offered throughout the *Aeneid*, as they identify the three admirals as a new triumvirate: Lepanto becomes Actium revisited; Jupiter and Venus function as allegories for God and Mary. But at other times the Vergilian influence takes on a different cast. Here the propagandistic elements are balanced by poetic concerns; the fact that the poets draw on the *Eclogues* and *Georgics* (and *Culex*) as well as the *Aeneid* suggests that an imperial agenda is enriched by other interests, including lamenting the plight of the conquered and meditating on the role of the poet, especially in a time of war. In these instances Vergil offered a matrix for reflecting on the complexity of the event in an imperial setting. Many of the poems celebrate the battle as an advance for militant Catholicism against the Muslim-majority Ottoman Empire. But others mourn the horrific violence, air sympathies with Ottoman fighters, and report misdeeds by the victors. The poem by Juan Latino is a case in point. Here we are confronted often with a jarring juxtaposition of points of view: within two lines the poet veers from stating clear pro-Western sympathies to complicating that propaganda with anti-imperial examples. For example, a rare depiction of an enslaved Muslim rower on a Spanish galley initially relies on stereotypes of Moorish duplicity. After giving voice to the Spanish commander's threat of summary execution should he fail to row steadily into battle against the Turks, the narrator instead offers a moving depiction of the slave's longing for his lost home. Other examples abound: descriptions of the naval battle echo not only scenes from the shield of Aeneas in Book 8 but also vignettes from the boat race in Book 5 (which nuances the question of winning and losing) and echoes from the storm in Book 1, where the Trojans are struggling to survive; underworld scenes draw on *Aeneid* 6, as well as on *Georgic* 4, mixing the brightness of Elysium with the dark shadows of Orpheus. References to the story of Dido and Aeneas recur, but both sides are evoked: as often as there are quotations of Mercury exhorting Aeneas to continue the mission to Rome, there are also allusions to Dido as she watches the Trojan ships sail away from Carthage.

The purpose and power of poetry, a concern for Vergil throughout his works, shows up in a variety of ways here. In the *Ecloga Nautica* of Giovanni Antonio Taglietti (XVI), a Turkish poet's death is lamented (ll. 290–98), and in Moizio's epyllion (XXI) the horrors of gunfire are described as a kind of anti-poetry (ll. 641–

76). But it is in the use of Fama that the strongest statement about this theme is made. Even as the new technological advances of gunfire were changing the landscape of battle forever, so the development of another kind of transmission, the printing press, would forever change the place that news — and poetry — would occupy. The Vergilian figure of Fama, negative in the *Aeneid*, is sanitized here to become a personification allegory for the advances in communication offered by the increasing number of print publications. Lepanto, reported and examined in print with astounding speed, was a watershed event that parallels today's internet revolution or, perhaps more, the powerful effect of television in the broadcasting of news, striking for its pervasiveness and immediacy. Lepanto's immediate international resonance, amplified through broadsheets, letters, and printed poems, is the Renaissance news story that comes closest to a "news event" of our time, surpassing earlier news sensations in the Mediterranean, such as the Siege of Malta and the Fall of Rhodes.[11] This seismic shift accounts at least in part for the large number of prophetic poems about the battle: the speed of printing gave the impression that people were hearing about the event before it happened, following old prepress rhythms and expectations.

The importance of broadcasting the news through publication put Venice — whose print shops maintained their preeminence in the international book trade — on the front lines. Craig Kallendorf has argued eloquently for the twinning of Vergil and Venice at the start of the printing revolution.[12] But the impetus in these poems seems to be slightly different. Here we find again and again an insistence that Vergil belongs not to Venice but to Rome: many more of the poems that show strong Vergilian influence also show a bias toward the western Mediterranean, Rome and Spain in particular. It seems plausible to suggest that one reason for turning to Vergil in the aftermath of this particular victory was to insist on his Romanness, taken in two ways: as a victory for the Rome Aeneas founded and as a victory for the much beleaguered Roman Catholic Church.

A recent novel, *Altai*, by the Italian collaborative group, Wu Ming ("Anonymous"), offers a final insight into Vergil's contribution to this poetry. In the novel, Lepanto is presented as the disastrous end of the era that began with the destruction of Babel, an event misunderstood throughout history. To these authors, Babel was a gift God gave to ensure difference among people through language. Lepanto, with its imperialistic overtones, threatens that diversity and, as a result, threatens poetry.[13] Of all the poets, Vergil was best able to represent both sides perhaps because he often focused on the power and limitations of poetry. What is Vergilian about these poems is only superficially imperial—that is certainly there in the language, meter, manifest destiny. But the more interesting poets are those who sense exactly what Wu Ming senses—that poetry was threatened by Lepanto *because* difference was under siege—and they use Vergilian verse to counter this. As counterintuitive as it seems, it is precisely the apparently univocal language these poets choose—Latin over vernacular—that highlights the polyvocal quality of the experience. More broadly speaking, the multiple voices in Vergil's corpus offered opportunities for nuanced reflections on the Muslim adversary, even as Vergil offered a poetic language in which to celebrate and scrutinize empire.

A volume of this scope does not come to light without the support of many. To begin, we thank our editor, Leah Whittington, for her tireless work and thoughtful emendations. The University of Georgia has aided in multiple ways, from undergraduate and graduate research assistants Sam Baroody, John Bodin, Natalie Fort, Drew Lichtenstein, Rebecca Marshburn, Buck Pennington, and Ashley Vann; to the Departments of Classics and Romance

Languages, especially budget managers Rebecca Holcombe and Maryanna Axson; the Franklin College of Arts and Sciences; the Office of the Vice President for Research; the Willson Center for Humanities and Arts; the Office of Sponsored Programs; the Office of the Senior Vice President for Academic Affairs and Provost; Thomas Jordan of the Department of Geography; and the Athletic Association.

For funding received from external sources we are very grateful to the National Endowment for the Humanities, The Rockefeller Foundation: Bellagio Center, and the American Philosophical Society.

We are particularly indebted to the librarians of the Pierpont Morgan Library; Houghton Library, Harvard University; Rare Book and Manuscript Library, Columbia University; Biblioteca del Monumento Nazionale di Santa Scolastica (Subiaco); Biblioteca Angelica (Rome); Biblioteca Casanatense (Rome); Newberry Library, Chicago; Biblioteca Nacional de España; Real Biblioteca (Madrid); Biblioteca Histórica Marqués de Valdecilla (Universidad Complutense de Madrid); Biblioteca de la Casa de Velázquez (Madrid); and the Archivo General de Simancas (Valladolid).

We acknowledge a deep debt to scholars, colleagues, and friends who offered invaluable feedback on the project. In particular we thank Brendan Rabon, whose help at the critical moment with the notes was greatly appreciated. We also thank Noel Fallows, Michael Putnam, Doris Kadish, Geoffrey Parker, Alessandro Schiesaro, the participants of the Romance Languages and Classics Department Colloquia at the University of Georgia, and the students in Ancient and Renaissance Epic, especially Sara Hobe.

And last but not least we thank three patient partners, Antonio Quiroga, Johanna Lemons, and James McGregor (with an added doff to Ned); and we dedicate this volume to David Ferry and the memory of Anne, without whom this collaboration never would have come about, and to Icarus Lemons, as a *primum munusculum*.

NOTES

1. The last systematic examination of Latin poetry on Lepanto was Nunzio Vaccaluzzo's 1909 study, "Dei poeti latini della battaglia di Lepanto." There is an article forthcoming by Claudia Schindler, "'Barbarico tingi sanguine vidit aquas': Darstellungen der Schlacht von Lepanto in der neulateinischen Dichtung," (in *Krieg und Frieden in der Frühen Neuzeit*, edited by Marc Foecking and Claudia Schindler). For vernacular poetry of Spain, see López de Toro, *Los poetas de Lepanto*; and Randel, *Historical Prose*, 93–111; and for Italy, Dionisotti, "Lepanto nella cultura italiana."

2. We have selected essential sources from the voluminous bibliography on Lepanto, basing our account of the battle on Guilmartin, *Gunpowder and Galleys*, 235–68; and Capponi, *Victory of the West*. For recent studies of Lepanto targeted to generalist readers, see Barbero's detailed chronicle, *La battaglia dei tre imperi*; and Crowley's highly readable *Empires of the Sea*, which takes the story of conflict back to the 1453 fall of Constantinople.

3. For Preveza, Djerba, and Malta, see Guilmartin's *Gunpowder and Galleys*; and Capponi, *Victory of the West*, 42–66. On Granada's Morisco revolt, see Coleman, *Creating Christian Granada*, 181–66; and Hess, "The Moriscos."

4. See Guilmartin, *Gunpowder and Galleys*, 260.

5. See, for example, Giovanni Pietro Contarini, *Historia*, fol. 55v.

6. Readers can trace the contours of the debate by comparing Hess's seminal "The Battle of Lepanto," with assessments by Guilmartin (*Gunpowder and Galleys*, 253) and Capponi (*Victory of the West*, 370–72).

7. See Casale, "Ethnic Composition." For Ottoman perspectives on Lepanto, see Inalcik, "Lepanto in the Ottoman Documents"; and Lesure, *Lépante*. For Ottoman battle lines, see Giovanni Pietro Contarini, *Historia*, fol. 43v–47v. On the durability of Moorishness in Spanish culture, see Fuchs, *Exotic Nation*.

8. Hankins, "Renaissance Crusaders."

9. Capponi's *Victory of the West* does engage Ottoman chronicles, particularly Katib Çelebi's chronicle (in 1697 Italian translation), Ibrahim Peçevi's *Tarih*, and Mustafa Selânikî's *Tarih-i Selânikî*.

10. In addition to the Gherardi anthology, the numerous Latin poems circulated shortly after the battle are attested in Silvio Barsi's edition of the 1573 *De bello turcico* by Bernardino Leo as well as in two anthologies that featured Latin poetry along with poems in other languages, the 1572 *Raccolta di varii poemi Latini, Greci, e Volgari* and Luigi Groto's 1572 *Trofeo della vittoria sacra*. For bibliographies, see Göllner's *Turcica* (ca. 1572–ca. 1600); for Italy only, see Mammana's *Rime per la vittoria sul Turco*.

11. On Lepanto as news, see Barbarics and Pieper, "Handwritten Newsletters," 65–78; and Jordan, *Imagined Lepanto*. For further on the portrayal of Fama in Renaissance literature, see Hardie, *Rumour and Renown*.

12. See Kallendorf, *Virgil and the Myth of Venice*.

13. Wu Ming, *Altai*. On this collective, see http://www.wumingfounda tion.com/index.htm.

Figures

ʘ

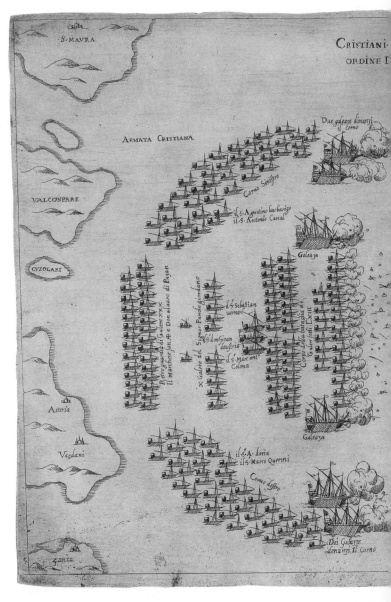

HI IN
ATE

C. fìgalo

ARMATA TVRCHESC HA

Natlico

Galato

Lepanto

dardanello

COLFO DE LEPANTO

dardanello

della gu. di Rodi

Cap della guardia d.Alessand

Partau bassa

Cap. della guardia de Metellin

Allì bassa

Cap' della guardia ti Algieri

Sirocco Cap'

O. Gialì

Ala

patras

Canigriza

Trapano

Cortopeli

Soline

racossa Cap'

int shops in Rome and Venice rushed to produce detailed depictions of Lepanto as soon
reports of the unexpected victory reached Italy. A popular iconographic program, shown
re, dramatized the first cannonade from the galleasses in the Holy League vanguard,
ile also representing the battle formations and the battle's exact geographic location.

FIGURE II. Martino Rota, "View of the Battle of Lepanto," Venice, 1572? From Newbe[rry] Library, Chicago, Novacco 4F 106. Photo Courtesy of The Newberry Library, Chicago.

...ry and cartography, history and myth, intertwine in this visualization of intense ...bat, in which Jupiter wields his thunderbolt for the Holy League in the top left, while ...Devil stands on the Ottoman shore side (top right). On the left, a hexameter poem al-...s to the three fleets joined by treaty and evokes the Holy League as another Holy Fam-...with Venice exalted as "alma urbs virgo" (gracious maiden city).

FIGURE III. *Map of the Mediterranean, ca. 1571. Prepared by Thomas Jordan, University of Georgia, Department of Geography.*

POLAND

LITHUANIA

MUSCOVY - RUSSIA

ia

Carpathian Mountains

Vistula

Kiev

Dniestr

Podolia

Dnieper

Don

Buda

Transylvania

Moldavia

Azov

HUNGARY

Khanate of Crimea

Mohacs

Temesvar

Sea of Azov

ia

Belgrade

Wallachia

Caffa

Transylvanian Alps

Bucharest

BLACK SEA

nia

SERBIA

Morava

Danube

Sarajevo

Monte-
Negro

Kosovo

Bulgaria

Sofia

Cattaro

Albania

Skopje

Macedonia

RUMELIA

Maritza

vo

Durazzo

Thrace

Valona

Monastir

Istanbul

Bosporus

Otranto

Thessaly

Salonika

Athos

Gallipoli

Ankara

RÛM

Corfu

Epirus

Mount
Athos

Hellespont

SEA OF MARMARA

Prevesa

Mytilene

Actium

Lepanto

*AEGEAN
SEA*

ANATOLIA

Cephalonia

*Gulf of
Corinth*

Zante

Athens

Morea

Paros

Naxos

Taurus Mountains

Tarsus

AN SEA

Cerigo

Stampalia

SEA OF CRETE

Rhodes

Finike

Aleppo

Canea

Candia

Castellorizo

Nicosia

Retimo

Crete

Cyprus

Famagusta

Tripoli

DITERRANEAN SEA

Syria

of
ra

Alexandria

Cairo

Nile

EGYPT

THE BATTLE OF LEPANTO

Nereidum Cantus ad Serenissimum Ioannem, Austriacum Caroli V. Imp. Aug. Filium

Carlo Malatesta

Litore cum primum classem deduxit Ibero,
et cursum Hesperiae magnae convertit ad urbes
invicti soboles pulcherrima Caesaris heros
Austriacus, mediis illi Nereides undis
5   laetitia oblatae ingenti plausuque fremebant.
Alma quibus myrrhae Tethys fragrantis odore
sparserat effusos humeris a vertice crines,
et studio incumbens cultuque ornaverat omni,
muscosos subter thalamos et murmure rauco
10   assidue flantis Zephyri, fluctuque strepentes,
quos intra aequoreae celebrant convivia nymphae,
Oceanoque patri caelesti nectare libant.
Unde abeunt laetae, si quando e gurgite vasto
prodire egregiisque viris occurrere gaudent.
15   Ut perhibent culto divini carmine vates
Argolicis illas heroibus occurrisse,
qui primi indomitos ausi transmittere fluctus
et tumidum curva pelagus sulcare carina,
velleris aurati spolium, laudemque petentes.
20   Ut quae ferunt multis manifesto in lumine visas,
auditas simul, Carolo trans aequora vecto
dum comites irent, quascumque adverteret ille
Austriadum famam protendens victor ad oras.
Illae igitur magni memores herois, ut ipsum
25   viderunt iuvenem gemmis ostroque decora
inductum chlamyde atque auro fulgentibus armis,

Song of the Nereids to the most serene John of Austria, son of Charles V, Holy Roman Emperor

Carlo Malatesta

When John of Austria, magnificent son of the unconquered emperor, first led his fleet from the Spanish shore and directed his course to the cities of great Hesperia, the Nereids rose from the depths of the waves to meet him, and they greeted him with great 5
joy and praise. Nurturing Tethys sprinkled their hair, cascading from crown to shoulder, with the scent of fragrant myrrh and carefully arranged it with great skill. Inside the damp caves resounding with harsh sounds from the ever-blowing west wind and 10
the waves, the water nymphs were celebrating feasts within, pouring offerings of heavenly nectar to their father, Ocean. They depart gleefully, joyful in the hope that if they rise up from the depths of the sea, they might catch sight of these famous men. For 15
the prophetic bards in their learned songs say that the nymphs came to meet the Argive heroes who first dared to cross the untamed ocean and plow the swollen waves in their curved boats, seeking glory and the spoils of the Golden Fleece. They also say 20
that nymphs were seen by many in broad daylight, and heard as well, when Charles traversed the waters with his company, extending the fame of the House of Austria to all the shores where he ventured. Now the nymphs were reminded of that great hero when they caught sight of the youth wearing a purple cloak deco- 25
rated with gems, and bearing weapons that flashed with gold.

quem proceres circumstabant, et lecta iuventus,
actutum agnovere, alacresque attollere voces
exorsae, has illi referebant ordine laudes,
30   Aonio late mulcentes aequora cantu:
     'Advenis optatus nobis dux inclyte votis
omnibus, ac laetam venienti assurgere iam nunc
Italiam cernes, quo te laus excitat ingens.
Instructumque opibus summis, et classe potentem
35   auspicio divum quo te rex maximus orbis
mittit, ut auxilio populis florentibus adsis,
praesidiis auctos vestro pro foedere qui se
cum videant tantis, iungant quas protinus omnes
expediunt nusquam deiecti in proelia vires.
40   Tum qui muneribus durisque laboribus acris
militiae praestant obeundis, undique claro
exciti sonitu, coeunt insignia laeti
sub tua, quae media praefers extantia puppi.
     'Hos animi praestans inter, pulchrisque sub armis
45   conspectus sese Farnesius inferet heros.
Romulidum commista duci de sanguine claro,
quem soror in lucem simul edidit ac tua; partu
felici Aeneadumque urbem et Latium omne beavit.
Hunc gladiis accincta phalanx comitatur acutis,
50   et iuvenum magna primi cinxere caterva
bellandi studio quoscumque aut Martia Roma
instructos ferro primis eduxit ab annis.
Assueti quicumque graves obiisse labores
venantum; rapidoque feras praevertere cursu
55   Eridani latis campis, seu rupibus altis
praecipiti fertur quas inter flumine Tarus.
     'Ipsa tibi auxilio transmittit et Umbria pubis
laeta ducem floremque suae, quem laudis avitae
accendit stimulis haud mollibus aemula virtus.

4

They recognized him immediately, surrounded by noble lords and chosen officers, and began to raise their delicate voices, singing his praise in turn as they soothe the waters far and wide with Aonian   30 song:

"You have come, glorious leader we have long prayed for. You will now see Italy rise in joy at your coming. Great praise awaits you there. Furnished with the utmost wealth and a powerful fleet, the greatest king of the world sends you with the blessing of the   35 gods, to offer aid to the flourishing people of Italy. When they see they are backed by the support your treaty promises, the Italians, never defeated in battle, will offer all the forces they can make ready. Then the soldiers, whose talent and fierce, steady efforts   40 outmatch any they encounter, will rise up on all sides with a clear shout and happily join together under the standards you display at the center of your ship.

"The Farnese hero will be among them, outstanding in his   45 bravery, distinguished in noble arms. Your sister married a duke from the famous family of Romulus's sons, and she bore her son on the same day that you were born. With this fortuitous birth she blessed the city of the sons of Aeneas and all Latium. A phalanx, bristling with sharp swords, accompanies him; his best young warriors surround him in a great throng, all raised by martial   50 Rome from earliest childhood, instructed in arms and endowed with a zeal for fighting. Every one is used to enduring the tough labor of the hunt, to overtake wild beasts in a speeding chase on the wide fields of the Po, or on the high cliffs where the Taro races   55 with its swift current.

"Fertile Umbria sends you her leader and the flower of her youth as reinforcement. Ambitious virtue and the harsh goads of

60   Ultro aderit magni monitis opibusque parentis,
     tum propria fidens virtute ac pectore forti.
     Tyrrheno exultans iam nunc et litore sistit
     advectus celeri montana per oppida cursu.
        'Huic et amore pari, cognato et sanguine iunctus,
65   it comes insigni forma et florentibus annis
     spectatus puer. Etrusci gens accola ponti,
     quem studio observat multo, placidoque parentis
     laeta sub imperio, nec segnes exigit annos.
     Gens dura, et manibus duros convellere montes
70   rupibus immanesque excindere sueta columnas,
     quae Parium vincant marmor candore nivali.
        'Quin Tiberis pulchra comitatus ad ostia classe,
     caelatam clypeo fulgenti ex aere columnam
     arduus attollens, sese feret obvius heros
75   inclytus. Haudquaquam mentis confidere sanctae
     consilium veritus pater est, cui maximus ille,
     plurima quem sacri penes est custodia cultus.
     Necnon et praestantem animi dimittere ad urbem
     egregiam, Adriaci egregiam decus aequoris urbem,
80   nimirum invigilat sancto cum foedere patris
     provida mens urbi regem adiunxisse potentem.
     Nunc etiam voti compos, hunc omnibus auctum
     auxiliis, ducis et defunctum munere summi,
     victorem bello toties, clarumque triumphis,
85   communes auspiciis laetis immittit in hostem.
        'Quisque igitur quanto divinae laudis amore
     accensus magis, hoc propius fortissime ductor
     ille tuis comitem properat se adiungere signis:
     seu pulchra Ausonia, regnisve oriundus Iberis,
90   quos tu consilio prudens moderabere multo.
     Et tua per benefacta oculos volventibus illis
     ardua quaeque dabunt divi superare ferendo.

ancestral glory spur him on. He comes of his own accord, bringing   60
with him the advice and wealth of his great father, while trusting
in his own virtue and brave heart; exultant, he now stops at the
Tyrrhenian shore, borne through the mountain towns on his swift
journey.

"With him, one in love and joined by the bonds of kinship and
blood, comes a boy admired for his looks and flourishing years.   65
The nation that borders on the Tuscan sea watches over him with
doting attention, happy under the placid rule of his father, and
he has not yet reached sluggish years. Theirs is a tough nation
accustomed to break hard rocks from the cliffs with their hands   70
for fashioning huge columns that surpass Parian marble in snowy
whiteness.

"Now the glorious hero, accompanied by his handsome fleet at
the mouth of the Tiber, will come to meet them, lifting the en-
graved column high on his flashing bronze shield. The Holy Fa-
ther did not hesitate to entrust the plan of his divine mind to that
great man responsible for guarding the sacred rites. No wonder   75
then that the pope with his farsighted mind took such great care
to send a man so outstanding in spirit to that remarkable city, the
pride of the Adriatic Sea, to join the mighty king with that city in   80
a holy alliance. Now his prayers are answered, and the pope calls
for Colonna, having completed his duties as grand admiral, so of-
ten victorious in battle and famous for his triumphs. He arms him
with reinforcements and blesses all the men before he sends them   85
out against the enemy.

"Every leader that burns with the desire for divine praise now
hastens courageously to join up as an ally under your standard.
You will govern them wisely with great counsel, whether they hail   90
from beautiful Ausonia or the kingdoms of Iberia. When the gods
have become aware of your good deeds, they will ensure that you
meet every challenge with perseverance. The monuments of your

Sic tibi magnanimi fuerint monumenta parentis
obvia, flectenti quaecumque ad litora classem.
95 Tum memori recolens animo sua fortia facta
invia nulla tuae virtuti erit aequoris unda,
obstabuntque tuis nullae conatibus urbes,
extremos donec protendas victor ad Indos
Austriadum nomen terris fatale regendis.
100 'Ite igitur summi ductu ducis, ite frequentes
invicto proceres spectati robore et armis.
Quaque viam virtus aperit, qua gloria vobis
monstrat iter, spondet qua Iupiter ipse triumphum
hostibus insignem victis contendite cursu.'
105 His dictis finem facerent cum deinde canendi
Nereides, Zephyrique implerent vela faventes,
continuo nova lux pelago terraque refulsit;
heroumque chorus candenti in limine caeli
astitit, ac roseum demisit ab aethere nimbum,
110 felices animae mortalis tempora lucis
defunctae, quae nunc vita meliore fruuntur.
Rodulfus generis clari, regumque ducumque
Austriadum priscus pater, ac felicibus olim
Romanum Imperium fatis sortitus. Et alter,
115 quod toties pugna victor superaverit hostes,
iure Triumphator pulchro cognomine dictus.
Proximus huic, verum spatio haud ita proximus aequo,
iustitiae pacisque ante omnia cultor et aequi
longaevus Federicus, et hunc prope filius orbis
120 imperium aeque iustitia tutatus et armis,
connubio felix nati felixque nepote
post patrios reges cui dives Iberia cessit
Austriaco commissa deum haud sine numine regi.
Tum gemini fratres aevi duo lumina nostri:

courageous father will be there to greet you, no matter what shore
you direct the fleet to. No wave of the sea that remembers his   95
brave deeds shall block the path of your virtue, nor shall any cities
stand in the way of your efforts until you, victorious, extend the
name of the House of Austria, fated to rule over kingdoms, to the
far reaches of India.

"Therefore, follow the direction of the supreme commander.   100
Go, crowds of noblemen, admired for your invincible strength and
martial skill. Wherever virtue opens the way, wherever glory shows
you a path, wherever Jupiter himself promises you a glorious tri-
umph, strive to conquer the enemy in your way."

With these words, the Nereids finished their singing, and, as   105
the favoring west wind filled the sails, a new light shone steadily
on sea and land; a chorus of heroes stood at the bright threshold
of the sky and sent down a rosy cloud from the heavens, blessed
souls who now enjoy a better life in heaven, having completed   110
their span of mortal light.

There was Rodulfus from a noble family, ancient father of the
kings and dukes of Austria, who inherited the Roman Empire
from the blessed Fates. Next, a man rightly called by the noble
name Triumphator, because he had so often been victorious   115
against the enemy in battle. Near him, but with a greater space
between, stands ancient Frederick, who upheld justice, peace, and
fairness for all; and near him his son, who guarded the empire of   120
the world with justice and arms. He was blessed in the marriage of
his son and blessed in a grandson, into whose hands, after its an-
cestral rulers, rich Iberia passed, entrusted to an Austrian king by
the divine will of the gods. Then the two brothers, the twin lights

125 Palladis et magni Carolus Mavortis alumnus,
qui totum implevit factis illustribus orbem,
Augustaeque recens sobolis decus, et pater et rex
optimus, ac veterum nulli virtute secundus
Ferdinandus. Ab aetheriis qui sedibus omnes
130 pro regali ostro gemmisque aurique corona
caesariem stellis redimiti ac luce decori
ostendunt sese interdum mortalibus: et nos
nostraque nunc etiam solita pietate tuentur.

of our age: Charles, child of Pallas and great Mars, who filled all 125
the earth with illustrious deeds, newest glory of the House of
Augustus, both a father and noble king; and Ferdinand, second to
none in the virtue of his ancestors. Seated on their heavenly
thrones, their hair encircled with stars and glorious light amid 130
royal purple and gems and a crown of gold, these souls reveal
themselves to mortal men from time to time. And they will watch
over us and our affairs with the same devout attention now and
always.

II

In foedus ictum inter principes Christianos

Belisario Gadaldini

Clarior en solito exsurgens natalibus undis
Cynthius afflicto passim nova gaudia mundo
nuntiat, haud sortis venturique inscius aevi:
scilicet ut reges inter sancita fideles
5   foedera sint hodie Venetam vulganda per urbem.
    'Surgite io iuvenes, manibus date lilia plenis,
spargite humum foliis, superumque altaria divum
muneribus cumulate piis pro munere tanto.
O quae fatidicae nobis felicia Parcae
10   tempora promittunt; o quae saecla aurea surgent,
cum Libyae extremo devictus Marte Tyrannus
occidet atque omnes una cum nomine Turcae.
Cernite ut ante alios firmati foederis auctor
ipse ingens pietate Pius, cui rector Olympi
15   turbine in hoc tanto terrae commisit habenas,
florentes populos inimica in proelia mittat;
quot rex Hispana gentes tellure Philippus
effundat bello assuetas et fortibus ausis;
quot Veneti cogant acies peditumque equitumque;
20   Italaque ut pubes animis ardentibus arma
arma fremat, raucoque simul clangore tubarum
et nemora, et silvae reboent collesque supini.
    'Parte alia innumerae leviter spirantibus Austris
carbasa tendentes scindunt vada caerula puppes,
25   barbaricamque petunt concordi foedere classem.
Quis tibi nunc, hostis, cernenti talia sensus?
Quove metu trepidas cum litora fervere late

: II :

On the treaty struck between the Christian leaders

Belisario Gadaldini

Behold! Apollo rises brighter than usual from the waves of his birth, bringing joyful news to the downcast world far and wide (for he is not ignorant of fate and of the age to come), that the holy alliance between the faithful kings be made known today 5 through the city of Venice.

"Rise, io! Young men, give lilies by the handful, sprinkle the ground with leaves, and pile the altars of the high gods with due offerings in thanksgiving for such a blessing. O, what blessed times the prophetic Fates foretell for us. O, what golden ages will rise, 10 when the Tyrant of Libya falls, beaten down in the final battle, and all the Turks fall, together with their name. See how before all the rest Pius himself, mighty in faith, author of the affirmed alliance, to whom the ruler of Olympus entrusted the reins of this troubled 15 world, sends his prosperous people into deadly combat. See how many people accustomed to war and great feats of daring King Philip pours forth from the Spanish land. See how many lines of infantry and cavalry the Venetians command. See how the Italian youth clamor for arms, with spirits blazing for battle, how the 20 glades and the forests and sloping hills echo with the harsh clanging of horns.

"Nearby, countless ships raise their sails to the lightly blowing east wind, slicing through the cerulean streams. United by their 25 treaty, they seek the barbarian fleet. What are your thoughts, enemy, when you see such things? Do you tremble with fear when you see the shores seething far and wide, and the whole sea cleft

13

prospicias totumque dehiscere classibus aequor?
Siccine iactabas tete, dum foedere rupto
30 Adriacis partem Cypri multo agmine nuper
cepisti? Tumidusque novo praecordia regno
non hominum, non ulla deum saeva arma timebas.
     'Iam video Oceano in magno concurrere utrimque
ardentes in bella rates, classemque rebellem
35 funditus everti, vastumque tumescere pontum,
dum rapido fractas absorbet gurgite naves
scuta virum, galeas, devotaque corpora morti.
Inde Dei classem victricia signa movere,
fervidus angustis qua faucibus Hellespontus
40 aestuat et longo sulcat duo litora tractu.
Hinc equitum turmas, peditumque hinc ire catervas
regnisque et populis stragem exitiumque minantes.
Euphratem Gangemque metu trepidare sub imis
fluctibus, et septem gemini tremere ostia Nili.
45 Iam video exanimem pulso cum milite terga
vertere et ad Scythicos cursum contendere saltus
Selimum ac sese extremis abscondere silvis,
illum sectari Hesperios animamque nefandam
eripere et media resupinum linquere arena;
50 atque ita devictis divino nomine Turcis,
urbibus eversis totoque Oriente subacto,
victores praeda immensa spoliisque potitos
in patrias urbes magnis remeare triumphis.
Tunc foliis redimita comas felicis olivae
55 candida Pax late populos inviset ovantes,
quam pia Religio incessu comitabitur aequo.
Tum fera bellandi rabies, et tristis Erinys,
tum Maomethaeae exitialia semina pestis,
Tartareasque domos horrentiaque antra subibunt.

with ships? Is this how you gloated when you broke the treaty
with the Venetians and captured part of Cyprus with a large   30
army? Swollen in your heart with pride in your new kingdom, you
did not fear the savage arms of men or gods.

"Now I see the ships come together on the great sea, eager for
battle; the rebel fleet is utterly destroyed, and the vast sea swells   35
up, as it swallows in a rushing whirlpool shattered ships, shields
and helmets of men, and bodies destined to death. Then I see the
fleet of God wave the standards of victory, where the seething
Hellespont writhes in its narrow jaws and cleaves a furrow be-   40
tween two shores with its broad current. I see squadrons of cavalry
marching here, and troops of infantry there, all portending slaugh-
ter and ruin to kingdoms and nations. I see the Euphrates and the
Ganges tremble with fear under their deep waves, and the seven
mouths of the twin Nile shudder. Now I see Selim, half-dead with   45
fear, his soldiers routed, turn his back and fly to the Scythian for-
ests to hide in the distant woods. I see the Hesperians pursue him
and end his hateful life, leaving him lying on his back in the mid-
dle of the sand; and when the Turks have been conquered in the   50
name of God, when their cities have been overthrown, and the
whole Orient is brought to its knees, I see the mighty victors re-
turn to the cities of their fatherland in triumph with great plunder
and spoils. Then brilliant Peace, her hair wreathed with lush olive
leaves, will visit the people rejoicing far and wide, and pious Reli-   55
gion will accompany her with an even step. Then the fierce hunger
for war, and sad Erinys, then the deadly seeds of the Muham-
madan plague will sink down to the dwellings of Tartarus with its

60   Aureaque laeto nascentur saecula mundo,
        saecula quae ventura olim volventibus annis
        veridici vates praesaga mente canebant.
         'Surgite io iuvenes, manibus date lilia plenis,
        spargite humum foliis, superumque altaria divum
65   muneribus cumulate piis pro munere tanto.'

grisly caves. And a golden age will be born in the happy world, an   60
age which the truth-telling bards once told us would come with
the revolving years.

"Rise, io! Young men, give lilies by the handful, sprinkle the
ground with leaves, and pile the altars of the high gods with due
offerings in thanksgiving for such a blessing."   65

: III :

Proteus

Cornelio Amalteo

Aurea Tithoni coniunx subtraxerat umbras,
pronaque puniceo velarat sidera vultu,
cum Sol Eoö tollens e gurgite currus
illustri magnum detexit lampade mundum.

5   Tum subito Adriacis Proteus sese extulit undis,
quem comitabatur flavos resoluta capillos
Cymothoe atque Hyale, niveisque Arethusa lacertis,
atque aliae vatem Nereides admirantes;
ut ventum ad litus, passim hic vaccinia nigra

10   pallentesque legunt violas mollesque hyacinthos.
Mox omnes circumsistunt, et carmina poscunt.
In medio Proteus altum iubet aequora murmur
ponere et Aeolios stridentia flamina ventos;
quo iussu placantur aquae, placantur et Austri.

15   Ipse autem canit ut nutu suspenderit orbem
rex superum qualisque hominum concrerit origo
informi ex limo; nec non elementa per omne
fusa genus, caeloque etiam labentia signa.
Tum memorat Phoebi cursus, Lunaeque meatus;

20   quid ferat Arcturus, quid verno Pleiades ortu,
quid tristes Hyades, quid desolatus Orion.
    His addit Lapithum media inter pocula rixas,
et dirum exitium Cadmi, vultusque Medusae.
    Tum miserae Inachidos deplorat tristia fata:

25   'Infelix virgo, quondam tu nectare digna

III

Proteus

Cornelio Amalteo

Tithonus's golden consort had dispersed the night shadows and
eclipsed the setting stars with her porphyry face, when the Sun,
driving his chariot out from the abyss of dawn, lit up the vast
world with his brilliant torch. Just then, Proteus emerged from the 5
waves of the Adriatic; Cymothoe was beside him, her tawny locks
hanging loose, and Hyale, and Arethusa with her snow-white
arms, and the other Nereids, marveling at the prophet. As they
come ashore, they wander about, picking blackberries, pale pan- 10
sies, and tender hyacinths. Soon they gather around and ask him
to sing. Proteus, in the center, orders the seas to quiet their loud
roaring, and the winds, their hissing gales. At his command, the
waters and the easterly winds grow still. Now he begins to sing 15
about how the king of the gods created the world with a nod, and
what sort of race of men had come from formless mud; and about
the elements diffused through all creatures, and the signs that sail
across the sky. Then he describes the courses of Phoebus and the
paths of the moon, what Arcturus portends, and the Pleiades in 20
the beginning of springtime, and the sad Hyades, and solitary
Orion.

To these matters he adds the quarrels of the Lapiths in the
midst of their drinking, and the terrible death of Cadmus, and the
face of Medusa.

Then he laments the sad fate of the pitiful daughter of Inachus:
"Unlucky virgin, once you were thought worthy of nectar and 25

et dulci ambrosia thalamoque toroque deorum,
nunc autem foliis, et amaro gramine tantum
pasceris, atque sitim limoso flumine pellis,
gramineoque iaces septis inclusa cubili.
30 Infelix virgo, quoties tu verba referre
conaris, toties auras mugitibus imples.
Ah pater, ah rector superum miserere puellae
iam miserere tuae finemque impone labori.'

Hinc Procnen Tereo convivia foeda parantem,
35 candentesque humeros Pelopis, Nisique capillos
commemorat. Post haec miseros decantat amores
Bistonii vatis, qui quondam coniuge rapta
ausus inaccessas Erebi lustrare tenebras.
Tartareum potuit custodem flectere cantu
40 et reditum ad superos optatae aperire puellae,
sed tamen incautum metus, et dementia vatem
invasit, sociamque viae iam luce sub ipsa,
iam iam Taenarii egrediens e liminis oris
respexit. Tunc illa iterum se Ditis ad umbras
45 corripiens, Erebi leges atque impia fata
visa queri, miserumque viri incusare timorem.

Tum canit insignem sacris Helicona Camenis,
Parnasumque orbis medium, laetosque per agros
Aonidum blando labentes murmure fontes.
50 Te quoque Pyrenes decus et Mavortis alumne,
cuius ob imperium caelo caput Austria tollit,
hoc tandem celebrat divinus carmine vates:
'Macte animo princeps, genus alto e sanguine divum,
qui modo coniunctas aeterno foedere classes,
55 magnorum regum classes, Venetique Senatus,
sublimi e specula totum praetexere pontum

sweet ambrosia in the marriage bed and couch of the gods. Now
you graze on leaves and bitter grass, and you slake your thirst in a
muddy stream, and you lie enclosed in corrals on a grassy bed.
Unlucky virgin, no matter how often you try to produce words,   30
you only fill the air with lowing. Ah, father and ruler of the gods,
take pity on the girl—pity her for she is yours—and impose a
limit on her suffering."

   Then he tells of Procne preparing the hideous feast for Tereus,
and the white shoulders of Pelops, and the locks of Nisus. Next   35
he recites the pitiful love affair of the poet Orpheus, who, when
his wife was abducted, dared to traverse the inaccessible shades of
Erebus. He succeeded in appeasing the guardian of Tartarus with
his song and earned the return of his much-desired wife to the   40
world above. But then careless fear and madness overcame the
poet: just as his companion had come to the edge of light, and he
was passing the boundary of the Taenarian threshold, he looked
back. At that moment she was swept down again to the shades of
Dis, and seemed to protest the laws of Erebus and her dark fate,   45
and to condemn her husband's wretched fear.

   Then he sings of Helicon, famous for the sacred Muses, and
Parnassus, the center of the world, and the springs of the Aonides
flowing through fertile fields with a pleasing burble.

   At last the divine prophet sings of you also, splendor of Spain,   50
and child of Mars, by whose authority Austria raises its head to
the sky:

   "Take courage, prince, divine offspring of a noble race, as
you look down from your high watchtower on the fleets recently
joined in eternal alliance—fleets of the great kings and the Vene-   55
tian Senate that cover the entire sea and display their robust

despicis, et validas Neptuno ostendere vires.
Eia age terribili Thracum pete fulmine puppes,
fulmine, quo mundi moles operosa pavescat,
60   et gentem sceleratam imo demerge sub Orco.
   'Tunc Asiae ingenti perculsus clade Tyrannus
abscindet manibus crines atque unguibus ora.
Mox irae impatiens praerupto e vertice saxi
sese praecipitem demittet in aequoris undas.
65   Hinc iuga servitio solvent et Maurus et Indus,
fallacisque dei ritus legesque profanas
contemnent, genitumque colent e Virgine numen,
et Romana ferent patrias vexilla per urbes.
   'Tum Parcae unanimes Saturnia saecula reddent
70   et rursus terrarum orbem Pax alma reviset.
Sponte sua fecundus ager flavescet aristis,
sponte sua molli sese rubus induet uva,
aureaque aeternum pendebunt arbore poma,
ac passim vario pingetur terra colore.
75   Ilice praeterea stillabunt dulcia mella,
et pecudes multo distendent ubera lacte,
colludentque lupis mediis in vallibus agnae.
Quin etiam placidis sternetur fluctibus aequor,
nec Scyllam pinus metuet, nec nauta Charybdim.
80   Spirabunt Zephyri tantum, quorum omnia flatu
ridebunt, totusque adeo laetabitur orbis.
   'Quare age, ne prorsus desint haec otia terris,
magnanima heroum soboles, iam sume potenti
arma manu; teque his quamprimum accinge trophaeis,
85   te Bellona ferox et te Fortuna sequetur.

strength to Neptune. Now go, attack the Thracians' ships with a
thundering crash, a crash that causes the onerous bulk of the
world to shudder, and sink that sinful race under deep Orcus.   60

"Then the Tyrant of Asia, smote by that mighty scourge, will
tear his hair and rend his face with his nails. Unable to bear his
anger, he will soon throw himself headlong off a steep rock cliff
into the waves of the sea. Then the people of Africa and India will 65
throw off the yoke of slavery and scorn the rites and profane laws
of a false god, and they will worship the God born of the Virgin
as they carry Roman standards through the cities of their father-
land.

"Then the Fates with one accord will bring back the age of
Saturn, and nurturing Peace will come again to the world. All on 70
its own, the fertile field will turn golden with grain. On its own,
the blackberry bush will clothe itself with tender clusters of fruit,
and golden apples will hang eternally from the tree. And ev-
erywhere the earth will be painted in all manner of colors. What's
more, sweet honey will drip from the holm oak, and the flocks will 75
swell their udders with milk. Lambs will frolic with wolves in the
valleys. And even the sea will lie flat with calm currents. Ships will
not fear Scylla, nor sailors Charybdis. Only west winds will blow; 80
everything will welcome their breezes, and the whole world will be
truly happy.

"Now go, brave offspring of heroes, take up arms now in your
mighty hands so that the earth does not lack this peace for much
longer. Brace yourself for these victories; fierce Bellona and For- 85
tune will follow you.

'Quid loquar Heliadum lacrimas, mutataque membra,
quidve piae Clymenes fusas e corde querelas,
cum Phaethonta polo deiectum fulmine vidit?'
   Omnia quae Musis Helicon, quaeque Ismarus Orpheo
90 audiit, ille canit; resonos dant litora plausus,
donec ad occultas redierunt numina sedes.

"What shall I say of the tears of the Heliades and their trans-formed limbs, or the complaints that loyal Clymene poured from her heart when she saw Phaethon shot out of the sky by light-ning?"

He sings everything that Helicon heard from the Muses, and Ismarus from Orpheus. The shores give echoing applause until the 90 gods withdrew to their hidden halls.

: IV :

[Dilectae miseranda Cypri dum funera cemit]

Marc Antonio Tritonio

Dilectae miseranda Cypri dum funera cernit
alma Venus, roseum os lacrimis suffusa decoris,
ingemit, et liquidum singultibus aethera complet.
Sed pater omnipotens celsi regnator Olympi,
5   'parce malis Erycina,' inquit, 'formosa querelis:
me quoque quos foetu profudit terra nefando,
ter sunt conati aeterna depellere sede,
arida ter dirae detrusi in viscera matris.
Pulchrum, nata, tuum vastet gens barbara regnum
10 et mea Cretaeam cunabula terreat Idam,
Illyricos penetret scopulos, abducat opimam
bellatrix praedam, et magnum tremefecerit aequor.
Vidistin' nostri sublimi nube ministram
fulminis in saturas infelicesque volucres
15 descendentem aquilam? Talis de litore Ibero
Austriacus iuvenis (tuus ingens Carole sanguis
virtutem ob summam caelo decus addite nostro)
fertur in adversam classem maiora paternis
viribus atque animis meditans. Huic aurea rident
20 sidera, dat cursus Zephyri levis aura secundos,
et placidi hiberno subsidunt tempore fluctus.
Monstra cadent inimica mihi: pars bracchia vinclis
assuescet, piceo pars caesa vorabitur igne,
sanguine permixtas proprio pars hauriet undas;
25 Cyclades e pelago attollent capita admirantes.

IV

[*When nurturing Venus beholds the tragic ruin*]

Marc Antonio Tritonio

When nurturing Venus beholds the tragic ruin of her beloved Cyprus, her rosy face flushed with shining tears, she groans and fills the open air with lamentation. But the all-powerful father, ruler of high Olympus, consoles her: "Beautiful Erycina, spare 5 yourself this sad complaining: three times the hateful spawn of the earth have tried to expel me from my eternal seat; three times they have been thrust back into the shriveled womb of their ill-fated mother. That barbarous, warlike race may lay waste to your beautiful kingdom, daughter, and may terrify my cradle, Cretan Ida. 10 They may penetrate the cliffs of Illyria, make off with the best plunder, and cause the great sea to tremble. But do you not see the eagle descending from the lofty clouds, a minister of our vengeance against birds that are fatted and unblessed? From the Iberian shore the Austrian youth is born against the opposing fleet — 15 he is your own flesh and blood, mighty Charles, you, exalted to heaven as a radiance on account of your supreme virtue — and he is planning great things with his father's strength and strategy. The golden stars smile on him, the light west wind grants him an easy 20 voyage, and the placid waves subside even in the wintry season. All the monsters I loathe will fall: some will grow accustomed to having their arms in chains; some will be slaughtered and devoured by pitchy fire, some will swallow seawater mixed with their own blood. The Cyclades will raise their heads from the sea in awe. 25

'At puerum latis victoria conteget alis,
felicem puerum, duce quo mihi Gnossia tellus
tuta satis; tu diva Paphon atque alta Cythera,
Iuno Samon, Phoebus Pindi iuga, Pallas Athenas
30   laeta colet: posito flavescent saecula ferro.'
Sic ait, et nutu stellantem concutit orbem.

"Victory will cover this blessed young man with her broad wings; with him in command, my Gnossian land will be safe enough. You will cherish Paphos, as Juno cherishes Samos, Phoebus, the ridge of Pindus, and happy Pallas, Athens. The ages will turn golden as swords are put aside." Thus he spoke and shook the starry orb with a nod. 30

: V :

Ad eos qui in sacra pugna obdormierunt

Nicolò Paladino

Felices animae, felicia pectora vestra,
queis ante ora virum tot millia contigit orbis
oppetere ad scopulos Ithacae inter stragis acervos
naumachiae, Thracum sumptis e funere poenis.

5   Ne violasse ferant vestrum se foedus inultos,
vestram Threicio decorastis sanguine dextram.
Illustri pugna victores fronde virenti
Phoebea crines Europae cingitis, unde
dat longas vestris pompas laeta ipsa triumphis

10   sol radiat sine nube diesi, aurisque tepescunt
intempestivis Zephyri, autumnalia plena
arva rosis, vario ac florum vernantia odore.

     Vivida vestra dedit virtus haec saecula in armis
venturis omni veneranda nepotibus aevo.

15   Vos immortales mortali lege creatos
dis miscent superis laurique et carmina vatum.

To those who died in the Holy War

Nicolò Paladino

Blessed are the souls, blessed the hearts of those whose lot it was to die at the cliffs of Ithaca before the eyes of so many thousands of men, amid the confused mass of slaughter in that sea battle where the sins of the Thracians were paid for by death. Let them not claim that they violated your treaty unavenged, for you deco- 5
rated your sword hands with Thracian blood. As famous victors in the great battle, you wreathe the tresses of Europe with Phoebus's greening leaves; where on a clear day, the joyful Sun offers long 10
processions for your triumph, and the west winds, with unseasonal breezes, warm the autumnal fields full of roses, made spring-like with an array of floral scents.

This age will be praised by future generations forever, thanks to your remarkable strength in battle. The songs and laurels of poets 15
will mingle you, made immortal by mortal law, with the highest gods.

[Hectora dum recolit maerens, illique parentat]

Alessandro Allegri

Hectora dum recolit maerens, illique parentat
urbs Raetico postrema iugo et pia funera solvit,
quippe memor magni quo se complexus amoris
praesidii hic vigilem curam sanctissime gessit.

5   Exstructi in medio tumuli, mirabile dictu,
Hesperiae simulacrum ingens, cui pectora crines
obstruerent, et taetra femur cupressus obiret.
Astitit, et tristem macie lacrimisque madentem
attollens vultum, sic inter sacra locutum est:

10   'Heu numquam celebrande satis toto orbe levamen
nate meum spolia haec aris circumdata, suntne
inclyta quae carae spondebat dextera matri?
Quae cum gramineis deberem cernere sertis
ornatum, et reduci generosae figere fronti

15   oscula; terribili deplorem morte peremptum
te, sociosque tuos, et clara ex stirpe nepotem.
Et mente intuear crudelia vulnera, et artus
mancipii quos strage fera laniarit avari
abiurata fides in libera colla furentis.

20   'Ah dirum facinus: fers ne execrabile monstrum
hoc tellus? Nec scissa cavo iam perdis hiatu?
Haud simile exitium tua te, mi nate, manebat
in divos pietas. Nimium sed cognita virtus
hosti visa potens. Docuit Salamina Tyrannum

25   te vivo pendere suis cervicibus ensem,
sanguine qui Thracium districtus tingeret aequor,

: VI :

[*A city in mourning pays homage to Hector*]

Alessandro Allegri

A city in mourning pays homage to Hector near the Rhetic ridge, and offers its final respects at his tomb, piously performing the funeral rites. He was the city's faithful and vigilant guardian, who never neglected the great love that embraced him there.

From the middle of the raised burial mound, an enormous im- 5
age of Hesperia appears, a wondrous thing. Her hair covers her breasts and a dark cypress tree hides her thighs. She stands, lifting up her sad face, stained and wet with tears, and speaks in the midst of the sacred rites:

"Alas, my son, my solace, if the whole world glorified you, it 10
would not be enough. These spoils of war that are strewn on the altars, my child, are they the tokens of glory that I, your dear mother, promised you with my right hand? I should have seen you crowned with grassy wreaths, should have planted kisses on your noble brow as you returned. Instead, I mourn you taken from me 15
by a hideous death, you along with your allies and a grandson nobly born. In my mind's eye I must look upon your cruel wounds and your limbs, savagely mangled by a greedy, oath-breaking slave, raging to free his neck.

"Oh, beastly outrage! Earth, how do you tolerate this atrocious 20
monster? Why not split open and engulf him in a gaping fissure? Your piety toward the gods, my child, did not earn you such an end as this. But your virtue, when it became known, seemed too strong to your enemy. It taught Selim the Tyrant that while you 25
were alive a sword hung over his head, which once drawn, would stain the water with Thracian blood and blaze the way for your

33

victricibusque viam signis patefaceret ardens;
dum peteret latebras regno spoliatus Eoö
tergeminum temnens numen bellator iniquus.

30   'Sed postquam hinc visum est superis te poscere, et inter
Indigetes sacro conspersum membra cruore
sistere, et aeternum sidus componere caelo,
ne cesses precibus divinam flectere mentem,
quo videam invictis percussi foederis armis
35   Selimi eversum imperium beluamque cruentam
infandi dantem sceleris per compita poenas.'

Haec dixit, subitoque leves recessit in auras
atque abiens templum divino implevit odore.

victorious standards until, stripped of his kingdom in the East, the
brutal aggressor would slink to his hiding places, cursing the tri-
une God.

"But now that the gods have agreed to bid you come and long 30
for you to dwell among them, since your limbs have been sprinkled
with sacred blood, and to become an eternal star in the sky, do not
stop beseeching the divine will with your prayers for such a time
when I might watch the invincible arms of the Holy League over-
throw Selim's empire, and see that cruel beast pay for his unspeak- 35
able sins at every crossroad."

She spoke these things, and then suddenly faded into the clear
air, filling the temple with her divine fragrance as she disappeared.

: VII :

Hymnus in Divum Marcum et Divam Iustinam

Davide Podavini

Aurea Lux salve, salve Lux septima sacra
Octobris, nostros multum miserata labores.
O praeclara dies cunctis celebranda diebus,
tot radians spoliis, tantis decorata triumphis.
5   Urite tura focis, Arabes comburite odores,
spargite humum redolente thymo, suspendite ad aras
virgineas laurus myrtumque hederasque nitentes.
Ac cuncti—genibus nixi iuvenesque senesque
nec non intonsi pueri innuptaeque puellae—
10   corde preces et voce novas fundamus ad aras,
muneribusque piis meritos solvamus honores.
     Haec est illa dies, qua quondam maximus urbis
Romuleae insigni Marcus pietate sacerdos
transiit ad superos, semper victurus Olympo,
15   quaque caput triplici virgo redimita corona
(virgo fuit, martyr, regali sanguine cretaque)
exuviis Satanae, carnisque onerata triumphans
Iustina e Patavi patria stipata caterva
caelicolum modulis plaudente volavit ad astra.
20   Vos, o vos magni duo lucida lumina mundi
salvete, aetherei proceres salvete Tonantis.
Credimus hac vestris hostem victricibus armis
victum luce, sua amissa iam classe superbum.
     Sacra pii cives statuunt altaria vestris
25   numinibus; cunctis statuunt volventibus annis
munere cum magno solemnes solvere laudes,

: VII :

Hymn to Saint Mark and Saint Justina

Davide Podavini

Hail golden light, hail sacred seventh day of October that pitied our hardships. O famous day, to be celebrated on all other days, gleaming with so many spoils, graced with such triumphs. Burn incense on the altars, burn Arabian fragrances, scatter the ground 5 with redolent thyme! Hang virginal laurels on the altars, along with myrtle and glossy ivy! Let us all, young men and old, bow on our knees; along with unshaven boys and unwed girls, let us pour forth new and heartfelt prayers before the altars. And let us pay 10 our due respects with pious offerings.

This is the day when Mark, once a high priest in the city of Romulus, renowned for his piety, crossed over to the gods to live forever on Olympus. On this day the virgin Justina, her head en- 15 circled with a triple crown (for she was a virgin, martyr, and of royal blood), flew in triumph to the stars from her homeland of Padua, surrounded by a cheering chorus of heavenly souls, weighed down though she was with flesh and the trappings of Satan. You, O you two lights shining over the whole world, hail, 20 and hail you princes of the heavenly Thunderer. We believe it was by your victorious arms that on this day our enemy was conquered, still proud even when his fleet was already lost.

The pious citizens build holy altars for you, their guardian spirits. They decree that a great service of solemn thanksgiving should 25 be carried out for every year to come, and that the town should be ceremonially purified with rituals and sacred prayers in the pious

atque adeo lustrare pio de more parentum
et pompis precibusque sacris solemniter urbem.
O iam audite, vocant votis, assuescite votis
30   numina sancta. Deum veterum procul este caterva,
este procul, procul ite lares, vanissima turba.
Non Martis Bellona soror cristata trilingui
angue comas, saevoque manus armata flagello,
ferrea non strepitu diro Mars fulmina torquens,
35   non serpentigeram quatiens hastam horrida Pallas
est opus hic nobis absint; fortissima bello
numina sancta adsunt nobis, genus omne Scytharum
est nihil haec contra, genus insuperabile bello.
Ergo agite, o divi, vestris succurrite telis;
40   aspicite in terras, nostros spectate labores,
armorumque graves iras, quas suscitat Orcus.
In nos Turca ruit, toto ruit agmine, et armis
tentat, cuncta movet, totis conatibus urget;
Christicolas tamquam genus execrabile passim
45   persequitur, torquens vinclis, ferro, ignibus, undis;
depraedatur opes, pueros rapit atque puellas;
totius ingentes orbis iam sperat habenas.
O quot iam tenet imperia, o quot regna gubernat
impius ille, Orci soboles? Asiatica regna
50   cuncta tenet dicione ferox, premit Hellada totam;
occupat imperio, lata dicioneque frenat,
quod rigat illustris Ganges et flumine Nilus,
Threicias urbes, longinqua binominis Istri
hostia in Europa; regna inter barbara clarum
55   cernitis (ah pudet haec fari) praesepe Tonantis,
et sanctum, claudi voluit quo membra, sepulchrum.
Ah pudet, indignum; ipso res damnata sub Orco.

manner of their fathers. O listen now, holy ones; they call to you
with their prayers. Receive their prayers! Let the rabble of old gods   30
stay away. Let the Lares keep their distance, useless mob. We have
no need for Mars's sister, Bellona, with three-tongued snakes in
her tangled hair and a biting whip in her hand, or Mars himself
with the dreadful racket he makes brandishing his flashing iron, or
bristling Pallas shaking her snake-bearing spear. They can leave us   35
alone, for it is our divine guardians who are mighty in battle. The
whole Scythian race, though unbeaten in war, is nothing against
them. So come, blessed ones, and defend us with your spears.
Gaze down on the earth; behold our struggles and the savage fury   40
for fighting that Orcus incites. The Turk rushes against us — he
charges with his whole throng and tests us with his arms. He mar-
shals his forces and attacks with all his might, just as that hateful
race harasses Christians everywhere, torturing them with chains,   45
iron, fire, and water. They pillage our wealth and abduct our boys
and girls. They dream of holding the mighty reins of the whole
world. Oh, how many empires does that faithless son of Orcus
already control? How many realms? He holds all the kingdoms of
Asia in his ferocious power and occupies all of Greece. In his vast   50
domain he rules over all the land that the famous Ganges and the
Nile river soak, the cities of Thrace, the distant lands in Europe
on the river Ister, which is known by two names. Within his bar-
barous kingdom you will find — oh, how it shames me to say   55
this — the Thunderer's famous manger, and the holy sepulcher in
which he wished his body to be enclosed. Ah, what a disgrace that
this place is condemned to the gods below.

Tempus adest, quo regna velint haec cuncta reposci
foedera Christigenum una coniurata piorum.
60   Militiae ardet amore piae Pius ille sacerdos
maximus, ad claras cui sedes Tibridis undas.
Et leo terrificus rugiens orientis in anguem
et caput, et caudam nunc tollit et altius alas.
Regali Austriadum heroum de stirpe Ioannes
65   horrisono bello quo non praestantior alter,
iam cupit in Turcas totas effundere vires.
Belligeros servate viros, servate secundis
auspiciis divi vestris Mavortia corda.
His opus est ducibus, ducibus quid clarius ipsis?
70   Hos super, o divi, illustris quos Brixia mittit,
praeclara de gente viros, virtute nitentes,
navarchos titulis clarisque ornate trophaeis.
At Stygios arcete canes, contundite monstra
fulminibus, madeant hostili sanguine campi.
75   Audio iam lituos, quos dant tormenta, boatus;
armorum strepitu caelum tonat, undique terra
pulsa tremit, resonant rupesque cavae, Indica clamant
litora, et accensus pulvis solemque polumque
involuit, nimbisque insuetis clauditur aer.
80   Horribilis Thracum consurgit ad aethera clamor;
dant strepitus lacerae puppes, iam gurgite vasto
merguntur toto, volitant per inane virorum
et capita alta, pedesque excisaque bracchia truncis.
Aequora purpureum referunt mutata colorem.
85   Ah divi, servate pios certamine in isto,
extentos prohibete arcus tormenta Scytharum,
et quicquid molitur Arabs Mahometus; at hostes
praecipites Acheronta petant, Phlegethontaque dirum,
atque ibi perpetuis crucientur in ignibus annis;

The time has come when the Holy League of pious Christians
must find the resolve to reclaim all these kingdoms. Pope Pius,   60
who resides by the gleaming waves of the Tiber, burns with the
desire to raise an army of the faithful. The dreadful lion roars at
the dragon of the East; he lifts high his head and tail, and his lofty
wings even higher. Born from the regal stock of Austrian heroes,
John is second to none in the din of battle. Now he wants to re-   65
lease all our forces against the Turks. Watch over our warriors,
blessed ones, and protect their warlike hearts with good omens.
We need leaders, and what leaders are more brilliant than these?

O blessed ones, adorn those sailors that famous Brescia sent   70
with titles and glittering trophies, for they are heroes of an illustri-
ous race, radiant with virtue. But ward off the Stygian dogs, strike
the monsters with lightning, let the fields drip with enemy blood.
I now hear the trumpets and the blasts from the cannons. The   75
heavens rumble with the crash of arms. The stunned earth trem-
bles and the hollow cliffs resound. Shores as far away as India
groan, and the burning dust envelops the sun and the sky, and the
air is choked by unfamiliar clouds. The horrible cries of the Thra-   80
cians rise to the sky. Mangled ships give a shriek before they
plunge into the vast abyss. Men's heads fly high through the air,
with feet and arms blown from their trunks. The sea takes on a
crimson shade.

Ah, blessed ones, watch over the faithful in this battle. Con-   85
found the Scythians' drawn bows and cannons, and whatever else
the Muhammadan Arab is scheming. Let the enemy rush straight
to Acheron and dreadful Phlegethon, and burn there forever in

90   spes foveat nulla illos, nulla piacula solvant,
quos non ulla tenet Christi pietasve timorve;
sed nostris, quibus oppetere heu contingit, apertos
caelituum liceat divorum intrare penates.
     Texite serta, rosae contexite suave rubenti
95   lilia, Apollinei laurus, hederaeque virentes
adsint, et sacrae frondes candentis olivae;
cingite martyribus meritis cava tempora sertis.
     Salvete illustres animae, gaudete beati
caelicolae Manes, quibus haec accessio tanta
100 facta, poli tantos o qui meruistis honores.
Sed quos incolumes servant caelestia fata,
iam date caelicolae, Marce et Iustina, potentes
ire per Armeniam signis victricibus atque
Threicias urbes, Libycas, Asiatica regna
105 atque Palestinae in primis arva inclyta magno
natali insignis Christi tumuloque nitentis,
et quicquid magno retinet curvamine Turca,
imperio lustrare, sacrum paeana canendo;
aurea sic tandem positis pax floreat armis.

fire. Let no hope encourage them, let no sacrifice redeem them; for 90
no Christian piety or fear held them back. But for those whose lot
it is, alas, to die, let them enter the welcoming homes of the heav-
enly gods.

Weave wreaths, intertwine blushing roses with sweet lilies,
bring out Apollo's laurel, the green ivy and the sacred leaves of the 95
glistening olive. Gird the spacious temples of the martyrs with
well-deserved garlands.

Hail, glorious souls! Rejoice, O blessed, heavenly shades; it was
you who fought this great battle, and you who deserve the honors 100
in heaven. But as for the men that the celestial Fates keep safe,
grant it to them, Mark and Justina, you heavenly powers, to march
through Armenia with conquering standards, and to gather under
their sway as they sing holy songs the cities of Thrace and Libya,
the kingdoms of Asia, and most of all the fields of Palestine, re- 105
nowned for Christ's great birth and the tomb where he lay so radi-
antly, and whatever else the Turk holds in the sweep of his great
power. When they finally lay down their arms, let golden peace
flourish.

: VIII :

In Mustafam

Giovanni Canevari

Ergo tot heroas, tot lectos Martis alumnos,
tot claros virtute viros, tot lumina belli,
adversus pactamque fidem foedusque receptum
ausus es indigna, Mustafa, extinguere morte?
5   Quorum et tu bello partum admiratus honorem,
et memoranda tuae stupuerunt gesta phalanges.
Testes, quos Lycia et latis Bithynia terris,
quos Babylon populos, quos solibus usta Syene,
quos dives palmis in proelia misit Idume,
10   pessime servorum Thracis, Mustafa, Tyranni;
divini, humani iuris temerator et hostis,
perfidiae monstrum saeclis infame futuris,
morumne exactis hanc faecem ducis ab annis
spadones inter viles et regia saepta?
15   An scelerum et dirae iampridem conscia mentis
hoc animo virus Stygia inspiravit Erinys?
Cum tibi tam celebris morderet gloria facti
pectus et invidiae stimulis agitaret iniquis;
parva quod innumeros Cypri pro moenibus hostes
20   sustinuit manus intrepide totiesque cecidit,
submovit, dedit in praeceps, conamina fregit?
An, cum non aliter domino praestare furenti,
spirantique minas tumide iactata valeres,
belli arte invictos toties expertus et armis
25   fraudibus exsuperas, et proditione nefanda?
Sanguineque illorum proprium delere putasti

: VIII :

On Mustafa

Giovanni Canevari

Mustafa, how could you dare snuff out so many men in a death
they did not deserve — so many of Mars's chosen followers, so
many brilliant, virtuous men, beacons in the fray — in violation of
the trust we offered and the treaty we sealed? Even you marveled 5
at the honor they won in battle, and your phalanxes were stunned
by the momentous deeds they carried out. Those men that Lycia
sent into battle can bear witness, Mustafa, as well as those from
broad-fielded Bithynia, and Babylon, and Syene with its burning
sand, and palm-rich Idume, that you are the worst of the Thracian 10
Tyrant's slaves, a defamer and an enemy of both divine and human
law, and a notorious symbol of treachery for ages to come. Are you
simply acting out the filthy habits you acquired from years spent
among vulgar eunuchs and royal stables? Did some Stygian Fury 15
who knew your sins and your cruel disposition long ago instill this
poison in your mind? When a small force of fearless men held
countless enemies at bay before the walls of Cyprus and killed so 20
many; when it then dislodged them, attacked them headlong, and
broke their ranks, did the grandeur of such a glorious exploit gnaw
at your breast and scourge you with envy's cruel whips? Or, when
in the same way you, who so often encountered men unmatched
in the art of war and weapons, failed by any other means to prevail
over your lord as he raved and spewed out threats in his arrogance,
did you overwhelm him with tricks and unspeakable treachery? 25
Did you think you could wash away your shame with the blood of

dedecus atque animum vel sic explere Tyranni?
Mancipii insignem laudem egregiumque triumphum,
si, quorum armatus virtutem atque arma timebas,
30   foederis obtentu prodens occidis inermes.
Non veritus Nemesim versantemque omnia sortem,
Fortunaeque vicem, ac eadem tibi posse rependi?
Debuit ingenuo saltem satis esse latroni,
contentum spoliis redimendae parcere vitae.

35   Heu quae te rabies, quis te furor impulit amens?
Laudem promeritos non una morte trucidas,
carnificis manibus crucias; crudeliter omnes
dilanias artus, foeda atque indigna relatu
omnia perpessis inter tormenta, necemque
40   obiectas Christum, probra ingeris, omnibus illos
traducis populis taetri spectacula facti.
Ipse suos fertur casum indignatus Apollo
avertisse oculos, facinus ne immane videret.
Infandique soli timuit contagia Nereus,
45   et tetigit trepido Salaminia litora fluctu.
Vicinaeque urbis refluens sub moenia Nilus
sustinuit dubium septena per ostia cursum,
contigua oppositae ne attingeret aequora terrae.
Aeolus indecorem referentia carbasa praedam
50   infamesque duces Boreali turbine adortus
non tulit insonti temeratum sanguine foedus,
sed fremitu horrendum increpitans et murmure saevo
contorsit, repulit, totum disiecta per aequor
allisit scopulis infestisque obruit undis.

others and in this way satisfy the will of the Tyrant? Glory worthy of a slave, a singular triumph indeed, if under the pretext of a treaty, you betray and kill unarmed those whose strength and fire- 30 power you feared even while armed. Are you not afraid that Nemesis or chance that turns all things, or the vicissitude of Fortune, will requite you in kind? As a natural-born thief, you should be happy enough to give up only your spoils in exchange for your life.

Alas, what madness, what insane rage drives you? You refuse to 35 slaughter praiseworthy men in one quick death, and instead you have your murderous minions torture them. You tear their limbs to pieces and, between their torture and their death, make them suffer things too foul and shameful to utter. You spurn Christ, and inflict such abuses, dragging those men before all of the people 40 like exhibits of your hateful actions. Apollo himself, they say, averted his eyes so as not to see this great atrocity, so appalled was he at these events. Nereus feared contagion from that unspeakable land, and so covered the shores of Salamis with a foamy wave; and 45 the Nile, retreating under the walls of the city it neighbors, held off its wavering course from the seven-mouthed delta, lest it come into contact with the waters that touched the opposite shore. Aeolus attacked the ships carrying these infamous leaders and their 50 unseemly spoils with the gusts of Boreas, for he could not bear that they had broken the treaty with the blood of the innocent. Roaring menacingly with thunder and fierce cloudbursts, he tumbled and tossed them about on the water, wrecked them on the cliffs, and sank them in the perilous waves.

55   At vos illustres animae, haec terrestria quondam
        corpora sortitae, caeli nunc regna tenentes,
        pro patria quibus et pro religione peracti
        mansuram et faustam patriam peperere labores,
        perpetuum quorum famae vix tempus et unus
60   vix satis orbis erit; pretio incertique brevisque
        temporis aeternae meruistis praemia vitae
        invideat vestris famam virtutibus hostis,
        aethereo invideat felices lumine sedes.

You, glorious souls, who once were allotted earthly bodies but   55
now inhabit the kingdom of heaven: the work you did for your
fatherland and your religion kept your country safe and flour-
ishing. One world and an endless span of time will scarcely be
enough for your fame. For the price of one brief and turbulent   60
lifetime, you have earned the reward of eternal life. Let the enemy
envy the fame of your virtues; let him envy your blessed home in
the ethereal light.

[*Luna ego, me Martis circumdedit undique terror*]

Maffeo Galladei

Luna ego, me Martis circumdedit undique terror
    et quo confugiam vix patet orbe locus.
Per terram fugiam? Leo saevit maximus armis.
    Per mare? Sunt Venetum carbasa tensa Notis.
5   Aera per vacuum? Volucrum regina fugavit.
    Per caelum? Petrus regna beata tenet.
Quid faciam moneas? Redde omnibus omnia; amicum
    te excipiet caelum, pontus, et aether, humus;
ni facias Styx atra manet, Letheaque regna
10   Cocytus, Phlegethon, Cerberus, Eumenides.

[*I am the moon; the fear of war has surrounded me*]

Maffeo Galladei

I am the moon; the fear of war has surrounded me on all sides,
and there is almost no place left on earth where I can take refuge.
Shall I flee by land? The mighty Lion rages there with his arms.
By sea? The sails of the Venetians are taut in the south wind.
Through the clear air? The queen of the birds has chased me   5
away. Through the heavens? Peter guards the blessed kingdom.
What would you advise me to do?

   Restore everything to its rightful place. The kind heavens, the
sea, the sky, and the land will receive you. If you don't, then the
black Styx and the realms of Lethe, Cocytus, Phlegethon, Cer-   10
berus, the Eumenides, await.

Inferorum Concilium Halysque Desperatus

Giovanni Battista Oliva

Duxerat armatas Euro spirante Liburnas
Halys amens, remisque frequens est vecta trieris
aequor in Ionium et Naupacti ad litora tuti.
Tunc omnis capta est, tunc Halys gurgite in alto
5   obruitur, miseramque animam depromit, et ipso
sanguine perfusus pelagi devolvitur imo,
Ausoniis ictus telis et caesus Iberis.
Nereidumque choris seu regnis Halys abactus,
Halys, qui nullos caelo terraque receptus
10   invenit: 'O nimium Manes aditure severos,
quaerenda en Ditis sunt subterranea regna,
quaerendi et Manes Stygio nunc gurgite nigri.'
    Ille petit vastas rupes, quaeritque Sicanas,
quae via sit miseris cunctis animoque revolvit,
15   mox lucos aditumque explorans Halys Avernos,
Tartareis regnis cupit ille abscondier imis,
exclamans, 'Positi sub terra o numina mundi,
ferte citi hinc Halym, Halymque irremeabilis unda
claudat, Styxque vadis liventibus ambiat atra
20   me invisum superis, Phlegethon perlustret anhelis
gurgitibus, rapidis flammis, quique aestuat igne.
Horrida me teneant vario nunc flumina cursu
errantem, resonans Cocytus sanguinis atri
vorticibusque furens spumanti in gurgite captum
25   me, me habeat magnis divis regique deorum

: X :

The council of the damned and Ali in despair

Giovanni Battista Oliva

In a mad panic Ali Pasha spurred on the war-ready Liburnian gal-
leys; the east wind was blowing, and his ship was borne onto the
Ionian Sea by steady strokes of the oars, all the way to the shel-
tered shores of Naupactus. His ship is seized, Ali is engulfed in
the deep abyss, and there he gives up his wretched soul. Drenched   5
in blood, he plunges down to the depths of the sea, pierced and
hewn by Ausonian and Spanish swords. Ali is driven away even
from the Nereids' kingdoms and choruses, Ali, who found no asy-
lum in heaven or earth: "O you who travel to the dreadful shades,   10
seek out the underground kingdoms of Dis and the black shades
in the Stygian abyss."

Ali seeks, he searches for the vast Sicilian cliffs, and ponders in
his mind the path all the wretched dead must take. He looks for   15
the groves and entrance of Avernus, and longs to hide himself in
the deepest kingdoms of Tartarus. He cries out, "O deities of the
underworld, quickly bear Ali away from here, and let the wave
from which none returns enclose him; let the black Styx encircle
me with its gloomy shoals — for I am hated by the gods — and let   20
the raging, fiery Phlegethon pour its stifling tides and consuming
flames over me. Let the horrid currents hold me as I tumble in
their turbulent flow; let echoing Cocytus, roaring in eddies of
black blood, seize me in its frothing whirl. And let the swamp by   25
which the gods and their king deign to make their oaths, the

iurari dignata palus, Styx sulphura volvens
sedibus et nigris Acheron me claudere discat
fluctibus ut exspes Lethaeis condar in altis.'
    Portitor ast senior, cymba qui flumina tranat
30   vidit ut has sontes animas Halymque superbum
astitit atque animam fugientem ad Tartara vexit.
Ille etenim gaudet Stygias innare per undas,
quem vectare iuvat praedam et depellere ad Orcum.
Ianua (dum levia incessit) devincta catenis
35   extemplo patuit, Ditis tunc regia nigri
et magnae scelerum facies, immania monstra.
Admittuntque Halym maerentem et fata vocantem
tristia. Tunc videas Manes occurrere eunti,
noctivagasque umbras, larvas, Lemuresque minaces,
40   tergeminumque canem, taetro qui ianitor antro
latratu aeternum Plutonia regna trifauci
custodit (referens horresco). Territus Halys
obtutu est primo, lacrimis luctuque tremiscit
arrectaeque comae misero et formidine presso
45   vox haerens. Tardos nequicquam extendere cursus
velle videtur et mediis conatibus aeger
substitit incassum; tenebris nam vinctus in ipsis
ducitur ad regis Rhadamanthi tecta vetusti.
    Aeacus Europae, Rhadamanthus crimina discit
50   Gnosius Aurorae populorum, Asiamque domando
fit solio iustus iudex spectabilis alto.
Continuo erumpunt portis, et sedibus illis
fit strepitus; nigros implexae crinibus angues
Eumenides adsunt, accurrit pallidus Orcus,
55   accurruntque umbrae passim, Luctusque Pavorque
adventante Haly, nec tristis mortis imago
longe aberat; comites veniunt ex ordine dirae.

sulfur-churning Styx, take me, and let Acheron learn to enclose
me in its black realm so that I may hide in despair in the deep
waves of Lethe."

The old ferryman, who crosses the river in a skiff when he sees
these guilty souls, stopped for proud Ali and carried his fugitive   30
soul to Tartarus. He is happy to sail through the Stygian waves; it
delights him to carry his plunder and cast it down to Orcus. Then
the doors, which are kept bound by chains as long as the insub-
stantial souls are there to attack them, opened suddenly to reveal   35
the kingdom of dark Dis, great shapes of sin, and gigantic mon-
sters. They let Ali in, weeping and calling on his sad fate. Then
you could see the departed souls rush to greet him as he enters,
and the night-wandering shades, ghosts, and menacing Lemures
and the triformed dog, which forever guards the door to the foul   40
cave, protecting Pluto's kingdom with its three-throated barking (I
shudder to remember). Ali is terrified at first sight, and begins to
quake with sobs of grief; his hair stands on end, and his voice
sticks, overcome with misery and fear. In vain, he seems to wish to   45
prolong his sluggish journey and limps along feebly, intermittently
starting and stopping. But it is to no avail, for, bound by the dark-
ness itself, he is driven to the house of the ancient king, Rhada-
manthus.

Aeacus examines the crimes of Europe, while Rhadamanthus
the Cretan king reviews the sinners of the East, for it was by con-   50
quering Asia that he became a just and glorious judge on his high
throne. Souls continuously break through the doors, and shrieks
rise from the halls. The Eumenides are there, with black snakes
woven in their hair; pale Orcus runs in, and the shades rush   55
around everywhere, and with them Grief and Fear. As Ali enters,
the sad face of death is not far absent. His fearful companions
come in one by one. He addresses the king and does not hesitate

Ille vocat regem et Plutonia quaerere regna
haud dubitat; tetra sedet iste inglorius arce
60   flammarumque globos volvens lucemque perosus.
Scire optat Manes adeat cur ille profundos
actutumque vocans Halym, cur lapsus ad imum
tunc Erebum, ad Stygias numquam revocabilis undas
venerit, effari iubet atris sedibus Halym.

65   Incipit has miseras veniendi expromere causas,
edocet atque umbras Halys, spargitque per omnes
tunc Erebi sedes: combustas igne triremes,
armorum fremitu captas seu turbine belli,
adventante Deo Christo, mersasque sub undis,
70   Thussagetas omnes vinctos, Selinumque trementem,
horrentemque diu pugnam (sic fatur et inquit)
perfusus lacrimis, lamentis, atque ululatu,
imperium extinctum iam iam dubitare, timere,
quaerere suppliciterque rogans tunc illius ergo
75   auxilium petere, et Ditis sua numina velle.
Convenere omnes umbrae, pater ipse vocatque
concilium Pluton, accurrunt undique Manes
Tartarei; facies omnes per stagna per antrum
itque reditque clamor sequiturque hunc infera Iuno,
80   nam neque Persephones valuit pietasque fidesque,
nostra nec Eurydice potuit compescere nigros
umbrarum coetus; strepit omnis gurgite daemon.
    Rexque Erebi regnum Christi producier usquam
non tulit immensum, non aequa mente tulitque
85   luctifica Allecto; Dirae hoc vetuere sorores
nocturnas ante aras, et solio sedet alto
immitis Pluton, quem progenies mala multa
circumstant, nigri concurrunt undique vultus

to ask about the Plutonian realms, while the king himself sits in-
gloriously in his foul citadel, whirling balls of fire and disdaining   60
the light; straightaway he summons Ali, wishing to know why he
visits the boundless shades, why he has fallen to the depths of
Erebus and come to the Stygian waves without hope of redemp-
tion. From his black throne, he orders Ali to speak.

Ali begins to explain the sad cause of his coming, and to in-   65
struct the shades, spreading the story through all the haunts of
Erebus: how his galleys were consumed by fire, captured in the
clash of arms or the confusion of battle; how at the coming of
Christ our God, they were submerged under the waves and all the
Thussagetae were put in chains; how Selim trembles and the bat-   70
tle still rages on. So he speaks, pouring out tears, laments, and
howls, and he tells them that even now he doubts and fears and
wonders whether the empire has been destroyed, and humbly begs   75
for the aid and the power of Dis on its behalf. All the shades as-
sembled, and Father Pluto himself convenes a council. From all
sides the shades of Tartarus rush in; they come through the
marshes and caves in every shape and form, raising a great ca-
cophony, and infernal Juno comes with them. For neither the piety   80
nor the faith of Persephone prevailed, nor could our Eurydice re-
strain the dark horde of shades; every demon in the abyss roared.

The King of Erebus did not allow the vast kingdom of Christ
to extend this far, and neither did doleful Allecto; the Dirae sisters   85
protested before their nocturnal altars, and so cruel Pluto sits on
his lofty throne. His many evil offspring surround him, and black
faces crowd around their king from all sides. You could see the

ad regem, videas umbrarum adstare phalanges:
90   Luctus, et ingentes Morbi, tristisque Senectus
et Metus atque Dolus, Curae stant, stat quoque Egestas
horrendae visu facies, Letusque Laborque,
et tenues umbrae simul omnes luce carentum.
Conciliumque petunt tales per limina pestes,
95   et Sopor et Bellum atque Atae concordibus ipsa
insinuans artes varias pacemque repellens.
Ulmus et annosa hic pallentes excitat umbras.
His Briareus adest flammisque armata Chymaera,
Gorgones, Harpyae, virosae et belua Lernae.
100   Monstra deum omnigenum obscuris qui sedibus orti,
nil nisi verba sonant ultricia plena minarum:
Tantalus, Ixion, Tytion, Sisyphusque, Diesque,
Noxque atra, et male suada Fames, Acherontis imago
Tartarea accurrens subito, praesensque Megaera,
105   et soror in tortis communis sibilat hydris,
haec eadem regis dictis obtemperat atri
acta malo, Allecto Stygiis se concitat alis;
natae Erebo ultrices dirae, Rabiesque, Scelusque,
et consanguinei simul omnes, Ira, Furorque,
110   maturare iubens gressum tunc Gorgone saeva
Ornaeo celeri invecta est pernicibus alis,
ocior est Ethonis vento, Nycteusque fremendo
currit Alastor equus, regis dum iussa facessunt.
    Haud mora, et ille furens animarumque agmina in unum
115   compellens Erebi dux mentem animumque poposcit
nigrarum umbrarum, et verbis ita fatur et inquit:
'Ecquid erit tandem rebus labentibus ultro?
Caelicolum regnum et Christum patiemur in omnes
terrarum fines labi, et sua numina pandi?

ranks of shades standing ready: Grief and grave Illness and sad   90
Old Age and Fear and Fraud and Worry are there, and even Pov-
erty — their faces terrifying to see — and Death and Labor, along
with the faint shades of those who lack the light. All these great
Plagues cross the threshold to the council chamber, with Sleep   95
and War and Delusion herself, who winds her cunning arts into
friendly factions to break their peace. Here the ancient elm rouses
the pale shades. Briareus is here, and the Chimera armed with
flames, the Gorgons, the Harpies, and beast of slimy Lerna. Mon-
sters come from every race of gods who rose out of the dark   100
realms, uttering nothing but vengeful and abusive words: Tanta-
lus, Ixion, Tityus, Sisyphus, both Day and black Night and unap-
peasable Hunger. The Tartarean spirit of Acheron rushes in, and
Megaera is there and her sister with her coiled, hissing snakes.   105
There is Allecto, heeding the words of the dark king, driven by
evil, soaring on Stygian wings. The cruel avenging sisters are there,
daughters of Erebus, and Ferocity and Depravity and with them
all their kindred: Anger and Fury ordering them to hasten their   110
step, along with the savage Gorgon, who is borne by swift Or-
naeus on nimble wings, faster than the wind of Ethon, and Nyc-
teus and the steed Alastor run in a frenzy as they perform the
commands of the king.

　　Without delay, the great ruler of Erebus rages and rallies the   115
troops of souls together, commanding the minds and souls of the
black shades. He speaks aloud and asks: "What will come of the
events that transpire above? Are we going to allow Christ's heav-
enly kingdom to reach all the ends of the earth, and his power to

120 Ventum ad supremum, socii. Spes omnis adempta est.
Scandite nunc superas simul omnes currite ad auras,
Aurorae et populis, animo, mentique Deoque
quem falso colere hi non cessant, prospicite omnes.
Tartarei proceres, rebus succurrite fessis.

125 Laeta modo en Christus passim sua gaudia pandit:
quidque Halys referat, quae nunc iam victa reportet
proelia dis superis, audistis; pellimur omnes
Tartareis regnis, Stygiis revocamur et undis,
ni prius ultrices iras mittamus in hostes,

130 Thracia ne subeat Christi monumenta Deique;
omnis Arabs, omnes dominentur iura Sabaei
nostra diu, nunc surgat adhuc Discordia in oras
aethereas, solvat pactum iam foedus, et Atae
omnia disrumpat. Selynus sua numina adoret.

135 Continuo exsiliant umbrae, nec sedibus istis
ulla quies adsit, superis furor, iraque mentem
praecipitent Italis, neu possint rumpere in oras
Thussagetas.' Celeres adlabi Strymonis undas
linquere Tartareas sedes, et regna malorum

140 certatim hoc studio Manes cupiere nocendi.
Erumpunt alacres portis Fraudesque Timorque,
terribiles visu formae, spargitque venenum
quaeque suum atque adeunt praestanti nomine reges
magnanimosque duces, populos, sanctumque senatum,

145 et coniuratos agitans Discordia fratres
nequicquam effundit virus, sed victa fatiscit.
Irrita concilia atque odiis agitata nefandis
cernere erit, frustraque animis elata superbis.

swell? Allies, the end has come; all hope is lost. Rise now and go,   120
all at once, to the air above. Watch over the people of the East,
their hearts and minds, and the false god they never cease to wor-
ship. Chiefs of Tartarus, help their worn-out cause. See how   125
Christ spreads his happy blessings all around. You have heard
what Ali reports, the battles he claims have already been won by
the gods above. We shall all be banished to the realms of Tartarus
and called back to the Stygian waves, unless we first unleash the
wrath of vengeance on our enemies. Do not let the monuments   130
of Thrace fall to Christ and God. Let every Arab and all the Sa-
baeans long have rightful dominion there. Now let Discord rise to
the heavenly shores and dissolve the treaty they made, and let
Delusion shatter everything. Let Selim worship his gods. Let the
shades rise up as they will, and give their homes no peace or quiet;   135
let rage and wrath swoop down on the lofty Italians, so that they
cannot breech the Thussagetan shores." The shades long to slip
through the swift currents of Strymon and leave the Tartarean
realms and the kingdoms of the wicked, vying with each other in   140
their eagerness to do harm. Fraud and Fear, fearful shapes to see,
swiftly break through the gates. Each spreads his own poison; they
go to famous kings and noble dukes and their people and the holy
Senate. Discord torments sworn brothers, but injects her venom   145
to no avail and collapses in defeat. You will behold assemblies
stirred by unspeakable hatreds, but to no purpose; the arrogant
spirits interfere in vain.

     Haec eadem dubitas diras voluisse sorores
150   commaculare arma, et foedus disrumpere initum?
     Cedite Cantharides, cessent odia aspera vobis
     lucifugi coetus Manes, umbraeque procaces
     cedite, deiectae flagranti flumine Olympi
     immundae facies, saeclis labentibus omne
155   aeternumque Dei regnum, Christique sacerdos
     ante aras stabit, plena qui spargat acerra
     continuo myrrhae liquidos, qui fundat odores.
     Intactae Ausoniis stabunt per saecula leges.
     Et Selyni regnum nostris popularier armis
160   quisque dabit, quamvis Manes, Orcusque timorque
     infernique omnes adsint, et regia Ditis
     suspiciat Selynum lugentem, et fata dolentem.
     Ergo agite, o sacros fontes, pia numina, divos
     qui colitis, bello audentes, armisque potentes
165   este precor firmis animis, rebusque paratis.
     Vincere nam vestrum, victos concurrite in hostes.
     Spiritus et cessent picea caligine nigri,
     nunc omnes sileant umbrae, Manesque profundi
     adventante Deo Christo, divisque beatis
170   caelicolis, adsint praesentia numina coeptis.
     Interea iussu Rhadamanthi iudicis Halys
     obrutus est tenebris, ut caeco carcere opacis
     aeternosque focis vitam traducat in annos.
     Nunc inter luctus, lacrimas, uncosque tridentes,
175   Hydras, seu Sphyngas, interque horrentia monstra.

Do you doubt that the Furies resolved to stain these arms and 150
break the treaty that was sealed? Give way, you poisonous flies: let
the shades of this light-fearing assembly hold back your bitter ha-
tred. Yield, insolent shadows, you vile forms cast down from the
fiery river of Olympus. As the centuries pass, the entire eternal 155
kingdom of God and Christ's priest will stand before the altars,
sprinkling and pouring fluid fragrances of myrrh from the laden
incense box. The Ausonians' laws will remain intact through the
centuries. The pope will turn over Selim's kingdom to our armies
to be destroyed, even as the shades, and Orcus and Fear, and all of 160
the damned stand by; and the palace of Dis will look on at Selim
as he grieves and laments his lot. So go, you who worship the sa-
cred fountains, the saints, and the gods, you who are daring in
battle and mighty in arms, I pray you, keep in good spirits for the 165
work you have begun. For victory is yours; charge against the con-
quered enemy and let the dark spirits retire to the pitch-black
gloom. Now let all the shades and the abysmal Manes be silent at
the coming of Christ our God and the blessed, heavenly saints. 170
Let the divine powers attend these undertakings. Meanwhile, by
the order of judge Rhadamanthus, Ali is buried in darkness to
spend endless years in a blind prison, amid dark fires — among
groans, tears, and hooked tridents; among Hydras, sphinxes, and 175
bristling monsters.

In pictorem eandem Victoriam fingentem

Anonymous

En Phlegrea phalanx dum versat remige pontum
excidium Hesperiae intentans; dum fulmine saevo
perfidus Endymion in terras arietat hostis,
ut cadat, ut magni pereat sub lege tonantis.
5   En pater omnipotens tandem miseratus ab alto
immeritas clades, inimica in proelia misit
tergeminam coniunctam aciem, quae classibus agmen
protinus infandum liquidis immersit in undis.
Obstupuit caelum; tonuit domus ardua Olympi.
10   Infremuere undae, circum tremere omnia visum est,
pugnacisque dei strepitus formidine stravit
Naupactum pugnas e litore prospectantem.
    Sed quamquam tantas strages lux finiit una,
ut trepident meminisse sui fata horrida regis
15   Ismariae gentes, opifex monumenta tabellis
dat mirus pictis centum evasura per annos.
Interea dum picta aderunt fracta agmina chartis,
Fama ipsa Ionio assistens pernicibus alis,
ore ingens, clangore ingens, praecordia centum
20   voce movens, late cunctas vulgabit in urbes
regnatorem Asiae supremo Marte cadentem,
et nostras ventura feret per saecula palmas.

On the painter portraying the same victory

Anonymous

Behold the Phlegrean phalanx that now churns the sea with row-
ing, intent on the destruction of Hesperia. See how the infidel
Endymion batters the lands of his enemy with a savage lightning
strike, so that it might fall and perish under the law of the great
thunderer. Behold the all-powerful Father, who, having pitied the   5
undeserved slaughter from on high, has at long last sent a three-
fold allied army into a vicious battle, which immediately sank the
unspeakable throng in the deep with its fleet. The heavens stood
still in wonder; the lofty house of Olympus rumbled. The waves   10
crashed, and all around everything appeared to tremble, and the
din of the bellicose god overwhelmed Naupactus with fear, look-
ing on at the battle from the shore.

But even though a single day brought an end to such massacres,
a marvelous craftsman painted these historic panels to last for a   15
hundred years, so that the Ismarian people will shudder as they
remember the horrible fate of their king. For as long as the broken
battle lines appear painted on the canvas, Fama herself, coming to
Ionia on her ruinous wings — with her huge mouth and mighty
cry, moving a hundred hearts with her voice — will spread news of   20
the fall of Asia's king in the greatest battle to all cities far and
wide, and will carry our victory palms for all ages to come.

De Actiaca victoria ob profligatum Turcarum classem

Agostino Fortunio

Ut pelago incubuere rates, iam iamque propinquae
hostiles puppes propius cernuntur ab hoste,
ilicet exsurgit spes de victoria utrimque:
it clamor caelo, atque instructo Marte phalanges
5   haud mora cunctae ad tela ruunt Vulcaniaque aptant;
hortatique duces socios navale corona
hinc inde adversi validum labuntur in hostem
procursu rapido, ut solet ad praedam Leo ferri.
Eminus explosa ignivomentia ut aera dedere,
10   principio tonitrus, ac crebris ictibus ignes:
iam mare, iam caeli horrendum intonat axis,
iam gemitum tellus dat litora singula circum.
    Interea classis pia Christigenum ocius ecce
perque hostes, ignesque ruens, celeresque sagittas,
15   turbinis ac fumi nebulas media agmina vastat.
Dumque instans hostis vires ac vulnera miscet,
hunc superans tanta prosternit imagine mortis
virtute ac ferro, rubeant ut caerula caede
ingenti, vix tot capere utque cadavera possint.
20   Actiaca Augustum huc fecit victoria clarum,
totius ac mundi imperio merito inde potiri:
Actiaca huc rursus facit en victoria claros
Christicolas; trino ut summoque Deo duce, et uno

On the Actian victory over the depraved fleet of Turks

Agostino Fortunio

When the fleet had reached the open sea, hostile galleys from the enemy were seen approaching ever nearer, and now hope for victory rises up on both sides. A shout goes up to heaven, and the ranks of soldiers ready for war all rush to their weapons and   5
swiftly suit up their armor. The leaders rally their men in naval formation, then turn and fall on their powerful opponent with a fierce charge, as a lion attacks its prey. The cannons, still at long range, offered the first fire, hissing and belching rounds of thunder   10
and fire in repeated blasts. Now the sea, now the expanse of the sky rumbles terrifyingly, now the earth gives forth a groan that echoes on every shore.

But now, behold: the pious Christian fleet rushes swiftly through the enemy ships, raining down flames and whizzing arrows, clouds of gunfire and smoke, and devastates the middle of   15
the enemy lines. For as long as it bears down on the main enemy force, it inflicts great damage, laying them low in so many shapes of death, stronger both in virtue and in sword; the sky-blue sea grows so red with the slaughter that they can hardly recover the bodies.

Victory at Actium won Augustus his fame, and from then on   20
he held the whole world as his rightful empire; behold, another Actian victory brings fame to the people of Christ. With the God of the whole world, who is three in one, as their guide, let pious

67

totius hinc mundi invadant mox (Maure), Tyranni
25   regna pii reges, pietas nisi iusque peribit.
Actiacos ludos instaurent ergo Quirites
auspiciis magni diademate tempora patris
tergemino ornati; hos Veneti, ac rex magnus Iberus
atque pius populus, magno qui sparsus in orbe est,
30   sectentur, maiora experti gaudia numquam.

kings invade the Tyrant's kingdoms, Moor, if their faith and oaths   25
do not fail them. Let the Quirites celebrate Actian games, and
take the auspices, their temples adorned with the triple crown of
the great father. Let the Venetians, the great Iberian king, and
all the pious people scattered around the great globe accompany   30
them, never having known greater joy.

: XIII :

Ad Sebastianum Venerium, Venetae classis ducem

Giovanni Battista Amalteo

Ausa Dei classem sociasque lacessere puppes
impia gens, Euris sinuosa in vela vocatis.
Horruit adversas acies, fractasque superbae
vidit opes Asiae, raptis spoliata trophaeis.
5   Illa per Ionios centeno remige fluctus
ibat ovans tristesque minas et bella ferebat;
impuleratque duces Cretaea a strage recentes,
rursus in arma vehi et duro discrimine, rursus
hostiles petere exuvias et Martia signa,
10   obvia cum triplici sese tulit ordine classis,
auspicio iam freta Dei caeloque secundo,
evertitque trucem validis in cursibus hostem.
Tum superum delapsa cohors plaudentibus alis
irruere, et vacuas visa est rutilare per auras,
15   et nunc barbaricas pelago submergere puppes,
nunc invisam aciem rapidis incessere flammis
aut pugnare manu, mediisque insidere transtris
Aeneadum, et Venetae defendere robora pubis
pars autem clypeis venientes excipit ictus;
20   aut stipata levi circumvolat agmina gyro,
non secus ac rigui si quando ad stagna Caystri
candentes liquido glomerantur in aethere cycni,
imbellesque agitant volucres, et inertia caedunt
agmina, sanguineas Zephyrus rotat aere plumas.
25   Cinge triumphali victricia tempora lauro
dux Venetum, cui clara suae cognomina gentis
dat Venus, et spolia ampla tuo cape debita Marti,

: XIII :

To Sebastiano Venier, admiral of the Venetian fleet

Giovanni Battista Amalteo

The impious race that dared challenge God's fleet and his allied
navy now stood trembling before the opposing battle line, as the
southeast wind beat against the billowing sails. They saw the
wealth of proud Asia broken, stripped of its stolen trophies. They
had sailed exultantly through the Ionian waves with a hundred   5
oarsmen, bringing with them menace and destruction. They had
compelled their leaders, fresh from the slaughter at Crete, to take
up arms again, to seek spoils and trophies again from their ene-
mies, despite the extreme danger. Suddenly, a three-columned fleet   10
blocked their way. Backed by God's promise and favorable skies, it
halted the relentless progress of the savage enemy. All of a sudden,
a band of angels descended on beating wings, and as they rushed
in, they seemed to glow red in the clear air. Now they sink the   15
barbarian ships down into the sea, now they attack the enemy
battle line with swift volleys of fire, or fight hand to hand, seated
on the middle of the thwarts with the sons of Aeneas. Some de-
fended the Venetian troops, intercepting oncoming blows with
their shields or flying around the dense troops in a smooth circle,   20
just as when, at the marsh of well-wat\ered Cayster, white swans
gather in the clear air and attack helpless birds. The torpid flock
yields; the west wind whirls bloody feathers in the air.

Bind your victorious brows with triumphal laurel, Venetian   25
commander, protector of the land you saved, that land to which
Venus gave the glorious name of her people; seize the ample spoils

servatae columen patriae. Tu maximus ille es
aequoreae, qui primus inis certamina pugnae
30   cladem Asiae intentans divi comitantur euntem,
et Curae vigiles et ovanti Gloria plausu;
ultricesque rates, et aenea mittis in hostem
fulmina, suscepto igne cavis impulsa metallis,
quo sonitu tremuere undae perculsaque longe
35   Ambracia, et pavidae latuere sub aequore nymphae,
et refluo trepidans Achelous inhorruit amne.
Nec te ullae belli facies, amissaque terrent
regna, nec avectae diverso ab litore praedae
nec te animi vigor et seris grave robur in annis
40   deserit, et fracto exuvias ex hoste reportas,
eque tua prior emicuit victoria puppi.
      Tum iuvenem imperio insignem, quem Caesare magno
progenitum, Virtus per grandia facta parentis
evehit, et caelum promissaque sidera monstrant.
45   Attonitae videre acies in proelia versum
quo pietas, quo laudis amor, quo gloria traxit,
et belli molem regere, et virtute tueri,
qualis Atlas humero stellantem sustinet axem.
His quoque ab auspiciis tantae pars maxima pugnae,
50   curarumque comes sacris Antonius armis
turbabat cuneos, inimicaque signa premebat
vi superans, quantas crebris maria alta procellis
secum hiems, Eurosque trahens et nubila perflans
verberata Orion, fluctusque illidit arenis.
55   Quem duo sectati varia in certamina fratres,
iuncti animis ambo, cognato sanguine iuncti
Romulidae proceres per barbara tela, per ignes
irrumpunt Martemque acuunt, spoliisque superbis,

you have earned in this battle. You are the master of the sea, the
first to enter the fray of the battle, intent on the destruction of
Asia. The gods accompany you on your journey, along with watch-   30
ful Care, and Glory with its triumphal applause. You send aveng-
ing ships and bronze thunderbolts against the enemy; the waves
trembled at the sound of gunfire bursting from the cannons. Far
away, Ambracia shook, the nymphs took refuge under the water in   35
fright, and Achelous shuddered with fear in his ebbing stream.
But the shapes of war do not frighten you, nor fallen kingdoms,
nor plunder taken from foreign shores. Neither your courage nor
your robust strength abandons you in later years. You carry away
the spoils of the broken enemy, and your deck glitters with the   40
trophies of other victories.

Then Virtue brought forward a young man, offspring of great
Caesar, destined for power by the great deeds of his father; the
heavens and the waxing stars make known that it is he. The men
looked on in awe as he turned toward the battle, where piety, love   45
of praise, and glory urged him on. He takes command of the en-
gines of war and comforts the men with his virtue, like Atlas bear-
ing the starry globe on his shoulders. With these good omens,
Marco Antonio Colonna, who had the greatest part in so great a
battle, an ally in the arms of the sacred cause, drove his troops into   50
wedge formation, pushing back the enemy standards, surpassing in
strength, just as winter brings with it storm after storm on the
deep sea, and Orion, driving the east wind and blowing the beaten
clouds, dashes the waves on the beach. His two brothers accom-   55
pany him into the thick of combat, bound by blood and fighting
spirit. These noble sons of Romulus rush in and fight fiercely
through the savages' spears and fire; often they decorate their col-
umn with huge piles of proud spoils, just as once the Tyndaridae,

saepe suam decorant ingenti mole columnam,
60   ceu quondam Oebalias soliti ductare cohortes
Tyndaridae, adverso spoliabant milite castra
insignes paribus clypeis, quibus aureus ensis,
et iam tum gemino radiabat sidere cassis
aurea, puniceae volitabant vertice cristae.
65   Nunc pharetras Lyciosque arcus perfractaque tela
fluctus agit, laceraeque natant in gurgite pinus
et iam trunca virum, discerptaque corpora passim
litoreae sectantur aves, proiectaque pascunt
viscera, et effuso late rubet unda cruore.
70   Atque aliquis, Naupacte, tuas dum tendit ad oras,
et pugnata refert sanctis nova bella sub armis,
dumque peregrina legit Actia litora pinu,
'Ecce,' ait, 'hinc pugnas iterum prospexit Apollo
bisque triumphatis Aegyptia signa carinis.'
75   Sic ait et celeri percurrit Echinadas aura.
Defer ad externas victricia nomina gentes
Fama, novas memorans pugnas partosque triumphos,
Quae vetera heroum obscuris monumenta sepulcris
subtrahis, aeternisque duces interseris astris,
80   dic actos in bella viros socia arma ferentes
Hispanos, Venetosque intermixtosque Quirites,
nunc primum Ionio in magno iunxisse carinas,
at contra Euboicas summa in certamina classes
mentitosque deos viresque Orientis agentem
85   regem Asiae domitum, tremefactaque saxa Capharei.
Scilicet hoc dudum precibus votisque petisti,
sancte heros, qui sceptra Dei sedemque tueris
idem aperis, idem caeli penetralia claudis
dum tu neglecta pro religione laboras,
90   et Vaticanas toties prostratus ad aras
sacra facis, sanctasque vocas in foedera gentes,

distinguished by their paired shields, led the Oebalian cohort to 60
despoil the enemy camp. They each had a golden sword and a
golden helmet that even then shone with twin stars, and crimson
plumes fluttered on their heads. Now the sea churns with quivers, 65
Lycian bows, and broken spears, and the battered boats drift on
the tide, along with torsos of men; here and there, shore birds
swoop down on their dismembered bodies and feed on their ex-
posed entrails; far and wide the water reddens with spilled blood.

And now one bird rushes toward your shores, Naupactus, bring- 70
ing news of a battle fought even now under holy arms. She points
out the shore of Actium with its gathering fleet, and says, "Behold,
Apollo looks down on another battle here; for a second time he
sees Egyptian standards on conquered ships." So she speaks and 75
flies toward the Echinades on a swift breeze.

Now, Fama, bear the names of the victors to foreign nations.
Recount these recent battles and the triumphs they brought, pass-
ing over the old monuments of heroes lying in obscure tombs, as
you enfold the leaders among the eternal stars. Tell of men led into 80
battle bearing allied arms—Spanish, Venetians, and Romans in-
termingled; now tell how the ships first joined forces in the great
Ionian sea for a mighty contest against the Euboean fleet, and how
the King of Asia, who led the false and lying gods and the forces
of the East, was subdued and the rocks of Caphareus were made 85
to tremble.

It was you, to be sure, holy hero, who contrived this victory
with your prayers and vows; you who watch over the scepter and
throne of God, you who open and close the inner sanctum of
heaven while you labor on behalf of a slighted religion and, so of-
ten prostrate at Vatican altars, make sacred offerings and call for 90
treaties among God-fearing nations. You order them to take back

Iordanemque iubes, Solymasque reposcere sedes,
atque implacatae superare Propontidis oras,
salve operum tantorum auctor, qui numina nobis
95   concilias, et diu tuis paris otia terris.
At tibi, dux Venetum, nunc alter ab Hercule magno,
qui gravidam colubris hydram, qui Thracia monstra
exsuperas, iterumque Acheloia cornua frangis,
quando etiam maiora manent superanda Propontis,
100   Rhetaeique sinus, proavitaque regna petenda.
Iamque tuis Rhodos et Salamis, Naxosque receptae
accedent titulis, et iam concussa tumultu
Mygdonia, et tristes expavit Achaia pugnas.
Te celsi iuga Taygeti, te frigida Tempe,
105   Aoniumque vocat nemus, et Permessides undae
et tua Pieriae responsant nomina silvae.
Tempus erit, cum rapta sacris solatia Musis
restitues fontesque suos, suaque antra recludes,
nunc dira illuvie et silvestribus obsita dumis,
110   et sua iam profugi recinent ad flumina cycni.
Hinc et ad aequoream victor provectus Ioppem
antiquas Solymorum arces et sceptra reposces
Ausoniae imperio, ac Romanis debita regnis.
Et tibi Carmeli rupes, tibi plaudet Idume
115   et tibi crescentes surgent ad sidera palmae.
O sacrae Libani valles, o palmifer Hermon,
en erit, ut vestros liceat penetrare recessus?
En erit, ut lustrans Syrias pius hospes arenas
caelicolum signata legam vestigia plantis?
120   Bethlemiaeque domus supplex sacraria visam?
Et propiora Dei cunabula pronus adorem?
Felices properate citis decursibus anni,
concordesque iterum fatalibus aurea pensis
saecla neant Parcae, meque haec ad vota reservent.

Jordan and the kingdom of Jerusalem, and to conquer the shores of Propontis, still unreconciled. Hail, author of these great tasks; you gain us favor and at long last earn holy peace for your lands. 95 As for you, Venetian commander, another come from great Hercules, you who conquer another snake-bristling hydra and Thracian monsters, and who break again the horns of Achelous, since even greater monsters remain to be vanquished in Propontis, seek out the Rhetean bay and your ancestral kingdom. Now that 100 Rhodes and Salamis and Naxos have been reclaimed they will be added to your titles, but Mygdonia and Achaea, already under siege, fear worse battles. The ridge of lofty Taygetus calls to you, frigid Tempe, the Aonian grove, and the Permessian waves; the 105 Pierian woods echo your name. The time will come when you will restore to the sacred Muses their lost home, and you will uncover their springs and their caves, now dark with filth and overgrown with rough thorns. Then the swans, now fled, will sing again on 110 their river. Sailing victorious from here to sea-blue Joppa, you will take back the ancient citadels of Jerusalem and the scepters owed to Roman dominion for the empire of Ausonia. The cliffs of Carmel and Idumaea will applaud you; for you growing palms will 115 rise up to the stars. O sacred valleys of Liban, O palm-bearing Hermon, will it ever be that we enter your hidden groves? Will it be that I come as a devout guest to look upon the sands of Syria, in the hopes of discerning the footprints of the gods? Might I come as a suppliant to see the sacred home in Bethlehem and 120 might I prostrate myself in adoration in the presence of the cradle of the Lord? Happy years, hasten on in your swift course, and let the Fates again agree to weave golden ages with their fate-defining spindles and to watch over me according to my prayers.

125   Adspice dum properant alios tibi fata triumphos,
       ut maria, ut tellus nobis, ut largior aether
       rideat, et nitido ostentet nova sidera caelo
       illustres animas, quae prodiga pectora vitae
       ausae omnes, dum fata dabant, hostilibus armis
130   obiicere et letum pro religione pacisci.
       Has sedes peperere sibi, qua lactea fulget
       orbita, et aeterni candent fastigia mundi,
       et modo pacatis diffundunt gaudia terris.

Look, as the future hastens to bring new triumphs to you, how the   125
sea, the land, and the bountiful heavens smile on us. New stars
appear in the shining sky: glorious souls, lavish with their lives,
who all dared, while the Fates were favorable, to bare their chests
to hostile arms and suffer death for the cause of their religion.   130
They earned these thrones for themselves, where the Milky Way
shines and the summit of heaven glitters bright, and they bring joy
to the now peaceful world.

: XIV :

Centum carmina: ad Urbem

Anonymous

Semper honoratus veniet, pulcherrima rerum,
hic tibi iure dies, posthac meliusque nitebunt
soles, Roma, tibi magno redeunte Columna.
Ecce tuus sanguis, rerum tutela tuarum,
5   cui genus a proavis clarum clarumque paternae
est laudis nomen, decorat quem regia mater.
Multus gentis honos, verum sua plurima virtus
quem merito celebri fama super aethera tollit.
En decus Italiae spoliis Orientis onustum
10   advenit, egregia parto sibi laude triumpho.
En trahit Ismarios, genus insuperabile bello,
spiculaque clypeosque, ereptaque rostra carinis;
en signa, en gladios, abiuratasque rapinas;
en tibi Christicolum, Christi en tibi nominis ultor
15   maximus, en tua spes, tua gloria, maxima rerum.
      Quos modo, Roma, vides manibus post terga revinctis
maestos ire, tui sunt, inclyta, nominis hostes,
qui captivorum populantur tempora raptis
auribus et truncant inhonesto vulnere nares;
20   gens inimica Deo populi, quos usque recentes
convectare iuvat praedas et vivere rapto;
qui modo tot dederunt crudelia funera nostris
militibus, qui tot viduarunt civibus urbes,
qui miseris latos vastant cultoribus agros;
25   qui scelus omne, dolos omnes qui turpiter audent,
qui manibus tumidi magnum rescindere caelum
aggressi, superisque Deum detrudere regnis.

: XIV :

One hundred verses: to the City

Anonymous

This day will be ever honored by you, Rome, most beautiful of
cities, and even better days will shine for you ever after, now that
great Colonna returns. Behold the guardian of your affairs — your
bloodline, which his regal mother adorns, his family made famous
by his ancestors and his name made famous by the glory of his   5
father. His great honor comes from his family, but his own cour-
age, greater still, rightfully lifts him above the skies through his
celebrated fame. Behold, Italy's glorious son, laden with spoils
from the East, arrives in a triumph he won for himself with great   10
renown. Behold, he leads in the Ismarians, that race once invinci-
ble in war, with javelins, shields, and the prows taken from their
ships. Behold, standards, swords, and perjured plunder; behold,
your mighty avenger, vindicator of Christians and the name of
Christ; behold, your hope, your greatest glory.   15

    Glorious Rome, those wretched men you now see passing by
with their hands bound behind their backs, they are the enemies
of your name. They are the ones who beat the brows of their cap-
tives, rip off their ears, and cut off their noses with a disfiguring
wound. This is a race of people hateful to God, a people al-   20
ways eager to carry off fresh spoils and live off their plunder. It was
they who recently dealt so many cruel deaths to our soldiers, wid-
owed so many cities of their citizens, laid waste to the wide fields
of wretched farmers. They dare any sin, any treachery without   25
shame; and, swollen with pride, they undertook to cleave the vast
sky with their hands and depose God from his lofty kingdom.

I nunc, bella ferox, polluta pace retracta:
promissam nunc rumpe fidem, Venetosque lacesse;
30   impia foedifragi nunc iussa capesse Tyranni.
Maiores dabitis poenas: Acheronta sub imum
ibitis inferiae Diti; mox truncus arena
Selimi, et longis singultibus ilia tendet
et modo honoratum pascet sine nomine corpus
35   effera avis; moremque malum, ritusque profanos
Christicolum eiciet virtus, natosque patresque
cum genere extinguet Turcarum nostra iuventus,
sacra nisi in melius referant, Christumque salutent.
      Maxima res effecta quidem, timor omnis abesto.
40   Omnia tuta vides. Ingenti, Roma, Columnae
ne trepides adnixa; duce hoc nam sospite numquam
res Romana cadet: solido ex adamante Columna est.
Nil timet illa maris, terrae, caelique periclis
tot defuncta; malis haud cedet nescia vinci.
45   Hic vir hic est, cuius rursum virtutibus aucta
imperium terris, animos aequabis Olympo,
cuius et auspiciis Saturnia regna redibunt.
Quam tali auxilio, quam defensoribus istis
tempus eget, quam magna Pii prudentia Quinti est.
50   Seu pacem, seu bella gerat, huic maxima rerum
verborumque fides; amat hunc et pectore toto
maximus. Huic ope, huic sancito foedere, eundem
magnanimo Austriadae Venetisque potentibus addit,
ductoremque suae classis iubet esse supremum.
55   Adiuvat et votis, tot namque evadere casus
haud potis ille foret, ni mox pia cura resistat,
perpetuis supplex onerans altaria donis.
Sic propria virtute Pii multoque rogatu
atque Dei est heros fatis defensus amicis.

Go now, savage war, for the peace has been sullied and broken. Break the sworn treaty, attack the Venetians; now carry out the impious commands of the pact-breaking Tyrant. You will pay for 30 what you have done, when you go under deep Acheron as an offering to Dis. Soon Selim's body will lie on the sand, his entrails convulsed in prolonged death agony, and savage birds will feed on his nameless corpse, once so honored. The Christians' virtue will 35 repel your evil customs and profane rites, and our young men will destroy the sons and fathers of the Turks along with their entire race, unless they change their religion for the better and welcome Christ.

Let this last task be carried out, and let all fear be gone. You see that everything is safe. Do not fear, Rome, while you lean on great 40 Colonna. While he is safe, the Roman State will never fall. Colonna is made of solid steel. He does not fear death in the struggles of the sea, land, or sky: not knowing how to be conquered, he will not yield to evil.

This is the man, Rome, by whose virtues you will again extend 45 your empire on earth and match Olympus in courage. Under his good auspices, the age of Saturn will return. How these times need such aid and such defenders! How great is the wisdom of Pius V! Whether he wages war or peace, the greatest responsibil- 50 ity for deeds and words falls to Colonna. Indeed, the pope loves him with his whole heart: with his work, with his sworn treaty, he allies this man with the courageous John of Austria and the powerful Venetians, and commands him to be the supreme leader of his fleet. And he lends help with his prayers, for Colonna would 55 never be able to survive so many misfortunes, unless pious care steps in, a suppliant loading the altars with endless gifts. And so with his own virtue and the many requests of Pius and of God, the hero is protected by friendly fates.

60   En laeti reditus, expectatique triumphi:
ecce venit summo fundens de vertice lumen.
Accipe nunc eadem magnum, quem magna tulisti
semideum, et laeto laetum clamore saluta.
Iam reducem gratare, venit; clamore resultent
65   alma tui colles? Meritos illius honores
testatur tellus, croceis quae floribus halat
laeta sub extremum brumae intractabilis imbrem;
comprobat et caelo meritos Deus ipse sereno.
Aeneadae rerum domini divumque propago
70   iam servatorem meritis extollite vestrum
laudibus: hic vestram properando restituit rem,
pro patria letum, et pro religione pacisci
nil metuit, rursum caput obiectare periclis
nil trepidat. Christi pro libertate tuenda
75   prodigus ipsam animam superis devoverat olim.
      En venit! Eia alacres manibus date lilia plenis.
Quantum habet hic patrii Martis; virtute nec ausis
haud ulli inferior veterum. Sub Tartara misit
mille die, victor disiecit mille carinas.
80   Et fortes humeros et fortia pectora bello
ardentesque notate oculos: qui spiritus illi,
qui vultus, quae vox divini signa decoris?
      Ingredere auspiciis urbem, alte Columna, secundis.
Aureus ipse tuae referas saecla aurea genti.
85   Magne, veni: haud aequum meritis iam sume triumphum,
sed qualem potuere tui, dux inclyte, cives.
      Afforet Austriades utinam, qui laude coronam
promeruit primam, Caroli fortissima proles.
Ille animi praestans, iuvenili in corde virilem
90   ille gerit curam: ingens fama, ingentior armis.
Afforet et Venetus nulli dux Marte secundus.
Quas nunc te terras, et quanta per aequora vectum

Behold his happy return and long-awaited triumph! Behold, 60
a light pours down from the sky's lofty peak. Receive now this
great demigod, whom you, great Rome, have borne, and salute this
blessed man with a joyful cry. Give thanks for his return, for
he has come. Do not your hills, nurturing Rome, resound with 65
shouts? The land itself bears witness to the merit of his honors,
happy and fragrant with yellow flowers, under the last rain of
rough winter. God himself confirms his merits in the calm sky.
Sons of Aeneas, lords of the city and offspring of the gods, extol
now your savior with deserved praise. This man has restored your 70
state with his decisive action. He did not fear to risk death for the
cause of his homeland and religion. He does not hesitate to expose
himself to danger once again. Generous in the cause of preserving
the liberty of Christ, he devoted his spirit wholly to the gods once 75
and forever.

Behold, he comes! Go quickly now, give lilies by the handful.
How much of his father's warlike spirit he has! Neither in virtue
nor in brave deeds is he less than any of the ancients. On that one
day, he sent a thousand men down to Tartarus. In victory, he
dashed a thousand ships to pieces. Observe his mighty shoulders, 80
and his chest, mighty in war, and his blazing eyes. That spirit, that
countenance and that voice: are they not the signs of divine grace?

Enter the city with favorable omens, mighty Colonna. Since
you yourself are golden, may you bring golden ages to your nation.
Great one, come, and take your triumph. Though it will not be all 85
that you deserve, glorious leader, it will be as great as your citizens
can offer.

If only John of Austria were here, he who earned the crown
of highest praise, most mighty offspring of Charles. Outstanding
in spirit, he bears the wisdom of a grown man in his youthful 90
heart: great in fame, still greater in arms. If only the Venetian
admiral were also here, second to none in war. How many lands
did you pass through and how many seas did you cross before we

accipimus? Quantis iactatum, magne, periclis.
Ingredere o patriam aeterno cumulatus honore;
95   iam grates superis reddas, fige oscula summi
pontificis pedibus sanctis; amplectere dulces
iam natos, sociamque thori, optatamque parentem.
    Felix, dum stabit Capitoli immobile saxum,
dum caeli clavesque Pater Romanus habebit,
100   semper honos, nomenque tuum, laudesque manebunt.

·

receive you now? How many dangers did you encounter, great one? Enter your fatherland, laden high with everlasting honor. Now give thanks to the gods and plant kisses on the holy feet of   95 the supreme pontiff. Now embrace your sweet children, your wife, and your long-desired mother.

Blessed man, as long as the immoveable rock of the Capitoline stands, and as long as the Roman Father holds the keys of heaven, your honor, your name, and your praise will always remain.   100

: XV :

[Laeta sub auspicio felici et numine sancti]

Anonymous

Laeta sub auspicio felici et numine sancti
pontificis nunc gesta canens virtuteque clari
Austriaci invicti, stupeant ut saecla futura,
pandere terreno possim quo carmine digno,
5   summe pater? Ni tu solus qui cuncta gubernas
movisti et remis cursus certamina rostris
succurras? Carmen ni fundat gratia caeli?
Namque tibi tantum cedit victoria: nostri
victi animi culpis gravibus, discrimine tanto
10   demissas fudere preces laetique potentis
arma tuae petiere manus. Victoria, Christe,
haec tua: sit nobis non parva hinc gloria, sitque
corpora quod pro te spectaris mersa sub undis
vulneribus decorata suis occurrere morti.
15   Hinc fisus tua facta, Pater sanctissime, nunc te,
Quinte Pie, aggredior, meritis spectande per orbem,
spectantur terris maiora ut lumina caeli.
Namque tuae pietatis, opus non invida mundi
improbitas delet, pulchris nec candida palmis
20   gloria plena tuis Lethea se abluet unda.
Tuta, composito per te iam foedere sancto,
omnia tunc properans, ductorem arcessere pugnae
commotasque alto nostris erroribus iras
a nobis, Pie, non cessas avertere in aris.
25   Venturae fuerat tua mens tunc prescia sortis,
ardenti vultu atque opibus cum tanta fatigat
cura Patrem, quocum curas partitur ab astris

: XV :

[I will now sing of the happy deeds]

Anonymous

I will now sing of the happy deeds done under the power and
good auspices of the holy pontiff and by the virtue of the famous,
invincible John of Austria. What earthly song would be sufficient
to reveal these events, highest Father, and make future ages marvel
at them, unless you come to my aid, you who alone govern all   5
things, who guided our rowers on the voyage and our ramming
prows in the battle. How, unless the grace of heaven inspires my
song? This victory falls to you alone. Our souls, burdened by
heavy sins and dismayed in the face of such a crisis, poured forth
humble prayers, and sought the protection of your powerful hand.   10
This victory, Christ, is yours. Let just a little glory come down to
us, and let the bodies, which you saw sink under the waves for
your sake, meet death glorified by their wounds. Now relying on
your deeds, holiest Father Pius V, now I turn to you, admired   15
throughout the world for your virtues, as the stars in heaven are
admired from earth. For the jealous spite of the world will not
erase your piety's work, and the shining glory that fills your re-
splendent palms will not be washed away by Lethe's wave. When
you gathered together the Holy League, ushering along every-   20
thing in safety, you summoned the commander of the expedi-
tion, and you did not fail at the altars, Pius, to ward off the rage
stirred by our mistakes on the sea. With piercing foresight, your   25
mind anticipated even then what fate held in store. Care with
her flushed face and many duties wearies you, Father, whenever

ipse Deus, quocumque aperit venientia saeclo.
Iamque gregem sine fine tuum per tuta vagantem
30   cernis et aequati per dulcia litora ponti.
Non metuent posthac matres ex urbe raptos
aut gremio dulces natos seseque peremptas
spectare aut Scythicos truces ornare triumphos.
Non, Pater: atque virum coniunx, non coniuge capta
35   connubia ante oculos consors polluta videbit
non optare necem has miseras, inferre nec illos,
aut nato aut natae carae, nec stringere ferrum,
damnatis nequeant iussis servire superbis.
Te pastore Pio fata haec immania Averni
40   iam sedes petiere; premant crudelia fata
infernos manes Ditemque et Tartara dira.
Te duce mutatis in prospera tempora rebus
alternat fortuna vicem, non amplius altis
eruptis Euris cymbam male fluctibus actam
45   undanti pelago dubiae sub imagine mortis,
sed placidam cernes laetamque innare per undas,
ceu Deus adfuerit subitoque ad tuta reducens
depulerit ventos aeternum et clauserit antris.
Discat terra omnis, discant nunc aequora victo
50   victore immani, vires submittere sacris
viribus. Haec iam pro cunctis victoria pugnis
certavit, cunctis arcet nos ista periclis,
et faciem mutat rebus, laeta otia terris,
et dulcis pacis cursus sine limite ponit.

55   At postquam mandata patris dux audit Iberus
clavigeri, interno flagrans virtutis amore,
Hispani regis magni tunc iussa capessens
ardet abire. Fugam classi sociisque per altum

God himself shares his concerns with you through his heavenly signs, and whenever he reveals what is to come in the world. And now you see your flock wandering freely along the safe and 30 pleasant shores of the calm sea. From this time forward, mothers will not fear that their sweet sons will be snatched from their city or from their very laps, or that they will see themselves sold or used to decorate savage Scythian triumphs. No, Father, every wife will have her husband, and no husband will see his marriage de- 35 filed before his very eyes by the rape of his bride. These pitiful brides will not have only death to hope for, nor will their husbands have to bury a son or dear daughter, nor draw a sword, nor obey the arrogant commands of infidels. With you as our shepherd, Pius, already these calamitous monsters have taken their place in Avernus; may the cruel Fates crush those infernal spirits, 40 along with Dis and the scourges of Tartarus. With you as our leader, our fortune turns again; our times become prosperous. No more will you see the skiff tossed about on the high waves of the undulating sea when the east wind breaks forth, facing a near- 45 certain death; instead you will see it float through the waves, peaceful and happy, as if God were on board, and in an instant restored it to safety, driving the winds away and closing them in their caves forever. Let the whole world learn, and the seas learn as well, to surrender their strength to your holy power, now that the 50 conquering fiend is himself conquered. This victory was fought for all other battles. It keeps us safe from all dangers, and changes the very state of the world. It confers a welcome respite on our lands and lays a path for sweet peace without end.

Now that the Spanish commander has received the commission 55 of the key-bearing Father, he burns with a deep love of virtue; he yearns to be off to carry out the orders of the great king of Spain. He prepares the fleet and its men for departure on the sea and

comparat atque ipsam multo vel milite complet.
60 Iam Phoebus biiugis caelo laxarat habenas,
obvius armato proceri, cum Sirius ardet;
caelestem et cursum remis, et lumina velis
aequabat tumidis, ipsum iuvenemque potentem
conspiciens et sistit equos, et talia fatur:
65 'I, mea lux, sequere Italiam ducentibus astris,
ac ducente Deo, dum te Victoria praesens
te sequitur, dum fata volunt, dum numina poscunt,
dum miseris instant caedes, incendia, raptus,
nulla dies umquam memori te subtrahet aevo:
70 tu referes lucem populis in proelia victis,
Lucifer Eois fulgebis gentibus alter.'
    Interea Zephyris late spirantibus alto
Italiam properans Hispano ab litore ductor
vicinas Ligurum sedes, portusque petivit.
75 Hic voluit fessis requiem studioque videndi
descendit puppi, lustrat quoque passibus urbem,
optatus populis caris, inhiantibus olim
heroem mirari animis, formaque decorum.
Hinc ad Parthenopen vehitur, Tiberinaque longe
80 flumina prospectat, celsa et monumenta suorum
moeniaque et magnae renovata palatia Romae,
dum causam Christi tantam, saevo hoste minanti
excidium Italiae, properans nunc sustinet unus.
Fernandum, quem magna tulit Mendocia proles,
85 pontifici summo prudens iam miserat ante,
nuntiet adventum classis, mentemque animumque
esse suum, iussis subeat res bellica sanctis,
Hispanum haec mandasse duci atque ante omnia, regem.
Dicenda et multa illi adiunxit maximus heros,

mans the navy with a great host of soldiers. Now in the sky, Phoe- 60
bus had loosened the reins of his two-horsed chariot, rising to
meet the armed commander, and all the while the Dog Star
blazes. He charted his heavenly course to follow their oars, so that
his light would track their billowing sails. Then, catching sight of
that mighty youth, he drew his horses to a halt and said these
things: "Go, my light, seek Italy with the stars and God as your 65
guides. As long as Victory follows you close at hand, as long as the
Fates are willing and the divine powers demand, as long as mas-
sacres, fires, and pillage still threaten people in misery, no day will
ever efface you from the memory of time. You will bring light to 70
the people you conquer in battle, and like another Lucifer you will
shine down on the nations of the East."

Meanwhile, the commander speeds toward Italy from Spanish
shores, far out on the sea where the west wind is blowing. He has
reached the neighboring lands of the Ligurians and their harbors.
Here he decreed a rest for his exhausted crew, and in his eagerness 75
to see the sights, he descends from the poop deck and traverses the
city with his steps, welcomed by the friendly crowds, who gaze
with wonder at this great man, so courageous and so handsome.
From here he sails to Naples, and looks out toward the distant
Tiber River, the majestic monuments of his ancestors, and the 80
walls and the newly rebuilt palaces of mighty Rome. All the while
he hastens on alone to perform his great mission for Christ, for
his brutal enemy threatens to destroy Italy. In his great wisdom,
he had already sent Fernando ahead, born of the great Mendozan
stock, to announce to the supreme pontiff the arrival of the fleet: 85
that his heart and mind were his, that all matters of war would
be submitted to holy decree; and that the Spanish king had en-
trusted these matters and everything besides to his commander.
The mighty hero added even more for the messenger to report:

90   affectus magni, summi signa, amplaque honoris.
Excipit ingentem iuvenem tunc regia pompa
Parthenopes, regem demonstrant omnia, vultus
verbaque, nec possunt expleri corda tuendo;
regis iussa facit, maiora et robora cogit
95   et vires renovat, surgentia dura resolvit
ut sese velis, remis commitat et undis.
     Utque fides pelago, classem de litore solvunt.
Attulerat Phoebea suos ter candida vultus
vix caelo, Phoebus ter flammea lumina, quaeque
100   Messanam aspiciens puppim cum advertere terrae
visa ratis curvoque simul se condere portu.
     Nunc, Messana, tuos referam, Messana, labores,
aemula virtutis, fidei, tunc aemula pompae
Parthenopes pulchrae, regnis certantibus hinc hinc
105   internos aperire animos et corda suorum,
Austriaco magno magnos subeunte triumphos.
Hic dux cum vidit Venetas adstare carinas,
Romanas etiam, explorat tum robora classis,
convocat heroas praestantes consiliumque
110   afferri in medium cunctis iubet. Undique magnis
mens haec una viris, lapsis succurrere rebus,
audacemque arcere hostem populosque frementes
hostili rabie et saevis defendere ab armis;
sic validas vires atque omnia debita victa
115   classibus adiungunt, sedes portumque relinquunt.
     Audentem tunc te viderunt, maxime ductor,
Ioniis fluctus magni, nymphaeque precantes
aequoreos flexere patres, Eurumque furentem;
cum te laeta videns Corcyra, exercita dudum
120   heu nimium Scythicis armis flammisque rapinisque
auxilia agnovit, pietatem atque arma suorum;
insula securis tunc flexibus accipit omnes,

94

tokens of great, nay the greatest, affection, and full of honor. Then   90
Naples welcomes the remarkable young man with royal proces-
sions. Everything about him—his expression, his words—reminds
them of the king, and their hearts cannot get their fill of seeing
him. He executes the king's commands, and gathers even greater
strength as he replenishes his forces. He prepares for the coming   95
hardships, entrusting himself to the sails, oars, and waves.

When they can trust the sea, they launch the fleet from the
shore. Gleaming Phoebe had scarcely lifted her face three times in
the sky, and Phoebus three times his flaming light, when a Mes-   100
sanian ship is spotted; the galley turns toward land and conceals
itself in a curved harbor.

Now Messina, I will speak of your deeds—Messina, rival of
Naples in virtue and faith, now also rival in pomp and ceremony;
the two kingdoms vie with each other to show their deep spirit   105
and joy, as great John of Austria celebrates his great triumphs.
When the commander sees the Venetian and Roman ships at
hand, he inspects the strength of the fleet. He summons the
highest-ranking officers and commands that each immediately give   110
their report. In all respects these men share one mind: to bring
help where all else has failed, to fend off the brash enemy, and to
defend the desperate people from their evil rage and savage arms.
So they add their powerful forces and all the necessary provisions
to the fleet and leave the settlements and the harbor behind.   115

Then the great Ionian waves saw your daring, great leader. And
beseeching nymphs appeased their fathers, the water gods, and the
raging east wind. Corcyra watched you with joy, for she had re-
cently suffered terribly, alas, from Scythian arms with their fires   120
and theft. She recognized the help, piety, and weaponry of her
own men. The island then receives them all in the safe curves of its

hi tandem portus latos sedesque requirunt.
Nec mora, cum nostras fama huc pervenit ad aures
125 ad Naupacteas undas consistere Turcas,
duxque ardens conferre manum cum Thrace recondit
navibus auxilia accelerans, aut offerat illi,
inferat aut pugnam, tentet vel fortia quaeque
digna suis ausis genitore et Caesare digna.
130 Et Cephalenem adfert Venetum tuta insula parva
Hispanam atque Italam classem redituque suorum
Turca ferox, monitus iam hostes adstare propinquos,
commovet ardentes animos, et robora sumit
in nostram caedem atque accensus perfidus ira,
135 nota suos circum praeceps dat signa recessus;
illi equidem subito exercent tunc omnia, iussi
incumbunt remis, vento dant carbasa laeti,
et sonitu strepituque fero lata omnia complent.
Non aliter quam cum cornu commota repente
140 venatum exercens prima sub luce resurgit
turba canum latrans, et praedae assueta propinquans,
corpore alit rabiem, morsu dum vulneret apros.
Illi autem impavidi rumpentes obvia quaeque
prosternunt feriuntque canes et dente recidunt,
145 hi remanent silvis diris avibusque lupisque
putens esca, fugit subito quam saepe viator;
diffugiunt alii ad latebras et vulnera lambunt
vix ulli remanent, sese stabulisque recondunt.
    Interea Austriacus neque enim datur hora quietis,
150 angusto portus spatio detentus et undae,
litora quae Cephali nunc abluit utraque ponto;
ardet abire loco et latas se extendere in undas,
fortunam monstrante Deo divinaque sumens
consilia adverso fluctus Aquilone secabat.

harbor, for after all they need an ample haven and a place to rest. None too soon: the news had reached our ears that the Turks were taking position in the waters of Naupactus, and our leader, yearn- 125 ing to try his hand against Thrace, stayed hidden while rapidly supplying his ships. Either John of Austria would offer battle to his enemy, or he would begin it himself; either way he would un- dertake to perform acts of courage worthy of his past bravery and worthy of his father, the emperor. Now the small, secure island of 130 the Venetians comes to Cephalonia to assist the Spanish and Ital- ian fleet. The barbarous Turk, warned by the return of his scouts that the enemy lay nearby, kindled the burning spirits of his men and directed their strength toward our destruction; the infidels, inflamed with rage, rush to send familiar signals throughout their 135 hiding places. At once they snap into action and prepare their fleet. The rowers are commanded to lean into the oars, and they rejoice to lift their sails to the wind, filling the wide expanse with noise and savage cries. Just as when, at the sound of the horn, a barking pack of dogs suddenly rushes forward on the hunt in the 140 first light of morning and, drawing near the familiar grounds of their prey, stoke their bodily hunger until they attack wild boars with their jaws. But the fearless boars, smashing whatever is in their way, flatten and ravage the dogs, cutting them down with their tusks. The dogs are left in the woods as stinking carrion 145 for the ghastly birds and wolves; how often does some passerby quickly flee from such a sight. Others scatter to their lairs and lick their wounds. Scarcely any remain, and they hide themselves in their dens.

Meanwhile, John of Austria has no time for rest, confined as he is by the narrow space of the harbor and the waves, which wash 150 either shore of the sea of Cephalus. He yearns to leave the place and spread his forces across the wide waves. He takes up his for- tune and divine counsel, with God showing the way, and cuts the waves with the north wind blowing against him.

155 Iam vix extulerat caelo sua lumina Phoebus,
Christicolae cum vela vident inimica secundis
Euris, vela suas Euris visura ruinas.
Omnia conspiciens hinc atque magnus Iberus,
hortarique omnes iterum non iam datur hora;
160 horribilem pugnam subeunt non ante superna
quam petat auxilia, et supplex animoque sereno
confixum ligno Christum sic ore precatur:
'O spes sola viris, virtus fidissima nostri,
ad te conversos nos qui respicis, unus
165 qui peccata luis pietate et pectora sanctis
post renovas curis hominum roburque tremendum
iustitiae in pravos, nocuos, inque impia facta,
sustineas vires nostras in proelia tanta
nunc tua, quod petimus, vincas tu sanguine nostro:
170 haec est nostra quidem pietas nunc debita sancto
sanguineo lateri, vires tua dextra ministret
in saevos, Pietas, hostes, in perfida signa;
hac adsis nobis, Pater optime, et optime sumas
iustitiam hac illos contra, in tua sacra nefandi
175 foedatos vitiis commissis. Aut tibi mens si
est aliter, tali peccans nec dignor honore,
ante pios saltem digner procumbere vultus,
nec fidos videam in populos servire Tyrannum,
ante pedes sacrasque manus atque ora salutis
180 exitio in misero tollentes lumina frustra.'
Absistitque prece imperterritus alta volutans
secum corde audens dux ille atque omnia cernens
imperat audaci pugnas accendere cursu
fortes inde duces, quaeque et certo ordine poni,
185 vexillo sacro erecto, quod rite dicatum
divinae tantum virtuti, ipsique superno
defensori ardens Pater atque ante omnia caro

Phoebus had scarcely raised his light in the sky when the   155
Christians saw the enemy sails filled with the favorable east wind,
sails which were about to see their own ruin by that same wind.
The great Spaniard was attentive to everything, and there was now
no time to encourage the men again. They would undergo a hor-   160
rible battle, but not before he calls on divine assistance and, kneel-
ing, his mind at peace, prays to Christ crucified on the wooden
cross: "O only hope of mankind, our most trusted strength, you
alone watch over us when we turn to you; you cleanse our sins   165
with your piety, and then spur the hearts of men to holy tasks,
restoring our great strength for justice against the wicked and
hurtful, and against impious deeds. May you sustain our strength
in these great battles which are now also yours, for we ask that you
conquer with our bloodshed. We owe what faith is ours to your   170
holy, bloodstained side. May your right hand supply us with
strength, O holy Piety, against our savage enemies and against
their false standards. May you be here with us, supreme Father,
and may you exact justice here against those who are stained by
the unspeakable crimes committed against your holy rites. Or else,   175
if your intention is otherwise, and sinner that I am, I am not
deemed worthy of such honor, let me at least be thought worthy
to die before pious faces. Do not let me see the faithful people
become slaves to the Tyrant, lifting their eyes in vain, in their mis-
erable ruin, before the feet and holy hands and the face of salva-   180
tion." And, devoid of all fear, the daring leader ends his prayer,
turning over deep thoughts in his heart. Looking out for every
contingency, he orders his mighty commanders to plunge straight
into the battle with a bold charge. He commands everything to be   185
prepared in proper order: the holy flag is raised, duly consecrated
only by the power of divine inspiration. In his zeal, the pope had

miserat Austriaco, signum insuperabile bello.
Prudens nam Christus fulgens atque aureus omnis
190 affixusque cruci patiens hic imminet altae.
Candida purpureus signabat pectora sanguis
ornabantque caput sanctum spineta coronis.
Hanc spectare velis media inter proelia et hostes,
nec scelerata pio perrumpere corpora ferro?
195 Iisdem nec nostros animos armare venenis,
armavere manus quae puro in sanguine saevas?
Quem pavidum crux haec dirum non pungat in hostem?
Quique sinat patrias redeuntem hunc victor ad oras?
Signa sinat suaves sacros spirantia odores
200 direpta heu canibus, foedis redolere triumphis?
  Iam puppes Scythicae instantes tumida ora gerebant,
duxque iubet Venetas magnas praevertere cursu
tunc socias puppes, pugnae et praedicere signum.
Collocat audentes Venetos in parte sinistra,
205 et classis triplicis dextram tenet Auria magnus,
cornua bina pari virtute et robore firmo;
ipse autem in media consistit fulgidus armis,
in medio et procerum, magnos quos utraque mittit
Hesperia, insignis, caelo demissus amico,
210 promptus ad auxilia et fessis succurrere rebus
invictoque animo fortem concurrere in hostem:
hostem, quem nullae poterant superare carinae,
quem non Germanae vires, Pannonia tota,
nec mare, nec terris adiuncta potentia regum.
215 Haeret Romanae classis dux, alta Columna
Austriaco, Venetus dux atque Venerius haeret.

sent his insurmountable war standard to his own heavenly de-
fender, John of Austria, who was dear to him above all. On it, wise
Christ hung overhead, radiant and golden, and suffering, affixed   190
high on the cross. His bright red blood marked his chest, and
thorns adorned his holy head in the shape of a crown. How could
we see this on the sails in the thick of the battle among our ene-
mies and not pierce their sinful bodies with our pious steel? How
could we fail to fortify our minds against the very same poisons   195
that stirred their savage hands against our pure blood? Who was
so afraid that this cross did not goad him against the cruel enemy?
Who, if he were victorious, would allow the enemy to return to
the shores of his homeland? Or allow these standards, still giving
off their sweet, sacred odors, to be torn — alas! — by dogs in some   200
foul triumph?

Already the Scythian ships were moving into position and turn-
ing their rising prows. The commander ordered the great Venetian
galleons to take the lead in the charge, out in front of the other
allied ships, and give the signal to fight. He placed the bold Vene-
tians on the left wing; great Doria with his triple fleet held the   205
right side, a two-pronged horn with balanced forces and solid
strength. John himself, however, took the center, brilliant in his
armor, and in the midst of these lords, great men sent from all
parts of the West, he was preeminent, as one sent down from a
heaven that favored him. He was as quick to give relief and lend   210
help when supplies were exhausted as to charge with indomita-
ble courage against the mighty enemy: an enemy which no ships
had ever been able to defeat, which German forces, all of Hun-
gary, and all the combined powers of our kings had not met on sea
or on land. The commander of the Roman fleet, towering Col-   215
onna, holds close to John of Austria, as does Venier, the Venetian
admiral.

Et iam iam strepitu ingenti et clamore resultant
aethera barbarico primum tremefacta superbo;
et reboat missis in Turcas ictibus aether
220   aere cavo, obscurus fumus ferit aethera summa.
Ictibus excussae merguntur in aequore puppes,
a fumo trepidae facies sumpsere colorem.
Aethereae caelumque ruens timuere volucres,
atque caput subitis pennis mersere sub undis;
225   monstraque tunc pavidi pisces nymphaeque marinae
heu pelagi sese occuluere in vallibus imis.
Moxque rates iungunt ratibus, prorisque propinquis
agglomerant acies. Exercent cominus enses
urentesque faces immitunt undique saevas,
230   mortales ictus ferri, crudelia saxa
atque arcu volucres, nimium spissasque sagittas,
qualis cum caelo demissi grandine nimbi
aera scindentes, densi turresque domosque
oppositos feriunt vultus hominesque ferasque
235   nulla salus his est, subito ni se abdere tectis;
omnia misceri subito, perque omnia cernas
horribiles caedes, raptus, incendia saeva,
hunc ferro extinctum misere, hunc atque ignibus atris
exhalantem animam, perfixum pectora quemvis
240   in puppi proprio revolutum sanguine multo.
Sanguineis rivis ponto hos dare colla tumenti,
Thraxque natat pavitans inimica per aequora, frustra
flagitat et vitam. Nostri se fidere ponto
quam potius Thraci, superat cum forte triremem
245   iam nostram, gaudent hostem submergere in undis
atque suos etiam, falsa sub imagine vultus,
sic fumus strepitusque, furor sic improbus ardet,
et stupidos reddunt visus mentemque oculosque
inque necem nostram saevimus lumine capti.

And now the sky resounds with a great crash and clamor, shaken by the haughty cries of the barbarians. The air echoes with the blasts fired against the Turks from the hollowed bronze. Thick   220 smoke strikes the height of heaven. Ships breached by the gunfire sink in the water. Frightened faces assume the color of the smoke. The birds of the air feared the crashing sky, and with a sudden flutter of wings, plunge their heads under the waves. The sea monsters and the panic-stricken fish and the sea nymphs all hide   225 themselves, alas, in the deep valleys of the sea. Soon, ship locks with ship, and oars with oars, and the battle lines close ranks. They wield their swords hand to hand, and throw savagely blazing torches everwhere. They trade deadly blows of iron, merciless can-   230 nonballs, and speeding bowshot, and a thick shower of missiles, just as when clouds sent from heaven, so dense with hail that they split the air and crack towers and homes, strike any faces (whether of man or beast) in the way, and there is no safety for them unless   235 they swiftly duck under their roofs. You could see everything suddenly jumbled together, and in the midst of it all, terrible slaughter, pillaging, and ravaging fires. You could see one man killed miserably by the blade, another coughing out his life amid black flames, still another pierced through the chest, slumped over on   240 the deck in a pool of his own blood. You could see these men give their necks to the sea, now swelling up with rivers of blood. A terrified Thracian swims through enemy waters, and pleads, in vain, for his life. Our men entrust themselves to the sea rather than to the Thracians when they chance to overtake one of our galleys, and rejoice to sink their enemies in the waves, and even some of   245 their own men, under the pretense of likeness: so much does smoke, noise, and relentless frenzy rage, and render vision, the mind, and the eyes senseless. And we who are deceived by our eyes struggle furiously toward our own death. Those who threw

250 Eiecti flammis tunc tentamenta salutis
quaerebant, infandum, horrenda per omnia nilque
obiicitur miseris, nisi desperare salutem.
Nil tutum ante oculos, oculi sua funera versi
cernebantque retro, cernebant undique ferrum,
255 undique ferventes strages, mortemque cruentam.
Heu quot saeva licet cerni tunc spicula, quotquot
vulnera Christicolum vix vivo haerentia cordi?
Queis tu conversis tunc ad te vulnera pandis
sacra tua ante oculos reddis tu, Christe, salutem,
260 atque novos animos infundis victor et armas
pectora cara tuae fidei, tunc debita morti.
    Tum demum Austriacus iusta iam fervidus ira,
non virtutis egens, propria statione relicta,
agmen agens procerum, summo fortique minanti
265 occurrit Thraci Aly, consurgensque, labores
indignans nostros, Venetis succurrit, et alte
prosternit rabiem hostilem atque aggressus eundem.
Ductorem magnum sternit, sternuntur et omnes
iam celsa in puppi fundunt cum sanguine vitam,
270 signa hic divina extollit tunc victor in auras
acer et hinc celeri cursu post tendit in hostes
indomitosque alios atrum demittit in Orcum,
detectos longum remis, duraque catena.
Nulla quibus fuerat spes umquam nulla salutis,
275 eripiunt saevis manibus pro nomine Christi
et multos servant captos in turbine belli:
barbariem nostros visuram mille triumphos,
regales fratres ambos praedamque superbam.
Regalesque animos servant regalia tecta.
280 Litore desertae puppes quaerentibus amplis
in silvis vitam cum surgunt horrida quaeque,
et spolia atque aurum in flammas solvuntur inanes

themselves overboard to avoid the fires were now begging for   250
promises of safety even through all the horrors—it is unspeak-
able!—but nothing is offered the poor wretches, except to despair
of salvation. Nothing before their eyes is safe; their eyes, fixed on
their own destruction, looked behind, looked ahead: everywhere
was iron, seething havoc, and gory death. Alas, how many deadly   255
arrows are there to be seen? How many wounds can be added to
the scarcely living heart of the Christian soldier? To those who
turned to you then, Christ, you open your sacred wounds, offering
salvation before their eyes, and you inspire their hearts with re-   260
newed courage, Conqueror, arming those hearts that are true to
your faith, though destined to die.

Then at last John of Austria, now seething with righteous
anger, lacking no virtue, leaves his own post, and leading the
frontline, encounters the Thracian, Ali Pasha, in all his menacing   265
strength. Rushing forward, infuriated by our distress, he brings
relief to the Venetians and nobly stamps out the enemy's frenzy.
Then he falls on Ali. He lays low that great commander, leveling
everyone on the high deck. They poured out their lives along with
their blood. With this, the conqueror raises God's flag in the   270
breeze, and turning his swift course back toward the enemy in all
his ferocity, he sends more of their savage lot to black Orcus. Oth-
ers he sentences to sit naked at the oars in cruel chains. These men
never had any hope of salvation, and they snatch them away with   275
ferocious hands in the name of Christ. They take many captives in
the whirl of battle: all the barbarians, including both noble broth-
ers, will watch our myriad triumphs and glorious spoils. Royal
defenses protect royal souls. Ships are abandoned on the shore   280
by men who seek life in the thick woods whenever some dan-
ger appears before them. Spoils and gold are destroyed in waste-
ful flames. The rest of the massive plunder is carried away in

ceteraque Ismariis ampla huc deducta carinis
partiri passim et laetantur ludere rapto.
285 Aurea laetantur subnectere Thracia collo,
et pharetras humeris, enses aptare superbos
iam lateri, capiti revolutaque lintea magna;
ingens laetitia ingentem sequiturque rapinam.
Heu quantum captiva phalanx invidit et illis,
290 quos hinc tunc patrias fugientes vidit ad oras,
quantum atque extinctis crudelia funera passis.
Vosque Scythas reduces quantis terroribus actos
afficit Hispanum nomenque Italumque subacta
successu tali Selynum qui numine sancto
295 cernitis imperia. Heu quantum faciesque pudendae,
verba tremorque loquens, et plurima mortis imago
deterrent alios, quos sors vocat ultima victos.
Quae regi regum vestro referetis inormes?
Et quae pro meritis miseri det praemia vestris?
300 O quantas Deus omnipotens crudelesque sagittas
atque faces vidit ferientes aethera tantum
in se conversas quas aura benigna reductas
in pelagum sancto vultu diverterat, atque
affixas malo puppes vel vidit acutas.
305 Haerentes sanctis signis, insignibus altis,
quae pietas, quae sancta manus non tacta reliquit?
Divinae virtutis opus, miracula pravis
credita non Scythicis: habeant sed digna suorum
iam scelerum capiti cruda et miracula victi.
310 Denique victorem Austriacum dum cuncta fatentur,
nec fraus, Occiali, tua perfida, nullaque iam vis
pro scelere extremo valet in certamine tanto
virtutem Liguris pugnando avellere dextra
remis vita datur rapidis, minimeque decebat

Ismarian keels, to be distributed widely, and the men amuse them- selves by trying on what they have seized; they strap Thracian gold 285 around their necks and quivers on their shoulders, and they fit haughty swords on their hips, and tie strips of the great sails, torn down from the mast, around their heads. Great rejoicing follows the great plunder. Alas, how that captured phalanx envied those they saw flee from there to their home shores; how they envied the 290 dead, even those who suffered wretched ends. The names of Spain and Italy haunt you, Scythians, as you are driven to retreat from such horrors, you who see Selim and all his empire broken by this turn of events and this holy power. How disgraced now are your 295 faces, your words, I tremble to say. The frequent sight of the dead frightens off others who are called to their final fate in defeat. What luxuries will you carry back to your king of kings? What reward might he give to you wretches for your services? Oh, how 300 many cruel arrows and torches did almighty God see hurtling up to the sky, when some benign wind threw them off course, and turned them back on themselves or into the sea, as though by di- vine will? He saw ships either transfixed by their own masts or cut to a sliver. What piety, what holy hand unfelt spared those who 305 clung to the holy standards, the high-flying flags? It was the work of divine power, miracles not believed in by the shameless Scythi- ans. Let the conquered now also have cruel miracles, worthy of the architect of their heinous crimes.

Indeed, while all declare John of Austria the victor, neither your 310 treacherous ploy, Uluj Ali, nor any force for evil succeeds in steal- ing virtue from the Ligurians in such a great battle. On the right flank, he gives life to the swift oars, for it was hardly fitting for one

315 spernentem Christum, proque infido hoste negantem
     laetitiis Christi, sacris et adesse triumphis.
     At fuge, te haec eadem semper fortuna sequetur,
     inque tuo vivet vultu victoria nostra.
     En infida ratis fugiens sine fine cruorem
320 sulcabat proprium; plenus iam sanguine pontus,
     sanguine tincta ratis, quem barbara corpora mersa
     impavidas timuisse umbras testantur Averni.
     Sit cruor is testis Mauris Libycisque pavoris
     infamis, quo te decoras nomenque tremendum,
325 barbare trux, assuete olim furtisque rapinisque.
     En tetigit Caracossa tuam cum sanguine puppim,
     audentem nimium fortis cum dextera clari
     semper Honorati propriaque in puppe coegit
     Tartareas tentare vias et linquere vitam.
330 At quo te claro nunc tollam nomine, princeps
     Farnesi, lumen magnum dignumque parente
     ac matre Austrica, amborum cura alta parentum:
     virtutem ex his primo qui sub flore iuventae
     discis, namque animi invicti tu signa dedisti.
335 Non te segnitie, et vili quis, magne, timore,
     arguat at nimis ausis, dum lumina Phoebus,
     corpora Neptunus rubris mersere sub undis.
     At postque caedes, clamor rabiesque inimica,
     noxque simul siluere, omni iam Thrace subacto,
340 omnia cui cedunt, primum Deus intonat alto
     collucens fuscam scinditque per aera noctem,
     illustrat caelum flammis, totumque resultat,
     laetitiae signa, Austriacos testantia honores.
     Namque dies sua signa dedit: sol ipse reclusit
345 surgens et clausit decedens lumine laeto
     vix aequatam animo victoriam et omnia cursu
     detulit ignotis per totum gentibus orbem.

who spurns and denies Christ in favor of the infidel enemy to be   315
present for the rejoicings of Christ and his sacred triumphs. But
flee, for your fate will always follow you, and our victory will live
on in your face. See how in retreat the infidel's ship was plowing
through the endless stream of his own gore. The sea is now filled   320
with blood, each ship stained with the blood that the drowned
barbarian corpses had shed in proof that they dreaded the fearless
shades of Avernus. Let this gore bear witness to the Moors and
the Libyans of the infamous fear with which you adorn yourself
and your terrible name, fierce barbarian, though once you were   325
quite used to pillaging and plundering. Look how Kara Hodja
stained your ship with his blood, when the strong right hand of
Onorato Caetani forced him in his over-boldness to test out the
road to Tartarus on his own ship and leave his life behind.

But under what glorious title should I celebrate you, Farnese   330
prince, great light, worthy of your father and your Austrian
mother, great hope of both your parents. From them, you learned
virtue in the first flower of youth, for you have shown signs of
your indomitable courage. No one could reproach you for weak-   335
ness and base fear, great one. If anything, you acted too boldly
until Phoebus dipped his light and Neptune sank bodies under
the red waves. But afterward, when the slaughter and the roar and
the enemy's rage and the night grows silent, when the Thracian is
entirely subdued, God, to whom all things give way, thunders   340
from on high, lighting up the dark night and splitting the air. He
brightens the heavens with flames, and the whole sky resounds:
signs of joy, testaments to the glory of Austria. For the day sup-
plied its own omens. The sun itself opened in its rising and closed   345
with a happy glow in its setting on a victory scarcely equal to its
spirit, and along its course it conveyed the news to unknown races

Ipsae etiam gentes norunt obedire triumphis
Ioniis, dux magne, tuis et cernere, sub quo
350   numine felici sua surgant aurea saecla,
non tua sors ullas, non virtus maxima metas
iam videt imperiis, rumpas nunc aequore cunctas
atque moras terris, terrae et maria omnia laetis
expectant animis, vincit tua fama sedendo.
355   Te te etiam vincis, maior victoria, nam tu
hanc Christo cedis. Spolias te nomine tanto
victoris reddisque humilem, dum gloria maior
non assueta viris, infert te, maxime, caelo.
Care Deo et terris, post hac fortuna superba
360   te tantum renuet ducibus servire superbis:
inque armis rebusque aliis Victoria magnis
iam sine te duce nescia erit vel vincere terris.

Aggrediar nunc te, tanti pars magna laboris,
communis dudum dubiae spes certa salutis,
365   gloria priscorum proavum, iam maxime Marce
Antoni, quem sors lapsum demisit in aevum,
ambiguis nam tu rebus tu foedera sacra
iungis, componens animos, parcisque labori
numquam indefessus, communem et restituis rem.
370   Flectere virtutem antiquam terraque marique
non potuit Fortuna tuam semperque resurgens
maior in adversis superas hanc fortior heros.
Te Tyrrhena prius vexarunt aequora vastis
fluctibus Hesperiam velox dum tendis in altam,
375   tuncque preces caelo, tunc gazam fudit in aequor
navita, cui pavibus pallor iam tinxerat ora.
At postquam Christi causam nostramque salutem
tutari properas, tollis te interritus undis
Hadriacis hinc hinc undantibus, alta Columna,

across the whole world. They know to take heed of triumphs in
Ionia, great leader, and to pay attention to yours in particular. For
under your blessed, divine power, their golden age may rise. Nei-   350
ther your fate nor your mighty virtue establishes any limit to your
domain, so now break off all delays on land and sea. The lands
and all the seas await you in high spirits; your fame triumphs
wherever it comes to rest. You even triumph over yourself—a   355
greater victory still—for you concede this victory to Christ. You
despoil yourself of the great name of "Conqueror," and while you
humble yourself, mighty one, a greater glory, one not often given
to men, bears you to heaven. Now that you are dear to God and to
all nations, proud fortune will forbid one so great as you to serve   360
proud leaders. In war just as in other great affairs, Victory will no
longer know how to conquer without you leading her.

I shall turn now to you, mighty Marco Antonio Colonna, who
played a big part in this great endeavor, the unflinching hope of
our common salvation when it was in doubt, the glory of our an-   365
cient ancestors. Fate sent you to our fallen age, for you brought the
Holy League together despite all uncertainties, calming minds and
always tireless in your work. You restored the common cause. For-
tune was unable to break your ancient virtue on land or sea; but   370
always rising back up ever greater for the adversities you faced,
you, the braver hero, overcome her. First the Tyrrhenian Sea buf-
feted you with its wide waves as you headed swiftly toward noble
Italy. Then a sailor, his face blanched by a fearful pallor, first   375
poured forth prayers to heaven, then poured your treasure into the
sea. But after that, you were quick to defend the cause of Christ
and our safety. Undaunted, you raise yourself, now here, now
there on the surging Adriatic waves, like a towering column.

380 et tandem accesti tutus Diomedis ad undas.
Quas referam hinc saevas iras per flantibus antris,
et praeceps caelum, nimbos, abscissaque vela,
montibus aequatam puppim tunc fulmine tactam
deiectum Illyricas cum te spectavit ad undas
385 Proteus et pavidae fleverunt undique nymphae?
At fretus pietate tua, tu robore cinctus,
vexatus toties, doctus te opponere morti,
teque tuos servas ad facta ingentia magnus
Aeneas alter, fatis servantibus et Dis.

390 Vixit et in virtute tua tanta omnis inhaerens
vita Italum; haec novit Pater optimus omina caeli
imperiumque dedit belli pro nomine sacro,
et iuvenem bello adiunxit comitemque nepotem.
Arma dedit viresque tibi sed fortia virtus;
395 hinc tibi florentes intexens Martia honores
Roma suos, palmis te nunc miratur ovantum.
Ne coeptis desiste ingens, invicta Columna,
aereum lumen divinum in turbine rerum.

Nec minor illuxit tua gloria tanta Veneri,
400 quem Deus et patria aerumnis tunc acta supremis
intrepidum accendunt ad bella in fine senectae;
canities animo superata est sera sed ingens
vis irae forti vel tunc non invidet ulli.
Te novere patres Veneti cum summa dederunt
405 imperia in magnum hostem, te hostis, maxime, novit
paenituitque suos casus et fata dolentem.

Tuque ultam patriam vidisti et Cypria regna,
Barbarice, tuis defensa viribus ingens,
dum te victorem sequitur mors invida pulchri.

At last you safely reached the breakers of Diomedes; why should I   380
recount the savage fury raging through the blustering caves, and
the precipitous sky, the clouds, and torn sails, the ship raised to be
level with mountaintops and then struck by lightning—and all the
while Proteus watched as you were tossed to the Illyrian waves,
and the frightened nymphs everywhere wept? But trusting your   385
piety and endowed with strength—how many times was it tested!
—you learned to set yourself against death. And you keep yourself
and your men safe for more important deeds, like another mighty
Aeneas, while the Fates and the gods watched over you.

He survived, and the well-being of all Italians depended on the   390
virtue that was yours. The highest Father recognized these omens
from heaven, and he offered this man supreme power in war, on
behalf of his sacred name. And he joined his descendant with the
youth, as a companion in battle. To you, he gave not only mighty
arms and fighting forces, but virtue as well. Now warlike Rome   395
weaves you blooming garlands and wonders at you with lifted
hands. Great, unconquered Colonna, do not give up on what you
have begun. You are a divine, ethereal beacon in the maelstrom of
earthly affairs.

No less did your great glory shine, Venier, whom God and   400
your fatherland, now beset with great trials, spur into battle un-
daunted, even at the end of your life. Gray old age was conquered
by your courage, and your great wrath, even then, envied no man's
strength. The Venetian patriarchs knew you well when they gave
you the highest authority against their great enemy. Even the en-   405
emy knew you well, mighty one, and you grieved for his losses and
fate.

And you, mighty Barbarigo, saw your fatherland avenged, and
the kingdom of Cyprus defended by your efforts. All the while

410　Iamque cadens, surgis, caelo et te condis in alto;
　　iamque patres laeti matres et vivida pubes
　　sese ornant decorantque tuo sic sanguine fuso.
　　Unda triumphali Veneta luctatur arena,
　　grata tuos patria haec meritos servabit honores.
415　　　Leucadiae iuga summa diem servate supremum,
　　ultas Romanas acies quae et nomina Christi
　　Maumethem saevum ferro flammisque cadentem
　　vidistis, iuvenem redeuntem mille carinis
　　Hispanum signis amplis spoliisque superbum.
420　Hinc tua laeta olim florebunt arva quietis
　　fluctibus, aeternum, sacrum spirantia odorem;
　　gaudete, o iuga summa, arva et gaudete superba.
　　Caesareis te et tolle animis. Rex maxime, fratre
　　Austriaco, iam iam felicia et omnia cerne
425　auspiciis magni iuvenis, quem regia virtus,
　　religio atque ornans humilem prudentia summa
　　acceptum dis, ac populis sanctoque potenti
　　pontifici, aeternum qui te iam suspicit illo.
　　Huc tu adsis spes magna et nostro occurre labori,
430　extremis votis, animisque inhiantibus omnes
　　te nam te solum optamus, te Roma resurgens
　　exspectat, visura tuo sua gaudia vultu,
　　visura et cladem extremam caedemque Tyranni;
　　non terrena tuos decorat modo regia pompa
435　invictos animos, successus, inclyte, tales.
　　At tua magnanimi victricia signa secuti,
　　quique sibi optarunt pulchram per vulnera mortem
　　atque triumphantes animae caelestia serta
　　caelestesque parant ad compita longa triumphos.

death pursues you, conqueror, jealous of your nobility. Now, in 410
falling, you rise and seat yourself in high heaven. Now happy fa-
thers and mothers and lively young men array themselves with
festive ornaments because of the blood you spilled. The waves
crash on the triumphant Venetian shoreline. This grateful country
will observe your well-deserved honors.

High peaks of Leucadia, watch over that final day: you who 415
saw the Roman fleet and the people of Christ taking their ven-
geance, and the brutal Muhammadan fall before sword and fire.
You saw the Spanish youth return with a thousand ships, proud
with his banners and his vast spoils. From now on your fertile 420
fields will blossom with waves of peace, exhaling a sacred, eternal
fragrance. Rejoice, high peaks, and rejoice proud fields! Raise
yourself with Caesar's spirit. Mighty king, with your Austrian
brother, see now all the blessings that come under the auspices of 425
that great youth. Regal virtue, faith, and high wisdom decorate
his humility. He is welcomed by the gods and the people alike,
and by the holy power of the pope, who supports you, always,
through him. Be with us here, great hope, and bring aid to our
cause, for we all put our faith in you and you alone, even with our 430
last prayers and our halting breath. Rome, rising again, awaits you,
hoping to see its joy mirrored in your face, and hoping to see its
last calamity with the death of the Tyrant. No mere earthly regal
procession celebrates your unconquered courage and achievements 435
such as these, famous one. Those greathearted men who followed
your victorious flag, and who chose a noble death through their
wounds, together with the triumphant angels prepare heavenly
garlands and divine triumphal processions at the wide crossroads.

440   Hos inter medius magni regnator Olympi
victorem tantum caelo mirabitur alto;
intrantique urbem sanctam laeta omina pandet,
et plaudent floresque dabunt sacrasque coronas
caelestes animae, caelestia munera, pompas.
445   Iam venias memorande omni terraque marique
et superis, prima et fulgens lux addita caelo
praeclaram solare urbem, solare superbum
Tybrim, luminibus campos solare decoris
amplexuque Pii Patris omnia numina coeptis
450   sume novis; magnum teque in nova proelia mitte.

In their midst, the Lord of great Olympus will admire your great   440
victory from high heaven. Happy omens will attend your entrance
into the holy city, and the heavenly spirits will applaud you and
give you flowers and holy wreaths, and heavenly gifts and parades.
Now come, you who are celebrated in every land and on every sea,   445
and by the gods above, as the first shimmering star added to the
sky to cheer the famous city, to cheer the proud Tiber, and to
bring joy to its fields with your radiant glory. And in the embrace
of Father Pius, go with all his powers on new endeavors. Throw   450
yourself, mighty one, into new battles.

: XVI :

Ecloga Nautica (seu Christianorum et Turcarum navale certamen)

Giovanni Antonio Taglietti

Euridamas. Idmon.

Dic age Pieridum princeps, dic maxime Apollo
proelia caeruleas Neptuni gesta per undas,
dum stimulis acti Eumenidum gens effera Thraces
Christicolumque acres pugnat manus. O bona, Musae,
5   progenies, primis colui quas semper ab annis,
ecquae erit e vobis, quae me graviora canentem
laurigeras inter silvas Heliconis ad undas
sistat et optata cingat mihi tempora fronde?
   At tu, quem dulces venientem in luminis oras
10   Astraea, Autumni portas, Chelasque relinquens,
ipsa suas docuit leges, cuique innuba Pallas
diversos caeli motus stellasque micantes
et dedit occultas rerum cognoscere causas;
macte tuis, Federice, actis, et sanguine avito,
15   huc ades et nostris faveas precor optime votis.
Non iniusta peto, tu nam persaepe recessus
Aonios lustras et dum felicia condis
ipse tua intentus miratur carmina Phoebus.
   Gnosius Euridamas, quo non praestantior alter
20   per vada salsa citam remis impellere puppim
et regere, et soles tempestatesque futuras
praecinere, et variae faciem cognoscere lunae,
instantes cupiens sollers vitare procellas.
In loca tuta ratem impulerat portumque tenebat,

: XVI :

Nautical Eclogue, or The naval contest of the Christians and Turks

Giovanni Antonio Taglietti

Euridamas. Idmon.

Sing now, leader of the Muses, sing, mighty Apollo, of the wars waged on Neptune's sea-blue waves, when, spurred on by the whips of the Eumenides, the wild race of Thracians fought the ferocious band of Christians. O blessed daughters, O Muses I have worshiped since I was young, which of you will set me among 5 the laurel-bearing groves by the waters of Helicon as I sing of weightier things and bind my temples with the green boughs I have hoped for?

But as for you, Frederick: Astraea herself taught you her laws 10 when you arrived on the sweet shores of life, as she left the gates of Autumn and the arms of Scorpio, and unwed Pallas showed you how to recognize the various motions of the heavens, the twinkling stars, and the hidden causes of things. Frederick, honored for your deeds and ancestral lineage, be with me now and 15 grant my prayers, I implore. I do not ask for anything unreasonable, for you often wander the secluded retreats of Aonia, and even Phoebus stands by with eager awe while you compose your blessed songs.

Euridamas of Crete was greater than all the others in rowing and steering a swift boat through the salty waves. He knew how to 20 read the sun and forecast the coming weather and to recognize the faces of the changing moon, all in his desire to use his skill to avoid the looming storms. He guides his boat to safe harbor and

25   qua formosa situ, gemina formosior arce
      Corcyra, aequoreas late prospectat in undas;
      dumque hic Fortunae ereptus, non horret aquarum
      agmina, vicino venientem in litore vidit
      Idmona, remigio doctum puppisque magistrum,
30   talibus atque illum compellat vocibus ultro:

Euridamas

      Fallor? An ista mihi quae nunc occurrit imago
      est umbra? An potius, quod mallem, est Cyprius Idmon?
      Idmon es; o dulci sospes quod vesceris aura,
      quam laetor dilecte mihi! Longaevus Amilcon
35   dixerat obsessae tendentem ad moenia Cypri
      atque arma atque epulas et Bacchi dona ferentem,
      effugere armatas classes atque agmina Thracum
      non potuisse; imis quin te vel mergeret undis
      dira manus nimium, vel adacto in pectora ferro
40   heu miserum, aeternis noctis demitteret umbris?
      Sed te, quae tantis Idmon fortuna periclis
      eripuit? Nostris et quis te reddidit oris?

Idmon

      Euridama, ut senior multis narravit Amilcon,
      milite cum patriis cuperem succurrere terris,
45   et Cererem obsessis vectarem et vina; carinis
      Ismariis ego praeda fui, sed compede vinctus,
      et iussus validos manibus propellere remos,
      verbera et assiduae sensi fera vincla catenae,
      optatam donec fesso Deus ipse salutem
50   attulit et celso insontem miseratus Olympo est;
      nam dum Threiciam telis et remige classem
      et ducibus penitus spoliat, primosque trucidat

reaches the port where beautiful Corcyra, stunning with its twin 25
citadels, looks out over the watery waves. Now he is safe from di-
saster, and does not fear the march of the waves. He spots Idmon,
skilled in rowing and master of his boat, approaching on the
neighboring shore and addresses him directly with these words: 30

Euridamas

Am I mistaken or is that a ghost now coming toward me? Or, is it
Idmon of Cyprus, which I would greatly prefer? You are Idmon!
O how happy I am that you still breathe the sweet air, my dear
friend. Old Amilcon had told me that you were trapped at the 35
walls of besieged Cyprus — bringing arms and platters and gifts of
wine — and could not get away from the armed ships and Thracian
battle lines. How is it that some dreadful horde did not submerge
you in the deep waves or send you, with a sword thrust to the
chest, poor man, into the eternal shades of night? What good 40
fortune, Idmon, snatched you from such great danger? And who
brought you back to our shores?

Idmon

Euridamas, as old Amilcon reported to many, I wanted to support
my fatherland by joining our fighting men. I would carry both 45
grain and wine to the people besieged. But I was taken for ransom
by Ismarian ships, bound at the ankles and ordered to ply the
strong oars with my hands; I suffered whips and fierce chains in
this unsparing captivity until, when I was nearly exhausted, God
himself brought me hoped-for help from lofty Olympus and took 50
pity on an innocent man. For when a select band of Christians
pillaged the Thracian fleet of weapons and oars and leaders, killing

Christicolum delecta cohors, mihi pristina tandem
reddita libertas, spoliisque oneratus et auro
55   en adsum, non umbra quidem, sed Cyprius Idmon.

Euridamas

Tu ne igitur praesens tanti certamina belli
horrida vidisti, ductorum et funera noscis?
Haec nobis avidis dum singula quaerimus, ante
fama loquax, obscura tamen, narrare solebat,
60   non veris vera involvens. Tu protinus ista
dic quaeso dilecte Idmon; pendebimus omnes
ore tuo, en iam te nautarum turba coronat.

Idmon

His oculis, his inquam oculis haec proelia vidi.
Dicam igitur, magna est etiam meminisse voluptas.
65   Threicius, miserae post diruta moenia Cypri,
ereptis laetus spoliis regnoque Tyrannus
iam tercentenis sulcabat puppibus aequor,
scilicet ut pelago, Venetoque Leone subacto,
et frena et magno leges imponeret orbi,
70   demens, qui tantis contraria numina votis,
nec vidit capiti ultrices instare sorores,
acer Halys, crudelis Halys, quem patre Doriclo
conceptum furtim gelidas ad Strymonis undas
edidit Alcimede, primis assuetus ab annis
75   ferre arma et celerem cornu torquere sagittam
atque pedum cursu ventos superare, et in orbem
vertere cornipedem rapidum cursuque citato
comminus adversos hastas effrangere in hostes
frigora tum solesque pati Boreaque furente,
80   huc illuc vastum ratibus lustrare profundum.

them first, then at last I was returned to my former liberty, and here I am, weighed down with spoils and gold: not a ghost at all, but Idmon of Cyprus.   55

Euridamas

Do you mean you were there to witness the horrible conflict of that great war, and you know about the deaths of its leaders? When we were eager to ask her for details about this event, Fama, previously so talkative (if also obscure), was inclined to spin stories, intertwining truth and lies. Please tell me right away what   60 happened, sweet Idmon; we all hang on your every word, for already a crowd of sailors surrounds you.

Idmon

With these eyes — I swear — with these eyes I saw these battles. So I will tell you about them, for my desire to remember these things is great. After the walls of pitiful Cyprus were torn down, the   65 Thracian Tyrant, pleased with the spoils and the kingdom he took, was already cutting through the waves in three hundred ships. He fully intended to impose his laws and reins on the whole world, now that the Venetian Lion had been captured. Brutal and   70 cruel Ali Pasha — son of Doriclus, born in secret by Alcimede at the cold waves of Strymon — was not in his right mind, so he did not perceive the forces that opposed his vows, the avenging sisters looming over his head. He had learned to bear arms at an early   75 age, to shoot a rapid arrow from his bow and, running on foot, to outstrip the winds, or turn a galloping horse in a circle and, in a swift charge, break his spears against the enemy in close combat. He had learned to endure heat and cold, and to sail the vast sea   80

Primus erat classis ductor, quem proximus, armis
consilioque valens sequitur Portunus, et audax
Sirrochus medias remis transire procellas,
nec non et Libyae solio sceptroque potitus
85   Ruzzalis, Occhialiden populi cognomine dicunt.
    Ergo ubi fama Pii Pastoris nuntia ductu
Hispanas properare manus Latiasque cohortes,
et cecinit lati magnas per marmora ponti
adventare rates, ultro quae bella lacessant
90   horrida, et Ismarias valeant excindere gentes,
armorum classisque novae numerique potentis,
non bene certus Halys varias sub pectore curas
volvebat, tandemque animo sententia sedit,
certior armatos illi dum nuntius hostes
95   narraret classemque mari decedere aperto,
Naupactique sinus tutos portumque tenere.
    Et iam Cimmeriis properans nox humida ab antris,
duxerat obscuras mundum complexa tenebras,
solaque candentes nobis Latonia vultus
100   ostendens, tremula vestibat caerula luce;
cum solitus praedas vectare et vivere rapto
Carcozza, humentis per amica silentia noctis
mittitur, exploret nostrae qui robora gentis,
telaque et excubias classis, numerumque reportet.
105   Nec longum in medio tempus, cum nare per aequor
Christicolum pictas cernit Carcozza carinas,
dumque acie cunctas numerare et cernere acuta
nititur, eripiens misero mentemque aciemque
ipse Deus, nigra velavit lumina vitta;
110   nam classis numerosa, potens, magnumque futura
Thracibus exitium, segnis, nec idonea bello,
nec posse Ismariae visa est concurrere classi.
Vix Aurora polum roseo patefecerat ortu

even against the raging north wind. He was the chief commander of the fleet. Pertev Pasha, strong in arms and council, follows him closely, as does audacious Sulus Mehmet Pasha as they row through the middle of storms, and even Uluj Ali, now in charge of the throne and scepter of Libya; his own people call him by the 85 name Occhiali.

Then Fama reports that by the order of Pope Pius the Spanish troops and their Latian cohorts are rushing to embark on their great ships across the expanse of the wide sea. Of their own free will they incite horrible wars and summon their strength to cut 90 down the Ismarian people. Ali Pasha, uncertain of his artillery, his new ships, and the strength of his numbers, was meditating cares in his heart. Finally, a plan forms in his mind, when a trusted messenger reports to him that his enemies are armed and their fleet is 95 departing on the open sea: he decides to protect the harbor and port of Naupactus.

And now humid night rose quickly from the Cimmerian caves, wrapping the world in obscuring darkness. Only Latona showed us her glimmering white face, swathing the sea in a tremulous 100 light. Kara Hodja, accustomed to carrying off booty and living on plunder, is sent through the friendly silence of the damp night to determine the strength of our side. He is to report on our weapons and sentries, our boats and numbers. Nor is there long to 105 wait, for sailing out in the middle of the water, Kara Hodja soon spies the painted ships of the Christians, and while he tries to count them and precisely discern them, God himself snatched away the pitiful man's mind and sight, veiling his eyes with a black band. The large, powerful fleet, soon to be the great ruin of the 110 Thracians, appeared sluggish to him, not fit for war, nor able to hold up against the Ismarian ships. Hardly had yellow dawn

lutea, cum fati ignarus, sortisque futurae,
115 ecce hilaris Carcozza redit, mox talia fatur:
     'Christicolae pereant omnes, victoria nostras
laeta super volitat puppes, optataque nobis
iampridem, felix tandem sors obtulit ultro.
Hesperias nuper, lustro dum cuncta, triremes
120 perspexi numero exiguas atque artis egentes,
militis, armorum atque ducum: quid bella moramur?
Linquite ductores portus et aperta petamus.'
     Talia dum memorat, subito per inania magnus
auditur multo mixtus stridore volatus,
125 dumque oculos Thraces mirati ad sidera torquent,
acriter ecce vident multo cum vulture magnum
pugnantem Iovis armigerum atque hostilia aduncis
unguibus et saevo rapientem viscera rostro,
sanguinis unde ingens supra caput affluit imber.
130 Turbati stupuere omnes, quidque omina poscant,
quidve ferant, tremula perquirunt voce. Ducumque
primus Halys dubias mentes et pectora firmat.
     'Auspicia e caelo nobis patefacta sereno
Christicolas horrenda petunt, gaudete potentis
135 Strymonii regis proceres et bella parate.
Nam qui nos avium tinxit cruor, omina nobis
dat certa: Hesperio fluxurum sanguine pontum,
dum nostrum illorum reserabit pectora ferrum.'
     Sic fatus, socios ad pugnam hortatur ovantes
140 et portum linquens latum migravit in aequor.
Ipse audax primas acies Carcozza regebat,
Sirrochus dextras agit, Occhialidesque sinistras,
piratum scelerata cohors postrema coercet;
hos inter spes magna suis, Portunus et ingens
145 ibat Halys, mediique ambo, media agmina ducunt.

unveiled the pole with its rosy glow when, behold, cheerful Kara 115
Hodja, ignorant of fate and his future destiny, speaks:

"Let all the Christians perish: joyful victory flies over our ships,
and fortunate destiny, which we have anticipated for a long time
now, appears to be at hand. While I was reconnoitering just now, I
saw Hesperian galleys, small in number, lacking in skill, troops, 120
weapons, and leaders. Why should we delay the fight? Captains,
leave the ports and let us seek the open sea."

While he was delivering his report, suddenly an object appears,
flying through the still air, accompanied by a great shriek. When
the stunned Thracians turn their eyes to the stars, behold, they see 125
an eagle, mighty arm-bearer of Jove, fighting with a flock of vul-
tures, snatching at their entrails with its curved talons and sharp
beak; above their heads a great shower of blood pours down.
Troubled, they are all stupefied and ask with a trembling voice 130
what the omens might mean or what they might portend. First
among the leaders, Ali calms their doubting minds and hearts:

"The frightful omens displayed to us in the serene sky are
meant for the Christians. Rejoice, captains of the powerful Stry- 135
monian king, and prepare for war. The blood of the birds that has
bathed us offers a clear sign: the sea will be flooded with Hes-
perian blood when our swords slash their bowels."

With these words he rouses his exulting allies for war. Leaving 140
the port he moves into the wide sea. Bold Kara Hodja himself was
leading the first battle lines. Sulus Mehmet Pasha drives the right,
Uluj Ali the left; a wicked cohort of pirates brings up the rear.
Among these goes Pertev Pasha, the great hope for his own peo-
ple, and huge Ali, both leading the middle ranks. 145

    Interea iusti succensus Martis amore
magnus Ioannes, Augusti invicta propago,
Hesperiae cladis et sparsi sanguinis ultor,
ad bella hortatus socios superosque precatus,
150   agmen agens aderat magnum, classemque pararat
quae posset densas Turcarum evertere turmas,
cui comes it Venetum spes magna Venerius heros,
et Latiae columen gentis lumenque Columna
magnus et Ursini gemini duo fulmina Martis,
155   Corneaque Ascanius ductor clarissimus armis,
atque simul medias ducunt miro ordine puppes;
at Ligurum decus egregium, Diis aemula proles
bella fremit forti praecinctus milite, princeps
Aurius et dextrum ducit latus; inde sinistrum
160   Barbadicus agit fortis, cui cruda senectus
non minuit validae vires animumque iuventae;
Alvarus et rigidi priscus Mavortis alumnus
posteriora tenet, magnae anteriora triremes.
    Ut primum mira tot ductas arte carinas
165   tot signa, et proceres tantos, tot lintea vidit,
maestus Halys, multa pressus formidine pectus
obstupuit, siccisque diu vox faucibus haesit.
Iam quid agat, nescit, placidos nunc denique vellet
Naupacti tenuisse sinus, tamen ipse timorem
170   dissimulat classemque truces convertit in hostes.
Nec mora, Christicolae occurrunt castusque sacerdos
ostendens vexilla crucis sublimia, Turcas
territat et magna clamans sic voce profatur:
    'Aeternum celso suspensus stipite Christus,
175   aeternum vivat, vivant quicumque sequuntur
dilectae vexilla crucis; mittantur ad umbras

Meanwhile, burning with zeal for a righteous war, great John, invincible offspring of the emperor and avenger of the massacre and spilled blood of Hesperia, urged his allies on to war and prayed to the gods. He appeared at the head of a huge force: he had assembled a fleet that could overturn the close ranks of the Turks. His companions are the hero Venier, the great hope of Venice; the mighty Colonna, pillar and luminary of the Latin race; the twin Orsini, thunderbolts of Mars; and commander Ascanio della Corgna, most famous in arms: they lead the middle division of the fleet together in a wondrous array. Admiral Giovanni Andrea Doria, great glory of the Ligurians, a young man who rivals the gods, presses for war surrounded by his strong troops, leading the right side; brave Agostino Barbarigo drives the left, his vibrant, youthful strength and courage undiminished by sluggish old age; Álvaro de Bazán, ancient veteran of stern Mars, guards the rear; the great galleons hold the front.

When he perceived so many ships with standards and sails led by miraculous skill and such great leaders, Ali stood somber and still, his chest tight with fear, and his voice stuck in his dry throat. Now he does not know what to do; now at last he wished that he had stayed in the harbor of Naupactus. Nevertheless, he hides his fear and turns his fleet against the ferocious enemy. Without delay, the Christians engage, and a chaste priest, displaying the lofty standard of the cross, terrifies the Turks and, shouting, speaks in a great voice:

"Let Christ eternally raised high on the lofty tree live forever, and let whoever follows the banners of the beloved cross live as well; let the perfidious race of Thracians be sent to the shades of

Tartareas, Erebique domos, gens perfida Thraces.
Sic erit, ecce tonat laevum Deus, ipsaque nobis
carbasa felici complet turgentia vento.'
180   Ergo utrimque pari concurrunt impete classes.
Fit fragor, et clamore virum, clangore tubarum
aequora lata sonant magno, caelumque remugit;
aerque et strictis collucent ensibus undae.
Maiores aliis Venetum armataeque triremes
185   et sponte ante alias prima in certamina missae.
Saepius aeratas valido conamine glandes
sulphureo iaciunt igni, quo murmure magnos
aequoreis credas scopulis concurrere montes.
      Tunc igitur laceraeque rates, caesaeque cohortes
190   Turcarum salsis late labuntur in undis.
Cum tot pestiferas caedes, tot damna suorum
respiciens furibundus Halys, iubet ocius omnes
ictibus ignitis auferri et credere puppes;
sed nec iussa valent: densae nam grandinis instar
195   ferrea pila ruit, Geticas quae densa triremes
quo se umquam ferant, lacerat, sternitque premitque.
Sic igitur caecas Orci demissus ad umbras
Thrax perit, et subito lunatum solvitur agmen.
      Instaurant acies, adduntque minantia verba
200   pro se quisque duces Getici, pugnamque capessunt;
atque hic tormentis iaculisque et milite saeptus
Sirrochus, medias acies circumdare tentat
Christicolum, ancipiti qui tunc certamine nixi
comminus Ismarias contra pugnare catervas.
205   Non tulit hoc sollers et nostrae causa salutis
magna, sed adversum tunc Barbadicus in hostem
agmen agit propere adveniens atque impedit orsa,

Tartarus, the home of Erebus. So it will be: behold, God thunders
on the left and fills our swelling sails with a favoring wind."

So on both sides the fleets engage with matched violence. 180
Havoc erupts, and the wide sea resounds with the shouts of men
and blasts of cannons, and the sky echoes the sound; the air and
water flash with drawn swords. The galleons of Venice, larger than
the others and heavily armed, are sent eagerly ahead of the rest 185
into the first contest. They fire bronze shells in continual volleys,
blazing with a sulfurous glare. The rumble was such that you
would think great mountains had crashed into cliff-like waves.

Then on all sides the shattered ships and slaughtered cohorts of 190
the Turks sink into the salty waves. Ali goes mad, seeing so much
disastrous carnage, so many losses for his people, and orders all
ships to withdraw swiftly from the fiery missiles and seek shelter;
but his orders are useless, for iron javelins fly, thick like hail, and 195
wreck the Getic galleys wherever they go, laying them low and
beating them down. And so it was that the Thracian perished,
sent to the blind shades of Orcus, the moon-shaped battle line
abruptly scattered.

The Getic leaders each reassemble their own battle forma-
tion, as they shout threatening words and rekindle the fight. Pro- 200
tected by catapults and javelins and his own militia, Sulus Mehmet
Pasha tries to surround the central battle line of the Christians,
who were then debating whether to close around the Ismarian
troops in hand-to-hand combat. Wise Barbarigo, our great source 205
of strength, could not endure this, but swiftly comes to drive his
fleet against the opposing enemy and impede the onslaught. He

nec cessat, donec telis atque igne voraci,
et glande, hostiles, capto ductore, carinas
210   perdat, et innumeros mittat sub Tartara Thracas.
      At Carcozza manu fidens levibusque sagittis,
Sirrocho amisso manet imperterritus atque
saevit et Ausonium pharetram consumit in agmen;
sternit Atyn, sternit Lalagem, sternitque Theronem,
215   et Fabarim, et puerum Lausum, et spem patris Abantem
Adriaci, invito is genitore ad bella profectus,
unica progenies, matris pulcherrima cura,
aeternum miseros liquit sine prole parentes.
Additur his iuvenis Superantius; hic prius acrem
220   senserat emissam corpus strinxisse sagittam,
ergo dum manibus vulnus bis terque retractat,
ecce illi Ismarium penitus cava tempora telum
traicit. Ille dolens crudeli vulnere, leto
volvitur, et Venetas moriens reminiscitur oras.
225   Talia per nostram geminat dum funera classem
Carcozza, assuetus prima tormenta iuventa
tractare et celeres ex illis mittere glandes,
Cenomanum genus, illorum quos Tropica vallis
educat, hunc torvo iamdudum lumine Pentheus
230   aspicit et motus gressusque observat ovantis,
si quando valeat tantos abolere furores,
classibus et veterem Latiis arcere ruinam.
Vix apicem puppi extulerat, cum protinus illi
glans violenta cavo contorta ut fulmen ab aere
235   transadigit galeam cerebrique in ventribus haesit.
      Interea mediis utrimque in classibus, ardens
saevit Bellona et resonat clamoribus aether.
Nam cupiens Thracum miseras ulciscier umbras,
et regi magno sese iactare triumpho,
240   clamat Halys saevumque gemens et fervidus ira

does not stop until he has captured their leader with weapons, devouring fire, and bullets, sunk the enemy ships, and sent innumerable Thracians down to Tartarus. 210

But Kara Hodja, trusting his aim and his slender arrows, remains undaunted, even though Sulus Mehmet Pasha is lost. In a rage he empties his quiver on the Ausonian troops. He lays low Atys, Lalage, Theron and Fabaris, the boy Lausus, and Abas, the 215 hope of his father Adriacus, who set off for war against his father's will, an only child doted on by his mother. He left his parents miserable and without heirs. The youth Soranzo is added to these: he first had felt the sharp arrow graze his body; then, while he 220 tried twice and three times to pull it out from the wound with his hands, suddenly an Ismarian shaft pierced him deep in his hollow temples. Suffering from this cruel wound, he succumbs to death and thinks of the Venetian shores as he dies.

While Kara Hodja redoubles his massacre throughout our fleet, 225 Pentheus, who learned in early youth to handle cannons and fire their swift shells, sees with a grim glance the Cenomanian troops, who were raised in the Tropic valley; he watches the movements 230 and steps of his jubilant enemy, wondering if he might check such great furor and ward off old ruin from the Latian ships. He had scarcely raised his head from the deck when a violent shot, twisted like lightning, from a bronze cannon pierced his helmet and bur- 235 ied itself in the depths of his brain.

Meanwhile blazing Bellona rages among the ships on both sides, and the ether resounds with her shouts. Ali cries out, wanting to avenge the pitiable shades of the Thracians and boast of a great triumph to his king. He groans and, boiling with rage, leads 240

ipse suam furibundus ad horrida bella triremem
ducit et instat agens. Nec mente minora volutat
Augusti proles, celeri sed puppe propinquat,
utrasque innectunt donec retinacula puppes
245   mutua, et alternis in pugnam viribus itur.
Fit sonus, hic ingens, hic pugna asperrima surgit,
quanta nec ipsa umquam vidit longaeva vetustas,
nec nostra inspexit, nec cernet serior aetas.
Threicii iaculis et curvo fortiter ense,
250   glandibus Hispani et rutilis mucronibus instant,
pix et flamma manu ferrumque et saxa sudesque
sparguntur, coeunt mixti, pereuntque vicissim
Hispani Thracesque simul mixtique Latini,
et pede pes manibusque manus miscentur, euntque
255   quo vel pugna magis saevit, vel densius agmen.
Hic videas passim remos et trunca natare
corpora et hinc illinc magnas ardere triremes.
Sanguineisque ingens consurgere fluctibus aequor.
    Ipse suas medius lorica et casside fulgens
260   Austriades tali compellat voce cohortes:
'O pubes lecta, o magni genitoris alumni,
o fortes pugnate viri, nunc denique tempus
Eoas Christi vexilla extendere in oras.'
    Sic fatus, magnum confestim fervidus ensem
265   vibrat utraque manu et medios prorumpit in hostes.
Quem primum, quem postremum, fortissime princeps,
sternis? Et aequoreis miseros quot mergis in undis?
Ipse tibi ante pedes ingentem stragis acervum
constituis, te saevus Halys, te Thracia classis
270   horret et adversum dum das tot corpora leto
advenisse putant Haemi de culmine Martem.

his own galley into the thick of the battle, threatening as he goes.
Matters no less momentous weigh on the mind of the emperor's
son, and so he drives near in his swift ship, until the cables lock
both ships together, and they both enter the battle in alternating 245
thrusts. Now a great sound rings out, now a bitter struggle begins,
such as antiquity never saw, nor our current times, nor any era
soon to come. With Thracian javelins and curved swords, with the
bullets of the Spanish and with flashing swords, each side presses 250
on. Chunks of pitch, flame, iron, rocks, and pikes, all mixed to-
gether, are hurled by hand, and Spaniards and Thracians all at
once, with Latins mixed in, perish one after another. Foot en-
twines with foot, hand with hand, and they run to where the bat-
tle rages more hotly or where the battle line is denser. Here you 255
would see oars everywhere, maimed bodies floating here and there,
and great galleys all ablaze; the huge sea roils with bloody waves.

In the midst of the fight, John of Austria with his breastplate
and helmet flashing drives his men on with these words: "Fight on, 260
chosen youth, children of our mighty Father; fight, brave men.
Now at last the time has come to carry the banners of Christ to
the eastern shores."

He spoke, brandishing his great sword violently in both hands, 265
and breaks into the middle of the enemy. Who was first, who last
that you laid low, bravest prince? And how many wretched souls
did you drown in the watery waves? You pile a huge heap of
slaughter before your feet; harsh Ali shudders before you, and the
Thracian fleet opposite; while you send so many bodies to death, 270
they think that Mars has come down from the peak of Haemus.

Quae dum Threicius miratur funera ductor,
nec videt Hispano iam posse obstare furori,
seque suamque ratem, innumeras resonante carinas
275   voce vocat, vocat et Geticas clamore phalanges
ingenti atque ducum tot millia cogit in unum,
scilicet ut laetam successu et Marte secundo,
Hispanam expugnet geminato robore puppim.
Primus, ut insidias sollers cognoverat: 'Ergo
280   nos erimus segnes ad bella?' Venerius inquit,
et simul in Geticum iam puppes verterat agmen.
Hunc super accurrere equites, equitumque magister
quos Melite insignis misit, venitque Columna
intrepidus magnae nitidissima gloria Romae,
285   Corneaque et ferro Ursini facibusque corusci.
Non mihi centenas tribuant si numina linguas
oraque Nestoreo sint nostra imbuta lepore,
tot pugnas saevasque neces, tot vulnera possim
dicere, tot valeam laceras numerare triremes.
290   Viderat Ismarium de puppe Venerius Acin,
qui doctis carus Musis falsique sacerdos
Maumethis, magna Maumethem voce vocabat.
Protinus ecce senex ardentem lampada torquet
incauti in faciem illius diadema reluxit
295   linigerum; accurrunt socii, properantque voracem
undanti lympha manibusque extinguere pestem;
non tamen haec prosunt, miseri quin flamma rubentem
consumat vultum et totos descendat in artus.
Inde alias aliasque faces iacit impiger, illae
300   consumunt tabulas ratibusque hostilibus haerent,
dumque viri trepidant intus Vulcaniaque omnes
militiae obliti certatim incendia vitant,
cum ratibus mediis subito exponuntur in undis;
extemplo his actis, aeratam corripit hastam,

The Thracian leader looks in amazement at the destruction, and he does not see how he and his boat can stand against the Spaniards' rage. He calls out to many a ship with his resounding voice. He calls the Getic phalanxes with a huge cry, gathering many thousand chiefs against this one man, clearly intending to attack the Spanish ship with redoubled strength, while it revels in its success and the turning tide of battle. Shrewd Venier was the first to recognize the ambush: "Will we then be slow to fight?" he asks, and turns his ships against the Getic troops. The knights and their commander also charged, those great Malta sent; then came undaunted Colonna, the brilliant glory of great Rome, and Ascanio della Corgna, and the Orsini flashing with swords and torches. If the gods should give me a hundred tongues, and my speech was endowed with the eloquence of Nestor, I could not tell of all the clashes, cruel deaths, the wounds—I could not name all the mangled galleys.

From the deck of his ship Venier had spotted the Ismarian Acis, a favorite of the learned Muses and priest of false Muhammad, who was calling the name "Muhammad" in a loud voice. But look, the old man hurls a burning torch in the other's face while he's off his guard and sets his linen turban on fire. His comrades run to help and hurry to extinguish the consuming fire with water and hands. But their effort comes to nothing, and the flame consumes the poor man's reddening face and descends over all his limbs.

Then tireless Venier throws more and more firepots, and they consume floorboards and cling to the enemy ships; while the men tremble inside and forget their military duties in their struggle to avoid Vulcan's flames, they suddenly find themselves exposed on their ships, in the middle of the waves. At this, Venier snatches

305   datque neci hostiles turmas agitatque cadentes
      per mare, et ingenti redeuntes cuspide pellit.
          Parte alia clypeo fulgens atque ense Columna,
      magnanimusque Ursinus adest Thracumque vicissim
      innumera aeterno demittunt corpora somno.
310   Portunique ratem, Getico qui milite nuper
      sperabat magnae properare ad moenia Romae,
      cum domibusque Dei sacrata evertere templa,
      invadunt; ille Ausoniae tot robora gentis
      aspiciens, pugnae inceptae oblitusque pudoris,
315   dat terga atque suam ducibus dat habere carinam.
          Et iam in Baeticolum valida comitante caterva
      Austriades, Thracum primos, primamque triremem
      atque ipsum superarat Halyn. Furit impete vasto
      Hispanum generosa cohors; lacerantque cremantque
320   undique, et hostilis spoliatur remige puppis.
      Cum fractos cernens socios ereptaque signa
      maestus Halys, manibus fulgentia proiicit arma,
      et tali Austriaden compellat voce ruentem:
          'Per fortunatas invicti Caesaris umbras,
325   per te, per magni felicia fata Philippi,
      me saltem aetherea captivum vescier aura,
      magne, sine, ingentes sulcant mihi caerula puppes,
      est Thracum mihi magna phalanx, sunt divitis auri
      pondera. Tu spoliis tantis praedaque potitus
330   omnia solus habe.' Austriades cui talia reddit:
          'Non auri me sacra fames, non denique praeda
      impulit, ut Geticas delerem Marte catervas,
      sed Christi me vera fides, quam, perfide, tantum
      persequeris: morere infelix.' Et talia fatus,
335   cum galea infidum valido caput amputat ictu,
      illud et arrecta gestandum fixit in hasta.

his bronze spear and sends the hostile squadrons to death; he   305
drives them headlong into the sea and pushes away any who come
back up with his huge sword point.

Nearby stands Colonna, with his shield and sword flashing,
along with the noble-hearted Orsini, and they send innumerable
Thracian bodies, one after another, to eternal sleep. They board
Pertev Pasha's ship, who not long before had hoped to reach the   310
walls of great Rome with Getic troops and overturn the houses
and sacred temples of the gods. Now, seeing the great strength of
the Ausonian race, heedless of the battle underway and his shame,
he retreats and leaves his own boat for the leaders to capture.   315

And now John of Austria, accompanied by a powerful throng of
Spaniards, overtakes the foremost Thracians, the flagship, and Ali
himself. The noble cohort of Spaniards surges forward with an
enormous charge, burning and laying waste to everything, and   320
stripping the enemy ships of their oarsmen. Seeing that his allies
are broken and their standards taken, Ali yields his flashing arms
in despair and addresses the approaching Austrian with these
words:

"By the fortunate shades of the unconquered emperor, by your-
self, and by mighty Philip's blessed fates, at least allow me to   325
breathe the air as a captive, great one; my huge ships slice the blue
sea, I have a great army of Thracians and tons of rich gold. Take
these great spoils and plunder: they are all yours to have."

John of Austria responded to him with these words: "It is not   330
accursed hunger for gold or plunder that drives me to obliterate
the Getic hordes in war, but the true faith of Christ, which you,
treacherous man, attack so vigorously: now die in disgrace." Saying
these words, he cuts off the infidel's head with a strong blow and   335
has it fixed on an erect pike for display.

Atque ea dum nostris felici Marte geruntur,
Marte potens, pelago assuetus patiensque laborum
Occhialides, flammis ferroque et glande ruenti
340   Ausonidum armatas penitus, lectasque triremes
straverat atque viros lucis spoliaverat aura;
et Liguris nisi dextra ducis, praeclaraque virtus
obstasset fortique viro, atque immania coepta
turbasset, nunc laeta minus nobisque profecto
345   esset cum multo victoria parta cruore.
Hostibus ille igitur caedes ac damna rependit
glandibus, igne, manu, saxis, ferroque rigenti;
Occhialidisque ratem saltu petit atque trucidat
Turcarum proceres multos, et turbinis instar
350   fulmineus, gladio nunc hos, nunc excipit illos,
atque metu trepido multos petere aequoris undas
cogit, et infirmis pontum tranare lacertis.
Cum tandem Thracum media inter funera vidit
Occhialides ardens, illumque affarier orsus:
355   'Non Ligurum calcas puppes, non Itala cernis
agmina, sed medium cingunt hostilia tela
hostilesque duces; ergo spolia ista relinques
atque animam, et nostris moriens addere triumphis.'
Dixerat, et celerem magno stridore sagittam
360   curvato cornu subito contorquet, at aurae
excipiunt vulnus; ductor nulla Aurius olli
dicta refert, magnis sed vibrans protinus ensem
viribus adversum properat furibundus in hostem,
extemplo gladium praeceps fugit ille cruentum
365   inque aliam ex alia sese iacit ipse triremem,
hortaturque suos, 'validos impellite remos
o socii; properate fugam, mihi terga flagello
Mars quatit, et nostris iam non favet amplius actis.'
Talia cui Ligurum ductor responsa remittit:

140

While our men are carrying out these things in the good fortune of battle, Uluj Ali, mighty in war, no stranger to the sea and unyielding even in great suffering, had laid low armed, elite Ausonian galleys with flames, iron, and rushing bullets and killed their men. If the right hand of Doria, leader of the Ligurians, and his outstanding courage had not stood in the way of this strong man, and put a stop to his cruel undertakings, our victory now would be less joyful, won at too high a price. But he repays his enemies for the slaughter and loss with bullets, fire, hand, cannonballs, and his rigid sword; he leaps into Uluj Ali's boat and cuts down many of the Turkish chiefs and, as destructive as a hurricane, slays now these, now those with his sword. He forces many men trembling with fear to plunge into the waves of the sea and swim through the ocean with wounded arms. But when his raging eyes fall on Uluj Ali in the middle of the Thracian slaughter, he addresses him with these words:

"You do not stamp out the Ligurian ships, nor cut off the Italian troops; enemy arms and enemy commanders are closing in around you: so it is that you will leave behind those spoils along with your life, and, in death, add to our triumphs."

As he finished speaking, he suddenly fires a swift arrow with a great shriek from his curved bow, but only the air receives the wound. Commander Doria speaks no words to him, but brandishes his sword with great strength and suddenly rushes forward, raging against the enemy. Immediately, his opponent flees from his blood-soaked sword, and throws himself headlong from one boat into another. He orders his men: "Lean on the strong oars, comrades; hasten our flight. Mars cracks his whip at my back and no longer favors our efforts." To him the Ligurian commander responds:

340

345

350

355

360

365

370 'Quo fugis, Occhialide? Meritum ne linque triumphum.
En adsum: spolia ista habeas.' Nihil ille, sed aequor
verrit, et obscuras quaeritque optatque latebras.
Et fugiens socios duro in certamine linquit,
et miseras audit voces gemitusque cadentum.

375 Sic Thracum classe absumpta, ducibusque fugatis
et caesis, nostris favit Victoria votis.
Ductores spoliis et praeda divite laeti
Hesperii, multis complent clamoribus auras
certatim, et caris dum multum amplexibus haerent

380 laetitiae dant signa novae, et dum singula lustrant,
armaque flexibilesque arcus pictasque pharetras
tormenta ereptas puppes ereptaque signa,
seminecesque duces, et dum quam plurima Thracum,
corpora caesa vident et millia captivorum

385 innumera, expleri nequeunt, gratesque Tonanti
et superis reddunt, onerantque altaria donis.
At nobis qui Turcarum fera vincula passi
Christicolis, veteres solvunt adimuntque catenas.

Quid dicam, Euridama? Cunctis quam plurima pectus

390 gaudia pertentant atque haec maiora fuissent,
ni Barbadicus longo deflendus in aevo
turbasset laetas inopino funere mentes.
Ille etenim hostiles superat dum Marte triremes,
Threicio periit lumen confossus ab arcu.

395 O decus eximium patriae lumenque tuorum,
Marte senex celeber, celeber praestantibus actis,
en te pro meritis alti plaga lucida caeli
suscipit et variis cingunt tibi tempora sertis
aetherei proceres: en nos lacrymas gemitusque

400 fundimus atque tuo geminamus dona sepulcro.
Tempus et illud erit, Pario cum marmore et auro
excelsum simulacrum ingens, patria optima ponat,

"Where are you running, Uluj Ali? Do not leave the triumph   370
you deserve. Look, here I am: claim your spoils." The other says
nothing, but he skims the surface of the sea, searching and hoping
for dark hiding places. As he flees, he leaves his friends behind in
the cruel contest, he hears their pitiful voices and the groans of the
dying.

And so, with the Thracian fleet in ruins and its leaders routed   375
or cut down, Victory smiles on our prayers. The Hesperian cap-
tains, happy with their spoils and rich plunder, vie to fill the air
with repeated shouts. And now they cling to each other in warm
embraces and give signs of renewed happiness, and now they   380
look over the spoils one by one: the arms, the curved bows, the
painted quivers, artillery, captured boats and standards, and half-
dead commanders, as well as the many slaughtered Thracian bod-
ies and countless thousands of captives. They cannot get enough   385
of what they see, and they give thanks to the Thunderer and the
gods, and they weigh down the altars with gifts. They unshackle
and remove the old chains from our Christians who suffered the
fierce captivity of the Turks.

What shall I say, Euridamas? Great joy filled everyone's heart,   390
and this joy would have been even greater if the unexpected death
of Barbarigo, long to be remembered, had not disrupted our hap-
piness. For while attacking enemy ships in the battle, he was
pierced in the eye by a Thracian arrow and perished. O extraordi-   395
nary glory of your fatherland and light of your people, celebrated
even as an old man for your tremendous accomplishments in war.
Behold, the bright expanse of the lofty sky welcomes you because
of your merits, and the princes of heaven decorate your brows
with many-colored garlands. Behold, we pour forth our tears and
groans and redouble the gifts on your tomb. A time will come   400
when your cherished fatherland will build a soaring statue of you
out of Parian marble and gold and will hail you as the father of

teque sui et Latii libertatisque parentem,
dicat et aeternis mandet tua nomina chartis.

Euridamas

405 Sic Thracum infaustas, Idmon carissime, pugnas,
sic et Christicolum narras felicia facta
noctibus ut tecum totis tecumque diebus
esse velim, et tantos persaepe audire labores.
Sed vos, o socii, postquam Deus ipse ferocem
410 contudit et nostris pepulit de finibus hostem,
adsitis precor unanimes, et templa petamus
votaque turicremas illi solvamus ad aras.

your country's freedom and the freedom of Latium; they will enter
your name in the rolls of eternity.

Euridamas

My dear Idmon, you recount the ill-fated assault of the Thracians   405
and the blessed deeds of the Christians so that I want to stay with
you night and day to hear more of such great labors. But you, al-
lies, now that God himself has beaten back the ferocious enemy   410
and expelled him from our borders, I pray that you remain united;
let us go to the temples, and let us fulfill our vows to him at the
incense-burning altars.

: XVII :

Ad Reverendissimum D. Paulum Odescalcum
Patruum Episcopum Atriensem

Giovanni Antonio Odescalchi

Annuite, o Musae, paulo maiora paranti
dicere, et immensi seriem perstringere facti,
et Scythicam cladem et victam percurrere classem;
magna quidem, divae, sed non indebita posco.
5   Nec deerunt, grandi victum qui carmine pontum,
barbaricoque canant fluctus undasse cruore,
divini vates clarosque heroas in astra
deducant atraeque vetent succumbere morti.
Non ego me demens illis adscribere tentem.
10   Huic quoque nunc faveas, sunt haec tua iussa, labori,
Paule; manent etiam tantae non ultima laudis
te decora et parti pars haud neglecta triumphi.
Te Pius ille hominum pastor divumque sacerdos,
ostia cui parent uni bipatentis Olympi,
15   ingentes volvens accenso pectore curas,
magnanimum ad iuvenem, triplex cui credita clavis,
misit; ei magni memoras mandata parentis
subiciensque acri stimulos, hortaris inertes
praecipitare moras rebusque instare gerendis
20   atque viros magno succendis laudis amore.
    Nec mora, Sicanio solvuntur litore puppes,
prosequeris manibus iunctis votisque secundis
voce vocans superos, finem requiemque laborum,
et laetum cunctis reditum et spolia ampla precatus.

: XVII :

To the most reverend Paolo Odescalchi,
Bishop of Penne and Atri

Giovanni Antonio Odescalchi

Look favorably on me, Muses, as I prepare to speak now of greater things, to narrate in brief this series of momentous events, and to touch upon both the slaughter of the Scythians and the defeat of their fleet. I ask great, but not unwarranted things of you, divine goddesses. There will be no dearth of holy bards to sing of the 5
conquered sea in lofty song, and the waves that churned with barbarian blood; let them escort famous heroes to the stars and keep them from succumbing to black death. I am not so foolish as to try to write about these things myself. May you also, Paolo, shine 10
the light of your favor on this work, for these things are done on your orders; not the least reward of such great praise is reserved for you, and no small part of the triumph won. Pius, the shepherd of men and priest of the gods, whom alone the doors of twin-gated Olympus obey as he ponders great cares in his burning 15
heart, he sent you to the courageous youth, to whom is entrusted the triple key. You relate to him the Holy Father's commands, adding stern incentives; you urge him to cast off sluggish delay and prepare for all that must be done; and you inflame the men with 20
the great love of praise.

Without delay, the ships set sail from the Sicilian shore. You follow with hands joined in prayer, calling on the gods to look favorably on your petitions and to grant a peaceful end to the struggle; you pray as well for a happy return for all and ample

25   Audiit omnipotens Genitor, subitoque fragore
      intonuit caelum et late lux clara refulsit.
      Illi abeunt, Zephyris curvantur vela secundis.
      Omnibus unus amor pulchrae succedere pugnae,
      et conferre manum atque audaces cordibus ardent.
30   Qualis Massylum patriis generosus in arvis
      ingreditur leo, sive fames stimulavit edendi
      sive illum virtus, animique in proelia mittunt.
      Horrescit cervix caudaque immania terga
      verberat et tumidas ingens assurgit in iras
35   atque aliquam in magna cupiens occurrere silva
      forte feram, saevo fremit implacabilis ore.
        Iamque Corinthiaci sulcabant aequoris oras,
      et sparsae mediis cernuntur Echinades undis,
      haud procul apparet nautis nemorosa Zacynthos,
40   atque Ithace; ast alia notissima litora fama
      Actia parte iacent et tellus dives Achivum.
        Est in secessu ventis immotus et ingens
      portus, iactatis statio benefida carinis:
      Lepantum patrio dixerunt nomine Graii.
45   Hic hostis sese ripis portuque tenebat.
      At nostri missa speculantur caerula cymba,
      explorantque locum certi decernere ferro,
      cum subito Eoam agnoscunt longo ordine classem
      litora deserere et latis procedere campis.
50   Una omnes illic videas ruere agmine denso
      cum fremitu, visu horrendum; ferit aethera clamor,
      spumea et aeratis scinduntur caerula rostris.
      Qualis si pelago evulsa ab radicibus imis
      incedat silva aut qualis Latonia Delos
55   errabunda olim medio natet insula ponto.

spoils. The almighty Father listened, and suddenly the sky re- 25
sounds with thunder, and lightning flashes far and wide. They
speed away, the sails filling with favorable west winds. One love
binds them together, and the brave men burn in their hearts to
clash in glorious battle and fight hand to hand. Just as when a 30
noble lion strides through the fields of his fatherland in Massylia;
whether ravenous hunger prods him on or virtue, his courage
sends him into battle. His neck bristles, and he whips his huge
back with his tail, rearing up large in his rising anger. He longs to 35
happen upon some wild beast in the vast forest, and he roars re-
lentlessly with his ferocious mouth.

Now they skimmed the shores of the Corinthian Sea, and the
Echinades appear scattered amid the waves. Not far away woody
Zacynthus comes into the sailors' view, then Ithaca; over there 40
lie the celebrated shores of Actium and the fertile land of the
Achaeans.

There is a vast harbor tucked back and protected from the
winds, a trusted outpost for storm-tossed ships: the Greeks called
it Lepanto in their native tongue. Here the enemy was holed up 45
on the banks and in the port. But our men send a skiff to recon-
noiter the waters and explore the area, certain that they will settle
the issue by sword, when suddenly they spy the Eastern fleet leav-
ing the shore in a long line and putting out to the open sea. Then
you might have seen them all rush together with a shout into a 50
close formation, terrifying to see. The noise strikes the heavens,
and the foamy deep is sliced with brazen prows. Just as if a for-
est, torn up from the depth of its roots, strode out to sea, or as if
Latonian Delos, the wandering island, floated once again in the 55

Puppibus auratis fulgent atque aere corusco,
horret et Ismariis acies armata sagittis.
Scilicet incautos nimium spes vana fovebat
haud laturum hostem, et turpi caedenda daturum
60   terga fugae: tanta est priscae fiducia famae.
Parte alia, aspectu horribili haud exterrita classis,
oblatam gaudens aequo certamine pugnam
alta secat magnosque animis affectat honores.
    Ipse dari signum belli tunc imperat ore
65   stans celsa in puppi, sociosque accendit in hostem
Austriacus ductor: 'Nunc o mihi lecta iuventus,
nunc o tempus,' ait, 'patriae pugnate, larisque
et Christi memores; meritum sua quemque manebunt
praemia, certum omnes hodie sperate triumphum
70   me duce.' Sic fatus princeps, tunc pergit in hostem
impavidus ducibusque aliis sua munera didit.
Hostibus at gelidus subita formidine sanguis
ima petit, postquam venientem cernere contra,
instructasque acies possunt fulgentibus armis.
75   Illico direxere suas de more catervas
et sensim iuncti lunatis cornibus ibant.
Ecce autem horrifico pelagus tonat omne fragore:
contremuere undae nimboque involvitur atro
aether et magno quatitur cum murmure tellus.
80   Auditur clamorque virum sonitusque globorum
litoribus Graium et belli praenuntiat horam.
Continuo saevit Mavors adamante superbo
tectus, at ignivomis ardet galea horrida cristis,
instigatque acies, stimulisque haud mollibus urit.
85   Dux erat ante alios, rerum cui credita summa,
insignem ducens auroque et murice pinum,
quadringenti illum, gens bello experta, sequuntur.

middle of the ocean. They flicker with their golden ships and glimmering bronze, and the armed battle line bristles with Ismarian arrows. It seems they had rashly nursed the vain hope that the enemy would not give battle and would retreat in shameful flight to be hacked to pieces — so great was their confidence in their for- 60 mer reputation. Nearby, our fleet is not at all perturbed by their fearsome appearance, but looking forward to a fair fight, cuts through the deep and strives courageously for great glory.

John of Austria orders the signal for war to be given, standing 65 high on the deck of his ship, and he rouses his comrades against the enemy: "Now, my chosen young warriors, now is the time: fight for your fatherland and your homes, always remembering Christ. Due reward awaits those who earn it. With me as your leader you can all hope for certain triumph today." After he fin- 70 ished speaking, the prince then sets off fearlessly against the enemy; he allots duties to the other commanders. The enemies' blood, frozen in sudden terror, contracts inward once they are able to see him coming against them and the fleet fitted out with its artillery flashing. Immediately they drew up their own squadrons 75 in their usual pattern, and slowly move into the shape of a horned moon. But behold, the whole sea thunders with a horrific noise; the waves tremble, the sky is enveloped in a black cloud and the earth shakes with a great crash. The clamor of men and the 80 sounds of cannon fire are heard on the Greek shore, announcing the hour of war. Mars rages incessantly, covered in proud steel, and his bristling helmet blazes from its fire-spewing crests. He stokes the battle lines and kindles their ardor with biting whips.

Before all the rest comes the Turkish commander, entrusted 85 with this critical mission, commanding his boat decked in gold and purple. Four hundred men follow him, a race well tried in

Huic natam haud laetis sociaverat ante Tyrannus
auspiciis, procerum hic fuerat gratissimus illi,
90   huic solitus, si quid versabat pectore magnum,
arcanas uni fidens committere curas.
Ergo ausus tardam cursu praecedere classem,
ut crucis auratae vidit volitantia signa,
instratamque ostro puppem, dux fertur amici
95   hac, ait: 'hic nullo victoria parta labore
vobis, o iuvenes, leto si sternimus illum.'
Nec minus Austriades nautis obvertere proram
imperat et caeli aspectans convexa precatur.
    Nec mora, concurrere, uncisque haesere catenis.
100   Accendunt exempla ducum et praesentia cunctos;
ter nostri Scythicam ingressi superare carinam,
ter cessere loco et gressum retulere coacti.
Hic belli moles, summis hic viribus omnes
contendunt: neque enim levia aut ludicra manebant
105   praemia victorem. Quae vos hic fortia facta
editis, o memoranda manus? Quot sternitis ense
corpora Medorum? Nil illos tela vel arcus,
nil validae iuvere manus? Occumbis et ipse,
infelix, tibi et Hesperius caput abstulit ensis,
110   dux o Turcarum, et nigro demitteris Orco.
Austriadae laeti clamorem ad sidera tollunt;
victores praeda et spoliis potiuntur opimis.
Inde citi flectunt cursum, qua plurimus hostis
urget, et insani gliscunt incendia Martis.
115   Extemplo Turcis solvuntur inertia duro
corda gelu, cessit defectis mentibus ardor,
ut videre ducem primo in certamine victum.
Attoniti torpent et pallida mortis imago

war. The Tyrant had married his daughter to this man, but with unlucky omens. He had been the most trusted of his advisors: when considering any great matter in his mind, the Tyrant used to trust him alone to carry out his secret devisings. Now the commander dares to sail ahead of the slow fleet, borne on the ship of his ally, the Tyrant, when he saw the flying standard of the golden cross and the ship covered with royal purple, and he says: "Here is victory delivered to you without effort, my young men, if only we lay that one low." John of Austria also orders his sailors to turn aside the prow, and looking at the dome of the sky, he prays.

Right away they engage and grapple with hook and chain. The examples set by the leaders, indeed their very presence, inspire all; three times our men move to take the Scythian ship, three times they stop in their tracks and retreat in close formation. Here is the struggle of war; here men fight with all their strength. The rewards that await the victor are neither slight nor trivial. What brave deeds did you perform, renowned soldiers? How many times did you lay low the bodies of Medes with the sword? Their javelins, bows, and strong hands do nothing to help them. You fall, unblessed leader of the Turks: the Hesperian sword takes off your head, and you are sent to dark Orcus. John's men raise their shouts to the stars; as rightful conquerors, they take plunder and the best spoils. Then they turn their path quickly to where the enemy presses down in greater number, and the fires of Mars in his madness flare up. All at once the slack hearts of the Turks melt like congealed ice, their burning rage vanishes from their tired minds, as they see their leader conquered in the first clash. They grow numb in their astonishment, and the pale image of death and

occurrit trepidis et inexsecrabile fatum.
120 Agnoscunt venisse diem, qua poscere poenas
perfidiae visum est superis ob foedera rupta.
Heu nimium rebus fisi, elatique secundis
vos manet ira Dei iustissima, vulneris alti
compensans gravitate moras. Te, rector Olympi,
125 te colimus, tua certa fides, nec iam impius hostis
audebit populis demens illudere Christi.
Quocumque Austriadae victricia signa tulerunt,
caede rubet pelagus; nullus concurrere contra
audet et obsceno miscentur cuncta pavore.
130 Illi autem caelo venientis fulminis instar
horribili late stragem fecere ruina.
Nec minus interea cornu pugnatur ab omni,
hostis ubique cadit, morientia pontus ubique
corpora volvit aquis, clypeos, galeasque micantes.
135 Victos caecus agit furor atque insania praeceps;
in mortemque ruunt, pelago merguntur in alto
complures salsosque absorbent pectore fluctus,
flamma vorax alios mediis absumit in undis.
Tandem ubi nulla fugae spes est et nulla salutis
140 praetendunt dextras, pacem veniamque precantur
supplicibus dictis infaustaque proelia damnant.
Ergo superba gravi religantur colla catena,
abiciunt tela, et manibus post terga revinctis
praeclari speciem visi praebere triumphi.
145 O miseri hae vires, haec magna potentia vestra est?
Siccine producti fines, aequata parentum
gloria, et Hesperiis ingens timor additus oris?
Discite nunc caelo iustum regnare Tonantem.
Vix demum e tanto fugerunt agmine pauci,
150 quos metus acer agit, ceu quondam in montibus altis

their loathsome fate runs through their alarmed minds. They real-
ize that the day has come when the gods have decided to exact   120
punishment for their treachery and the treaties they broke. Alas,
you who trusted too much in your joyful success, the righteous
wrath of God awaits you, making up for the delay with the sever-
ity of the deep wound. Ruler of Olympus, we worship you, your   125
promises are assured; for now our impious enemy will not be so
mad as to dare deceive the people of Christ. Wherever they carry
John of Austria's victorious standards, the sea reddens with blood-
shed. None dares to challenge him, and all disperse in craven fear.
Like a thunderclap coming from the sky, they wreak havoc and   130
horrible destruction far and wide. Meanwhile, the battle is waged
on both flanks, and everywhere the enemy gives ground; the sea
churns up dying bodies, shields, and shining helmets in the waves.
Blind fury and heedless folly drive the defeated, and they rush to   135
their deaths. Many drown in the deep sea, swallowing down salt
water in their lungs. Devouring fire eats up others in the middle of
the waves. Finally, when there is no hope of flight or safety, they
lift up their right hands and beg for grace and mercy with beseech-   140
ing words, as they curse the ill-fated fight. Their proud necks are
then clapped in heavy chains; they throw down their weapons and,
with their hands bound behind their backs, seem to suggest the
very image of a glorious triumph. O wretched men, is this your   145
strength, your great power? Is this how your end is to come about,
is this the glory worthy of your parents, the great fear you inspired
on Hesperian shores? Learn now that the Thunderer who rules in
heaven is just. Now at the end only a few make their escape,
driven by biting fear, just as in the high mountains, when a dog is   150

conspecto cane cerva fugit praeruptaque saxa
et cautes superans silva se condit opaca,
ille nemus late latratibus implet acutis.
    Victores gaza innumera spoliisque potiti,
155 re pulchre gesta, missis tot millibus Orco
Parthorum, insignem nacti post saecla triumphum,
constituunt superis dignos indicere honores.
Quas tibi nunc omnes magni pulcherrima proles
Augusti tanto laudes pro munere reddent?
160 Quem tibi vel summis belli virtutibus umquam,
vel pietate parem, felicia saecla tulerunt?
Tu noctem Europa, tenebras tu discutis atras,
sol veluti radiis obstantia nubila pellens
divinaque refers terris nova gaudia luce,
165 et propius merito divis accedis honore.
    Quid vos? O quantum gaudetis nomen adepti
ductores alii? Bello praeclarus, et armis
emicat ante omnes, laetoque Columnius ore
Romulides, clari praefulgens sideris instar,
170 atque suam aeterno collustrat lumine Romam.
Ille autem magnis patruum virtutibus aequans
Auria, temporibus fulvo radiantibus auro
caelo exultat ovans. Videsne ut pulcherrima tollat
fama virum magna circum plaudente corona?
175 Non ego te Venetum tacitus, fortissime ductor,
praeteream, nec iam vano tua funera fletu
prosequar; oppositos audax dum tendis in hostes,
torta manu valida lumen sibi fixit harundo.
Occumbis victor, sed fortia facta tuorum
180 ante tibi et partum licuit spectare triumphum,
tum caelo ascendens, aeterna ibi pace quiescis.
Salvete aeternum, nostrae decora inclyta gentis.

spotted, the deer flees and hides itself in the dark forest, leaping over broken rocks and crags while the dog fills the grove far and wide with its keen barking.

The victors acquired countless treasures and spoils, the deed was gloriously done, and so many thousands of Parthians were 155 sent down to Orcus. Having won this great triumph after so many centuries, they decide to proclaim honors worthy of the gods. What praises shall they render unto you, noble child of the emperor, for such great service? Who will ever be your equal in the 160 highest valor of war for blessed ages to come? You dispersed the night and its dark shadows from Europe, like the sun scatters the intervening clouds with its rays. You bring new joy to the earth with divine light; with the honor you have earned, you approach 165 closer to the gods. What of you, great commanders? How much will you rejoice in the reputation you have won? Colonna, child of Romulus, is foremost in battle and shines before all in arms: his happy face flashes forth like a brilliant star as he looks over his 170 Rome with an everlasting eye. But famous Doria, matching the great virtues of his ancestors, lifts his exultant joy to the sky, his temples adorned with tawny gold. Do you see how such magnificent fame can raise a hero up, surrounded by a large, applauding crowd? Bravest leader of Venice, I shall not pass over you in si- 175 lence, nor follow your funeral marches with empty tears. While you were boldly plowing into the enemy host, an arrow bent by some strong hand fixed itself in your eye. You died in victory, but before you were able to see the brave deeds of your men and 180 the triumph you earned. Ascending to the sky, you rest there in eternal peace. Hail forever, famous glory of our people; no age

Nulla umquam vestrum delebunt saecula nomen,
nulla prement tantas ingrata oblivia laudes.
185 Dum prisco in solio, pastor Romane, sedebis
maiorum, et placida terras moderabere lege,
dumque diem rebus Phoebi lux alma reducet,
egregii semper facti monumenta manebunt,
audiet et patrum titulos ventura iuventus,
190 et pugnas canet atque aeternum prodet in aevum.

shall ever erase your name, no thankless oblivion shall silence such
great praise. So long as you sit on the age-old throne of your fore-   185
fathers, Roman bishop, you will rule the lands under your gentle
law, and as long as the nourishing light of Phoebus brings the day
back over your kingdoms, the monuments of your magnificent
deeds will always remain. The rising generation will hear the
honor of their fathers and sing of their wars and pass on the tradi-   190
tion forever.

[*At Latio tandem pallentes dispulit umbras*]

Ottaviano Manini

At Latio tandem pallentes dispulit umbras
exoptata dies et lucem reddidit almam.
Iam rediit vigor et bello iam vivido virtus
ad resides animos desuetaque corda triumphis;
5   vicimus et largo foedarunt sanguine fluctus
Ionios sceleratae acies invisaque divis
agmina pontus habet. Sol o pulcherrime salve,
salve nobilibus gaudens Victoria palmis,
et saecli melior tandem surgentis origo.
10   Quid primum memorem? Qua linguam in gaudia solvam
voce prius? Natat ecce mari disiecta profundo
atque Asia atque Oriens et vasto gurgite fractae
Threicii iactantur opes et sceptra Tyranni.
Ipse autem longe vacua turbatus in aula,
15   nuntius excidii ut tanti gravis impulit aures,
qualis ubi ante aras percussus colla securi
procubuit taurus, mugitibus aera complet
abscinditque humeris vestem proiectaque calcat
tegmina Achaemeniae capiti direpta tiarae,
20   et nunc multa fremit iactatque minantia verba;
nunc gemit, et tristi secum sub pectore versat,
quas condat sese in latebras, quae limina quaerat,
Riphaeasne petat glacies Tanaimque nivalem,
an campos Nomadum arentes; stipante suorum
25   anne manu magna, an solus cum remige solo
traiciat fauces inglorius Hellesponti.
Ille quidem ad rapidi nuper vada concitus Hebri

[The long-desired day at last dispelled the fading shadows]

Ottaviano Manini

The long-desired day at last dispelled the fading shadows from
Latium and restored the nurturing light. Now strength and cour-
age for the pressing battle returns to our sluggish souls and our
hearts now unused to victory. But we have triumphed, and the   5
battle lines of the wicked have stained the Ionian waves with copi-
ous blood, and those troops hated by the gods now lie in the sea's
grasp. Welcome, most beautiful day, and welcome Victory, rejoic-
ing in our noble victory palms. The dawn of a better age is come
at last.

   What should I recount first? With what words shall I first   10
loosen my tongue in joy? Behold, Asia and the East have been
scattered across the deep sea, and the shattered wealth of Thrace
and the scepters of its Tyrant are tossed about in the vast abyss.
Far away in his empty palace, the Tyrant is troubled as the grim   15
news of such a great defeat strikes his ears. Just as when before the
altars, a bull is struck at the neck with an ax and falls, filling the
air with his bellowing; so he tears the cloak from his shoulders,
pulls the wrapping of the Achaemenian crown from his head,
tosses it down, and tramples it, and now he rages wildly and sput-   20
ters threatening words. Now he groans and in his sad heart con-
siders what hiding places he might cower in, what shores he might
seek: should he make for the icy mountains of Ripheus and the
snowy river Tanais, or the dry fields of the wandering Numidians?
Should he pass through the jaws of the Hellespont surrounded by   25
a great band of his own people or alone with a single oarsman?
Not long ago he rushed to the shoals of the swift-flowing Hebrus,

Italiam contra flammantia lumina torquens
sanguineamque aciem, bella horrida bella ciebat,
30   poscebatque, nefas! magnae sibi moenia Romae,
Adriacaeque urbis sedes atque aurea sceptra.
Demens qui vires alias et numina divum
defensura pias acies non crederet aut tot
posse coire manus aeterno foedere iunctas.
35   Ah nonne indignum fuerat tot stare per annos
infandi caput hoc monstri implacabile terris?
    Perfidus hic praedo, cui nec fas, nec pudor ullus,
nec pietatis honos, nec dulcis pignora pacis,
sed tantum imperii et caedis scelerata cupido,
40   victor ovans tot regna armis et divite cultu
fortunata olim, dum res stetit Itala, bello
evertit? Lateque premens parere coegit
interea Europa infelix discordibus armis
certavit? Propriamque amens in viscera dextram
45   condidit? Ille ferox ampla regnavit in aula,
impune heu nostris erepta regibus aula?
At sceptris etiam nondum contentus avitis?
Quod superest, inhians animis vastabat opimam
periurus Cyprum iamque arces culmine summo
50   iam dederant divum atque hominum tecta alta ruinam.
At parte ex alia spumabant caerula remis,
pineaque Aegeum moles medium impellebat,
Thraciam in Italiam portans et tristia fata.
Qualis ubi hiberno consurgens turbine nimbus
55   incubuit pelago tempestatemque sonoram
agglomerans equitat fluctus, et litora vento
ingenti plangit; iam foedam instare tremiscunt
agricolae stragem campis; ruet ille, labores

turning his flaming eyes and bloody gaze toward Italy, and set in
motion war, horrendous wars, and demanded for himself—impi- 30
ously!—the walls of mighty Rome and the holdings of the Adri-
atic city and its golden scepter. He was out of his mind if he
thought that the powers of the gods would not defend our forces
and our pious battle lines, or that so many legions of men would
not band together, joined by an eternal pact. Surely it is an insult 35
that this merciless head of an unspeakable monster has lasted on
earth for so many years already?

Is this treacherous thief, who recognizes neither divine right,
nor shame, nor the glory of piety, nor pledges of sweet peace, but
only the shameful desire for power and slaughter—is this the con- 40
queror who delights in overthrowing so many kingdoms that once
flourished in arms and rich culture, as long as the Italian empire
lasted? Is this the man who forced downtrodden nations far and
wide to obey him while miserable Europe contended with civil
wars, and who, like a madman, buried his own right hand in his
guts? Was it he who ruled defiantly in his massive palace—a pal-
ace, alas, that was taken from our kings without retaliation? But 45
even then was he not content with his ancestral scepters? Coveting
in his heart all that remains, that oath-breaker laid waste to rich
Cyprus, and now the citadels of the gods on the highest peaks and 50
the lofty roofs of men's homes are given over to ruin. But else-
where, the sea was frothing with oars, and pine-timbered hulks
forced their way through the Aegean Sea, carrying Thrace and sad
omens to Italy. Just as when a cloud rises in a winter tempest and
looms over the sea, it grows in rumbling turbulence, and rides in 55
on the waves, beating the shores with a mighty wind. Already the
farmers begin to tremble at the sickening ruin that threatens their
fields; the storm rushes in and flattens their happy labors with a

prosternet laetos effusa grandine et anni
60 spem longi franget. Sed quae sine numine divum
stent vires? Superum auspiciis hinc Itala virtus
et vis consilii haud expers, et robora pubis
Hispanae cursu placido maria alta secabant.
Tuque adeo caelo iuvenis demisse sereno,
65 altera progenies, magnum et patris incrementum,
Augusti imperiis iam nunc ingentibus aucte,
cui moles et summa rei commissa Latinae,
tune decus nostri et donum mirabile saecli?
Tune velut clarum procedis Caesaris astrum?
70 Et tremulum roseo perfundis lumine pontum?
I, quo te virtus vocat et fortuna secunda.
I, felix, i: maior avis atavisque redibis.
Iamque mari magno tota hinc Europa vehit se,
barbaricas acies contra mirantur et undae;
75 miratur Nereus vastas innare carinas,
Tritonesque feri se fluctibus exeruerunt
et procul e saxo spectant immania monstra.
      Est locus Ionio in medio spumantia contra
litora Naupacti, quo sese plurima cogit
80 atque Ithacae scopulis illisa remurmurat unda.
Huc actae coiere utroque ab litore gentes,
Actius Eoas hic rursum aspexit Apollo.
Hesperiasque manus armis concurrere, rursum
instructo adspexit Leucaten fervere Marte.
85 Altera classis erat Stygiis damnata tenebris,
altera laetantes iam iam visura triumphos.
Ista deos secum placidos in proelia ducit,
illa importuna prognatas Nocte sorores.

deluge of hail, shattering the hope of a long year. But what good is   60
brute strength without the power of the gods? With the gods'
blessings the might of Italy (indeed, a force not without guidance)
and the strength of Spain's youth were cutting through the high
seas on calm waters. And you, young man, sent down from serene
heaven, the other child and great scion of your father, made   65
greater now by the emperor's vast realm—to you has been en-
trusted the final destiny of the Latin world. Are you the glory of
our people and the wondrous gift of the ages? Do you come forth
like the clear star of Caesar, bathing the tremulous sea in rosy   70
light? Go where virtue and good fortune call you. Go, blessed one,
go: you will return greater than your grandfathers and great-
grandfathers. Already all of Europe assembles here from across the
great sea, and the waves gape at the barbarian battle lines that op-
pose them. Nereus watches in awe as the huge ships swim by.   75
Fierce Tritons drag themselves out of the waves and watch the
hulking monsters on a rock from afar.

There is a place in the middle of the Ionian Sea opposite the
foamy shores of Naupactus, where waves gather and echo as they
crash against the cliffs of Ithaca. Men driven from both shores   80
have come together to this place. Here Actian Apollo again watches
the eastern and western troops assembling their arms, again
from Leucate he watches them as they prepare for war. One fleet   85
was already condemned to the Stygian shades, the other, soon to
see triumphs of exultation. This fleet led the gentle gods with
them into battle. That one, ill-omened, brought the sibling daugh-
ters of Night. On the high deck of this ship sat the guardian and

Hinc celsa aethereae custos et ianitor aulae,
90   illinc Tartareus residebat navita puppi.
Quo ruitis, dirae heu pestes? Quo lintea venti
plena ferunt? Iam iam adversa reflabitur aura
carbasus; haec horae momento mille trophaea
detrahat, haec victis ingens dabit unda sepulchrum
95   et iam constiterant imitantes cornua lunae;
hinc atque hinc geminae classes, iam fluctuat aequor
aere repercussum, dubiis iam saevus in armis
horrebat Mavors intentaque tela tenebat.
Cum nostras super advolitans Victoria puppes,
100   'quid dubitatis adhuc, o natae ad fortia dextrae,
magnanimi heroes, crudelem exscindere gentem?
Ferte faces, remos impellite, vincite; vobis
ipsa adero, ingentique duces sub cuspide frangam.'
Dixit, et ipsa manu signum dedit; ipsa carinam
105   impulit, ipsa gravem prima hastam intorsit in hostem.
Venturamne diem audistis, quae subruat arces
orbis, et emoto volvantur cardine cuncta
in praeceps? Montesque novo rapiantur in altum
impetu? Non aliter tunc agmina concurrerunt.
110   Non aliter fragor horribilis ferit aethera; credas
Ismaren aut Rhodopen vasto concurrere Olympo;
fumidus ad caelum densa caligine nimbus
volvitur, ex oculisque diem eripuere tenebrae.
Et iam pronus equos agitabat Phoebus anhelos;
115   tum vero horrificae penitus patuere ruinae,
et fera Tisiphone, luctusque et mortis imago,
heu dirae facies medio in discrimine visae;
fragmina remorum passim, fluitantia passim
transtra natant, proras demersis aequora rostris

doorkeeper of the heavenly halls above; on that, the ferryman of   90
Tartarus. Where are you rushing, accursed plagues? Where do
your wind-filled sails carry you? Now a hostile breeze will billow
your sails. May these hours take back your thousand trophies in a
single moment; when you are beaten, this ocean will provide you
one giant sepulcher. And now on one side, they had already drawn   95
themselves up, taking the shape of the horned moon; and on the
other were the paired fleets. Now the sea grows choppy as it is
struck by bronze, now Mars rages fiercely amid undecided skir-
mishes and keeps his weapons drawn. Then Victory flies over our
ships, saying: "Why, O soldiers born for brave deeds, great he-   100
roes — why do you still hesitate to cut down this brutal race? Bring
the torches, lean on the oars, defeat them! I myself will fight with
you; I will break their leaders beneath my immense blade." So she
spoke and gave the sign with her hand; she added momentum to   105
the ship and was first to turn her heavy spear against the enemy.
Have you heard that there will come a day which will tear down
the citadels of the world, when all will be overturned, unhinged,
and pitched headlong? When mountains will rise into the heavens
with a new upthrust? No differently did the troops then rush;
no differently did their terrifying noise strike the heavens. You   110
would have thought that Ismaria or Rhodope had crashed into
vast Olympus. A smoky cloud rises to the sky in a dense fog, and
the darkness snatched the day from their eyes. And now Phoebus,
leaning forward, was driving his panting horses. But then the hor-   115
rible destruction was laid bare, and fearsome Tisiphone, and the
images of Grief and Death — dreadful forms — were seen in the
middle of the fray. Fragments of oars and waterlogged crossbeams
float here and there, and the deep waters flood the prows whose

120   ima bibunt; superant flammae quibus unda pepercit.
        Corpora iam tot volvit aquis quot pontus arenas.
        Singula quid memoro? Longa est mora, gaudia nec me
        plura sinunt. Vicere pii, gens impia poenas
        expendit; numero ex omni vix una superstes
125   puppis ad ignotas contendit remige terras.
        Necte humeris pedibusque novas, age nuntia tantae
        Fama rei pennas et nubila transvola et Euros,
        quaque diem condit Vesper, qua promit Eous,
        et maria et terras his laetis vocibus imple:
130   advenisse diem, qualem longaeva vetustas
        non umquam vidit, non speravere minores,
        viribus eximiis regnorum et corpore toto
        Europamque Asiamque inter discrimine magno:
        certatum, palmam tanti pretiumque laboris;
135   post superum regem quis proxima sceptra teneret,
        barbaricam nostra excussam cervice securim;
        et iuga sub pedibus nostris perfracta iacere
        quae nuper veriti sumus. O felicia saecla!
        O quam nos faustum superi servastis in aevum!
140   Surge triumphales age victrix indue cultus,
        Ausonia, et gemmis splendente auroque corona
        regales ornata comas solemnia vota
        exsequere in primis solemnes instrue pompas.
        Velentur lauri victrici fronde per urbes
145   omnibus in templis arae, nec munera desint,
        quae metit Assyrius cultor felicibus arvis.
        Omnibus in templis casta cum virgine mater
        et coniunx reducem iam iam amplexura maritum,
        solvite quae toties fudistis pectore vota
150   sollicito, procul hinc curae et dolor omnis abesto.
        Quod si cui dulces reditus patriosque negavit
        Fortuna aspectus (neque enim Mars omnibus aequus)

beaks had been submerged. Flames overcame those whom the 120
waves spared. The sea was already churning as many bodies in its
waves as grains of sand. How could I recall them individually? It
will detain us too long, and more joyful tidings urge me on. The
pious were victorious, the impious race paid the price; hardly one
surviving ship from all their number managed to row to unknown 125
shores. Bind new wings to your shoulders and feet, Fama, and go,
announce the news of these great events. Fly through the clouds
and east winds to where Evening conceals the day or where Dawn
brings it forth, and fill the seas and the lands with these happy
words: that there has come a day such as long-lived old age has 130
never seen and younger men have not hoped for, a day fought be-
tween Europe and Asia in one great clash with all the outstanding
strength and all the substance of their kingdoms; tell how it was
fought, and the palm and prize of such a great struggle; who now
holds the next best scepter after the king of the gods; how the 135
barbarian's ax has been shaken from our neck; and how the yoke
we recently feared now lies broken under our feet. O blessed ages!
For what a happy time you have saved us, O gods!

Rise and clothe yourself in triumphal attire, victorious Ausonia; 140
adorn your regal tresses with a crown of jewels and shining gold,
and fulfill your solemn vows: first of all to prepare solemn proces-
sions. Let the altars be wreathed with the leaves of the victorious
laurel in all the temples throughout the city, and let them not lack 145
offerings harvested by the Assyrian farmer from his blessed fields.
In all the temples mothers with their chaste daughters and wives
will embrace their returning husbands. Fulfill the many vows you
poured forth from your anxious heart; let all cares and sorrows be 150
far from your minds. But if Fortune denied anyone these sweet
reunions or the sight of his father (for Mars is not fair to all), it is

non huius velut extincti lacrimabile fatum,
non huius fas est in funere solvere crinem,
155 aut manibus lacerare genas aut pectora pugnis.
Vivitis, illustres animae, quae sanguine vestro
servastis patriam; nec vos ulla auferet aetas,
Letheae rapient nec muta silentia ripae.
Atque ipse, o utinam! vestri pars una fuissem,
160 et meus ingentes inter nunc spiritus umbras
erraret tenuis, per vulnera pulchra profusus.
O quali exceptos plausu vos credimus! O quos
credimus amplexus et gaudia quanta fuisse
per nemus Elysium secura in sede piorum!
165 Teque adeo te, magne heros, cui caerula Doris,
et centum Hadriaco formosae in litore nymphae
dona suprema ferunt, ut nunc mirantur. Et altis
circumfusi humeris astant decora illa Latina
Scipiadae, Decii, Favii, magnique Camilli!
170 Utque pari conferre gradu vestigia gaudent!
Vulneraque illa lavant, queis stat victoria nostra,
et fluidum siccant generosa per ora cruorem.
      Sed quo mens abiit mihi nunc? Aut quo feror? Unde
haec nova vis animo? Quis mi calor aestuat intus?
175 Fallor? An aethereas concepi pectore flammas?
Ante meos oculos hinc rauca Bosphorus unda,
cumque suis late versatur Thracia campis;
illinc Armeniae fines atque altus Araxes,
et populi Aurorae superandi, et litora rubra.
180 Haud bellum exhaustum est, haud hic vestigia plantae
figunt certa meae: plus est quod mente revolvo.
Maius opus meditor, pugnatum est alite dextro,
et virtus lato patefecit limite campum;
quod reliquum, expugnate alacres, et pergite porro,
185 ductores magni, et coeptum decurrite munus.

not right for you to weep over his fate as if he were dead, or to
wear loosened hair in mourning for him, to tear your cheeks with   155
your hands or beat your chests with blows. You who preserved the
fatherland with your blood live on as glorious spirits; no age will
bear you away; the mute silence of the Lethean banks will not
snatch you. Oh, how I wish that I myself had been one of you,
and that my tender spirit, poured out through noble wounds, now   160
wandered among you mighty shades. With what applause we be-
lieve you have been welcomed there! What embraces and what
great joy we believe is now in the Elysian grove, there in the man-
sions of the faithful free from care! You, great hero, you for whom   165
sea-blue Doris and one hundred beautiful nymphs on the Adriatic
shore perform last rites, how they admire you now; and around
your mighty shoulders stand those great lights of Rome, the
Scipios, the Decii, the Favii, and the great Camilli! How they re-
joice to match your steps with equal stride! They wash the wounds   170
on which our victory stands, and they dry the blood that trickles
over your noble face.

   But where has my mind gone now? Or where am I being
taken? Where does this new strength in my mind come from?
What heat warms my insides? Am I mistaken, or do I feel the   175
flames of heaven in my breast? Before my eyes, here is the Bos-
phorus in its clamorous stream, and Thrace reeling far and wide in
its fields. There are the borders of Armenia and the deep Araxes,
and the people of the East who are soon be conquered, and the
shores of the Red Sea. The war has not yet run its course; my   180
heels have not set firm footprints here. There is more to turn over
in my mind. I think of the greater work to come, how the fight
was fought on the right flank, and how their courage opened up
the field in a wide swath and conquered whatever was left. Keep
going, swift and mighty leaders, and finish the task you've begun.   185

Ipsa adeo soliumque superbum atque aula Tyranni,
urbs antiqua ingens, magnae quondam aemula Romae
ultro sese offert vincendaque moenia servat.
Quae mora? Quid tandem coeptis felicibus obstat?
190 Quin age surgamus genus omne et quicquid ubique est
gentis Romanae, quicquid sub vindice mundi
candida signa sequi gaudet, properemus ad unum
hoc caput; hoc nobis est denique pervincendum.
Nec prius inceptum fas est dimittere cursum,
195 quam se perpetua solvant formidine terrae,
accipiantque iterum leges, melioraque iura,
atque equidem, ni vana animum praesagia fallunt,
quos iam concursus? Quanto terramque polumque
turbine misceri video? Iam iam ultima pulsu
200 Bactra gemunt, fremit hinc Boreas, septemque triones,
hinc Zephyrus, trepidant septem Nili ostia, et Auster
nubibus; attonitus longe stupet arduus Atlas.
Scilicet hanc olim venturam certa canebant
fata diem, qua caelestum contemptor, et orbis
205 eversor Latiae subiectet colla catenae
suppliciterque pias humilis procumbat ad aras,
aut desolata cadat ingens truncus arena.
Nec mora, subiectas omnes longo ordine gentes
prospicias, Romane pater, tua templa petentes,
210 poplite submisso sacris ferre oscula plantis.
O ne mors fuscis caput hoc circumvolet alis,
nostra nec extrema claudantur lumina nocte,
dum videam, quae nunc confusus imagine miror,
et plectro graviore canam venientia fata,
215 virtutesque virosque et tanta exordia rerum:
omnia quae referens operoso carmine texam
Leminis ad patrii sacrum caput, aut ubi dictam

The Tyrants' haughty thrones and palaces, the vast ancient city, once the rival of great Rome, offers itself willingly and safeguards its walls for you to conquer. What is the delay? What, in the end, stands in the way of such happy undertakings? No, let us rise up 190 as a united people, and whatever remains of the Roman race, whoever rejoices to follow the gleaming white standards of the world's Savior, let us hasten to this one purpose: we must prevail at last. It is not right to abandon the path begun before these lands are free from eternal terror. Let them accept again our laws and better 195 governance. Indeed, unless vain prophecies deceive my mind, what clashes are these that I see already? In what a great tempest do I see the land and stars in turmoil? Already the farthest part of Bac- 200 tria groans at the blow; here the north wind clamors and the northern regions roar, there the west wind and the seven mouths of the Nile tremble, and the south wind with its clouds; thunderstruck from afar, steep Atlas is stunned. For the Fates sang true that a day would come when one who despises the gods and overturns the world would submit his neck to Latian chains, humbly 205 kneeling at pious altars, or he would fall, like a huge trunk on the lonely shore. Let there be no delay: may you, Roman Father, see subject nations in a long line seeking your temples to give kisses to 210 your sacred feet on bended knee. Do not let death fly around my head on dusky wings, do not close my eyes in final night until I see that which now I see only dimly, and until I sing the coming fates in a weightier key, and the virtues, men, and the great 215 beginnings of things. All this I will weave in a well-wrought song, returning to the sacred font of ancestral Lemine, or where

Varmius ipse suo de nomine praenotat arcem
Naiade caelesti fortunatissimus amnis.

220 Ipse canam; secura meis dabis otia Musis,
tu Grimane heros, quo tellus Ilvia gaudet
principe, quo melius nobis nil fata dederunt;
et modo quae canimus tua sunt non mollia iussa.
Atque utinam magni te caeli regia terris

225 non prius invideat, quam cernam saecula condi
aurea, nam pars huius eris tu magna laboris,
Tarpeioque Iovi propior propiora tenebis.
Quare ades, et placide aspira maioribus orsis;
huc ades atque animum prasenti numine firma.

Varmius himself brands the citadel named for him, a river most
fortunate in its heavenly nymph. I myself will sing; you will grant   220
carefree leisure to my Muses, you, great Grimani. The land of
Elba rejoices in no prince more than you, and the Fates have given
us nothing better. But the matters you have commanded me to
sing are not easy. Oh, would that the palace of mighty heaven
might not be so jealous as to claim you before I see the golden age   225
founded, for you will be a great part of this labor and, since you
are so close to Tarpeian Jove already, you will have what is becom-
ing of your station. Therefore, go breathe peace into these greater
undertakings: be here and bolster our courage while the divine will
is with us.

Lucens Carmen Ioanni Austriaco Victori Dicatum

Pompeo Arnolfini

Austriacos canimus, Musae, faveatis honores,
    et Capitolino parta trophaea Iovi,
disiectasque rates populataque in aequore castra,
    ponenda in Latio barbara castra solo;
5   et Venetum invictas acies et Iberica rostra,
    fregere insanas quae tibi Turca minas.
Bella cano. Vos o, quondam mea carmina, Amores,
    ite procul: dicta est bella puella satis.
Cantandi reges, mittendae in proelia classes,
10   tingendum Ioniae sanguine marmor aquae.
Scilicet hic magni primordia concinat orbis,
    nec bene digestum compositumque Chaos;
ut Deus hanc miro coniunxit foedere molem,
    et sortita suum sunt elementa locum,
15   unde hominum pecudumque genus, genus unde volucrum,
    quosque suo pisces gurgite pontus alit.
Alter terrigenum narret temeraria fratrum
    consilia, et summo bella parata Iovi,
et superimpositos turbata cacumina montes,
20   inque suae matris monstra sepulta sinu.
Crudeles alius Thebas, incestaque dicat
    connubia atque epulas gens Pelopea tuas.
Atque Agamemnoniis subversas ignibus arces
    Dardaniae, et profugi Troica signa viri,

A shining song for the victor, John of Austria

Pompeo Arnolfini

Look favorably on me, Muses, as I sing of the glories of John of Austria, of trophies offered to Capitoline Jove, of ships routed and camps destroyed on the sea, barbarian camps that were to be built on Latian soil. I sing of the Venetians' invincible battle lines and the Spanish prows that shattered your wild threats, Turk. I sing of battles. You who once were my songs, Loves, be gone: my pretty girl has been sung of enough. Now we must sing of kings, of fleets sent to war, of the surface of the Ionian sea dyed with blood. Let one man sing of the beginnings of the great world, and Chaos neither well ordered nor balanced; of the time when God united this shapeless mass in a miraculous alliance, and assigned each element to its proper place. From there the race of men arose and the herds and the birds, and all the fish that the sea nourishes in its current. Let someone else sing of the rash plans of brothers born from the earth, of wars devised against mighty Jove, of mountains heaped on shaken peaks and monsters buried in the bosom of their own mother. Let another tell of cruel Thebes, incestuous marriages, and your feasts, race of Pelops; of the citadels of Troy overturned by Agamemnon's fires and the Trojan standards of the

25 Romanamque urbem, toti quae praefuit orbi,
        quaeque etiam sacrum tollit ad astra caput.
    Cantent haec alii; Scythicae nos funera gentis
        et iuvat Austriaci facta referre ducis.
    Magna loquor: quod si vires et carmina deerunt,
30   tentasse in magnis gloria magna satis.
    Est Naupacteus Locrensi in litore portus,
        Evenus rapido qua fluit amne pater,
    et qua se Ionii profundunt aequora ponti;
        inque Corinthiaco clauditur unda sinu,
35 Crissaeo tandem quae vix retinetur ab Isthmo
        quo minus Aegeae murmura findat aquae.
    Hinc egressae atros fluctus Aquilone secabant
        Turcarum infaustae, robora vasta, rates.
    Pictaque fulgebant auratis aequora peltis,
40   non secus ac speculi fulgida plana micant,
    quas simul ut gelida Nereus prospexit ab acta
        fatidico tales edidit ore sonos.
    'Adverso aeratas solvisti numine proras,
        perfida gens, vasto praeda futura mari.
45 Eheu quam multo stabit tibi sanguine, divum
        consensu pactam deservisse fidem.
    Flectite iter, miseri, non vos periuria terrent?
        Sanctaque sacrilega foedera rupta manu?
    Flectite iter, magno laus est aequanda triumpho
50   fugisse Hispani tela tremenda ducis,
    qui modo ab Hesperiis Tirynthia signa Columnis
        expertas ducit victor in arma manus,
    ut clarum vestra referat de strage triumphum.
        Et forti Eoas milite frangat opes,

hero who fled, and the city of Rome that ruled the whole world   25
and even raised its sacred head to the stars. Let others sing of
these things. I prefer to recount the destruction of the Scythian
race and the deeds of the Austrian leader. I speak of great things;
if strength and song fail, it is enough of an honor even to have at-   30
tempted such important themes.

The harbor of Naupactus lies on the Locrian shore, where Fa-
ther Evenus flows in his swift current, where the waters of the Io-
nian Sea pour forth, and the surge is enclosed in the Bay of   35
Corinth: there the Crissaean Gulf barely keeps it from crashing
into the murmuring waters of the Aegean Sea. Sailing out from
here on the north wind, the doomed ships of the Turks in all their
vast strength cut the dark waves. The waters gleam, painted by
their golden shields, just as the blazing surface of a mirror flickers.   40

At that moment, Nereus, watching them from the barren shore,
uttered these prophetic words: "You have loosed your bronze prows
against God's will, treacherous race, soon to be plunder on the vast
sea. Alas, how much blood it will cost you to have abandoned the   45
treaty you joined with the consent of the gods. Turn back, you
wretched men. Do not your perjured oaths frighten you? And the
holy alliances broken by your impious hand? Turn back: there is
glory equal to a great triumph in having fled from the terrifying   50
weapons of the Spanish leader. Even now he leads experienced
troops and Colonna's Tirynthian standards from Hesperia into
battle to bring back a brilliant triumph from the slaughter of your
people. Let him break the Eastern forces with his mighty army
and spread the conquering eagle throughout the whole world, so

55   auspiciisque patris, cuius Germania nutum
      pavit, et experta est Africa tonsa iugum,
  victrices Aquilas toto circumferat orbe,
      progeniesque suis digna feratur avis.
  Hic, veluti summo demissum fulmen Olympo,
60   qua ruit aeternae dat monumenta viae.
  Nec quisquam irati vultus spectasse severos,
      vitasse aut dextrae vulnera certa potest.
  Non illo quisquam Vulcania fortior arma
      induit aut pulchro pulchrior ore nitet.
65   Aurea caesaries humeris atque aurea fulgent
      tempora vixque genas aurea pluma tegit.
  Qualem olim memini Troiana ad moenia Achillem,
      sanguine qui Hectoreo ter madefecit humum.
  Perfide Haly, et superum spretor Portune deorum,
70   quam male tam longum consuluistis iter.
  Deserit en vestras felix Victoria puppes,
      Hesperiasque petit diva superba rates.
  Haec erit illa dies, quae vos demittat Averno,
      vestraque in Ionio contegat ossa salo.
75   Iam video humano spumantem sanguine pontum,
      aequoraque armatis plena cadaveribus.
  Iam video vinctosque duces raptasque triremes,
      et tibi praedico iam Caracosa necem.
  Te quoque iam video celeri Ossialene carina
80   spectanda infami terga dedisse fugae.'
  Dixerat, et vasto senior se condidit alveo,
      Tritonumque petit Nereidumque choros.
  Illi indignantes remis vada caerula verrunt,
      et properant coeptam puppibus ire viam.
85   Interea Austriades Phaeacia liquerat arva
      Alcinoique altas, regia tecta, domos;

that a worthy race might spring from his line. He has the bless- 55
ings of his father, whose will Germany feared and whose yoke
shorn Africa felt. Like lightning sent from the peak of Olympus,
wherever he brings destruction, he leaves memorials of eternal life. 60
No one could survive the stern expressions he makes when an-
gered, or avoid inevitable wounds from his right hand. No one
wore Vulcanian arms more bravely than he, or radiated greater
beauty from his face. His hair shines golden on his shoulders, his
temples glisten like gold, and golden down only just covers his 65
cheeks. Just so, I remember, Achilles once stood at the walls of
Troy and soaked the ground three times with Hector's blood.
Treacherous Ali Pasha, and Pertev Pasha, condemner of the
mighty gods, the path you have chosen is as evil as it is long. Be- 70
hold, blessed Victory abandons your ships: the proud goddess
seeks the Hesperian boats. This will be the day that sends you
down to Avernus and covers your bones in Ionian seawater. Al-
ready I see the sea foaming with human blood, and the water full 75
of armed corpses. Already I see your leaders bound and your gal-
leys pillaged, and already I predict that death will come to you,
Kara Hodja. I also see that you, Uluj Ali, on your swift ship, have 80
already retreated in infamous flight."

The old man finished speaking, then sank into the vast depths
and sought the choruses of Tritons and Nereids. The disdainful
Turks sweep through the blue shoals with their oars and hasten to
follow the route they began with their ships. Meanwhile, John of 85
Austria had left the Phaeacian fields and Alcinous's tall houses and

lustraratque rates, sociosque hortatus euntes
    iam medium instructa classe tenebat iter;
et iam Leucadii nimbosa cacumina Phoebi,
90   Samenque et rupes, ardua saxa, Ithacas,
Dulichiasque aras, nec non nemora alta Zacynthi
    cernere erat medio procubuisse mari.
Cum Venus antiquae linquens Lacedaemonis arces,
    (huc etenim capta fugerat illa Papho)
95   Austriaci regis supra caput astitit atque
    ter micuit flamma conspicienda nova;
non illa aureolos per candida colla capillos
    sparserat, aut docta compserat arte caput,
nec niveos Cois ornarat vestibus artus,
100   candida nec Tyrias induerat tunicas
sed galea insignem divinae frontis honorem
    caelarat, flavas condideratque comas,
et teneras duro armarat thorace papillas
    atque gravi suras clauserat aere leves;
105   at dextra ingentem praedurae cuspidis hastam
    quassabat, clypei laeva regebat onus
et clypei auratum fulgebat in aequore malum;
    anguineam apponas Gorgona, Pallas erit.
Talis erat quondam Phrygiis immixta catervis
110   ad pugnam Argolicos ausa ciere viros.
Tunc quoque talis erat, Romanae vincula gentis
    vix una effugit cum Cleopatra rate.
Agnovere deam, et geminas sine labe columbas
    Austriadesque heros, Hesperiique duces,
115   at pavidae circum aeratae obstupuere phalanges,
    et tantae aspectu conticuere deae.
Tunc illa: 'O stirps invicti invictissima patris,
    Augustae Austriadum gloria magna domus,

royal palaces. He had inspected the ships and cheered on the allies accompanying him, and already held the halfway mark with his readied fleet. And now he saw the leafy tops of Leucadian Phoebus, and Samos, and the Ithacan cliffs, steep rocks, and the Dulichian altars, and the lofty groves of Zacynthus stretching out in the middle of the sea. 90

Venus then left the citadels of ancient Lacedaemon, (for she had fled there when Paphos was captured) and hovered over the 95 head of the Austrian prince, and she flashed her known torch three times so she would be recognized. She had not spread her golden locks around her white neck or arranged her hair with learned skill, nor had she decorated her snowy arms with Coan garments or dressed her beautiful form in a Tyrian tunic. Instead, 100 a helmet covered the clear grace of her divine forehead, and she had tucked away her blond locks. She had armored her tender breasts with a sturdy cuirass and enclosed her slender thighs in heavy bronze. In her right hand she shook an immense spear with 105 a sturdy point, and in her left she hefted the weight of a shield on whose surface flashed a golden apple. It will be you, Pallas, who carries the snake-haired Gorgon. Venus looked just as she once did, when, mixed in with the Phrygian warriors, she dared to pro- 110 voke the Argive heroes to fight, and just as she was when Cleopatra narrowly escaped the fetters of the Roman race with only one boat.

The Austrian hero and the Hesperian leaders recognized the goddess and her pair of immaculate doves, but all around them, 115 the bronze phalanxes were struck dumb with fear and fell silent at the sight of so great a goddess. Then she spoke: "O invincible child of an unconquered father, great glory of the imperial House of Austria, rule of the whole world will not be enough

eximiae cuius virtuti et fortibus ausis
120 unius imperium non satis orbis erit;
ne dubita armatae Parthorum occurrere classi,
  quae nunc invitas impia sulcat aquas.
Namque modo ingentem pariet tibi victa triumphum,
  et cadet ante tuos turba superba pedes.
125 Ecce tibi Mavors stricto tam perfurit ense,
  aegida iam Pallas, iam galeamque parat,
letalesque acuit Phoebus sua tela sagittas,
  et pater ipse deum fulmina saeva quatit.
Nec tibi ego clypeum frustra sumpsisse videbor,
130 sentiet illa meas gens inimica manus.
Nec longum sacrae spoliis Amathuntis onusta
  iactabit vanas Cypridos esse minas.
Turca ferox, salsas tune ergo impune per oras
  vectabis celsa rapta trophaea Papho?
135 Impune, infandum, deieceris aurea templa,
  impune et sanctas arseris igne domos?
Et mea regna, eheu, dextra vastaris iniqua?
  Et credar magni semine nata Iovis?
Unius ob culpam Pallas evertere classem
140 et potuit Danaum mergere rostra mari;
ast ego nata salo patrias volitare per undas
  impia Turcarum robora inulta sinam?
Nec potero Ausonia Parthorum arcere Tyrannum,
  et Capitolina pellere ab arce procul?
145 At potui quondam, norunt haec litora, forti
  barbaricas Itala tundere classe minas,
cum Cleopatra furens, saevisque Antonius armis
  haec freta complerat navibus alta suis;

for your outstanding virtue and the brave deeds you have done. 120
Do not hesitate to meet the armed fleet of the Parthians, which
now impiously cuts through the hostile waves. It will be beaten
swiftly, and the proud horde will deliver you a great victory as it
falls before your feet. See how Mars rages on your side with his 125
sword drawn; now Pallas prepares her shield and helmet; Phoebus
sharpens his lethal arrows, his weapons; and the father of the gods
himself shakes his cruel thunderbolts. You will see that I have
not armed myself for you in vain: that enemy race will feel my 130
strength. Though now weighed down by the spoils of sacred Ama-
thus, they will not boast for long that Cyprian threats are empty.
Ferocious Turk, will you carry off the trophies you took from lofty
Paphos across the salty shores without punishment? Unpunished, 135
will you destroy — it is unspeakable! — its golden temples? Unpun-
ished, will you set fire to its sacred homes? Will you destroy my
kingdoms, alas, with your iniquitous right hand? Will anyone be-
lieve I am born from the seed of mighty Jove? For the crime of one
person, Pallas was able to wreck the Greek fleet and submerge 140
their prows in the sea; must I, born from the sea, allow the ships
of the Turks to sail across my native waters without vengeance?
Will I be unable to keep the Parthian Tyrant away from Ausonia
and push him far from the Capitoline citadel? Once, these shores 145
know well, I was able to crush the barbarian's threats with a brave
Italian fleet, when raging Cleopatra and Antony with his savage
arms had filled these deep straits with their ships. The untamed

indomitumque genus Nomadum, pictosque Gelonos
150   duxerat excidio, maxima Roma, tuo.
Sed tunc Leucadio latrantem in gurgite Anubin
      vidimus, et versas in sua fata manus.
Nec Cleopatra tamen, patriaeque Antonius hostis
      tantum tentarant in mea damna nefas.
155   Quare agite, o lecti iuvenes, fortissima bello
      pectora, in adversum mittite tela Scytham,
Ionia ut rursum, infelix, mactatus in unda
      iam nova stultitiae det monumenta suae.
Tuque adeo decus o saecli, cui barbarus hostis
160   victori supplex bracchia capta dabit
tutare Italiam, quae se tete auspice freta
      sperat in antiquum posse redire decus,
et longum infestis Turcarum exposta rapinis,
      commisit dextrae publica vota tuae.
165   Nec timeas quamquam innumeris gens improba velis
      naviget, et multo remige frangat aquam.
Ipsa adero, et Boream quo nunc ruit illa secundo
      convertam in faciles, flamina blanda, Notos.'
Haec ubi dicta dedit, nivea cervice refulsit,
170   et late ambrosio sparsit odore locum.
Et subito aerias cursu delata per auras,
      obvia Parthorum ligna inimica petit.
Ac procul ut liquidum aspexit proscindere pontum,
      atque renascentis cornua ferre deae;
175   et lunae in speciem totam longo ordine classem
      caeruleum pelagi currere vidit iter,
'Frustra,' ait, 'in celsis fers puppibus ora Dianae,
      lunatas frustra cogis in arma rates.
Non his assueta est venari Delia campis,
180   figere nec celeres per vada salsa feras.'

race of the wandering Numidians and painted Gelonians would have led to your downfall, mighty Rome, but then we saw Anubis   150
barking on the Leucadian tide, and the pair's own hands became fatal to them. Yet not even then did either Cleopatra or Antony, enemy of the fatherland, attempt to do such unspeakable harm to me.

Now go, chosen youths, sturdiest hearts in war, attack the   155
Scythian enemy, so that, wretched and slaughtered as before in the Ionian Sea, he might yet have new reminders of his own folly. You are truly the glory of this age. After you claim victory, your barbarous enemy will come as a suppliant to offer you his shackled   160
arms. Watch over Italy; in the wake of your good fortune, it hopes to restore its ancient glory. It has been exposed to the violent incursions of the Turks for too long and now puts its prayers behind your right hand. Do not be afraid, even if the wicked race should   165
sail with countless ships and slice through the water with many oars. I myself will be there, and I will transform Boreas, now the prevailing wind, into gentle Notus with its pleasant breezes."

After she spoke these words, she flashed her white neck and perfumed the area far and wide with her ambrosial scent. Now   170
rising through the upper air, she moves to intercept the enemy line of the Parthians. From a distance, she saw them cutting across the choppy sea, bearing the horns of the reborn goddess; she sees the entire fleet in the shape of the moon, following the blue path of   175
the sea in a long line: "In vain," she says, "you bear the image of Diana on your lofty ships, in vain you gather your ships in a crescent for war: Delia is not accustomed to hunt on these shores, nor   180
to wound swift prey across the salty sea."

Nec plura. Obstantes telum coniecit in hostes,
    fulgidaque ingentes arma dedere sonos,
quo terrore animi cunctis cecidere minaces,
    horridaque infecit pallidus ora pavor:
185   quique prius certos volvebant mente triumphos,
    coeperunt turpes tunc agitare fugas;
quin flatus Boreas fertur posuisse secundos,
    et trepida adverso terga dedisse Noto.
Est locus, Ionii mediis ubi Echinades undis
190   amnis Acarnani numina spreta dolent.
Namque illas quondam castae servisse Dianae,
    et memorant festas concelebrasse dapes,
agricolasque deos sacra ad veneranda vocasse,
    et silvis blandos conservisse choros.
195   Immemores, Acheloe, tui: tu flumine tempto
    diceris et fusis intumuisse vadis,
saltantesque simul Dryades, silvasque sonantes
    voluisse in vastas, fervidus ultor, aquas.
Quas tandem memoresque tui, pavideque natantes
200   excepit gremio Doris amica suo,
quaeque olim fuerant, pulcherrima corpora nymphae,
    nunc versa in scopulos candida membra gemunt.
Huc ergo advectae diverso ex orbe catervae
    fixere in liquido pinea castra salo;
205   dixisses Venetum geminas in fluctibus urbes
    nutare, et celsas surgere in astra domos.
Interea horribiles edit cava buccina bombos,
    et variis resonant tympana pulsa modis.
Iam gelidusque pavor, laudumque innata cupido
210   utrisque in medio pectore corda quatit;

She spoke no more. She threw a spear at the opposing enemy, and her flashing armor made a great noise. The enemy's blustering courage shrank in terror, and pale fear colored their horror-stricken faces. Those who had expected certain triumph began to   185
consider running away in disgrace. And indeed, they say that when the north wind sent no favoring gusts the enemy retreated, their backs trembling in the opposing south wind.

There is a place in the middle of the Ionian waves, where the Echinades mourn the spurned divinity of the Acarnanian River.   190
They recall that they once served chaste Diana as they celebrated solemn feasts, summoned the gods of the fields to observe the holy rites, and joined in cheerful choruses in the forests. They were not thinking of you, Achelous: after you provoked the river, it is said   195
that you swelled up on your broad banks, and in your angry vengeance, enveloped both the dancing Dryads and the talking trees in your vast waters. They finally remembered you, and friendly   200
Doris took them in her lap as they swam around in panic. They had once been nymphs with beautiful bodies, but now their white limbs, transformed into rocks, only groan.

Here, then, troops gathered from all parts of the globe pitched naval camps on the flowing tide: you would have said that twin   205
Venetian cities bobbed in the waves, raising their lofty structures to the stars. Meanwhile, hollow war trumpets give forth horrendous blasts and drumbeats resound in varying rhythms. Now cold fear and an inborn desire for praise stir hearts on both sides. Now   210

189

iamque faces et tela volant, iamque aequora passim
    caede nova, et tepido sanguine tincta rubent,
et iam fulmineo caelum tonat omne fragore,
    et freta sulfurea condita nube latent.
215   Continuo ex oculis Phoebusque diesque recedunt,
    incubat Ioniis nox tenebrosa vadis.
Ingeminant crebras tormenta horrenda ruinas,
    et volat immiti concita ab igne pila.
Vela cadunt, remi franguntur, naufraga puppis
220   uritur, et saevas excipit alnus aquas.
Insequitur vasto morientum in gurgite clamor
    dissonus, et circum litora pulsa sonant.
Multos flamma vorat, gelidisque in fluctibus ardent,
    multi animam misto sanguine ab ore vomunt.
225   Nec pauci pelagi surdis periere procellis,
    instat Mors iaculis undique acerba suis.
Quis cladem immensam, Scythicae quis funera classis
    explicet? Austriaci quis decora alta ducis?
Gens invicta mari, certisque assueta trophaeis,
230   en tandem aequoreis piscibus esca iacet.
Pauci queis pontus, ferrumque ignisque pepercit,
    impia servili colla dedere iugo.
Vixque una sospes potuisti, perfide, navi
    effugere hostiles Ossialene manus.
235   Captiva aversis ducuntur robora proris,
    et gemina Austriades Nerea classe secat.
Neptunus placidum summis caput extulit undis,
    spectansque infidis aequora plena Getis,
'Ite,' ait, 'Adriacis posui quam fluctibus urbem
240   deiicite, inque Italo figite castra solo.'
Sed quid ego imbelli cythara, quid proelia tento?
    Proelia Maeoniis concelebranda modis.

torches and weapons fly, and now everywhere the water is dyed red
with fresh slaughter and warm blood. Now the entire sky thunders
with the crash of lightning, and the straits lie hidden, buried un-
der a sulfurous cloud. Suddenly Phoebus and daylight recede from   215
sight; dark night broods over the Ionian shoals. Horrible cannons
redouble the massive onslaught and mortar shells fly, launched by
cruel fire. Sails fall; oars are broken; a wrecked ship burns, and its   220
planks take in the raging water. Then follows the discordant noise
of the men dying in the vast abyss, and all around, the shores re-
peat the sounds that strike them. Flame devours many, and they
burn in the icy waves; many spew forth their souls from their
mouths mixed with blood; many perish in the deafening storms of   225
the sea. Armed with his javelins, bitter Death looms everywhere.

Who can describe the tremendous slaughter, the destruction of
the Scythian fleet, the noble glory of the Austrian commander? A
race unconquered on the deep, accustomed to uncontested victo-
ries, lies there at last, food for the fish in the sea. Those few whom   230
the sea, iron, and fire spared gave their impious necks to the yoke
of slavery. You managed to get away safely from the hands of your
enemy, treacherous Uluj Ali, with barely a single ship. Captured
boats are led away with their prows turned backward, and John of   235
Austria slices through Nereus's realms with a fleet doubled in size.
Neptune raises his placid head above the high waves, seeing the
water filled with these impious Geets; "Go," he says, "disassemble
the city I built on the Adriatic waves and settle your camps on   240
Italian soil."

But why do I try to sing of battles with a lyre not suited for
war? These battles are to be celebrated in Maeonian modes. Why

Quid studeo obscuris heroum inducere chartis
    nomina? Et invito tangere fila Deo?
245   Austriadae laudes cantet Capilupus, eburnam
    cui tribuit merito pulcher Apollo lyram.
Quique suum aequiparans cycnea voce Maronem
    Tybridis ad ripas concinit acta Pii.
Hesperiosque duces, Parthosque in proelia ducat
250   Angelius, clari gloria prima Dei,
qui nunc Hetruscis Arnus qua illabitur undis
    aeterno Cosmi carmine facta refert.
Cantuque Hesperiam per foedera iungat utramque
    Carga suo, et Phoebo carmina digna canat;
255   vitrea Felsinei qui nunc prope flumina Rheni
    Campegium heroem tollit in astra suum.
Nec tamen haec prima quae nos florente iuventa
    lusimus ad laudis murmura magna tuae,
despicias, dux magne, precor; sic Bosphora tantis
260   accedant titulis postmodo capta tuis.
Fors erit illa dies, plectro cum plenius aureo
    non dubitem heroas cogere in arma manus,
atque tua fractos decantem cuspide reges,
    ultimaque imperio subdita Bactra tuo.

do I try to add names of heroes to obscure pages and strike the
chord if God does not wish it? Let Capilupi sing the praises of   245
John of Austria; handsome Apollo has bestowed on him the ivory
lyre. Rivaling his beloved Vergil with his swanlike voice, he sings
the deeds of Pius on the banks of the Tiber. Let Angeli lead the
Hesperian and Parthian captains into battle, the foremost glory of   250
illustrious God. He now tells the deeds of Cosimo in eternal song,
where the Arno flows with its Tuscan waves. Let Carga join either
side of the West together in treaties with his poetry, and let him
sing songs worthy of Phoebus, he who beside the glassy streams of   255
the Reno of Bologna is now exalting the hero Campeggio to the
stars.

I only ask, great leader, that you do not despise these first ef-
forts: in my early youth, I have only practiced at muttering your
praises. Let the capture of the Bosphorus be added to your great   260
credits: perhaps that will be the day when I might decide to lead
heroic bands to arms with my golden plectrum, and I might recite
how kings are broken by your sword and the farthest edge of Bac-
tria is brought into your empire.

: XX :

Victoria Naupactiaca

Giovanni Baptista Arcucci

Quae divos celebras, et fortia facta virorum
dulcibus exornas numeris, aeternaque reddis,
Musa Iovis summi soboles pulcherrima Clio
laetitia precor; in tanta qua maximus orbis

5   terrarum late, ac septem cum collibus alma
imprimis Roma exultat domus inclyta divum;
pro clade ingenti Turcarum et classe subacta
Ionio in magno rursus cape condita plectra.
Nam quamquam nullo doctorum carmina vatum

10 sunt hodie in pretio, nec habent sua praemia Musae,
non ingrata tamen fuerit cecinisse voluptas,
et claram Europae famam extendisse per urbes.
Ergo age, diva, mihi memores ab origine prima
quis tanta intulerit Turcarum funera genti.

15   Ponto Asiae in medio sedet insula sacra Diones
formosae natae, et longe gratissima tellus,
clara viris opibusque, Cypron dixere Pelasgi.
Hanc Veneti patres multos tenuere per annos,
munere sed vitae Solymano et dulcibus auris

20 defuncto, simul imperium sceptrumque regendum
saevior accepit Selymus, dum latius optat
regnorum fines protendere, foedera rumpit,
magnanimis quae cum Venetis percusserat olim
armipotens genitor nullum violanda per aevum.

: XX :

The Victory at Naupactus

Giovanni Baptista Arcucci

Clio, my Muse, Jupiter's loveliest daughter, you who glorify the
gods and embellish the brave deeds of men with sweet rhythms to
make them eternal, I pray to you in my happiness. The whole vast
world rejoices, and most of all nurturing Rome with her seven   5
hills, famous home of the gods. Pick up the lyre you had put away
and celebrate the momentous defeat of the Turks and their fleet,
vanquished on the great Ionian Sea. Though today the songs of
learned bards are held in low esteem, and the Muses get no re-   10
ward, it will have been no idle pleasure to have sung and spread
this famous story through the cities of Europe. So start now at the
very beginning, goddess, and tell me who it was that brought so
many deaths to the race of the Turks.

In the middle of the sea of Asia there is an island sacred to   15
Dione's lovely daughter, a bountiful land, famous for its heroes
and its riches. The Pelasgians call it Cyprus. The Venetian fathers
possessed it for many years, but when Suleiman came to the
end of his life and stopped breathing the sweet air, the more bru-
tal Selim took control of both the state and the scepter; soon   20
he wishes to extend the confines of his kingdom, and he breaks
the treaties that his valiant father had once struck with the cou-
rageous Venetians, swearing they would never be dishonored.

25 Tum belli reserat portas et classe parata
  (quantam non umquam nostris audivimus annis)
  impius invadit Cyprum. Iamque oppida multa
  ceperat, et passim speciosas usserat urbes,
  cum Venus hunc miserans casum telluris amatae,
30 alloquitur sic maesta Iovem: 'Si filia vere
  sum tua, si de te vere me pulchra Dione
  suscepit, tua si venerans, rex inclyte, divum
  iussa sequor, cur heu pateris tu numina nostra
  contemni? Dilecta mihi (iam despice) tellus,
35 in qua ter centum sancte per templa colebar,
  uritur: ecquidnam meruit? Cur ille triumphat
  audax, contemptor divumque hominumque Tyrannus?
  Certe ego, si tanti sunt numina nostra, recedam
  caelo, et Tartareas habitabo ingloria sedes.'
40 Tum pater apprendens dextra, dedit oscula fronti
  atque ait: 'Ista quidem iustissima causa dolendi est,
  nata, meus sanguis, sed enim temerarius ille
  omnes adversus divos, numenque Tonantis
  nil veritus (quamquam magna cum strage suorum)
45 Cypron habet, ferroque et flammis omnia vastat.
  Haec ego permisi, fateor, dum turpia gentis
  Christiadum dignis ulciscor facta flagellis.
  Nunc illos toto ex animo quod poenitet, ac iam
  mutarunt mores (Stygii per flumina fontis
50 obtestor) terrae faciam pelagique potentes.
  Iam domus Othomani ruat, et quem classe superbum
  aspicis ingenti spatiosum currere pontum,
  victorem atque urbes capere, et regna addere regnis.
  Tempus erit, iamque accelerant ea stamina Parcae,

Then the treacherous king opens the gates of war, and when his   25
fleet is ready (a fleet such as I have never heard of in all my years)
he invades Cyprus. Now he had seized many of its towns, and ev-
erywhere had burned down its beautiful cities. Venus, pitying the
catastrophe of her beloved land, mournfully speaks to Jove: "If I   30
am truly your daughter, if lovely Dione truly bore me by you, if I
follow your commands with reverence, famous king of the gods,
then why do you suffer my divinity to be scorned? My beloved
land, where I am devoutly worshipped in three hundred temples,   35
is in flames — see for yourself. What has it done to deserve this?
Why does that insolent Tyrant triumph, scornful of gods and
men? If this is all our divine powers are worth, I shall retreat from
the sky and inhabit the realms of Tartarus in disgrace."

   Then, taking her by the right hand, her father kisses her fore-   40
head, and says: "Indeed, this is a valid cause for grieving, daughter
of my blood. It is true: that brazen man has taken Cyprus against
the will of all the gods, scorning the power of the Thunderer
(though with much slaughter of his own men), and there he lays   45
waste to everything with sword and fire. I confess I allowed these
things to happen to punish the shameful deeds of the Christian
people with righteous whips. Now they regret their transgressions
with their whole heart, they have changed their ways, and I swear
by the streams of the source of Styx: I will make them rule over   50
land and sea. Now let the House of Ottoman fall to ruin. You see
how he scurries around proudly on the vast sea with his huge fleet,
taking cities as he conquers, and adding kingdoms to kingdoms.
There will be a time — the Fates already quicken their spindles —

55 cum tantis spoliatum armis et classe videbis
  exutum, maerentem animo et sua fata gementem,
  extremis sese pavitantem condere Bactris,
  vel qua praecipiti cursu petit aequor Hydaspes.
  Reddeturque tibi pauco post tempore Cyprus.
60 Tu modo fac Italae feriant sacra foedera gentes,
  Hispanaeque. Tuus labor esto hic filia mentes
  mentibus atque animos animis connectere regum,
  quo simul in Thracum coniuret Roma Tyrannum,
  utraque et Hesperia, et Venetum Respublica dives.'
65 Dixerat. Illa polo Suada comitante loquendi
  artifice excessit, claramque ad Tibridis urbem
  contendit, magnumque Pium, regnator Olympi
  cui dedit in terris aperire et claudere caelum,
  affatur. 'Videsne ut Scythiae dominator avitis
70 tot regnis non contentus bella horrida rupto
  foedere magnanimis Venetis indixerit? Et iam
  claram expugnarit Cyprum victricibus armis?
  Quin et Corcyrae malus imminet? Hac quoque capta
  mox illum cernes Siculi sulcare profundi
75 aequora et huc etiam numerosa excurrere classe.
  Surge age, quid cessas? Tantis obsistere coeptis
  te decet in primis, genitor quem maximus unum
  esse dedit Romae columen, tutamen et omnis
  Ausoniae, pedibusque tuis regalia sceptra
80 subiecit. Tu fac coeant in foedera fortes
  Hispani Venetique, ac sese ingentibus ausis
  opponant Selymi; dabitur victoria tandem.
  Ne dubita, pater huc alto me misit Olympo.'
  Agnovit divam senior. Iubet ocius ergo
85 Hispanos Italosque simul componere foedus
  immortale sacrum, centum quod duret in annos.

when you will see him deprived of his arsenal and stripped of his   55
fleet, sad at heart and bemoaning his fate. You will see him hide
himself, shivering with fear in distant Bactria, or where the Hy-
daspes reaches the sea in its abrupt plunge. Cyprus will be re-
turned to you in a short time. You have only to make the peoples   60
of Italy and Spain strike a holy alliance. Let this be your labor,
daughter: to join kings together, mind with mind, and spirit with
spirit. In this way let Rome unite with Spain and the rich Repub-
lic of Venice against the Thracian Tyrant."

He finished his speech. With Persuasion, skilled in speaking,   65
accompanying her, Venus departs heaven, and hastens toward the
famous city of the Tiber. There she addresses great Pius, to whom
the ruler of Olympus gave jurisdiction on earth to open and close
heaven: "Can't you see that the Lord of Scythia, not content with
his many ancestral dominions, has broken the treaty and declared   70
terrible wars against the courageous Venetians? Can't you see that
they have plundered famous Cyprus with overwhelming forces? Is
this evil not a threat to Corfu? If it too is captured, you will soon
see him plowing the waters of the Sicilian seas, and intrude even   75
here with his innumerable ships. So come, rise, why do you delay?
It is your duty to thwart their enterprise, for the mighty Father
made you alone the safeguard of Rome and protector of all Auso-
nia. He has laid the scepters of kings at your feet. You must make   80
the mighty Spaniards and Venetians enter into an alliance and set
themselves against Selim's great daring. Victory will be granted
you at last. Have no doubt, for the Father has sent me here from
high Olympus."

The old man recognized the goddess. Quickly he commands
the Spaniards and Italians at once to make a timeless, sacred pact,   85
such as will last for a hundred years. Then he commands his

Deduci ingentem classem tum mandat in aequor,
acciri et iuvenem clara de stirpe deorum
Austriaden, belli referentem laude parentem
90   divinum, quo non praestantior alter in armis,
Alciden quamvis et Graecia iactet Achillem.
Hunc belli esse caput tanti voluitque phalanges
Hispanos Venetasque et magnam ducere classem
Christiadum. Calidi urebat iam terga Leonis
95   sol, et pacati ridebant marmora ponti,
cum dux Austriades Zephyris dat vela secundis,
fratris ab amplexu avulsus, cui plurima parent
oppida in extrema Hesperia, transque aequora late
alter cui mundus tellusque Antarctica servit.
100   Hispanis illum fauste cum solveret oris
filia magnanimi Iovis aurea Cypria duxit
per mare in Ausonias oras ad litora pulchrae
Parthenopes, ingens ubi classis et omnia tantis
opportuna orsis stabant iam rite parata.
105   Namque bonus regni praeses, pars magna senatus
Romulei, belli et pacis clarissimus arte
pernotus, cuius mira virtute regendis
in populis divus dum vixit Carolus, et nunc
Austriades regum rex utitur ipse Philippus,
110   arma, viros, naves, simul et quaecumque fuissent
illius ex usu belli instrumenta pararat.
Mox templo in magno sacris de more peractis
olli multa deos aurata in veste precatus,
sceptra et pontificis porrexit nomine sacrum
115   vexillum, quo tutus eat per tela, per hostes.
Talibus auspiciis heros de litore curvo
Parthenopes dat vela Notis duce Cypride diva.

immense fleet to put to sea, and sends for John of Austria, a young
man from the glorious line of the gods, who matches his divine
father in his renown for battle. No one was more outstanding in   90
arms, though Greece may boast of Hercules and Achilles. For it
was the pope's will that this man should lead them in such a bat-
tle, that he command the Spanish and Venetian forces and the
great Christian fleet. Already the sun was burning the back of the
fiery Lion and the marble surface of the placid sea was smiling,   95
when the Austrian commander sets sail on the favoring west
winds, pulled from the embrace of his brother, who rules the
many cities of distant Spain, the Other World far across the
ocean, and even the Antarctic land.

When he had embarked with favorable omens from the Span-   100
ish shores, golden Venus, daughter of high-minded Jove, guided
him across the sea toward the Ausonian shores, and to the coast of
lovely Parthenope, where the immense fleet and the necessary sup-
plies for such an undertaking waited, all properly prepared. For
Colonna, the noble guardian of the kingdom and key member of   105
the Roman Senate, famous in the arts of war and peace, had re-
ceived advance notice, and with the same marvelous instinct for
ruling people that divine Charles wielded—while he lived—and
now that king of kings, Philip of Austria wields, he had prepared
the arms, the men, the ships, and whatever other equipment they   110
would need in the conflict. Soon after the sacraments had been
celebrated according to custom in the great temple, he prayed to
the gods wearing golden vestments; then, in the pope's name, he
took up the scepter and unfurled the sacred standard, under which   115
he hoped to pass safely through spears and enemies.

Under these good omens, the hero raises the sails to the south
winds, setting out from the curved shore of Parthenope, with the
Cyprian goddess in the lead. He had just left behind the hills of

Et iam Pausilypi colles Nesidaque pulchram
liquerat a dextra, Prochytenque sacrumque Minervae
120 transierat montem, et quondam, dum regna manebant
Teleboum, Capreas armis opibusque potentes,
Sirenumque domos dulces ac litus amoenum,
naturae gaudentis opus, cum plurima turba
nympharum regno caput extulit Amphitrites,
125 mirantum, quaeque illarum pulcherrima Drymo
sic coepit, vocem reliquae tenuere sorores.
    'Non has, o iuvenis, fausto sine numine ad oras
venisti; poscunt unum te fata deorum,
perdita qui sceptra Italiae et decus omne reponas.
130 Ergo age, et invictus tanto ne cede labori,
quamvis Scylla tibi superandaque vasta Charybdis
Leucadiique maris scopuli Patraeaque saxa.
Quid tua non sternet virtus? Te gloria belli
attollet caelo. Nam postquam classe Corinthum,
135 Actiaque Augustis semper memoranda trophaeis
attigeris, hosti occurres, pugnamque lacesses
terribilem, crudelem, acrem, qua nulla fuisse
dicetur pelago maior, licet aspera multa
Xerxis cum Danais in caelum bella ferantur
140 et cum Romanis Cleopatrae illustre duellum.
Perge age, ne dubita, dextro maris aequora curris
omine.' Et his dictis vitrea caput abdidit unda.
Ille iter incoeptum properat felicibus Austris.
    Tertia iamque dies aderat, cum Trinacris orae
145 prospiciunt longe salientem ad nubila fumum.
Laetatur ducis adventu Sicania tellus
gaudiaque explosis centum testatur aenis
tormentis; magno reboant cava litora plausu.
Hic Venetum bonus occurrit cum classe manumque
150 Venerius iungit dux, et sacra foedera firmat.

Pausilypus and beautiful Nesis on the right, and had passed by
Prochyta and the mountain sacred to Minerva, and what were   120
once the kingdoms of Teleboes, the Capreans, mighty in arms and
riches, and the Sirens' sweet homes—he had just left that charm-
ing shore, the work of Nature in her joy, when a large group of
nymphs lifted their heads from the kingdom of Amphitrite to
marvel at him. And one of them, the most beautiful Drymo, be-   125
gins to speak while the rest of her sisters hang on her words:

"You have not come to these shores, young hero, without the
blessing of the divine. The fates of the gods call on you alone to
restore all the glory and the lost power of Italy. Go now, and do   130
not cease in this great labor, though you must prevail over Scylla
and immense Charybdis, and the cliffs of the Sea of Leucas, and
the Patraean rocks. What can your virtue fail to defeat? The glory
of this war will raise you to the sky. For after you and your fleet
have reached Corinth and Actium, which will always be remem-   135
bered for Augustus's conquests, you will meet your enemy, and
you will wage a terrible battle, brutal and vicious. No sea battle
will ever be thought greater, though Xerxes's many bitter wars
with the Danaans are known worldwide, as is Cleopatra's famous   140
fight with the Romans. Go, and do not delay: you race upon the
surface of the sea with favorable omens." And having spoken these
words, she hid her head under the glassy waves. The journey thus
begun is sped on by the blessed south winds.

On the third day they see far-off smoke from the Trinacrian
coast, billowing to the clouds. The Sicilian land rejoices at the   145
commander's arrival, and shows its joy with a hundred shots fired
from brass cannons. The curved shores resound with great ap-
plause. Good Venier, chief admiral of the Venetians, runs to meet   150
them here with his fleet, and joins hands with John to confirm the

Iamque simul placidas sulcabant Doridis undas
Hesperii Venetique duces, unaque Columnus
Romanae classis princeps; et sic ubi celsas
inveniant Cilicum puppes, maria omnia obibant.
155 Cum prope Brundusium fuit obvia navis Ibera,
innumeramque refert classem vidisse Scytharum
attollit qua se ponto nemorosa Zacynthus.
Imperat Austriades illuc advertere cursum
nostrorum proras, certus committere pugnam.
160   Ventum erat ad colles Naupacti, ubi maxima gentis
Heraclidarum steterant navalia quondam.
Hic procul ex alto Scythicas videre triremes.
'Arma, arma, o socii,' exclamat tunc maximus heros,
'Ecce dies toties votis optata refulsit:
165 pugnemus.' Celeri haec dicens rate singula lustrat
componitque acies bello. Nec segnius hostis
instruit ad pugnam naves, nostrisque propinquat.
     Quis classem Ismariae gentis tunc ductor agebat,
diva, refer pugnaeque modum? Genitore Thoante
170 ortus Alys, cui rex Asiae commiserat omnem
regnorum Europae molem, ac saepe horrida bella
gesserat eventu felici, et Marte secundo
in curvae speciem lunae miro ordine classem
Threiciam tumidus ducebat. Iamque trecentas
175 florentes armis opibusque virisque carinas
hinc atque hinc contra nostras instruxerat audax.
Ipse quidem torvis oculis et corpore magno,
quantus Sicana fuerat Polyphemus in Aetna.
Et latere a laevo pendebat maximus ensis,
180 effulgens cuius capulum decorabat iaspis,
ingentem dextra clypeum gestabat, Abantis

holy alliance. Now at once the Spanish and Venetian captains cut
across the calm waves of Doris; with them is Colonna, the com-
mander of the Roman fleet. Likewise when they meet the lofty
ships of the Cilicians, the seas grow calm before them. Near Brin-   155
disi an Iberian ship crosses their path and reports that it had spot-
ted the massive Scythian fleet, where wooded Zacynthus rears it-
self up from the sea. John of Austria commands our ships to turn
their course toward that place, ready to enter the battle.

They had come to the hills of Naupactus, where the great ships   160
of the sons of Hercules once took their stand. Far off on the deep,
they make out the Scythian galleys. "To arms, comrades, to arms!"
The great hero then calls out, "Behold, the day we have so often
wished for has begun to shine. Let us fight!" And saying this, he   165
inspects the fleet on his swift boat and readies the battle lines for
war. But the enemy is not slow to array its ships for the fight and
begins to draw closer.

Tell me, goddess, what leader was then commanding the fleet
of the Ismarian race, and what was his manner of fighting? Ali
Pasha, born the son of Thoante. It was to him that the King of   170
Asia had entrusted the burden of conquering the kingdoms of
Europe. Often the terrible wars he had waged turned out well;
Mars favored him when, swollen with pride, he led the Thracian
fleet in a wondrous array in the shape of a curved moon. And now
in his audacity, he sent three hundred keels, brimming with arms,   175
riches, and men against our ships. He himself was there with his
dreadful eyes and his massive frame, like Polyphemus on Aetna in   180
Sicily. And at his left side hung his mighty sword, its radiant hilt
adorned with jasper. His right hand carried an immense shield,

qui fuerat Lyciae regis, galeaque minaci
munibat caput, et pectus thorace rigenti
ex ferro, suras ocreis, hastamque ferebat,
185   ad pugnam his acuens Turcarum pectora dictis:
     'Gradivo quantum Geticis qui praesidet arvis
debemus Marti, o socii, summoque Tonanti?
Qui praedam hanc nobis nil tale putantibus ultro
obtulerint, gentem imbellem, quam saepius olim
190   fudistis, cunctam et misere obtruncastis ad unum.
Quare alacres committite proelia, vosque putate
cum totidem certare virum sub imagine Damis.'
     Maximus Austriades contra terno agmine classe
instructa ad pugnam divis comitantibus ibat,
195   formosus facie iuvenis flavoque capillo,
qualis erat Nireus, Phrygia vel raptus ab Ida.
Huic fabricata manu dederat Cytherea mariti
arma, quibus contra magnos insurgere divos
vel tutus poterat; consertam ex aere minutis
200   in primis loricam hamis, auroque argentoque,
insignes ocreas, galeamque ensemque coruscum,
cuius erat capulo viridis praefixa smaragdus,
et clypeum; medios alacer quibus ibat in hostes,
bis centum aeratas adigens in bella triremes.
205   Hic omnis flos Ausoniae, flos omnis Iberae
gentis erat: dextra Ligur Auria, Barbarigusque
legatus Venetum laeva; medium agmen agebat
ipse heros, quem circumstant duo fulmina belli
hinc dux Venerius, princepsque Columnius illinc,
210   atque alii. Tum sic pelagi formosa Cythere
compellat regem: 'Neptune tridentiger, omnes
quem supra divos uno Iove patre Tonante
excepto colui, da nunc felicibus Euris

which once had belonged to Abas, King of Lycia. His head was protected by a menacing helmet, his chest with a stiff breastplate of iron, and his calves with greaves. He also carried a spear. And he roused the hearts of the Turks to war with these words: 185

"How much do we owe to Mars, who rules as Gradivus over Getican fields, and to the mighty Thunderer? They have brought us these spoils in war of their own accord, without our even think-ing to ask for so much. How often in the past have you routed this unwarlike race; how often have you cut them down to nothing.   190 Therefore, make haste to enter the battle, and remember that you fight them with an equal number of forces, under the likeness of Diana."

On the other side, mighty John of Austria with his triple fleet goes into battle with the gods at his side. The young man's face is   195 handsome, and he has golden hair, as Nireus was, or the boy snatched from Ida in Phrygia. Cytherea had given him his armor, made by her husband's hand, arms with which he could even rise up against the great gods and be safe. He wore a coat of mail   200 joined together with tiny hooks of brass, and gold and silver; em-bossed greaves, and a helmet; and also a glimmering sword, on whose hilt a green emerald was set, and a shield as well. Wearing these he moved quickly to the middle of the enemy force, driving forward two hundred bronze-clad ships into battle. Here was the   205 flower of Ausonia, the best of the Iberian race. At his right side was Giovanni Andrea Doria from Liguria; Agostino Barbarigo, the Venetian legate, stood on his left. The hero himself was lead-ing the middle column. On either side, two thunderbolts of war flanked him: here commander Venier, and there prince Colonna. And there were others. Then beautiful Venus addresses the king   210 of the sea in this way: "Trident-wielding Neptune, whom I esteem above all the gods except thundering Father Jupiter alone, grant now that my John of Austria may fight in the favorable east winds

Austriades pugnet meus, infelicibus hostis.'
215 Sic illa, atque deus Veneris prece motus amatae,
Austriadae classem felicibus impulit Euris.

Iam fortes utrimque duces certare parabant,
cum turmas duri accendens in proelia Martis
Austriades celsa ex puppi sic ore profatur:
220 'Si Christi vos tangit honor, si gloria tanti
titillat belli, o socii, nunc fortiter armis
tendite in adversos hostes, conferre volentes
nunc acres in bella manus. Deus aethere pugnat
pro nobis, simul et venti, Neptunus et ipse,
225 sanctus et ille senex, Romae qui templa tuetur,
divorum et mentem novit; mihi maximus ille
omnia promisit dextra in certamen eunti,
vos estote viri tantum, victoria nostra est.'

Imperat his dictis mox classica mille tubasque
230 inflari ac magno explodi tormenta fragore
aenea, quo vasti intremuit domus ardua Olympi
Oceanusque imis caput occultavit in antris.

Quis stragem illius belli? Quis funera fando
enumeret? Magnis animis certatur utrimque.
235 Turritae Venetum naves, sex illa marinas
inter aquas castella, bonus quas fronte locarat
in prima Austriades, ingentia saxa pilasque
proiciunt ferri grandes, stragem ac miserandam
per classem dant adversam et simul omnia turbant.
240 Tum magnas Turcae iactant ad sidera voces:
exululant, immane fremunt Psylli, Garamantes,
Aethiopes, Daci, Morini, Cilicesque, Getaeque.
Occursant prorae proris. Fit maxima caedes.
Austriades medios sic irruit acer in hostes,
245 ut leo pascentes per gramina laeta iuvencos
si videat stimulante fame petit unguibus uncis

against this unblessed enemy." So she spoke, and the god, moved   215
by the prayer of his beloved Venus, backed the Austrian's fleet
with the favorable east winds.

Already the mighty leaders on both sides were preparing to
fight, when John of Austria spoke thus from his high deck to kin-
dle the spirits of his squadrons for the pitched battle:

"If the honor of Christ touches you, if the glory of such a battle   220
excites you, comrades, now press on valiantly in arms toward the
enemy we face; willingly lend your eager hands to the fight. God
fights on our behalf in the sky, as do the winds, and Neptune
himself, and that holy patriarch, who guards the temples of Rome   225
and knows the will of the gods. That great man himself promised
me that all things would favor my entrance into this contest. Be
men, and the victory is ours!"

After he said these things, soon he commands the thousand
trumpets and the horns to blow, and the bronze cannons to fire   230
with a great crack; at this the lofty home of vast Olympus trem-
bles, and Oceanus hides his head in deep caves.

Who could measure in words the slaughter of that battle, or its
devastation? It was fought with great courage on both sides. The
turreted ships of the Venetians, those six castles on the sea, the   235
good John of Austria positioned them in the very front. They
launch massive shells and mortars of iron, inflicting terrible car-
nage throughout the enemy fleet, and sending them all at once
into disarray. Then the Turks raise their great voices to the stars.   240
They howl. The Psyllians, Garamantes, the Ethiopians, Moors,
Cilicians, and Geets rage wildly. Prows run into prows. The car-
nage is unthinkable. John of Austria runs fiercely into the middle
of the enemy, like a lion prowling for calves that feed in the fertile   245
grass; anything he sees, he attacks, slashing with his curved claws,

dilacerans. Alyn ante alios tunc impete vasto
aggreditur rostroque ratem percussit acuto
ac tabulas late huc illuc disiecit in aequor
250 temonemque ipsum malumque et aplustria tota
abstulit explosis ingentibus aere cavato
saxis nigranti mista cum pulvere flamma.
Neve fuga se proripiat tum barbara puppis,
grandibus ex ferro tenet harpagonibus arcte
255 implicitam, magnis manibus, validisque catenis.
Ast Alys intrepidus turba stipante suorum
opponit sese nostris, et comminus ense
obtruncat quicumque manum conferre parasset.
Annuit et Barco celeres impellere proras
260 et ducis a tergo Hesperidum committere bellum.
Praesensit iuvenis fraudem, Siculisque carinis
imperat accelerent cursum Barcumque repellant.
Iam magnis late resonat stridoribus aether,
omnia complentur sonitu, bellique fragorem
265 Elide cum tota procul audiit alta Corinthus,
Pireneque sacer Musis, et pontus uterque.
Invadunt Turcae Austriaden, et spicula iactant
letali taxo et Scythicis medicata venenis.
Ille tegens clypeo septemplice tela repellit.
270 Hostilem tandem fortissimus insilit heros
in puppem, sequitur sociorum cetera turba;
atque Alyn intrepide pugnantem percutit ense
qua costae iecur abscondunt, Erebique coegit
ire domum et meritas Allecto solvere poenas.
275 Inde Agat obtruncat Dadagumque Caramque Casamque
Mustafamque uni fuerat cui barbara gaza,
omnis et illius commissa pecunia belli.
Quo tamen ense minus caderet, nil profuit aurum
argentumque sua multum quod puppe ferebat.

his hunger driving him on. Then he attacks Ali before the others
in a massive onslaught and strikes his ship with a sharp ram, toss-
ing planks in all directions over the sea; he tears off the forebeam
itself, and the mast, and the whole stern post with immense   250
cannonballs launched from the hollowed bronze by flame mixed
with the black powder. Nor did the barbarian ship wrench itself
away in flight, for he held her close, clenched with huge grappling
hooks of iron like giant hands, and with strong chains. But Ali,   255
fearless among the surrounding mob of his men, throws himself
against our troops, and at close quarters, slashes with his sword
any man who would try to oppose him. He gives the sign for
Barco to drive his swift ships around, and enter the battle with the   260
western fleet at our leader's back. The young hero senses the de-
ception and commands the Sicilian ships to quicken their course
and push Barco back. Now the air echoes far and wide with great
crashes; everything is enveloped by the sound. Far off, lofty Cor-
inth hears the clamor of war along with all the region of Elis,   265
and so does Pirene, sacred to the Muses, and the seas on either
side. The Turks attack John of Austria, and throw spears of lethal
yew, imbued with Scythian poisons. Taking cover behind his sev-
enfold shield, he fends off the weapons. The mighty hero leaps, at   270
last, onto the enemy deck and the rest of the crowd of his com-
rades follows. And he strikes at Ali, as he fights fearlessly, where
the ribs hide the liver, and drives him to the house of Erebus, to
resolve the debts he owes to Allecto. Then he cuts down Agat, and   275
Dadagus, and Cara, and Casa, and also Mustafa, whose charge
was the barbarian treasury, and all the wealth acquired in that war.
The gold and silver he was carrying in abundance on his ship did

280   Giafferrumque Osmanque Perumque trucidat et Affyn,
         et Prouyn et Ligeryn uno quos candida partu
         dicitur in magna quondam genuisse Libyssa,
         Liriope geminos concordi pectore fratres.
         Nam Prouys aeratam per costas impulit hastam,
285   cui mox auxilium Ligeryn afferre parantem
         adiungit fati comitem, mittitque sub Orcum,
         fulmineo medium mucrone in pectus adacto.
         Cappadocumque ducis Peribae, qui fortia leto
         corpora multa virum dederat, perfodit utrumque
290   tempus et undivagis proiecit piscibus escam.
         Atque Amet in tota regnantem Chalcide ferro
         traiecit medium, Caralymque trucemque Morattum.
            Quanta per adversos hostes det funera magnus
         Venerius, dic Musa Iovis clarissima proles.
295   Namque ducem contra Gyalum natosque Dragutti
         tendebat celeri invectus Pistrice per aequor.
         Iamque rates tres illorum combusserat igni,
         merserat atque duas pelago, cum puppe Nearchus,
         cuius erat torva cum fronte insigne Leaena,
300   a tergo prora Pistricem invadit acuta.
         Iamque virum mersisset aquis cum puppe decorum,
         ni sustentasset dextra Neptunus amica.
         Namque ferunt olim Hadriacis cum solveret oris,
         Venerium pulchrae Veneri vovisse patrique
305   Neptuno, cui stat Venetum Respublica curae,
         si sospes victis aliqua cum laude redisset
         hostibus in patriam, positurum maxima templa
         Neptuno in primis atque Idaliae Cythereae.
         Hostem Venerius sic increpat: 'Improbe, fraudes
310   iam tibi nil faxo prosint artesque dolique.'
         Dixit, et impellens rostro stridente Leaenam
         mersit aquis. Nusquam socii, nusquam ipse Nearchus

not prevent him from falling by the sword. And John killed Giaf- 280
ferrus, Osman, Perus, and Affys. Also Prouys, and Ligerys, both
of whom lovely Liriope was said to have borne once in a single
birth in great Libya; twin brothers with hearts in harmony. For
John struck his bronze spear through Prouys's ribs, and to him he 285
soon adds Ligerys as he tries to bring help, a companion to his
brother in death. He sends him down to Orcus driving his thun-
dering sword point into the middle of his chest. He pierces
through both brows of Cappadocus, commander of the Periba,
who had given many strong bodies of men to death, tossing him 290
overboard as food for the wave-wandering fish. And he transfixes
Amet right through the middle, he who rules in all of Calchis
with his sword, and Caralys, and savage Morattus.

Tell, Muse, most famous child of Jupiter, how much destruc-
tion great Venier deals out to the opposing host. For, conveyed 295
over the sea on the swift ship *Pistrix*, he was pressing against the
commander Gyalus, and the sons of Dragut. He had already set
three of their ships on fire and had sunk two in the sea, when on
his deck, Nearchus, whose ship was the Leaena, fearsome with its
painted bow, attacked the *Pistrix* from behind with its sharp prow. 300
And now he would have sunk this worthy man in the waters along
with his ship, had not Neptune held him up with his friendly
right hand. For they say that once, when he was leaving the Adri-
atic shores, Venier had vowed to beautiful Venus and to Father
Neptune, patron of the Venetian Republic, that if he returned 305
alive to his fatherland with glory, having conquered the enemy, he
would first of all raise great temples to Neptune and to Idalian
Venus. Venier rebuked the enemy thus: "Wicked man, I will
make it so that your deceits are of no use to you, nor your crafts, 310
nor your tricks." He spoke, and charging with his grating ram,
sank the Leaena in the waves. Never again do Nearchus and

amplius apparent. Tegit omnes caerula Tethys.
Mox et Monsorrem Delphinide puppe volantem
315   assequitur, teloque caput terebravit acuto,
Myrmillumque necat confosso pectore vastumque
Andraleonta feros Getula per arva leones
venari solitum rapidasque occidere tigres.
     Aspera pugnabat dextro Ligur Auria cornu
320   proelia, et ingentem Corinaei Tygrida puppim
ceperat, ac septem combusserat igne phaselos
audacis iuvenis Chelypi, quibus improbus omnem
Tyrrheni maris assidue vexaverat oram.
Mox magnum sternit Solymaeum, acremque Cloanthum
325   insequitur, claris qui tunc regnabat Athenis.
Excedens bello parva fugit ille veloce.
     Militiaeque duces Melitensis, clara propago
Martis, in adversos contendunt fortiter hostes,
et primi pugnas ineunt Turcasque lacessunt.
330   Non impune tamen miseri: namque agmine facto
insiluere feri violento pectore Thraces
ac late illorum tinxerunt sanguine pontum.
Iamque erat in tanto Melitae praetoria bello
capta, sed Hispanus propere tunc affuit heros,
335   auxiliumque tulit, saevoque ex hoste recepit.
     Pone sequebatur Romani principis auro
tota micans puppis et Christi signa gerebat,
in qua clarus erat dux ille Columnius aevi
prisci reliquiae et Romani roboris index.
340   Abstulit hic animam piratae ex pectore Brontis
iniectoque ussit tres illius igne carinas.
Luminaque eripuit forti iuveni Paralyppo,

his comrades appear. Sea-blue Tethys covers them all. Soon he
pursues Monsorres, sailing on his ship, the Delphinis, and im-
paled his head on a sharp spear, and he kills Myrmillus pierced   315
through the chest, and great Andraleo, who used to hunt wild li-
ons through the Getulan fields and kill swift tigers.

    Genoan Doria was fighting bitter battles on the right flank. He
had captured Corinaeus's immense ship, the *Tygris*, and set seven   320
light ships on fire that belonged to the bold, young Chelypus,
ships the wicked man had used relentlessly to harass the entire
coast of the Tyrrhenian Sea. Soon he lays low great Solymaeus
and pursues bitter Cloanthus, who then ruled in famous Athens.   325
Leaving from the battle, he flees in a tiny skiff.

    And the commanders of the Maltese forces, that famous prog-
eny of Mars, struggled bravely against the enemies they faced.
They were the first who entered battle to assail the Turks. They
did not do so unpunished — poor souls. For when the column was   330
formed, the savage Thracians attacked with violent intent and
dyed the sea with their blood far and wide. The command ship of
Malta had already been captured in the battle, but the Spanish
hero was then quickly on hand and brought help, retaking it from   335
the savage enemy.

    In the rear followed the ship of the Roman prince, all glittering
with gold, and carrying the ensign of Christ. On it was that fa-
mous leader, Colonna, all that is left of an older age, and a model
of Roman vigor. He tore the life from the heart of the pirate Bron-   340
tes, and burned three ships with the fire he tossed at them. He
tore the eyes out of the brave young Paralyppus, whose mother

quem genetrix olim Fauno commista crearat.
Et nati cum iam cuperet cognoscere fatum,
345 respondit genitor: 'Pulchro quem lumine laeta
arridere tibi cernis, si bella Latino
tum duce congressus committat in aequoris undis,
ipse quidem patriam vivus remeabit amatam.
Sed tamen hos ipsos oculos amittet acuto
350 percussus telo, iucunda et luce carebit.'
Ergo illum in silvis, interque parentis opacum
tempore servarat longo nemus anxia mater,
nec dabat in inde pedem proferre: sed improba tandem
sors vicit. Nam cum nitido se fonte lavaret
355 forte per aestatem, puerum piratica turba
vidit et abripuit. Crevit puer ac Solymano
sic gratus fuit ut late regnare per omnem
iusserit Arcadiam; cumque omnia fervere bello
cerneret, insignis pugnae succensus amore
360 ipse decem primus cum navibus affuit, ac se
addiderat Turcis comitem magnamque ciebat
nostrorum vasti tunc per maris aequora stragem.
Huic oculos telo ductor Romanus acuto
eruit inque fugam vertit. Mox eminus hasta
365 deiecit magnum transfosso gutture Sangam,
Dondomenumque ferum atque ingenti corpore Phydrum.
Atque ambos magni fugientes aequore natos
cepit Alys vivos, alta ad Capitolia curru
devinctos post terga manus ducturus ovanti.
370 Haerebat lateri gener huic, Carrafia proles
qui Lirim late princeps dominatur ad amnem,
clarus avis, et tela truces torquebat in hostes,
coniecta quamvis percussus crura sagitta
iam foret, et multus manaret vulnere sanguis.
375 Ipse quidem tanti generosum pectus amore

bore him after mingling once with Faunus. And when she desired to know the fate of her child, his father responded: "The boy 345 whom you now delight to see laughing at you with his beautiful eyes, if he goes to war on the watery waves and fights with the Latin leader, will return alive to his beloved fatherland. But he will lose those eyes of his when he is struck by a sharp spear, and will 350 lack his joyous sight." So his nervous mother had guarded him for a long time in the woods and in the dark forest of his father, and he was forbidden to set foot from there. But unlikely fate won out at last, for when he was washing himself in a bright spring in the 355 summer heat, by chance a pirate band spotted the boy and kidnapped him. The boy grew up, and was so favored by Suleiman that he was charged to rule over all of Arcadia. And when he saw all the kingdoms burning for war, the outstanding young man, stirred by the love of battle, was the first there with ten ships, and 360 he appointed himself as an ally to the Turks. He was calling for the slaughter of our men on the surface of the vast sea when the Roman commander tore out his eyes with his sharp spear and turned him to flight. Soon, from a distance, his spear struck down 365 great Sanga, impaled through his throat, and savage Dondomenus, and Phydrus with his immense body. And he took captive both the sons of great Ali Pasha alive as they fled on the sea, soon to lead them with their hands tied behind their backs to the high Capitoline on a triumphal chariot.

His son-in-law clung to his side, the descendant of Carrafa, a 370 prince who rules on the river Liris, of famous ancestry, and he hurled spears into the fierce enemies even though he had been struck in the thigh by an arrow and much blood flowed from the wound. He burned in his noble breast with love of such battle, 375

dum flagrat belli, deserta coniuge parvis
cum natis, Nerei sulcaverat humida regna
ancipitem Martem, et soceri vexilla secutus.
Illa sed expectans, et cunctos anxia casus
380 dum timet, heu misere morbo correpta mariti
prae desiderio primis intercidit annis,
ac multas lacrimas patrique viroque reliquit.
    Illustres alii proceres, fortissima corda,
magnanimi iuvenes, quos et Tiberinus et Arnus
385 Eridanusque pater fluviorum et magnus Iberus
et Tagus aurifera celeberrimus amnis arena
miserat in bellum pulchra pro laude ruebant.
Inter quos princeps Ursinae maxima gentis
gloria Paulus erat, clarisque micabant in armis.
390 Illius robur grandique in corpore nervos
obstupuere Getae, densos dum fortis in hostes
irruit, et cornu penetrat per tela sinistrum.
Mammettumque ducem nostrorum sanguine tela
tingentem et certo iaculantem spicula nervo
395 arreptum dextra interimit mergitque profundo,
Cassannumque Halymumque et vasto corpore Stassyn.
    Et te, Farnesi iuvenis, tum barbara classis
obstupuit pugnantem hasta; tua sensit Orontes
arma ferox, sensitque ferox tua saucius arma
400 Scyroccus versa quaerens sibi puppe salutem.
    Magnus et Urbini natus ducis ense corusco
fulminat et toto Scythicas agit aequore naves.
Non illum bello quisquam se attollere contra
audebat; solus Gurgut, qui regna tenebat
405 excelsae Smyrnae claro cum fonte Melete,
ausus conseruisse manum et decernere ferro
infelix mediis animam exhalavit in undis.

and leaving his wife behind with their young children, he had plowed the wet realms of Nereus in pursuit of uncertain war, and followed the flags of his father-in-law. But as she waited at home, nervously dwelling on all the possible outcomes, alas she was taken ill out of longing for her husband and died in her early years, leaving many tears for her father and husband.

Other noble chiefs, brave hearts, courageous young men, whom the Tiber and the Arno and the Po, father of rivers, and the great Ebro, and the Tago, the river most celebrated for its gold-bearing sands, had sent, died in the battle for the cause of noble glory. Among them, Paolo, the greatest glory of the Orsini family, shone foremost in his famous arms. The Geets were astounded by his valor and the strength in his mighty body as he ran bravely into the thick of the enemy and broke through the left flank with spears. He killed the commander, Mammettus, who was soaking his weapons in the blood of our men, and hurling pikes with great force, caught him in the right side, and sank him in the deep, along with Cassannus, Halymus, and Stassyn with his huge body.

And then the barbarian fleet was astounded by you, young Farnese hero, fighting with your spear. Brutal Orontes felt your arms, and so did savage Scirocco, wounded by your weapons as he sought safety for himself on his ship turned to flee.

The great son of the Duke of Urbino thundered with his flashing sword and drove back the Scythian ships over the whole sea. No one dared match himself against him in battle. Only Gurgut, who held the kingdoms of high Smyrna with the famous fountain of Meles, dared to fight hand to hand and battle it out with the sword. Unhappily, he breathed his last in the middle of the waves.

De nostris etiam pugnantum plurima turba
fuderunt dulces crudeli funere vitas.
410 Nam ferus Occyalus, Calabris quem montibus ortum
fama refert Christo lustrali in fonte dedisse
nomina, mox Arabis complexum dogmata vatis
falsidici, quem cum Libya simul omnis adorat
nunc Asia, Europaeque etiam pars maxima nostrae,
415 abiurasse Deum verum, rectaque parentum
deflexisse via. Qualis sub nocte silenti
egrediens silva lupus insidiatus ovili
dat magnam stragem pecoris, ruit aequore toto
fervidus, incenditque rates nostrosque trucidat.
420 Ille et Cardinei iuvenis, quo ditior alter
vix erat Hesperiis aut fortunatior oris,
cumque tot inter opes potuisset ducere vitam,
maluit Austriadae comes ire morique sub armis;
candida traiecit letali pectora telo.
425 Barbarigus multis occisis hostibus, igni
navibus incensis partim, partim aequore mersis,
fortia dum laevo pugnaret proelia cornu,
eminus impulsa confossus harundine guttur
occubuit; tanti latuit sed vulneris auctor,
430 nec sese illius iactavit funere quisquam.
Tum latus Armenio traiectus ab ense Soranzus,
Bisballusque atque Hispano qui carmine divos,
claraque praestantum celebrabat facta virorum
Mavorti simul et Musis Toraldus amicus
435 formosusque aevi primo sub flore Quirinus
occidit, Ioniumque infecit sanguine pontum.
Sacraque gens Melites, audacia pectora, Marte
durati longo iuvenes, quos barbarus hostis
saepe ad Byzanti portas et moenia vidit,

A great number of our men as well poured forth their sweet lives in the cruel carnage. For wild Uluj Ali, who was born, they say, in the Calabrian Mountains and was baptized in the purifying spring, but soon embraced the false doctrines of the Arab priests; who, the story goes, though once all of Libya and Asia and even the great part of our Europe honored him, foreswore the true God, and swerved from the righteous path of his parents; just as a wolf on a silent night, having sat in ambush in the woods by a sheepfold, leaps out and wreaks havoc on the flock, so he rushes raging over the whole sea, and burns ships, and cuts down our men. That young man, Cárdenas, richer than almost anyone on Spanish shores and so fortunate that he was able to lead his life among great wealth, preferred to ride with the company of John of Austria and to die in arms; his white chest was pierced by a deadly spear. While Barbarigo, having killed many enemies—some in the fire that burned their ships, some drowned in the sea—fought brave battles on the left flank, he was pierced through the neck by an arrow shot from afar, and fell. But the author of this great wound hid himself, and no one boasted of this man's death. Then Soranzo was struck in the side by an Armenian sword; and Bisbal; and Toraldo, who celebrated the famous deeds of outstanding heroes in Spanish song, friend at once to Mars and to the Muses. And handsome Quirini, in the first flowering of his age, died and stained the Ionian Sea with his blood. The Maltese contingent, bold hearts, young men hardened by long war, whom the barbarian host often saw at the gates and walls of Byzantium

410

415

420

425

430

435

440 ante oculos Selymi captas incendere naves
et passim populare suis cum civibus urbes,
vulnera per pulchra occubuerunt. Ite, beatae
o animae, quo regnator vocat aetheris; ite,
et capite insignes palmae immortalis honores.
445 Nec, quod marmoreis urnis tellure caretis
in patria, dolor hic angat; nam maximus aether
vos tegit et quantum rutila sol lampade lustrat.
Belli anceps fortuna diu stetit, aethere donec
despiciens divum genitor certamina tanta,
450 fatorum memor, et Veneri quae dixerat almae,
iussit ut in bellum descenderet acer Apollo
exitium clademque Getis et funera portans.
Namque ex Naupacti praecelsa rupe sagittas
in Scythicas puppes iaciebat acutaque tela.
455 Quo terrore feri sensim se abducere bello
coeperunt Turcae et nostris dare terga carinis,
etsi Bosphorio tum nil fuga profuit hosti.
Nam velut accipiter pavidas agit ille columbas
aera per vacuum, nec deserit impiger ante
460 quam cunctas rapiat victor; sic maximus heros
Austriades toto fugientes aequore turmas
insequitur, tantamque ciet per Dorida stragem,
ut iam se rubro mutaverit illa colore.
Bracchia truncatasque manus et crura pedesque
465 et capita aspiceres salsas fluitare per undas
perfusosque enses pharetrasque et tela cruore
intextasque auro chlamydes Phrygiasque tiaras.
Tanto de numero paucae evasere carinae
Occyalo duce, cladis iit qui nuntius ipsum
470 ad Selymum: capta est abductaque cetera classis.

burning captive ships before the eyes of Selim and everywhere   440
ravaging their cities along with their citizens — they all fell with
noble wounds. Go, blessed souls, to where the Lord calls you in
heaven. Go, and take the glorious honors of the immortal palm.
And do not let it be a cause for distress that you lack marble urns   445
in the earth of your homeland, for the great firmament of heaven
embraces you, indeed all that the sun bathes in luminous light.

For a long time, the outcome of the war remained doubtful,
until the father of the gods, looking down on such struggles from
the heavens, mindful of fate and what he had said to gentle Venus,   450
commanded that swift Apollo go down to the war bringing de-
struction, ruin, and slaughter to the Turks. And so from the high
cliffs of Naupactus, he launched arrows at the Scythian ships. At
this, the savage Turks began to break away from the battle in ter-   455
ror, and to retreat from our ships, even though flight was of no
advantage to the Bosphoran enemy. For just as the hawk drives
fearful doves through the empty air, and that swift conqueror does   460
not leave until he snatches them all; so the mighty hero John of
Austria pursues the fleeing battalions everywhere on the water and
instigates such slaughter through the Doridian sea that it changed
itself now to the color red. You could see arms, and severed hands,
and legs and feet and heads floating through the salty waves, and   465
swords, and quivers and spears, all covered with gore, and cloaks
woven with gold, and Phrygian crowns. From such a great num-
ber, a few ships escaped with the commander Uluj Ali, who goes
to bring news of the disaster to Selim himself. The rest of the fleet   470
is captured and led away.

Tunc lauro de more comas fortissimus heros
praecinctus tanta Austriades ex hoste trophaea
victor in Italiam retulit duxitque triumphum.
Ibant bis centum, nec habebant signa, triremes
475   captae ex hoste ducis post terga omnisque sonabat
pontus, 'io victor, Caroli dignissima proles,
Austriades bellator io,' passimque per urbes
Christiadum divis actae sunt omnibus aris
immensae grates et debita vota soluta.

Then the bravest hero, crowned with laurel in his hair according to custom, the conqueror John of Austria brings back to Italy great trophies from the enemy, and leads the triumph. Two hundred galleys passed by, no longer bearing their standards, taken from the enemy behind the back of their leader, and the whole sea   475
cried, "Io conqueror! Most worthy son of Charles, John of Austria; warrior, io!" and everywhere through the Christian cities, great offerings of thanksgiving are prepared on all the divine altars, and promised vows are performed.

De victoria Christianae Classis Carmen

Guglielmo Moizio

Surge age, Calliope, magni Iovis inclyta proles,
dulce decus rerum, quae mulcens aethera cantu
dona deum celebras et fortia facta virorum.
Tende chelym vocesque sono coniunge canoras,
5   magna fero; magna nobis nunc voce sonandum.
Nunc hymnis opus et cantu, nunc dicere grates
fas est caelitibus quorum clementia gentis
vota piae gemitusque polo respexit ab alto,
quorum ope Christicolae nuper concordibus armis,
10   pontificisque Pii divino foedere iuncti,
exarsere animis, inque aspera bella ruentes,
Ismarii classem numero superante Tyranni
disiecere mari toto Neptuniaque arva
caede nova late hostili infecere cruore.
15   Aeternum supplex mecum venerata parentem,
suspice, Musa, polum et caelestes incipe cantus.
Dicendus Pater in primis, qui condidit orbem
ex nihilo, sapiens, sine fine, bonusque potensque;
Filius et Patri consors, qui lapsus ab alto
20   aethere, mortales pretioso sanguine culpas
lavit et in ligno crudeli morte pependit
noster amor, nostri generis reparator Iesus.
Spiritui sua laus almo tribuenda, piorum
afflatu dulci qui corda illustrat et unit.
25   Virgo etiam dicenda parens, tutela reorum,
quae supplex hominum lapsus miserata, verendi
iudicis a nobis poenas avertit et iras;

⁂ XXI ⁂

Song on the victory of the Christian fleet

Guglielmo Moizio

Arise now, Calliope, glorious daughter of great Jove, sweet splendor, you who soften the air with song, extolling the gifts of the gods and the deeds of brave men. Tune your lyre and raise your sweet voice in song: I bear great tidings that are ours to spread abroad. Now is the time for hymns and music; now is the moment to give thanks to the heavenly gods whose compassion regarded the prayers and laments of our pious people from on high, and with whose help the Christians joined forces in the Holy League of Pope Pius and rushed ardently into harsh battle. Though vastly outnumbered, they scattered the fleet of the Ismarian Tyrant over the whole sea, and the fields of Neptune were dyed with fresh blood far and wide in the vicious slaughter.

Muse, look up to the heavens: as a suppliant with me entreat the Eternal Father, and begin the celestial song. Sing first of the Father who created the world from nothing, how he is wise, limitless, good, and powerful. Then of the Son, equal to the Father, who descended from high heaven to wash away our mortal sins with his precious blood, and hung from the cross in cruel death, Jesus, our love, the restorer of our people. Sing praise to the life-giving Spirit, who with his sweet breath illumines and unites the hearts of all believers. Sing also of the Virgin Mother, protector of the condemned, who pitied the fall of man, and implored the Venerable Judge to divert his penalty and wrath from us; and also of

    et Petrus ille Simon, audita voce Magistri,
    retia qui celerans pelagusque ratemque reliquit,
30   commissas qui pavit oves abeunte Magistro,
    arbiter et caeli claves qui gessit et Orci.
        Dii superi laus omnis, honos, et gloria vobis,
    et cantus festique dies debentur; agendae
    sunt vobis grates adolendaque tura per aras.
35   Gens pia, gens verax, sancto perfusa lavacro,
    pressa malis foedisque diu iactata procellis,
    numine iam tandem vestro, et caelestibus auris
    laeta reviviscit, recolens decora alta parentum,
    virtutem antiquam et priscas reminiscitur artes.
40   Irritata minis Getici et feritate Tyranni,
    qui ferro fines late populatur et igni,
    humano sedare sitim qui sanguine gestit.
    Ultro hostem petit et iustas ulciscitur iras.
        Rex hominum pastorque Pius Christique sacerdos,
45   puppe sedens clavumque tenens; in foedera reges
    advocat et gravibus iubet occursare periclis.
    Accedit socius laudataque foedera sancit,
    invicti proles Caroli generosa, Philippus,
    cui parent nostrum latissima regna per orbem,
50   alter et Oceani spatiis immanibus orbis
    seclusus, pendunt cui vectigalia linguis
    antipodes variis, alio Phaethonte calentes.
    Hinc Veneti iurant in foedera, quos dolor ingens
    exacuit, iustasque recens accendit in iras
55   foedifragi furor atque iniuria saeva Tyranni
    excisam ob Cyprum flamma ferroque nefando.
        Nec mora, rostratae passim navalibus altis
    deductae naves pronum labuntur in aequor.
    Litoribus nautae cunctis glomerantur et acres

Simon Peter who quickly left his nets, the sea, and his boat when
he heard the voice of the Master. Once the Master was gone, he   30
shepherded the faithful flock, and now carries the keys, deciding
who enters heaven and who enters hell.

   All praise, honor, and glory to you, gods on high. We owe you
songs and festival days, and offer you thanks and incense burned
on the altars. Your pious, truthful people, washed clean in holy   35
baptism, was for a long time oppressed by evil and tossed in the
tempests of sin, but now at last we come to life anew by your di-
vine will and the breath of heaven, remembering the great glory
of our forefathers, their ancient virtue and age-old skill. Once
hounded by the threats of the Geets and their savage Tyrant who   40
lays waste to our borders with sword and fire and quenches his
thirst with human blood, now your people seek out the enemy on
their own to avenge their just wrath.

   The king of men and priest of Christ, Pope Pius, sits on the
deck of his ship, holding the papal keys. He calls the other kings 45
into an alliance and orders them to set out to face grave dangers.
Philip, the pope's great ally, readily agrees, and he ratifies the
treaty and gives it his blessing—Philip, the noble offspring of in-
vincible Charles, who rules the widest kingdoms in our world, and
in the Other World separated by the immense reach of the Ocean;   50
to him the Antipodes, warmed by a different Phaethon, pay trib-
ute in their varied languages. The Venetians also take an oath to
uphold the treaty. Great sorrow goads them on: their recent out-
rage over the harsh offenses of the pact-breaking Tyrant kindles   55
them to a justified wrath, ever since Cyprus was toppled by flame
and wicked steel.

   At once, the beaked ships are led out from lofty shipyards and
slip into the calm water. Sailors from every shore gather together

60 exercent curas operique incumbere certant,
  milleque sternuntur magnis freta lata carinis.
   Conveniunt proceres, et capta cupidine Martis,
  auspicibus confisa deis generosa iuventus.
  Illinc Hispani ripis undantis Iberi,
65 atque Tago missi, quos primo flore iuventae
  Austrius aspersus prima lanugine malas
  ducit Ioannes Carolo satus atque Philippo
  fratre potens, belli cui credita summa potestas,
  Maurorum clarus spoliis et Marte secundo.
70 Ad laevam comes incedit praefectus Iberae
  vir magnus classi, rubra cruce pectus honestum
  ostentans, sacrique gerens decus ordinis ingens.
   Litora cum primum tetigere Ligustica magno
  ductori occurrunt, veluti duo sidera, quales
75 Tyndaridae caelo fulgent: hinc Feltrius heros,
  hinc et Alexander Farnesius, inclyta regum
  magnorum soboles, quem laetus avunculus ulnis
  excipit amplexuque premens atque oscula libans.
  Occurrunt Ligures laeti, quos Auria ducit
80 Andreas, illo non arva peritior alter
  Neptuni ratibus findit victricibus. Ille
  praedonum terror, vindex acerrimus alti
  aequoris, haudquaquam laudes oblitus avorum.
   Iordanus properat Tusco de litore Paulus,
85 ostentans latos humeros, pulcherrimus ore,
  atque duci magno gener additus et decus ingens
  Ursinae gentis. Campano litore surgens
  Parthenope regum atque ducum domus inclyta portis
  omnibus effundit fulgentes aere catervas.
90 Ter denae implentur generosae milite puppes,
  in quibus et Calabri furibundi Martis alumni.

and apply their honed skills; they compete as they lay into their 60
work. The wide channel is covered by a thousand great boats.

The leaders assemble together, along with the young men of
noble birth, spurred on by a desire for war and their trust in God's
blessings. On one side, John of Austria in the first bloom of youth,
his cheeks brushed with soft down, leads the Spaniards sent from
the banks of the flowing Ebro and from the River Tagus. He is the 65
mighty son of Charles, and, together with his brother Philip, was
entrusted with the high command of the war. Backed by Mars, he
is famous for ransacking the Moors. To his left is a great man, the 70
Prefect of the Spanish fleet, his companion, displaying a scarlet
cross on his sturdy chest, the venerable sign of his holy order.

When they first reached the Ligurian shores two men rush to
meet the great commander, shining like two stars, as the Tyndari- 75
dae shine in the heavens: on one side the Feltrian hero, Duke of
Urbino, on the other Alexander Farnese, famous offspring of great
kings. His happy uncle snatched him up in his arms, grasping him
in an embrace and covering him with kisses. The Ligurians arrive
joyfully, led by Andrea Doria; no one is more skilled than he in 80
plowing Neptune's fields with conquering boats. He is the terror
of pirates, the most feared defender on the high seas, never ne-
glecting his famous legacy.

Paolo Giordano hastens from the Tuscan shore, with his broad 85
shoulders and handsome face, the son-in-law of the great duke and
the great glory of the Orsini family. Naples, rising from the shores
of Campania, the famous home of kings and leaders, poured forth
from all its gates companies of men flashing with bronze. Thirty 90
noble ships are filled with soldiers, among them, the men of Cala-
bria, offspring of raging Mars.

Litoribus Siculis iam pridem stabat in armis
Marcus avis atavisque potens Antonius, ingens
Aeneadum decus et gentis spes fida Columnae.
95   Romanae ductor classis gentisque Latinae,
consilio praestans, invictus robore dextrae
casibus adversis prima veniente iuventa,
qui didicit belli duros perferre labores,
fortunaeque truces non exhorrescere vultus;
100   ut catulus fulvi Massyla per arva leonis
dura pati discit vento pulsatus et imbri.
Pontifici rebus solida virtute gerendis
spectatus pridem, qui saeva in bella Quirites
duceret, et classi magna dicione praeesset.
105   Dux pius Allobrogum causae communis amator,
quattuor instructas Alpino milite naves
miserat extremis in Turcica bella paratas
finibus Italiae veterisque ex arce Monoeci.
Haud procul unde caput viridanti fronde revinctum
110   attollit pater Eridanus, qui suspicit Alpes
vertice tendentes convexa sub astra nivali.
Implentur Siculis numero bis quinque carinae,
quos Messana genus Martis, quos clara Panormus
misit, et excelso gens circumiecta Pachyno.
115   Privatis opibus multi duxere triremes,
quos pietas splendorque domus, quos inclyta virtus
impulit in partem tanti properare pericli.
Magnanimi salvete viri, res publica vobis,
et decus Italiae, pietas super omnia caelo
120   debita cara fuit. Semper laus vestra manebit,
semper honos animo fixus mentique piorum.
Nostra salus manibus vestris adiuta deorum
munere certa manet. Magni venere magistri

On the shores of Sicily, Marco Antonio Colonna stood ready in arms, with all the power of his grandfather and great-grandfather, great glory of the line of Aeneas and trusted hope of the Colonna family; he led the Roman fleet and the people of Latium. Out- 95 standing in counsel and unmatched in the strength of his fighting hand, he encountered adversity early in his youth and learned to suffer the harsh labors of war, never shuddering at fortune's savage face. Just so the cub of the tawny lion in the harsh Massylan fields 100 learns to suffer hardships as he is pelted by the wind and rain. He was much admired for carrying out pontifical orders with integ- rity; he led the Romans into fierce battle and governed his fleet with great authority.

The pious leader of the Allobroges, supporter of the common 105 cause, had sent four ships furnished with Alpine troops ready for war against the Turks from the far edges of Italy and from the citadel of ancient Monaco. Not far from here, Father Eridanus 110 raises his head, bound with green leaves, and admires the Alps stretching out under the stars that arch over their snowy peaks.

Ten ships are filled with Sicilians, Mars's own people, some sent from Messina, some from famous Palermo, and some from the people living around lofty Pachynus.

Many led ships at their own expense; it was their piety, the 115 honor of their house, and glorious virtue that drove them to share in such peril. Hail, courageous men: the republic, the honor of Italy, and above all, the piety owed to heaven was precious to you. 120 Praise will be yours always, your honor is forever rooted in the hearts and minds of the pious. Our safety is sustained by your hands; it remains assured by the gift of the gods. Great leaders

post hos instructae Melitensi milite naves
125   exiguae numero, sed robore pluribus aequae.
       Adriacas findens undas atque aequoris oram
Illyrici relegens, et ventis acta secundis,
procedit Venetum classis pulcherrima, longo
ordine, dives opum, qua non instructior umquam
130   altera sulcavit proris stridentibus aequor.
Ductores lecti celsis in puppibus astant,
navi quisque sua, ferroque auroque nitentes
ostentant vires et saevi Martis amorem.
Indutus trabeam signis auroque rigentem,
135   regifico cultu proceres supereminet omnes
et saevis effert sese Venerius in armis,
imperiis pridem, magnis et honoribus usus,
canitie longa venerabilis, ore rubenti
vividus atque ferox, non illi longa senectus
140   vim dextrae aut animi valuit mutare vigorem:
consilio linguaque potens rerumque peritus,
cui patriae decus et belli commissa potestas.
Ille crucem fixumque Deum summissus adorat
pontificis, gentisque piae venerabile signum,
145   ductorem summum, sociosque exinde salutat.
Laetitia exoritur, summum ferit aethera clamor.
Laetificis longum resonant freta caerula bombis.
      Tum vero admirans numerum, stupet Austrius heros
turritas puppes, nec non latera ardua cernens
150   tormentis (visu horrendum) muralibus apta,
qualia Vulcanus procudit fulmina magni
cum dextram Iovis armat in horrida bella Gigantum.
Dant sonitum, scissa ceu nube tonitrua vasto

came after these, ships furnished with Maltese troops, scant in
number but a match for many more in strength.   125

The illustrious fleet of the Venetians cleaves the Adriatic waves,
picking its way along the shore of the Illyrian Sea. Driven by fa-
voring winds, it advances in a long line, laden with wealth. A fleet
so well equipped never plowed the water with crashing prows. The   130
chosen commanders stand on the lofty decks, each on his own
ship, shining with iron and gold that spoke of their strength and
love of savage Mars. Wearing a robe stiff with insignia and gold,
Venier shines over all the rest in his ferocious arms with splendor   135
fit for a king. He is long used to leadership and great honors, ven-
erable with his long white hair, his ruddy face flushed and fear-
some. Long old age has not yet succeeded in diminishing the
might of his right hand or the vigor of his mind. He was entrusted   140
with his country's honor and authority in battle, given his power
of strategy and speech, and his experience in action. Humbly he
worships the pope's cross and the crucified Lord, the venerable
standard of the pious people; then he greets his allies and the su-   145
preme commander. The crowd explodes with joyful shouts, and
the sound strikes the highest heaven. Far and wide the sea-blue
shoals echo with the sounds of rejoicing.

Then the hero John of Austria surveys the great host in admira-
tion, awestruck by the turreted galleys, amazed to see the steep
sides of the cannons (horrible sight) fitted in the hulls. Vulcan   150
struck similar thunderbolts when he armed the right hand of great
Jove in the horrible war against the Giants. They make a great
commotion; they terrify the ears of fearful mortals with a deep

murmure terrificant trepidis mortalibus aures.
155 Corda pavore tremunt; latebras genus omne ferarum
quaeritat aufugiens; immani turbine turres
disiectae ad terram ingentem traxere ruinam.
Oppida tot pelago credas innare, tot arces
totque imposta iugis vento castella moveri.
160 Has moles cernens, haec propugnacula, miles
concipit ingentes animos atque appetit hostem.
    Imperat actutum dux ordine castra moveri
Austrius ac pugnam iubet expectare paratos.
Curva legunt alacres Corcyrae litora; mox et
165 Actia Romanis gratissima litora priscis.
Accelerant, portusque petunt et tecta Zacynthi.
    Barbarus interea ductor, cui Turcica paret
classis, et innumerae gentes terraque marique
Illyricos fines ferro populatus et igni,
170 terrorem ancipitem Latiis incusserat arvis,
Hesperios temnens reges populosque Latinos
conversos in sese odio ac discordibus armis
perniciemque sibi per mutua damna ferentes;
ast ubi iam rebus praedo in contraria versis
175 foedere concordes animisque in bella paratis
adventare videt. Trepidus loca tuta requirit
moenibus Aetolis clausus portuque sinuque
fluctuat ancipiti distractus corda timore,
an fugiat metuensque famem stragemque suorum,
180 an pugnet stolidi metuens fera iussa Tyranni,
qui, procul a talis, stupris vetitoque Lyaeo
languidus, eructat tristes male sobrius iras
atque suis ducibus laqueosque sudesque minatur
ni captos referant hostes mergantve profundo.
185 Denique stat conferre manum mediosque per hostes

rumble, like thunder from a ruptured cloud. Hearts tremble with   155
fear; wild animals of every kind take flight and search out hiding
places; towers, thrown to the ground by the vast onslaught, drag
with them immense destruction. You would have thought that
many towns floated on the sea; citadels and castles fitted with row-
ing benches move in the wind. Seeing these masses, these war en-   160
gines, the soldiers entertained high hopes and longed to set forth
in pursuit of the enemy.

At once the Austrian commander orders the navy to move into
formation, and he commands the readied men to expect a fight.
Swiftly they skim the curved shores of Corcyra; soon the shores of   165
Actium appear, most beloved by the ancient Romans. They speed
ahead and seek the harbor and shelter of Zacynthus.

On the other side was the barbarian admiral, the man in charge
of the Turkish fleet and countless peoples on land and sea. Having
destroyed the Illyrian kingdom with sword and fire, he had shot
terror and doubt throughout the fields of Latium. He despised the   170
kings of the West, and the Latin people who had turned against
each other, inflicting great damage on themselves through mu-
tual losses in civil wars. But now this pirate sees that things are
changed: they have joined in a treaty and now approach with arms   175
ready for war; in fear, he takes shelter, protected by the Aetolian
walls. He hesitates in the curve of the harbor, distracted by the
wavering fear in his heart: should he flee, fearing deprivation and
the slaughter of his people, or should he fight, fearing the fierce   180
orders of the stolid Tyrant. Far removed from these concerns, half-
drunk and weak with fornication and forbidden wine, he spews
out his feeble rage and threatens his own leaders with the noose
and the rack unless they bring back their enemies captive or sub-
merge them in the sea. At last Ali Pasha decides to attack, to open   185

237

aut aperire viam ferro, aut occumbere morti.
Ter centum educit naves: pugnamque capessit.
   Octobres nonas Titan referebat in orbem
atque diem Domino festum praeclarus agebat,
190   cum vigil atque oculos intendens Austrius heros
adventare videt spumosa per aequora Turcas,
infaustas lunas aquilis victricibus ultro
atque salutiferis crucibus conferre paratos.
Stans celsa in puppi fulvo spectabilis auro
195   et ferro longe flammas vomitante coruscas,
flore nitens primo, pulcherrimus ore verendo,
qualis erat Phrygii quondam vastator Achilles
agminis; aut Geticis Mavors bellator in arvis:
qualis item Carolus genitor primoribus annis
200   imperii nuper sumptis insignibus; ostro
indutus, gemmis, auroque nitente corona,
saeva vel in Turcas intenderet arma vel Afros,
vota Deo supplex fundit dextramque reflectens,
et frontem et pectus signat cruce, nomine Patrem,
205   teque vocans Fili compar, te Spiritus alme;
esse, crucem tollens, ductorem classis Iesum,
quo duce fidentem fallat victoria numquam;
praedicat, atque loco se militis esse fatetur.
Hortatur proceres partes conversus in omnes,
210   nomine quemque vocans stimulatque in proelia pubem.
Pugnandumque docet pro religione focisque
pro laude in ferrum et pro libertate ruendum,
Hesperiae nunc gentis agi decus atque salutem.
Clamorem tollunt socii Christo auspice freti
215   ductorisque sui fausto verba omine firmant.
Collocat his dictis per cornua bina triremes,
perque aciem mediam. A tergo iubet esse paratas
subsidio certas. Mandat quod cuique gerendum.

a path through the middle of the enemy with his sword or die trying. He leads forward three hundred ships and he starts the fight.

Radiant Titan was bearing the Nones of October into the sky, ushering in the feast day of the Lord, when John of Austria, ever vigilant, spots the Turks approaching across the frothing waves. Their fleet bears ill-omened moons raised to meet the conquering eagles and healing crosses. He stands on the lofty deck, spectacular in tawny gold and holding a sword that sends flashing flames far and wide. Radiant in the first bloom of youth, his handsome face inspires devotion; he looks just like Achilles when he destroyed the Phrygian troops, or Mars when he fought on the Getican fields; he looks just like his father Charles in earlier years, when he took up the emblems of empire; when, dressed in purple, gems, and a crown of flashing gold, he menaced the Turks or Africans with savage arms. He pours forth entreaties to God and, raising his right arm, makes the sign of the cross on his forehead and chest, calling on the name of the Father, and you, his equal Son, and you, nurturing Spirit. Displaying the cross, he proclaims Jesus to be the leader of the fleet; with such a leader, victory could never elude the faithful. He prays, and acknowledges that he is here in the role of a soldier. Facing them all, he encourages the leaders, calling each by name, and motivates the young men for battle. He explains that they must fight for their faith and their homes, that they must rush into battle for glory and freedom, that the honor and welfare of the Hesperian race is at stake. The allies, trusting in Christ's guidance, raise a shout and affirm his words with predictions of success. When he is finished speaking, he orders the galleys to advance between the two horns in the middle of the battle line. He orders the ships in the rearguard to be ready

190

195

200

205

210

215

His actis addit capiti dux saevus et acer
220 horribilem galeam, et ferratam corripit hastam.
Undique signa canunt. Naves urgentur in altum.
Adsunt horrifico Turcae clamore minaces.
  Hesperii tendunt contra ventisque secundis,
auspicibusque deis. Propulsant ictibus hostem.
225 Ardescunt animis, inimico sanguine fluctus
inficiunt. Tormenta ignis displosa, sonore
terrifico aeratas diffringunt turbine puppes.
Tum fragor auditur; sonitu maria alta tremiscunt.
Conditur extemplo picea caligine caelum
230 et geminans longis resonat mugitibus aether.
Horribiles sonitus circum dirosque fragores
contremuit Calydon, Naupactus, et alta Corinthus,
et terris fugere ferae et pecus omne sub undis.
Exacuens iras medio Mars agmine saevit.
235 Multa cadunt passim bellantum corpora. Primi
excipiunt hostem Veneti (nam cura sinistri
obtigit his cornu) pugnant fortissima bello
pectora, nec dubitant animas profundere pulchris
vulneribus, redimant ut honesta morte salutem
240 dilectae patriae, cui barbarus imminet hostis.
Plurimus his labor et pondus grave Martis iniqui
incubuit; primos aditus tamen ilicet armis
illustres rupere viri stragemque dedere.
Morte horum egregia, multo velut empta cruore,
245 ostentare caput placidum Victoria coepit.
  Quem pigeat non ingratum meminisse virorum,
qui ducente Deo, votis precibusque piorum,
litoribus nostris saevo impendente Tyranno,
sanguine communem fuso adiuvere salutem?

with reinforcements, detailing what each must do. When all this
was done, the savage and fierce leader puts on his terrifying helmet   220
and takes up his iron sword. Both sides give the signal to attack.
Ships race forward on the deep. The Turks approach, threatening
with their terrifying cries.

The Hesperians line up opposite, with the winds and the gods
behind them. They drive off the enemy with their assault. Blazing
with courage, they dye the waves with enemy blood. The cannons   225
fire their blasts, tearing apart the bronze-clad ships with a terrible
assault. Then a roar is heard; the deep sea reverberates with the
sound. At once the sky is buried in pitch darkness and the echoing
heavens resound with long howls. Calydon, Naupactus, and high   230
Corinth tremble at the horrendous din and dreadful crashes all
around; wild animals flee inland and all the fish hide under the
waves. Mars rages in the middle of the troops, provoking their
fury. The bodies of many warriors fall on both sides. The Vene-   235
tians are the first to overtake the enemy (for it fell to them to
guard the left flank). Hearts bravest in war fight, never hesitating
to pour forth their lives from beautiful wounds, as they pay with
honest deaths for the safety of their beloved fatherland, now un-   240
der threat from the barbarian enemy. Great effort and the heavy
weight of unjust Mars looms over them; nevertheless these fa-
mous men made the first inroads straightaway with their weapons
and slaughtered many. Through their illustrious deaths, Victory,   245
though bought with much blood, began to show her placid head.

Who but the most thankless could fail to recall those selfless
men, who, with God as their guide and backed by the vows and
prayers of the faithful, chose to defend the safety of all with their
own spilled blood, as the harsh Tyrant closed in on our shores?

250   Dum Veneti Turcis laeva de parte resistunt,
nube sagittarum et plumbi per inane volantis
grandine, telorum necnon stridente procella,
obruitur, quisquis fortissimus audet in hostem
longius a sociis pervadere. Maximus armis
255   tum Barbadicus stimulis agitatus amaris,
impatiensque morae, prae cunctis poscit honorem
hunc sibi consertae pugnae primique laboris,
magnus, et a primo ductor ductore secundus,
provisor classis patrio sermone vocatus,
260   maximus in castris veluti sub rege tribunus.
Tum quinquaginta rostris ingentibus aptae
huic parent naves sancto mandante senatu.
Praemia remigibus spondet. Iubet ordine certo
navarchos sociosque sequi. Facto agmine proram
265   dirigit in Turcas violentus. Turbine magno
Campsani perculsa ratis demergitur undis.
Bis centum Rhodii, coeptae magno omine pugnae,
fluctibus absorpti fundo voluntatur in imo.
Ductores Veneti cunctis e partibus adsunt.
270   Conseritur proris proras urgentibus, atrox
pugna, ruunt fortes in mutua vulnera. Solem
densius obscurant volitantia tela per auras,
perculit heu pennis allapsa sagitta tribunum,
per caput acta senis. Letali vulnere victus
275   corruit in tergum. Lapsum traxere ministri.
Ille manus inter medicas, dum vellere ferrum
infixum, et fluidos trepidant siccare cruores,
defectum caput attollit clamore suorum
excitus leto, quibus et victoria cessit,
280   et prior ac maior tantarum gloria rerum.
(Nam calor huic aliquot mansit vitalis in horas)

While the Venetians assail the Turks on the left flank, anyone who   250
is brave enough to try to infiltrate the enemy detached from his
allies is covered with a cloud of arrows, a hailstorm of lead flying
through the void, or a shrieking storm of projectiles. Then great
Barbarigo, driven by bitter goads and impatient with the delay,   255
demands this honor for himself before all: that he be the first to
engage in the battle. He is the second in charge after the chief
commander, given the title "Provider of the Fleet" in his native
language, the highest commander in the field, just as he is in   260
court. By the order of the holy Senate, fifty ships fitted with vast
prows were under his command. He promises rewards for his
oarsmen; he orders his captains and their men to follow in a cer-
tain order. When the battle line is formed, he steers the prow ag-   265
gressively against the Turks. In the great frenzy, the ship of Camp-
sanus is struck and sunk in the waves. Two hundred Rhodians are
engulfed by the waves and overturned in the depths of the sea: a
great omen for the fight now begun. Leaders from all parts of the
Venetian Republic are present. As prow intertwined with pressing   270
prow, hideous battle is begun; brave men are soon wounded on
both sides. Cannon shells flying densely through the air obscure
the sun; an arrow flying on its wings hits the commander, driving
through the old man's head. Conquered by the lethal wound, he
falls back, and his attendants picked him up as he fell. Surrounded   275
by healing hands that try to pluck out the iron lodged in him and
dry the flowing blood, he raises his weary head, summoned back
from death by the clamor of his people as victory falls to them,
and, with it, the greater glory of their past. He praised God (for   280
the life force remained in him for a few hours) and drank in happy

laudavitque deos, oculisque natantibus hausit
laetitiam. Mors visa seni iucunda, triumpho
victricem patriam tanto qui linqueret auctam.
285   Insons mox anima, et nullius conscia culpae,
non secus atque rei properaret nuntia tantae,
voce Deum divosque vocans super astra volavit.
    Vertitur ingenti pinu per caerula vectus
Andreas animum turbatus morte propinqui.
290   Hunc cupit ulcisci Turcis immistus. Acerbis
indulgentem odiis et proeliae saeva gerentem,
opprimit illabens a vertice ferreus imber;
concidit et Landus medios invectus in hostes,
aspera bella movens, magnis audacius usus
295   viribus. Observant Mahumetes, Thracius hastam
coniicit et ferro pectus transfigit acuto.
Ille cadit. Sonitum dant ferrea suta cadentis.
Viribus Euboicos magnis Caterinus adortus,
audet in hostilem sese demittere navem:
300   mox urente cadit traiectus pectora plumbo.
Concitat in medios navem Superantius hostes;
multaque dat leto Turcarum corpora, multos
praecipites agit in fluctus, haud morte suorum
territus, ast longe violentior excitus ira.
305   Dum furit et stragem toto ciet aequore, fractus
turbine tormenti vitam exhalavit in undis.
Tum duo ductores invicti robore, siqua
inclyta tormentis virtus muralibus obstet,
hortati socios Hieronymus atque Marinus,
310   lux Contarenae clarissima gentis uterque;
navibus impulsis numeroso remige, Turcas
invadunt totoque ferunt fera proelia ponto.
Disiecti cecidere pilis, quas turbine vasto

sights through his swimming eyes. Death seemed pleasant to the
old man, for he left his victorious fatherland richer for such a great
triumph. Soon his guiltless soul, aware of no sin, will hasten, like   285
a messenger of great news, to fly off above the stars, calling on
God and the saints.

Borne through the sea on a massive boat, Andrea Doria turns
back, his soul troubled by the death of one so dear. He longs to
engage the Turks and avenge his friend. As he gives free rein to his   290
bitter hatred, inflicting savage wounds, a shower of iron falls from
overhead and strikes him down. Lando also falls as he is carried
into the middle of the enemy, stirring up sharp contests and mak-
ing a bold show of his great strength. The Muhammadans watch   295
him; a Thracian throws a spear and pierces his chest with sharp
iron. He falls, and as he falls, his iron coat of mail clatters. Cata-
rino, striking with great Euboean strength, dares to throw himself
onto an enemy ship; soon he falls, struck in his chest by a burning   300
bullet. Soranzo drives his ship in the middle of the enemy and
delivers countless bodies of Turks to death; he hurls many head-
long into the waves, undaunted by the death of his people, but
stirred to a still greater violence by his wrath. While he rages   305
slaughtering over the whole sea, he is knocked down by a storm of
cannon fire and breathes his last in the waves. Then two leaders
unconquered in strength — if any renowned virtue could stand up
to a wall of cannons — Gerolamo and Marino, together the leading   310
lights of the Contarini family, encourage their comrades: with
boats propelled by numerous oars, they infiltrate the Turks and
expand the fierce battle over the whole sea. They fall, blown apart

machina longa vomit referens ex aere canales,
315   sulfure contrito, rapidisque incensa favillis.
Cum Lauretano bonus et Pascalius armis
inclytus et clara cumulatus laude Quirinus,
navi quisque sua remis ferientibus aequor,
Turcarum invadunt magna virtute triremes.
320   Turbatos agitant ac multa caede repellunt:
et cogunt longe decedere terque quaterque.
Fidentes numero et saevis ululatibus hostes
eminus hos, magnamque manum per transtra virorum
et plumbo et baccis et contrivere sagittis.
325   Illustres genere et praestanti corpore fratres
quattuor ante aciem, soboles Cornelia, primam
pugnavere pares animis et robore; dispar
vix fuit his aetas paucis distinctior annis.
Omnibus unus amor fuit et concordia felix.
330   Quattuor in bellum germani viribus ibant
coniunctis animosa phalanx stragemque ciebant,
effera vis Martis raperet quocumque furentes.
Quattuor una dies uno certamine fratres
abstulit et matri solatia bina reliquit:
335   egregiam mortem atque aeternae praemia vitae.
Unum se patriae dixit genuisse Lacaena
accipiens mater pugnantis funera nati;
quattuor haec patriae natos largita, daturam
se plures dixit, si pignora plura tulisset.
340   Praeterea plures duro in certamine passim,
dicere quos fuerit longum et miserabile cunctos.
Egregii cecidere viri proceresque ducesque
horribiles inter strepitus dirumque fragorem
et resonante mari et saevo turbante tumultu,
345   conati patriae instantem depellere pestem,
pectoribus versis et honesta morte cadentes.

by the missiles that the long cannons spew forth from their brass
barrels in a heavy onslaught, as pounded gunpowder is ignited by   315
swift sparks. Then good Loredan and Pasqualigo, famous at arms,
and Quirini, heaped with renown—each in his ship with oars
striking the water—attack the Turkish galleys with great bravery.
They drive them into disarray and send them off with much   320
slaughter; three and four times they force them to fall far back.
The enemies, trusting in their numbers and their savage howling,
destroyed these men and their large squadron of troops on the
thwarts, with lead shells, bullets, and arrows.

   Four brothers famous for their lineage and outstanding beauty,   325
descendants of the Cornelii, fought right at the frontline; equal in
mind and strength, their difference in age was hardly more than a
few years. There was one love between them all, a blessed har-
mony. The four brothers went to war joined in strength, and their 330
courageous phalanx wreaked havoc, as the wild power of Mars
sent them raging every which way. One day took away four broth-
ers in one contest and left a twofold solace for their mother: a
worthy death and the rewards of eternal life. A Spartan mother,   335
receiving the news of her warrior son's death, said she had begot-
ten him for the fatherland alone; this one said that though she
offered four sons to the fatherland, she would have given more if
she had borne more children.

   It would be a long and miserable tale to give a full account of   340
the many others who perished on both sides in that cruel contest.
Outstanding men, leaders, and commanders died as they tried to
expel the plague that threatened the fatherland, amid the horrible 345
crashing and terrible din as the sea resounded and churned in the
fierce turmoil. They fell with their chests turned toward an honest

Vicit amor patriae, ne quem fudisse pigeret
pro templis animam et pro libertate parentum.
Illustres fortesque animae, vos nulla silebit
350   posteritas; longum fama vivetis in aevum.
In patria medioque foro templisque deorum
nomina marmoribus per saecula vestra legentur.
     Non tamen idcirco proceres, quicumque supersunt;
non reliqui cives conspecta morte suorum
355   demittunt animos, quin et stimulantur in iras:
esse nec illustres socios patiuntur inultos.
Viribus attritis saevo cadit impetus hosti.
Audentes Veneti renovata in proelia tendunt.
Nam volat excelsa Venerius puppe per agmen
360   sublimi patrium, bello dux opimus idem,
pugnatorque manu fortissimus. Omnis in illo
spes haesit patriae tanto discrimine rerum.
Providus intentis oculis rem prospicit omnem;
hortatur socios, animum bellantibus addit.
365   Commemorat paucis veterum decora alta parentum:
ingentes classes per caerula cuncta vagatas,
edomitos longe populos Orientis ad oras,
auditum Bactris Venetorum nomen et Indis,
saepius et fuso partos ex hoste triumphos,
370   imperium pelagi per saecula longa retentum;
urbem marmoream regum sedem atque deorum,
Italiae decus eximium, portum atque salutem
gentibus expositam, sacramque extorribus aram,
perfugium miseris, morum vitaeque magistram,
375   lucem hominum summam, terrarum insigne theatrum.
Civibus hanc patriam vel certa morte tuendam.
     Incusat resides, verbis exsuscitat iras.
Ille laborantes reficit. Citus ille labantem
subsidiis aciem firmat. Iubet ire triremes

death. Love for the fatherland so prevailed that no one was loath
to pour forth his soul for his church and for the freedom of his
family. Famous and brave souls, the future will not be silent about   350
you. Your fame will live on: in your homeland, in the heart of the
forum, and in the temples of the gods, your names will be read on
marble through the centuries.

But nevertheless, neither the surviving officers nor the remain-
ing soldiers lose heart when they see the death of their country-   355
men but are, instead, driven to rage: they will not allow their glori-
ous comrades to remain unavenged. Though their strength is worn
down, their blows continue to fall on the cruel enemy. The brave
Venetians direct their course to the renewed battle. Venier flies on
his lofty ship high through the battle line of his fatherland, the   360
best leader in war and the bravest fighter in close combat. All the
hope of his fatherland hinged on that critical moment. In his pru-
dence, he oversees every aspect with intense scrutiny: he encour-
ages his men; he lends strength to his warriors. Briefly he calls to   365
mind the great honors of their forefathers: the massive ships that
sailed over the entire blue sea; people conquered at the far shores
of the East; the name of Venice heard in Bactria and India, and
the triumphs often celebrated over the defeated enemy; the Em-   370
pire of the Sea held through long centuries; their city of marble,
seat of kings and gods, Italy's greatest glory, the harbor and its
safety open to all people, and the altar sacred to the exiled, sanctu-
ary for the poor, teacher of customs and life, beacon for humanity   375
and famous theater of the world; a country to be protected by its
citizens even in certain death.

Venier rouses the sluggish men. He excites their wrath with
words. He invigorates the men as they work. He swiftly rein-
forces the faltering battle line with reserves. He orders the galleons

380   ante aciem primam; cernit quascumque recentes
       et laceras retrahi postremum mandat in agmen,
       virtutem turbae patitur succumbere nusquam.
       Pugnat et ipse manu, nervo stridente sagittas
       contorquens ferit adversos obstantia passim
385   corpora dat leto; concussas mole carinas
       vastat et avertit trepidum terroribus hostem.
       Increpitans Turcas dictis compellat amaris.
       Infidos vocat atque deis celestibus hostes,
       invisam stirpem, quae rapto gaudeat et quae
390   gaudeat humanum sitiens haurire cruorem.
       Ignavum, servumque pecus, probrosa Selimi
       mancipia, expertes legum, sine more, ferarum
       degentes vitam, quos ferro excindere fas sit.
       Advenisse diem, populus quo concidat omnis;
395   esse mare ac terras scelerata gente levandas.
       Foedifragum votis exoptat adesse Tyrannum,
       illius et rigido praecordia rumpere ferro
       atque informe solo pedibus calcare cadaver,
       et monstrum infelix iunctis raptare quadrigis.
400   Incipiunt Turcae quassas inhibere carinas
       atque referre pedem. Conceptum corde pavorem
       arguit inconstans et raucus clamor ad auras.
       Hos agitans laevo Venerius in agmine saevit.
         Andreas dextro in cornu fera proelia miscet
405   Aurius et partes late circumspicit omnes,
       egregias validis adiungens viribus artes.
       Agmine tum medio varius labor extitit; acrem
       virtutem exercent late iuvenesque ducesque
       Romanus ductor non segnius hostibus instat.
410   Hortatus socios centeno remige pinum
       urget in adversos. Immani turbine Thracum
       icta ratis mediis depressa immergitur undis,

to the front line; he sees which ones are rested and orders that the   380
damaged ones withdraw to the back of the fleet; on no occasion
does he allow the bravery of the men to flag. He himself fights at
close range, shooting arrows to strike the enemy from his whizzing
bow. He kills the men he encounters; he devastates ships plowed   385
together in a heap and routs the enemy trembling with fear. Re-
buking the Turks, he accosts them with bitter words; he calls them
infidels and enemies of the heavenly gods, a hated race that re-
joices in pillaging and takes pleasure in thirstily drinking human   390
blood. Lazy, servile flock, shameful slaves of Selim, devoid of law
and morals, leading the life of wild animals, it is right to extermi-
nate them with the sword. The day has come when all their people
will die and both sea and land will be freed from their wickedness.   395
He wishes that the treaty-breaking Tyrant were present so he
might stab his heart with a stiff sword, trample the formless ca-
daver on the ground with his feet, and rip apart the unlucky mon-
ster with joined chariots. The Turks begin to curb their shaken   400
boats and retreat; their intermittent cries piercing through the air
redouble the panic that is taking root in their hearts. Driving them
on, Venier rages on the left flank.

On the right flank, Andrea Doria is in the midst of a fierce
fight, but oversees the whole situation, joining outstanding skill   405
with virile strength. In the middle of the formation, the strug-
gle appears uncertain; young fighters and their leaders both dem-
onstrate intense bravery, and the Roman commander actively
threatens the enemy. Encouraging his men, he keeps his hundred-   410
oared boat pressed against the enemy. A ship of Thracians is
struck by a huge volley and sinks in the middle of the waves. The

terga Getae trepidi vertere. Columnius heros
fraxineam quatiens hastam trepidantibus instat.
415 Corpora multa virum rubras deturbat in undas.
    Tum puer egregia praestans virtute Michael,
ante annos grave Martis opus durumque laborem
haudquaquam veritus, telum contorquet in hostem,
quem belli cupidum divinus avunculus ante
420 iusserat audentem pugnare et fidere divis.
Huic consanguineus praestanti robore Paulus,
iampridem bello spectatus, maior et annis,
luxque novumque decus Ghisileri nominis, una
sancto spes patruo prodendae gentis in aevum;
425 cominus in Turcas fertur violentus et hasta
proterit obstantes ingenti strage catervas.
Magnanimum Turcae falcatis ensibus hostem
excipiunt, summis adnixi viribus acrem
si vim forte queant tantamque repellere molem.
430 Non illum cohibent iam vulnera terna furentem.
Negligit undantem per candida membra cruorem,
ac magis ardescit; trepidos magis obterit hostes,
Turcarum magnis sua vulnera caedibus ultus.
Ut leo pro catulis venantum dissipat agmen,
435 cui cruor effusus per pectora lata, iubasque
maiores animos, maiores suscitat iras.
    Parmensis princeps proles Farnesia, Dacos
tendit in adversos et corpora turbat in aequor.
Illi par aevo princeps et sanguine iunctus
440 bella movet stragemque ciet duce natus ab Umbro.
Hostilem in navem saltu se coniicit ingens
Iordanus gladiumque rotans per transtra forosque
corpora dat leto vasta implens caede carinam.
Emicat ante alios rapido velocior Euro,

Geets retreat in terror. The hero Colonna shakes his ashen spear
as he looms over his trembling opponents. He throws many men's   415
bodies into the red water.

  Then Michele, a boy renowned for his extraordinary virtue,
precocious in the somber work and cruel labor of Mars and utterly
fearless, turns his spear against the enemy. When he desired to go
to war, his holy uncle had advised him to fight bravely and trust in   420
the gods. His kinsman Paolo possessed outstanding strength, long
before proven in war; a few years older, he was the promise and
new glory of the Ghislieri name, his venerable uncle's only hope
for continuing the family into the future. He is swept violently   425
into hand-to-hand combat with the Turks, and with his spear he
mows down the troops standing in his way with tremendous car-
nage. The Turks ward off the brave enemy with their curved
swords, striving with their utmost strength in the hope that they
might by chance repel such a massive force as his. Three wounds   430
at a time do not check him in his rage. He makes light of the
blood flowing down his white limbs, and rages all the more. He
brings greater harm to his frightened enemies, avenging his own
wounds by slaughtering many Turks. In the same way, a lion, pro-
tecting his cubs, can tear a troop of hunters to pieces as the blood   435
pouring over his wide chest and mane stirs up greater spirit,
greater wrath.

  The Prince of Parma, offspring of the Farnese family, presses
against the opposing Dacians and heaves bodies into the water.
Equal to him in age and joined by blood is Prince Paolo Giordano,
son of the Duke of Umbria; he now stokes the fight and stirs   440
up slaughter. Mighty Giordano throws himself onto an enemy
ship with a leap. Brandishing his sword through the thwarts and
benches, he delivers bodies to death, filling the ship with heaping
gore. He flashes in front of the others, swifter than the east wind,

445   fulminis in morem, cui non vis ulla resistat,
      non ferrum, aut moles saxo substructa vetusto.
      Tusca ratis, quae prima trium fert puppe sub auras
      erectum Stephani vexillum, quem fera saxis
      discipulum Christi Solymorum turba furore
450   percita contusum caelestes misit ad oras.
      Turcarum primas acies Etrusca iuventus,
      pectora cui longe fulgent cruce picta rubenti,
      disiecit, stragemque dedit toto aequore, magni
      non oblita ducis pulcherrima iussa: coactam
455   mitteret in bellum cum pubem, cumque iuberet
      Florentis populi veteres meminisse triumphos,
      et patriae retinere decus, laudesque parentum.
         Sfortia rostratam praegrandi corpore navem
      concitat in Cilicas remis findentibus aequor,
460   consilio dextraque potens florentibus armis.
      Pugnaces Siculi, simul et Campana iuventus,
      et Calabri genus acre virum per caerula vastam
      dant stragem, Geticas urgent franguntque carinas.
      Durior Alpinos socios fortuna fatigat.
465   Undique Turcarum numero maiore premuntur.
      Non tamen iis animus cadit aut in terga recedit.
      Opponunt clypeos densum glomerantur in orbem.
      Hortantur sese et solida virtute resistunt.
      Subveniunt Ligures. Turcis metus ingruit; instant
470   acrius Alpini et flammas spirare videntur,
      unius amissae stimulant quos damna carinae.
      Nec trepidum telis urgere sequacibus hostem
      absistunt geminas immani corpore donec
      Turcarum naves ventosa sub aequora mittant,
475   et cladem acceptam geminata clade rependant.

just like a lightning bolt, which no strength, no sword, no bulwark 445
supported by ancient rock can withstand. The Tuscan ship is the
first of the three to lift the pennant of St. Stephen from the deck
into the air — that disciple of Christ who was crushed with rocks
by a wild mob of raging Solymites and sent to the celestial shores. 450
The young men of Tuscany whose breastplates flash from afar,
painted with a ruddy cross, throw down the first line of Turks and
wreak havoc across the whole sea, not forgetting the noble orders
of their great lord: when he sent the assembled youth into battle, 455
he commanded them to remember the former triumphs of the
Florentine people and preserve the honor of the fatherland and
honor of their parents.

Sforza, mighty in his counsel and strong when brandishing
arms, steers the huge beaked ship against the Cilicians with their 460
oars slicing the sea. Sicilian fighters, together with young men
from Campania and the harsh race of Calabrian men, went on a
rampage across the water, hemming in and destroying the Getican
boats. Harsher fortune wearies the Alpine allies who are trapped
on all sides by a great number of Turks. Nevertheless, their cour- 465
age does not fail them, nor do they retreat. They raise their shields
and form a dense circle. They encourage each other and fight back
with solid bravery. The Ligurians come as reinforcement; fear
strikes the Turks; the Alpine men press more fiercely and seem to 470
breathe fire; the destruction of one lost ship spurs them on. They
do not stop bearing down on the frightened enemy with pursuing
shots until they send the twin ships of the Turks under the wind-
tossed water in one huge mass and pay back the slaughter they 475
suffered with twice the number of dead.

Ascanius Chabriasque duces iam tempora canis
aspersi pugnant, hos sueti ferre labores,
exemploque suo iuvenilia pectora firmant.
Pompeius Prosperque invicti robore fratres,
480   et Paravicinus numero obrutus et rate capta,
per medios hostes ausus se credere ponto,
atque animo praestans et pulchro corpore Pyrrhus
induit et ferro quos non incognita Musis
Brixia, quam decorat meus alto Gambara versu.
485   Gonzagae proceres et Tusci Marte feroces,
Insubrum longis soboles exercita bellis,
Felsinei iuvenes et pubes missa Tridento,
Italia lectum robur, flos lectus ab omni,
et cruce candenti insignis Melitaea iuventus,
490   quos inter Gallus flagrans Ramagasus acerbis
in Turcas odiis, Turcarum terror et ingens,
in bellum clamore ruunt. Pugna aspera surgit.
Hostiles obstant numero maiore carinae.
Durati bellis contorquent spicula Turcae;
495   Cappadoces, Daci, Cares, Cilicesque Getaeque
exululant, immane fremunt, caelum omne remugit.
Eventus belli ingentis dum prodere multos
conor et attingit varias mens anxia partes
me rapit invitum Melitensis casus; obortae
500   debilitant lacrimae, maesto de pectore fractas
singultus voces extrudit creber ad auras.
Dicendum tamen est adsit quaecumque facultas.
Impetus a sociis distraxit navibus unam
cum cruce candenti vexillum in puppe tenentem;
505   seu maris Ionii fluctus nimis impulit, ausam
Turcarum in medias remis penetrare carinas.

Ascanio della Corgna and the Chabrian leaders fight in different quarters. With a touch of gray already at their temples, the Chabrians are used to undertaking such missions; they encourage young hearts with their example. Pompeo and Prospero are brothers unmatched in strength; Pallavicini is overwhelmed by the enemy's numbers, and, when his boat is captured, dares to throw himself into the sea in the midst of his enemies; Pyrrhus, spirited and handsome, takes up the sword. He too hails from Brescia, not unknown to the Muses, since my Gambara celebrates it in lofty verse. The lords of Gonzaga, Tuscans ferocious in battle; Lombard offspring tested in long wars; the young men of Bologna and youth sent from Trent; the chosen strength of Italy, the best of them all; and the youth of Malta marked by the white cross; and with them Romegas the Gaul, the colossal terror of Turks, raging with bitter hatred against them—they all rush into war with a shout. The fight grows severe; hostile ships oppose each other in ever greater numbers. The Turks, hardened to war, fire arrows. Cappadocians, Dacians, Carians, Cilicians, and Geets howl, roaring savagely, and all the heavens echo back.

As I try to make known the many events of this momentous war, my anxious mind lights on different parts of the tale. Now, unwillingly, I turn to the fall of the Maltese; tears well up and sap my strength; constant sobbing from my sad chest sends broken words to the air. Nevertheless, the story must be told, whatever skill I may have. A strike drove one ship away from its allies, the one that was bearing the standard with the white cross on its deck; perhaps the waves of the Ionian Sea pushed it too hard, as it dared to penetrate into the middle of the Turkish ships with its

Agnovere truces Numidae, quos illa per alta
aequora praedantes victrix persaepe fugarat.
Circumstant unam naves ter quinque carinam.
510   Triginta proceres generosae stirpis, adeptos
egregia virtute crucis candentis honorem,
et comites centum, quingenti ac mille prehensos
circumdant incensi odiis memoresque malorum
piratae fremitu horrendo. Melitaea iuventus
515   pondere pressa gravi, tamen imperterrita mansit,
et pugnam horribilem ternas produxit in horas
obiectis clypeis conata repellere nubem
telorum saevi commista grandine plumbi.
Terque quaterque furens ingenti caede repulsos
520   disiecit Numidas et vertere terga coegit.
Succubuit numero virtus generosa sequaci.
Quin potius vicere viros ardentia fortes
fulmina cum bombis atque undique plurimus ignis.
Interea socii non subvenere vocati.
525   Dum reliquos plus parte suus labor occupat omnes,
subsidio caruere viri, miserabile dictu.
Ite, viri fortes, ad sidera. Regia caeli,
illustres animae, vobis patet. Ite beatas
ad sedes, animae felices. Fortibus illic
530   aeternam Deus omnipotens dat ferre coronam.
Vobis parta quies est sanguine, parta labore.
     Ocyalus caput infandum, contemnere quondam
ausus iura Dei et sanctum abiurare lavacrum,
faxque luesque hominum, ponti pirata, tyrannus
535   Massylos dicione premens, et classe superbus,
agmine postremo totis non viribus usus,
rem gerit; et cautus sua commoda mente volutans,
eventum pugnae puppi speculatur ab alta.
Urgeri socios Turcas ut vidit, in altum

oars. The savage Numidians recognized the boat, which had often driven them in flight as they carried out their raids on the deep sea. Fifteen ships surround the one small boat. Thirty leaders of 510 noble blood, who had won glory through the extraordinary virtue of the white cross, and one hundred soldiers (fifteen hundred already captured) were surrounded by hideously howling pirates, burning with hatred and recalling their misfortunes. The young men of Malta, pressed by this heavy weight, nevertheless remained 515 unafraid, and they extended the horrendous battle for three hours, trying to repel the cloud of projectiles (a hail of spears mixed with savage lead) with their shields raised. Three and four times the raging men routed the Numidians, repulsed them with much 520 slaughter, and forced them to retreat. But noble virtue gave way to persistent number. Overhead, thunderbolts flashing with explosions and intense fire overcame the brave men everywhere. Meanwhile their allies, though summoned, do not come to their aid. All 525 who are left are wholly occupied by their own tasks, and so the men had to fight without reinforcement. It is heartbreaking to speak of it. Go, brave men, to the stars. The kingdom of heaven stands ready for you, famous souls. Go, fortunate spirits, to your blessed thrones. There almighty God permits the brave to wear an 530 eternal crown. For your blood and for your labor, you have earned your rest.

The infamous captain Uluj Ali, who once dared to scorn the oaths of God and forswear his holy baptism, was the firebrand and plague of men. A pirate of the sea, a tyrant who rules the Massylians with his mighty authority, he drives on with purpose, proud 535 in his fleet, not yet having spent all his strength in the rear battle line. Cautiously mulling over his options, he watches for the outcome of the fight from his lofty galley. When he sees allied Turks

540 vela dat ac ventis convertit terga secundis,
     defensus tenebris fumi et caligine caeca.
     Infidumque ducem naves ter quinque secutae.
     Victores celer eludit, sociosque relinquit
     pallidus atque tremens, turpi formidine captus.
545 Ut lupus arma videns venantum densa canumque
     horribiles rictus, latratu territus acri
     arva secat cursu et silvis se condit opacis.
        Austrius interea ductor, quem regia puppis
     ordine remorum septeno concita portat,
550 per medias acies fertur sublimis, et agmen
     urgeri quacumque videt; iubet ire triremes
     subsidio certas, variis hortatibus illos,
     nunc hos exacuens. Densos ubi prospicit hostes
     obstare, intrepidus proram convertit in illos.
555 Caede furens late stragem ciet aequore toto.
     Hispanique duces, proceres quos misit Iberus,
     Hispalis, Emerita, et Gades, et Corduba, bello
     gens clara Oceano domito victricibus armis,
     decernunt lacerantque rates, sternuntque catervas;
560 vincentemque ducem laeto clamore sequuntur.
        Haec prospectat Halys, belli cui cura gerendi,
     iusque datum fuerat summum; robustus et acer
     atque manu promptus, tantae non inscius artis.
     Fecerat hunc sociata toro cognata Tyranni
565 clarum divitiis et pulchra prole parentem.
     Hesperium ductorem oculis animoque requirit.
     Hunc tribus a signis noscit, quae ventilat aura
     spirantis Boreae volitantia. Namque sinistrum
     ostentat clarum Venetorum insigne Leonem;
570 dextrum Aquilam gemino cum vertice fulget imago;
     inter utrumque Dei, fixum quem sustinet alta
     crux, populi regisque Pii venerabile signum.

hard pressed, he sets sail on the open sea and turns his back to the   540
favoring winds, protected by the smoky shadows and the blind fog.
Fifteen ships follow the faithless leader. Swiftly he eludes the con-
querors; pale, trembling in the grips of shameful fear, he leaves his
allies. Just so a wolf, seeing the dense arms of hunters and the   545
horrible snarls of dogs, is terrified by the loud barking and cuts a
path through the field and hides himself in the dark forest.

Meanwhile the commander John of Austria, borne on the swift
flagship with seven rows of oarsmen, is carried high through the
middle of the battle line and sees that one column is hemmed in   550
on all sides. He orders reliable galleys to bring reinforcements,
spurring on first these, then those with various encouragements.
When he sees that the enemy stands thickly in the way, he fear-
lessly turns his prow into them. Raging with slaughter he ram-   555
pages over the whole sea. The Spanish commanders and the
noblemen sent from Spain, from Seville, Mérida, Cadiz, and Cor-
dova—a people famous in war, that tamed the ocean with con-
quering arms—now they fight it out and destroy ships and slaugh-
ter the crews. They follow the conquering leader with a happy cry.   560

Ali Pasha observes all these things: he had been given the task
of conducting the war and the highest authority; he is robust and
sharp, ready with his fist, not ignorant of this great art. His wife,
the Tyrant's daughter, had made him famous for his wealth and a   565
father of beautiful children. He searches for the Spanish leader
with his eyes and mind. He recognizes him by the three standards,
which flutter in the breezes of the blustering north wind. The left
one shows the famous Lion, the emblem of Venice; and on the
right, the image flashes an eagle with twin heads; between both   570
the image of God, nailed on the lofty cross, the venerable sign of

Nec minus adversum noscit dux Austrius illum
picta tribus Lunis prae se vexilla gerentem.
575 Exarsit ducibus violentia saeva duobus,
vincendum egregie vel pulchra morte cadendum.
Credit uterque simul praeclaro ex hoste trophaeum
nunc sibi sorte dari; nunc fama, nunc decus ingens
affore, si spoliis victor laudetur opimis.
580 Concurrunt summi ductores: Thracius illinc
saetosa horrendus facie, iam grandior aevo;
Austrius hinc iuvenis levi pulcherrimus ore,
flammam oculis fundens rigidaque ferocior hasta.
Impulsae naves numeroso remige vastos
585 dant ictus. Proram magna vi prora suburget.
Nunc latus incumbit lateri atque carina carinam
altior adversam stringit. Revoluta per undas
alternis pinum pinus demergere ponto
tendit et immani iam verbere victa fatiscit.
590 Fragmina remorum fluitant agitata per undas.
Sublatus summum clamor ferit aethera. Bombis
tormenta horrisonis frangunt excussa carinas.
Undique tela volant. Quam plurima fistula ferro
vel producta cavo, producta vel aere corusco,
595 pluere sulfureo, flammaque incensa rubenti,
grandinis in morem glandes per inane volantes
liventis plumbi spargit, quo pulsa virorum
millia multa cadunt. Scloppum dixere magistri
eductum Stygiis (ut res docet ipsa) caminis.
600 Corpora trunca hominum, clypei galeaeque nitentes,
thoraces, gladii mixto glomerantur acervo.
Tormenta ingeminant ictus. Tremit aerea puppis.
Percussae crepuere trabes; ruere omnia credas.
Exundat fumus. Tum circumfusa repente
605 nox oculis adimit, nec non fragor auribus usum.

Pius's people and king. No less does the Austrian commander recognize his opponent, who flies the pennants before him painted with three moons. A beastly violence inflamed the two leaders, both eager to conquer or die an honorable death; each believes at the same time that fate has awarded him the trophy over his illustrious enemy, that now fame, and now great glory will bear witness whether the victor is honored with the general's spoils. 575

    The supreme leaders clash: on that side the Thracian, his coarse face bristling with hairs, now advanced in age; on this side, the young hero John of Austria, with his beautiful smooth countenance, with fire in his eyes, even more ferocious with his rigid spear. The ships sped forward propelled by many oarsmen and strike huge blows. Prow presses close to prow with great momentum. Now hull leans on hull, and, below the surface, keel scrapes against opposing keel. In turns, one ship weaves through the water trying to submerge the other in the sea until, weakened by the heavy blows, it begins to tire. Splinters of oars are tossed about on the waves. The rising clamor reaches the highest heaven. The cannons, reverberating with cacophonous blasts, strike the ships. On both sides the missiles fly. So many barrels, made either from hollow iron or from flashing bronze, rain with sulfur, and, ignited by gunpowder and ruddy flame, spread bullets of blue-black lead flying through the air like hail; struck by these, many thousands of men fall. This is what teachers meant by "scloppum," the blast of air that came from Stygian chimneys. Truncated bodies of men, shields, shining helmets, breastplates, and swords are heaped up in a confused pile. The cannons redouble their strikes. The brazen galley trembles. The floorboards shiver as they are struck. You might think that the world was collapsing. The smoke billowed in waves. Then night suddenly envelops them and deprives them of their sight, even as the blast takes away their hearing. Those who 580 585 590 595 600 605

Intrepidi pergunt ultro, quicumque supersunt:
in mortem haud dubiam et subiecta cadavera calcant.
In tormenta ruunt et contra tela feruntur;
ut feriant hostem sternantque ea sola voluptas.
610 Mors et vita viris tenui discrimine constat.
Vulneris accepti violentior ira dolorem
sentiri prohibit, gressus ne tardet euntis.
Pectora pectoribus, frontes et frontibus haerent.
Urgetur pede pes, et parmam parma repellit.
615 Luctantesque petunt per mutua vulnera mortem,
crudelemque ciet rabies vesana furorem.
Alter in alterius saltu transire carinam
nititur alteriusque alter statione potiri
turbatumque loco prosternere nititur hostem.
620 Cominus hic iugulum petit et praecordia ferro
rumpit. In adversos nervo stridente sagittas,
dirigit hic; alius duram iacit eminus hastam.
Insidiis multi ac pugna bellantur iniqua
protecti tabulis rimas qua monstrat hiantes
625 apta carina dolis. Igni ferroque latentes
eminus in densam dispergunt vulnera turbam
glandibus et plumbo dirum stridente per auras,
ignotique (nefas) dant fortia corpora leto.
  Heu cadis occulto iuvenis spectatus ab hoste
630 ante aciem primam tam saevo vulnere: gentis
Ursinae decus egregium bellator Horati,
Virgiliusque tuus. Nihil, o Romana propago,
te iuvit chalybis calida fornace recocti
durities, thorax fidum munimen ut esset
635 pectoribus. Diro cessit vis ferrea plumbo.
Sed tamen insigni tam letum nobile bello,
tot proceres inter virtus spectata ducesque

survive press fearlessly on to their own unquestionable death, and
they trample over the cadavers that lie nearby. They rush toward
the cannons and are thrown against spears: their only desire is that
they might strike the enemy and lay him low. Death and life are of   610
little difference to them. Wrath keeps them from feeling the pain
of any wound they receive, so their advance does not slow. Chest
clings to chest, forehead to forehead. Foot is crushed by foot and
shield repels shield. Grappling together, they inflict death through   615
mutual wounds, and the insane frenzy incites cruel fury. One tries
to leap into the other's boat; another tries to take one's post and
knock his enemy from his place in the confusion. Hand to hand,   620
he goes for the throat and cracks his chest with his sword. This
one casts arrows against the enemy from a hissing bowstring; an-
other throws a cruel spear from afar. Many wait in ambush, and
wage unfair war protected by planks with gaping cracks: the ships
are equipped with treacherous devices. Concealed from fire and   625
iron, the soldiers scatter wounds into the dense crowd from afar,
sending bullets and cruelly shrieking lead through the air, and
unseen — shamefully — they send brave bodies to death.

   Alas, you died from just such a cruel wound, youth, spotted in   630
the frontline by the hidden enemy: great glory of the Orsini fam-
ily, warrior of Horace and your very own Vergil. The toughness of
steel, child of Rome, did not help you at all, though your breast-
plate was newly forged in a hot furnace to serve as a faithful de-
fense for your chest. Iron strength yielded to vicious lead. But to   635
die in such a famous war is still noble: that your virtue was tested
among the noblemen and commanders will lessen the flowing

maestorum fusas lacrymas luctumque parentum
imminuet. Neque enim corpus miserabile nati
640   vulneribus fossum aspicies, Vicine, pudendis.
          Heu fraudem infandam, invisam superisque virisque
adversam egregiis. Heu detestabile telum,
letiferum telum, quo non praesentius ullum
virtutem extinguit, nec fortia corpora leto
645   plura dat, aut aperit damno maiore phalanges,
aeratasve acies, aut proterit agmina campis.
Igne oculos violat, sonitu aures, sulfure nares,
et miserum perdit crudeli vulnere corpus.
Hanc furiae Stygiis pestem invenere sub antris,
650   ne qua virum medio se virtus inclyta campo
inserat, aut parto pugnans laetetur honore.
Despecti manibus tractabilis atque pusilli
militis, oblongo ac tereti cava fistula ferro,
pulvere nigranti ac plumbo livente repleta,
655   angusto ad fundum terebrata foramine, flammam
sulfuream rapit ardenti succensa favilla.
Horribili crepitu atque immani turbine baccas
excutit. Ah miseri, quibus immedicabile vulnus
infligens, plumbo costas perfringit abusto.
660   Me vero, capiunt veterum quem scripta virorum,
Socraticae retinet quem longa insania chartae,
emeritumque senem; si bellicus ingruat horror,
detestata mihi, si fundat fistula glandes,
non platani trepidum genialis protegat umbra,
665   non clypeus tegat, aut iniusto pondere thorax.
Antra obscura petam; fugiam trans flumina praeceps,
trans montem oppositum, lati trans aequora ponti,
fistula dira meas ne bombis vulneret aures,

tears and sorrow of your grieving parents; you will not see the piti-
ful body of your son riddled with shameful wounds, Vicino.   640

Alas, unspeakable deceit, far from praiseworthy, hated by both
gods and men; alas, detestable gunfire, death-dealing gunfire, noth-
ing quenches virtue more quickly, gives more brave bodies to   645
death, or opens the phalanxes or brazen battle lines to greater loss,
or tramples more armies in the fields. It hurts the eyes with fire,
the ears with sound, the nose with brimstone and destroys the
wretched body with cruel wounds. The Furies unleashed this
plague from under the Stygian caves, so that the renowned virtue   650
of men need not show itself on the open field or any fighter rejoice
in the honor he achieved. Manageable even in the hands of the
despicable and weak soldier, the hollow pipe of oblong and tapered
iron, packed with black powder and livid lead, drilled all the way
through with narrow holes, when ignited by a burning spark,   655
catches sulfurous flame. They dispense bullets in a huge volley
with a horrible crack. Ah, poor wretches, on whom gunfire inflicts
untreatable wounds as it breaks through the ribs with burning
lead. But as for me in my worn-out old age, captivated by the writ-   660
ings of the ancients, gripped by the boundless follies of Socratic
pages: if the horror of war should erupt, if the barrel I loathe
should pour forth bullets, the genial shade of the plane tree would
not protect me, nor would the shield or weighty breastplate cover   665
me. I will seek dark caves; I will flee headlong across rivers, across
intervening mountains, across the waters of the wide sea, so that
the cruel barrels do not wound my ears with their blasts, so that I

ne videam latis cumulata cadavera campis
670   et decurrentes humano sanguine rivos.
Martis opus pubes exercet prodiga vitae.
Rem gerit hic tacitus; lingua tonat ille sonanti.
Ille gemit miserans. Hic verbis increpat hostem
voce minax. Magno miscentur caerula luctu.
675   Obstrepit unda maris, clamoribus intonat aether.
Nulla quies miseris medio concessa labore.
    Quis seriem rerum verbis aequaverit omnem,
arte valens summa? Nobis in carmina vires
exiguae. Sed nostra fidem (nec fallor) habebunt
680   difficilem, nisi forte die quis cogitet illo
ferrea corda viris animosque fuisse leonum.
Diditur extemplo magno discrimine summos
isse duces passim turbata per agmina rumor.
Accurrunt, densasque tradunt in bella triremes
685   egregii fratres et Halym servare parentem
contendunt vitamque volunt pro patre pacisci.
Subveniunt Partheus, Caracossius, Assis, et omnes
Bassarei populis sueti dare iura subactis
barbaricumque ducem numero gens barbara firmat.
690   Ductori Hesperio pariter venere carinae
undique subsidio. Properat Farnesius heros,
pectore sollicito cui fixus avunculus haeret.
Cognati capitis grave propulsare periclum
officii putat esse sui. Fert impetus illum
695   longius, audentem dolor, et temeraria virtus
in medios remis rapit impellentibus hostes.
Tum pudor in rabiem Turcas incendit, et unam
circumstant omni naves ex parte carinam
complures numero, proram puppemque tuetur

do not see bodies heaped up in the wide fields and rivers running   670
with human blood. The young, careless of life, perform the work
of Mars. This one works silently; that one thunders with a re-
sounding tongue. That one groans with compassion; this one,
menacing with his voice, attacks the enemy with words. The sea is
roiling with immense grief. The wave of the ocean thunders; the   675
air echoes with shouts. No rest is granted to the wretched in the
middle of the struggle.

   Who, even if he were a master of the highest art, could do jus-
tice to this series of events in words? My powers in song are slight,
and indeed my poems will be hard to credit (I do not lie) unless
by chance one believes that on that day men had hearts of iron   680
and the courage of lions. A rumor is suddenly spread throughout
the confused troops that their supreme leaders were engaged in a
duel. The renowned brothers rush on and drag packed galleys into
battle. They strive to protect their father, Ali Pasha, and they wish   685
to trade their lives for his. The Parthians, Caradossius, Assis, and
all the Pashas, accustomed to giving laws to subjected peoples,
come to his aid, and the barbarian race reinforces their leader with
their number. In equal numbers, the ships come from all sides   690
with reinforcement for the Hesperian leader. The Farnese hero
speeds on, his uncle clinging close with his troubled heart: he
thinks it is his duty to ward off serious danger from his kinsman's
head. But the attack carries his nephew far off; grief and reckless   695
virtue sweep him in his daring right into the middle of the en-
emy with driving oars. Then shame inflames the Ottomans into
a rage, and many ships surround that one boat on all sides, and a
dense ring of young warriors guards both the prow and stern,

700   et spondas iuvenum bellantum densa corona:
moenia qui Parmae liquerunt, moenia Castri,
quique Placentinam succinctam moenibus urbem
excelsis, Trebiam Tarumque per arva bibentes,
quosque ferax Bacchi, Cererisque Novaria misit,
705   lecta manus bello magna cum caede repellit
Turcarum assultus varios. Ululatus inanis
funditur, atque Italas frustra diverberat aures.
Bella manu non voce gerit, sed cominus armis:
et pede collato, longis exercita bellis,
710   nobilis Italiae, ferroque assueta iuventus.
Ipse autem iuvenis fortissimus insilit altam
in Peribis navem, virtus spectata Tyranno
cuius erat. Magno pro munere regia pellex
ditarat Peribem thalamo concessa beato.
715   Occurrit Peribes furiis agitatus, et illum
increpat horrendum stridens, miratus in uno
tantum animi superesse viro, duraverit aetas
quem nondum matura satis, securus ut altam
arripiens navem densos contemneret hostes;
720   non dubitat meritas quin mox audacia poenas
tanta luat, simul et falcato fulminat ense.
Se iuvenis clypeo collectum protegit; et vim
sustinet atque gradum dextro pede protinus addens
Hispano incautum gladio transverberat hostem.
725   Dat sonitum percussa ratis ductore cadente.
Agmina Turcarum fugiunt perterrita, victor
obtinet arreptam magna virtute carinam.
Te iuvenis memorande (licet si dicere) longe
disiunctum a sociis maioraque viribus ausum;
730   vox audita Deo patrui cognominis aras
ture pio pro te cumulantis, vota, precesque

as well as the benches: those who left the walls of Parma and the   700
walls of Castro, and the city of Piacenza, girded by lofty walls, and
those who drink the waters of the Trebbia and the Taro flowing
through the fields, and those sent by Novara, rich with grape and
grain; this company, chosen for war, repelled the repeated on-   705
slaughts of the Ottomans with much bloodshed. Mad howling
pours out of them, but strikes Italian ears in vain. They wage war
with their hands, not their voices, up close with arms: the noble
youth of Italy are trained for extended wars in close quarters and   710
accustomed to fighting with the sword. Now the bravest youth
jumps onto the high ship of Peribes, whose virtue had been no-
ticed by the Tyrant; for his great service, the royal concubine had
made Peribes rich when she was admitted to his fortunate mar-
riage chamber. Peribes rushes in, driven by the Furies, and scream-   715
ing, confronts that fated warrior, wondering how so much spirit
survived in one man (though mature age had not yet hardened
him to the point that he could fearlessly repel crowds of enemies
while seizing their high ship). He does not doubt that such audac-   720
ity will soon suffer the penalties it deserves. He suddenly flashes
his scythe-shaped sword. The youth retreats behind his shield and
defends himself. He harbors his strength and, quickly lunging
forward with his right foot, stabs his enemy off guard with his
Spanish blade. The ship makes a sound, struck by its falling com-   725
mander. The Turkish troops flee in terror, and the victor takes
charge of the ship he has seized with his great bravery. You, young
man, separated far from your allies, will be remembered (if I may
say it) for having dared even greater things with your strength; the
voice of your uncle was heard by God as he was heaping up your   730
family's altars with pious incense on your behalf. And so were the

reginae uxoris fusae, caraeque parentis;
et tua caelitibus pietas gratissima salvum
reddidit, ut spoliis magni praedonis onustum
735 Roma prius mox te Mavortia Parma videret.
    Dum gerit haec iuvenis Farnesius, Austrius illinc
dux minus urgetur; quin et vir maximus armis
adiuvat ad dextram classi praefectus Iberae.
Corripit adversum navem et deturbat in undas
740 fervidus obstantes Turcas oneratque catenis
progeniem regum veniam vitamque petentem.
Adiuvat ad laevam vibratque Columnius ensem
fulmineum ductor. Stragem ciet aequore vastam
a cruce dux sancta. Procerum manus adiuvat, ingens
745 pugna recrudescit. Summa certatur opum vi.
Viribus aequatis anceps victoria nutat;
lance duces aequa librat fortuna superbos.
    Dum Caietani generis lux magna decusque
pugnat Honoratus dextra de parte carinae
750 atque invadentes Turcas deturbat in aequor,
aversum iuvenem fallit Caracosius altam
in navem saltu delapsus parte sinistra
et perimit pubem Circeio in litore natam.
Conversus iuvenis magno turbante tumultu,
755 stringit utraque manu praelongum fervidus ensem
praedonemque premit per structa sedilia nautis,
lapsantem remos inter rigidasque catenas.
Praedonis caput abscisum praetervolat altos
influctus. Iacuit truncus per transtra volutus,
760 magnus et effundens spumantem sanguinis undam.
Cetera mox acies ingenti caede repulsa
desilit in fluctus et piscibus aggerat escam.

vows and prayers poured forth by your wife, the queen, and your
dear mother. Your piety, so pleasing to the heavenly gods, brought
you back safe, so that Rome first, then martial Parma would see   735
you laden with spoils of the great pirate.

While the young Farnese hero accomplishes these things, John
of Austria is pressed less on that side; for the commander of the
Spanish fleet, that mighty man in arms, lends support to the right.
He seizes the opposing ship, and boiling with rage, throws the   740
Turks in his way into the waves; he weighs the offspring of kings
down with chains as they beg for pardon and life. The commander
Colonna defends the left flank, brandishing his lightning-like
sword, and he stirs up vast destruction on the sea with the holy
cross. A band of noblemen lends assistance, and the huge battle
grows bloody. It is fought to the last strain of their strength. Vic-   745
tory wavers ambiguously between matched forces; Fortune weighs
the proud leaders in the trays of the balance.

While the great light and glory of the Caetani family, Onorato,
fights on the right side of the ship and throws invading Turks   750
overboard, Kara Hodja deceives his young enemy, dropping onto
the high ship from the left side with a leap, and he destroys the
young men born on the Circean shore. Young Onorato, whirling
around in the great maelstrom, angrily draws his long sword with   755
both hands. He presses the pirate through the benches set up by
the sailors, where he slips among the oars and rigid chains. He
cuts off the pirate's head and tosses it into the deep waves. The
great trunk rolls along the thwarts and then lies still, spewing a   760
frothing wave of blood. Soon the rest of the fighters, pushed back
by the immense slaughter, jump into the waves and add food for
the fish.

Contigit hoc etiam, dictu mirabile, multos
sacrificos corpus nullo munimine tectos,
765   isse per ardentes acies. Per tela, per ignes,
nudato capite, et reiecto in terga cucullo,
ingressos pedibus nudis laevaque tenentes
in cruce pendentem dominum de virgine natum
assiduis gyris, longo molimine dextrae
770   et recto, et verso signantes aera ductu,
implorasse Deum, psalmos, hymnosque canentes,
sordibus exactae vitae, maculisque remissis,
caesorum ad superos animas prodire iubentes;
ore alacres passim resonabant nomen Iesu:
775   'Christe, Dei mandata patris per cuncta libenter
aspera progrediens implesti, idemque subisti
in cruce pro nobis tormentum mortis acerbae,
pro quibus ille tibi donavit, magne redemptor
dulce, potens, sanctum super omnia nomen Iesu.
780   In caelis simul et terris Ereboque profundo
flectitur omne genu, cum vox auditur Iesu
hostis in hoc ipso flectatur nomine victus,
inque hoc Christicolae sint omnes nomine salvi.
Protege, Christe, tuos, animis et viribus auge.
785   Irrita tela cadant, quae torquet Turca profanus.
Sacrilegos Turcas male perdant tela piorum.
Este viri fortes. Animos attollite. Christo
fidite. Nobiscum faciunt pia numina caeli.
Perdite sacrilegos. Sceleratam excindite gentem.
790   Vincite magnanimi divosque in vota vocate.
Vertitur in manibus vestris nunc sancta deorum
religio, patriae libertas, gloria gentis
Hesperiae, decus atque salus: pugnate. Laborem
egregium iam iam victoria laeta sequetur.

Amazing to say, it happened that many holy men marched through the burning battle lines without any armor for protection. 765 They walk, feet bare, through weapons and fire with their heads uncovered, hoods thrown back, holding in their left hand the virgin-born Lord hanging on the cross; and with the persistent effort of their right hand, marking the air in continuous motion forward and back with the sign of the cross, they implored God, 770 singing psalms and hymns, bidding the souls of the slaughtered to go forth to those above, the filth and stains of their spent life now forgiven. Everywhere they called out the name of Jesus with glad voices: "Christ, as you passed willingly through all bitterness, you 775 fulfilled the orders of God the Father, and you endured the torment of an agonizing death for us on the cross; on account of these things, Great Redeemer, he gave to you the sweet, mighty name of Jesus, holiest of all. In the heavens, on earth, and in the 780 depths of hell every knee is bent; when the sound of "Jesus" is heard, let the enemy be swayed, conquered by this name itself; and in this name, let all Christians be saved. Christ, protect your people, and increase them in spirit and in strength. Let the weapons 785 of your faithful destroy the profane Turks. Let the weapons which the impious Turk hurls fall harmlessly. Be brave, men. Raise your spirits. Trust in Christ. The holy powers of heaven work with us. Kill the sacrilegious, destroy the wicked race. Conquer, courageous 790 ones; call on the gods with your prayers. Now the holy religion of the gods, and the liberty of the fatherland, along with the honor, glory, and safety of the Hesperian race, is in your hands. Fight! Even now blessed victory will follow your extraordinary effort.

795 Iam vos certa manent aeternae praemia vitae.'
Spem certam interea pugnans divinitus hausit
Hesperius miles fregitque audentius hostem.
Gratus et ille labor; cum vulnera multa ligaret,
erigeret lapsos, vim fessis ipse sacerdos
800 adderet ac dulcem ferret sitientibus undam.
O fortunatos nimium, vereque beatos,
corporis illecebras ausos contemnere, et omni
pauperiem Christi studio vitamque secutos.
Affuit illaesis fiducia tanta per agmen,
805 ut minus horrerent strepitus dirosque fragores
quam volitantis apis per candida lilia bombos.
    Austrius interea manet imperterritus heros
magnanimumque ferox pugnando sustinet hostem.
Ense ferit multos; multos umbone repellit.
810 Denique ductoris longum miserata laborem,
lecta manus iuvenum, quibus est Hispania mater,
prosilit arma movens. Huic stat sententia, saevo
difficilem pugnae nodum dissolvere ferro,
caedibus aut sterni certaeque occumbere morti.
815 Agmine densato tendunt per tela, per ignes,
quingenti numero per millia multa virorum.
Arripiunt navem insignem, quae maxima reges
ferre solet summosque duces per caerula vectos.
Ascensu exsuperant magno clamore carinam;
820 veliferum ad malum iam pervenere. Sed ingens
vis tormentorum circumtonat. Ignibus atris,
glandibus, et plumbi pubes pene obruta passim
crebra cadit membris disiectis, inter odorem
sulfureum fumique globos atramque favillam.
825 Pectoribus versis reliqui cessere parumper.
Respirant. Iterum invadunt pugnamque capessunt.

Now the certain rewards of eternal life wait for you." Meanwhile,   795
the Hesperian soldier has drunk in assured hope as he fights with
God's inspiration, and attacks the enemy even more boldly. The
priest's work is welcome; while he bandages many wounds and
picks up the fallen, he confers strength on the tired and brings   800
sweet water to those in thirst. O you lucky and truly blessed ones,
who dared to scorn the seductions of the body and follow the
poverty and life of Christ with complete devotion. So great was
their faith as they moved unharmed among the troops that they
feared the shrieks and explosions less than buzzing of bees flying   805
through white lilies.

Meanwhile, the hero John of Austria remains unafraid and
fights fiercely to hold back the strong enemy. Many he strikes with
his sword; many he repels with his shield. At last the chosen band   810
of youths, whose mother is Spain, pitying the long struggle of
their leader, grab their weapons and rush forward. They decide
they will either loosen the entangled knot of the fight with their
swords, or be overthrown by slaughter and succumb to certain
death. In tight formation they move through missiles and fire, fifty   815
in number through the many thousands of men. They occupy the
flagship which, being the largest, is accustomed to bear kings and
carry the highest leaders across the sea. They scale the keel and
capture it with a great cry; they have now reached the sail-bearing   820
mast. But the immense force of the cannons thunders all around.
Almost buried in black flames and lead bullets, young men fall on
all sides, one after another, limbs torn off, among the sulfurous
stench, clouds of smoke, and black ash.

Those who are left turn aside and withdraw for just a mo-   825
ment. They take a breath. Again they attack and resume the fight.

Tunc etiam fortes similis fortuna repellit.
Nulla mora, exoritur iam tertia pugna. Resistunt
horribiles Turcae contempta morte ruentes.
830 Assultu quarto Turcis atrocius instant
protecti clypeis: et magna caede peracta,
iam numero pauci tamen obtinuere carinam.
Nescit enim vinci, si quo est verissima virtus:
illa viam reserat sibi cuncta per ardua victrix.
835   Tum demum insultans longo certamine fessum
urget Halym iuvenis fortissimus. Inter et illum
transtra premens dura subversum cuspide, diros
edentem gemitus, geminato vulnere summum
ductorem summus ductor demittit ad Orcum.
840 Arma viri, chlamydem pictam atque insignia regum
cuncta legens, magnaque Deum ter voce salutans,
et grates peragens, spoliis laetatur opimis.
Detrahit e puppi lunae vexilla nefandae,
et vexilla crucis figens extollit ad auras.
845 Conspectamque crucem victoria laeta secuta est.
       Ast ubi capta fuit praetoria puppis et ingens
lancea ductoris sectum caput extulit alte,
territa Turcarum conversis agmina proris
diffugiunt. Ligures circum fugientibus obstant,
850 consilio ducis in gyrum curvo agmine ducti,
aversam ut classem premerent et terga ferirent
Cappadocum, queis non lapsus, non exitus esset.
Ut se comprensos Turcae sensere, gemiscunt.
Torpescunt animis. Manibus languore solutis,
855 spicula lapsa cadunt. Artus stupor occupat ingens,
in pecudum morem strati caeduntur. Ad Orcum
millia multa ruunt, implentur sanguine puppes.
Sanguine lata rubent freta, sanguine spuma rubescit.

Then a similar circumstance compels the brave men yet again. A third strike begins without delay. The horrible Turks resist the onslaught, rushing on with a contempt for death. On the fourth   830
charge, the allies assault the Turks more fiercely, protected by their shields, and they deal out much slaughter. Though now few in number, they capture the ship. The truest virtue, wherever it exists, does not know how to be conquered; victorious virtue opens a way for itself through all obstacles.

Leaping forth at last, brave John of Austria goes after Ali Pasha,   835
weary from the long contest. Standing on the thwarts, the one supreme leader sends the other to Orcus. Weakened by a double wound, Ali Pasha is overwhelmed by the fierce onslaught and emits sorrowful groans. Noticing the arms of the man, the painted   840
cloak, and all the insignia of the king, and loudly calling to God three times to give thanks, John rejoices in the rich spoils. Dragging down the standard of the unspeakable moon from the deck, he affixes the flag of the cross and raises it to the breezes. Victory follows happily when the cross is seen.   845

But when their commander's ship has been captured and a huge lance has lifted the severed head of their leader on high, the terrified fleet of Turks retreats, their prows turned away in flight. The Ligurians box them in as they flee, guided by the advice of their   850
leader to curve their column into a ring in order to pursue the enemy fleet and strike the backs of the Cappadocians, for whom there would be no escape, no exit. The Turks begin to groan when they realize they are caught. They grow sluggish in spirit. Arrows slip and fall from their hands, slack with exhaustion. An unnatural   855
numbness seizes their limbs. They are cut down, prostrate, like so many cattle. Many thousands rush to death and the ships are filled with blood. The wide straits redden with blood and the sea foam grows ruddy with death.

Ter denae tamen elapsae fugere biremes.
860   Alta petunt trepidi. Victor fugientibus instat
terga premens. Illis spes iam cadit irrita. Terram
obliqui arripiunt urgentque in saxa carinas.
Illisae crepuere rates. In litus anheli
sese coniiciunt. Pedibus via parta salutis.
865   Condunt se silvis per devia lustra ferarum.
Incendit victor fractas in litore naves.
Ignis edax longe flamma crepitante reluxit.
     Victores spoliis curam intendere legendis:
bisque rates centum laeto traxere triumpho
870   barbaricis opibus, gemmis, auroque refertas.
Captivi innumeri duras subiere catenas.
Millia multa etiam cupidi de gente Latina
compedibus passim et gravibus solvere catenis,
ad remum miseros quos ante ligaverat hostis.
875   Multa etiam duro in certamine caesa suorum
corpora cum gemitu, luctu, lacrymisque profusis
legerunt, patriis mox transmittenda sepulchris,
exequiis decoranda piis pulcherrimus ut mos
Christicolis constat; producere funera cantu
880   lugubri ad delubra deum, sacrasque per aras
aeternam requiem defunctis luce precari
inque hominum magnis conventibus ore diserto,
eloquioque gravi funebres dicere laudes,
commemorare genus, praeclaraque facta virorum.
885   Credimus hoc tamen, et freti bonitate fatemur
tum Patris aeterni, tum servatoris Iesu,
illustres animae, pro religione profusas
vulneribus pulchris vos in sublime volantes,
aethereas penetrasse domos sedesque beatas.

Nevertheless, thirty biremes slip away and flee. Anxiously they   860
seek the high seas. The victor pursues them as they flee, hard on
their tail. Now all their vain hope abandons them. They reach the
land at an angle and push their ships on the rocks. The ships are
dashed and burst apart. Gasping for air they throw themselves on
the shore and escape inland on foot. They bury themselves along   865
the uncharted tracks of wild animals in the woods. The victor
burns the broken ships on the shore. Hungry fire shines at a dis-
tance with its crackling flame.

Now the victors turned their attention to choosing their spoils.
In joyous triumph, they lead away two hundred ships crammed   870
with barbarian wealth, gems, and gold. Countless captives are
placed in harsh chains while they eagerly release many thousands
of the Latin race from their shackles and heavy bonds, those
wretched men whom the enemy had tied fast to the oars.

With moaning, lamenting, and a great outpouring of tears, they   875
retrieved many bodies of their own men, slaughtered in the harsh
contest, to be sent over to native graves and honored with religious
rites as the sacred Christian custom dictates; they will lead a fu-
neral procession to the shrines of the gods with mournful singing,   880
and at the holy altars pray for eternal rest for the dead, and in
their congregations, speak funeral eulogies with eloquence and
authority to commemorate their nation and the outstanding deeds
of their men.

But, renowned souls, we believe this and we confess, trusting in   885
the goodness of the Eternal Father and our savior Jesus: that you,
having poured out your lives for your religion in beautiful wounds,
are flying aloft to reach the heavenly halls and blessed seats.

890 Templa Dei laetae implestis rumore secundo.
Istic vestra fuit pulchri vox nuntia facti.
(Sic homines loquimur sensum moremque secuti,
omnia cum videat Deus haec, mentesque solutae)
nunc promissa Deus persolvit praemia vobis,
895 aeternum caelo iam nunc agitabitis aevum,
cum sanctis hymnum Domino sine fine canentes.
Tu Domine es sanctus, sanctus, ter denique sanctus,
atque exercituum Deus es. Tua dextera fortis.
Magne Deus, caelum ac terram tua gloria complet.
900 Felices animae, pro vobis sacra per aras
maximus antistes peragens solemnia, vobis
indulgens, fors si qua manent, commissa remittit.
Interea nostri memores, quia maxima belli
restat adhuc moles, aeternum orate parentem,
905 ipsius ut nutu victoria sanguine vestro
parta, piae genti pergat procedere, donec
victor Ioannes Byzantia moenia portis
effractis penetrans, pallentem morte Tyrannum
sternat humi Hispano traiectum pectora ferro.
910 Ut victi bello Turcae, Nasamones, et omnes
barbaries verum agnoscant, Mahomete relicto
mendaci, Dominumque Deumque sequantur Iesum.
      Aequoreis strages apparet maxima campis
(horrendum visu, non enarrabile dictu)
915 gaza ingens iactata salo, pretiosa supellex,
sanguine tincta natant rerum fragmenta per undas,
cristarum coni, perfracta hastilia, fundo
corpora, thoraces, galeae volvuntur in imo.
Ingentem luctum mox nuntia fama Selimo
920 afferet: amissam Ioniis in fluctibus esse
immanem classem, qua perfidus alta tenebat

Happily, you fill up the temples of God with cheerful news. From 890
there your voice tells of this noble event. (So we men say, follow-
ing sense and custom, since God sees all these things and our
minds are weak.) Now God pays you your promised rewards.
Now you will live an eternal life in heaven, singing hymns with the 895
saints to God forever. You are holy, Lord, holy, and three times
holy, and you are the God of hosts; your right hand is mighty.
Great God, your glory fills heaven and earth. Blessed souls, for 900
you the high priest performs solemn rites at the altar; mercifully
forgiving your sins, if by chance any remain. Meanwhile, be mind-
ful of our people, since the greatest labor of the war still remains,
and call on the Eternal Father, so that with his approval, this vic- 905
tory, born of your blood, may rouse our pious race to go forward,
until victorious John, entering the walls of Byzantium through its
breached gates, lays the Tyrant low, growing pale in death on the
ground, pierced through the chest by a Spanish sword. Let it be 910
that as they are conquered in war, the Turks, the men of Naxos,
and all barbarians may recognize the truth and, leaving behind ly-
ing Muhammad, follow the Lord and God, Jesus.

  Tremendous destruction appears on the watery fields — horrible
to see, impossible to describe — huge treasure tossed on the waves, 915
valuable furnishings; fragments of things stained with blood float
on the water: cones of helmet crests, broken swords; bodies,
breastplates, helmets all churned in the deep. Soon herald Fama
will bring enormous grief to Selim: how his vast fleet was lost in 920
the Ionian waves, the fleet he used treacherously to keep the deep

aequora iampridem populis infesta Latinis,
Christicolas vicisse mari, cecidisse sub armis
Turcarum gentem magno certamine victam,
925 exitium reliquis ingens instare paratum,
expertes belli Turcae quicumque supersunt;
Hesperios reges, modo stet concordia firmo
foedere, victores semper fore, milite quando
fortius occiduo nihil, aut pugnacius extet.

930 Si quid mentis habet, si quid resipiscere possit,
demittet fastus audita clade Tyrannus,
aequalem sese esse Deo qui credat, et illum
(triste nefas, scelus immane, intolerabile, dirum)
diviso velut imperio, caelestibus oris
935 contentum, iubeat reliquis absistere regnis,
aequora cuncta sibi, qui terras arroget omnes.
Tene pusille culex haec sic agitare? Selime,
poena luenda tibi. Tum, perfide, sera subibit
tantorum scelerum te conscia cura remordens.

940 Pulveris in morem, rapidus quem dissipat Auster,
te perdet Deus omnipotens, Deus ille superbis
adversus, tumidos qui vertit, et urget ad ima
et mites humilesque animo qui tollit ad auras.
Horrescet subito, magno turbante tumultu,
945 Turcica gens ignara Dei; gens impia vestes
induet atratas, saevos testata dolores.
Uxores multas cum vir sibi copulet unus,
pectora foedabunt pugnis atque unguibus ora
prorsus multa locis viduarum millia cunctis.

950 Caelestum magno, ac memorando munere, contra
tu, Pie magne pater, longum laetabere, cuius
consilio, cura, studio res tanta peracta est.
Audiit omnipotens genitor tua vota precesque,
et populi clemens gemitus respexit ab alto.

sea unsafe for so long for the Latin people; how the Christians had prevailed on the sea; how the race of the Turks was beaten in the great battle and fell in combat; how complete destruction was 925 planned for those who remained, and loomed ever closer (since any of the Turks who survived have no knowledge of war); how the Hesperian kings, if the alliance remains a durable pact, will always be victorious, since there exists nothing braver or more belligerent than a Western soldier.

If any of his reason remains, if he could come to his senses, the 930 arrogant Tyrant would put away his scorn when he heard of the slaughter, he who believes that he is equal to God and (a pitiful sin, a tremendous wickedness, both intolerable and dreadful) he would even order him, as though their empire were shared equally, to be content with the heavenly shores and stay away from the re- 935 maining kingdoms, arrogating to himself all the land and sea. Does this news bother you, little gnat? Selim, you must suffer the penalties. Then, traitor, the nagging awareness of your responsibility for such great sins will come too late. Just like the dust, which 940 the south wind rapidly scatters, almighty God will destroy you, that God who opposes the proud, who overturns them, sending all who are swollen with pride down to the depths, and who raises those meek and humble in spirit to the sky. The Turkish race, not 945 knowing God, will suddenly shudder in a great, whirling maelstrom. The impious race will dress in black clothes as witness to their savage sorrows. When one man may join himself to many women, many thousands of widows everywhere will defile their breasts with their fists and their faces with their nails.

For the great and memorable service you performed for the 950 heavenly gods, on the other hand, you, great Pope Pius, will rejoice for a long time; such great things came about through your counsel, attention, and devotion. The almighty Father heard your vows and prayers and considered the laments of the people from

955 Gens pia laetitiam ingentem testata per aras
vota Deo solvet laetos et concinet hymnos.
Perque domos, fora lata, vias, et compita passim
ignibus accensis resonabunt omnia cantu.
Maius opus numquam sol vidit, facta virorum
960 omnia per terras qui lustrat, laetus idipsum
vidit, et obstupuit; tanto discrimine rerum
enituit virtus. Maior victoria numquam
parta fuit gentique piae ducibusque Latinis.
Stabit Ioannis nomen memorabile, donec
965 arma viri, maria, ac terras, classesque loquentur.
      Ductorem summum proceres clamore salutant
victricemque manum proni contingere gaudent.
In caelum clamore Pius pater optimus, auctor
horum operum, nec non domus Austria tollitur. Una
970 tolluntur Veneti factis gens clara per orbem.
Suspiciunt caelum, laetis et vocibus hymnum
Ambrosii verbis cantant, quo rite solemus
ante aras laudare Deum Dominumque fateri.
      Conversis proris, contento litora cursu
975 nota petunt laeti et portu conduntur amico,
procedens caelo cum iam nitet Hesperus alto,
moratlesque monet serae decedere nocti.

on high with compassion. The pious people will make known 955
their great happiness, honoring the vows they made at the altars
and singing happy hymns to God. Fires will be lit in every home;
the wide streets, highways, and crossroads everywhere will resound
with song. The Sun, who sees all the deeds of man throughout the 960
lands, has never witnessed a greater work; he himself is happy and
amazed; for virtue shone forth in the moment of great crisis. No
greater victory was ever won by the people of faith or Latin lead-
ers. The name of John will be remembered for as long as they will
speak of the arms of men, seas and lands, and fleets. 965

The commanders hail their supreme leader with a cry; kneel-
ing, they rejoice to touch his conquering hand. Pius, greatest fa-
ther, author of these works, is exalted to heaven along with the
House of Austria. With them, the Venetians are exalted, a people 970
famous throughout the world for their deeds. They look up at the
sky, and with happy voices they sing the hymn in the words of
Ambrose, with which we are duly accustomed to praise God be-
fore the altars, and to declare him Lord.

With the prows turned homeward, the happy men seek known
shores at a steady pace and are embraced by the friendly harbor 975
when, appearing high in the heavens, Hesperus rises and urges
mortals to withdraw into the late night.

287

: XXII :

Austrias Carmen

Juan Latino

Liber Primus

Deza gravis meritis, pietate insignis avita,
cui dotes animi reddit natura benigne,
clarus ab officiis et regis munere praeses,
Garnatae missus fato, civilia iura
5   ut regere imperio, cives regnumque tueri,
urbibus ut posses aequas concedere partes,
patratus patriae nostris celebratus in oris,
militibusque pater gratus tutorque bonorum,
excellens ductor, Baetis tutela per orbem.
10   Diceris esse tuis consultus iuris in hostem,
quem columen gentis nostrae regnique salutem
alma fides fecit; virtus sibi conscia recti
praesidium regale dedit tibi sorte regendum,
ingens ut pietas, nostris dum praesidet armis,
15   afflictos cives, urbem, tua iura, Philippe,
sollerti ingenio tutans servaret ab hoste.
Pervigil ipse diu cognosti cuncta parari,
haereticosque dolos, fraudes Maurosque moveri,
artes, insidias, simulatas ordine technas,
20   antiquum foedus pactum caedesque piorum.
Secretum Mauris tunc alta mente repostum
iudicio mentis valuisti cernere princeps.
Magnanimus pondus belli motusque recentes

: XXII :

The Song of John of Austria

Juan Latino

Book One

Deza, dignified by your service and marked by your ancestral
piety, on whom nature generously bestowed all the gifts of mind
and soul; renowned official and leader of the royal chancery: des-
tiny sent you to Granada to administer civil law, to watch over 5
the kingdom and its people, and to grant equal privileges to its
cities. You are revered on our shores as the nation's emissary, a
kindly father to the soldiers, protector of the virtuous, skilled
commander, and world-renowned guardian of Baetis. Known by 10
your people as an expert in wartime laws, nurturing faith made
you the defender of our nation and the safeguard of our king-
dom. Virtue, knowing what is right, put you in command of the
royal garrison so that your boundless piety and sharp mind would
guard our soldiers and protect our oppressed citizens, the city it- 15
self, and your laws, Philip, from the enemy. Ever watchful, you
knew to anticipate all manner of dangers: the deceit of the infi-
dels, the betrayal of the Moors, their ruses and tricks, artifices
masked as truth—all part of their age-old conspiracy to destroy 20
the pious. Your mind's eye, great prince, was able to discern the
plot then still buried deep in the minds of the Moors. With your
steadfast bravery, you bore the burden of war during the recent

Maurorum portans vitasti incommoda regni,
25   incolumem populum servans urbemque tumultu.
Hospitio fratrem cepisti ad bella Philippi,
quem domus ista fori, regali splendida luxu
et lautis dapibus pavit grandemque cohortem
larga manus tenuit mensis opibusque paratis.
30   Audi gesta tui iam dantis vela Ioannis,
perlege victorem, quo non felicior alter
in bellum veniens Hispanos duxit ad arma.
Quod si gesta cupis regum percurrere, Deza,
si vacat annales nostrae cognoscere gentis,
35   contuleris si forte duces, si bella per orbem
prospera, si volvas felicis fata Ioannis:
Hector, Romanus Caesar, tum Graecus Achilles,
felix sic nullus pugnavit, ad Actia bella
Augustum fugiens sordet Cleopatra carinis.
40   Non audita retro fastis victoria mundi,
exoptata diu nostris iam regibus una
Christicolis, fatis Austridae en parta Philippo.
Res gestae ut pelago; memorandus in orbe Ioannes,
quas strages dederit victor, quae corpora ponto
45   obruerit, naves captas quot traxerit inde,
Turcas, Bassanes, Parthos, quos miserit Orco.
Carolides fratris deducens arma Philippi,
pontificis sancti puppes Venetosque viriles,
unus quos Christus coniunxit foedere sacro,
50   ut referant unum Patrem Natumque potentem,
Spiritus ut Sanctus iam iunctos servet in unum.
Accipias vates orat supplexque Latinus
en petit, ut grandi tu princeps mente revolvas,
quae numquam saeclis poterit delere vetustas,

Morisco uprising and avoided any harm to the kingdom, keeping   25
the people and city safe from disturbance. You received Philip's
brother as your guest as he set out for war; your palace of govern-
ment feasted him with royal luxury and sumptuous banquets, and
your generous staff supported his large entourage with food and
ready supplies.

Listen now to the deeds of your John as he set sail: read about   30
him in victory. No one more blessed than he has ever led the
Spanish forces into battle. If you wish to pore over the deeds of
kings, Deza, if time allows you to study our nation's annals, if you   35
compare generals and successful military campaigns the world
over, if you reflect on the deeds of blessed John: no commander
has ever fought more capably, not Hector, Roman Caesar, Greek
Achilles, not even Augustus as the humiliated Cleopatra fled him
in her ships at the Battle of Actium. Such a victory as this was   40
unheard of in the history of the world, and though it was long
sought by our Christian kings, it was the destiny of John of Aus-
tria to deliver it to King Philip. His exploits took place at sea. Let
John be remembered throughout the world—all the devastation
he wrought as he conquered, all the bodies he submerged in the   45
waves, how many captive ships he towed back, and the Turks, Pa-
shas, and Parthians he sent to Orcus. This son of Charles mar-
shaled the forces of his brother, Philip, the ships of the Holy
Pontiff, and the mighty Venetians, whom Christ himself had
joined in a sacred treaty, so that they might remember the one   50
Father and his powerful Son, and so that the Holy Spirit might
keep them safe, now united as one.

The poet Latinus, your suppliant, prays that you receive and
ponder in your mind, great prince, these events that time can

55 quamvis sustineas Augusta negotia solus.
    Aspiret coeptis ut nostris rector Olympi
    et verus mentem dictis incendat Apollo,
    iustitiae sol natus homo de virgine Iesus;
    Catholicae Musae faveant Hispana canenti,
60 versibus ut plenum pietatis condere carmen
    nunc valeam lotus Parnasi in gurgite sancto,
    Romanae Ecclesae dono virtutis aquarum,
    virginis auspiciis narrabo et nomine Christi.
        Viderat exactos Mauros Garnata rebelles
65 haereticumque malum, manifestae crimina gentis
    extinctumque genus penitusque ex urbe revulsum,
    supplicium iuste regem sumpsisse Philippum.
    Consiliisque tuis, felici et nomine, Deza,
    constantique fide Christo dum fervis, ab urbe
70 iam Christi populos gentem vitasse nefandam
    miranturque duces fatum vicisse malignos,
    urbem qui nostram flammis incendere et arcem,
    aggressi prorsus Christos absumere cunctos.
        Urbs Garnata Deo grates dum solvere templis
75 destinat; ipse viros dum iungit carmine laetos,
    dum pompas ducitque choros precibusque fatigat
    Christicolas Petrus Guerrero pastor ad aras —
    moribus et vita, doctrinis clarus in orbe,
    religio cui summa viro sanctusque recessus
80 orandi populos arcebat lege periclis.
    Dum pastor lustrat maculatam gentibus urbem,
    templa Dei saxo vivi fundata vetusto,
    aedes sanctorum, praesentia numina Christi
    invocat et cives hortatur vivere sancte.
85   Nuntia fama volans iam vulgi impleverat aures:
    felices cursus classis, iam rem bene gestam,
    ad votum nostris venisse et prospera fatis;

never erase, even as you alone shoulder the burden of imperial af- 55
fairs. May the ruler of Olympus breathe blessings on our under-
takings. And may the true Apollo—Jesus, the sun of justice, born
a man from a virgin—kindle my mind with eloquence. May the
Catholic Muses look with favor on me as I sing of Spanish deeds,
so that I might now be able to compose a song filled with pious 60
verses; having bathed in the holy waters of Parnassus, by the grace
of baptism in the Roman Catholic Church, I will begin to tell my
story with the Virgin Mary's blessing and in Christ's name.

Granada watched as the rebellious Moriscos—a notorious race 65
of evil heretics—were expelled, and their entire caste was wiped
out or driven from the city, as King Philip exacted his just punish-
ment for their uprising. On your orders, Deza, as you burned with
your unwavering faith in Christ's blessed name, the Christian 70
people banished this nefarious race from the city, and marvel that
fate defeated those wicked leaders who set out to burn our city
and its fortress and massacre all the Christians within.

The city of Granada then resolves to give thanks to God in the
temples: the archbishop Pedro Guerrero—renowned throughout 75
the world for his morals, way of life, and doctrine—joins the
grateful men in song, as he leads ceremonial processions and
chants, and leads the people of Christ in unceasing prayer at the
altars. His great faith and holy meditation kept the people from 80
danger with the rule of prayer. While the bishop cleanses the city
from the heathen stain, the holy sanctuaries, and the temples of
the living God built on ancient rock, he invokes Christ's divine
presence and exhorts the people to live devoutly.

Now the winged messenger, Fama, had filled the ears of the 85
common people with news: that the fleet's journey was successful
and the mission was accomplished; that prosperous times had

navali instructos pugna, tum Marte superbos
vicisse et fractas ponto sparsisse carinas
90 Austria quem peperit clarum virtute Ioannem,
Parthorumque duces submersas aequore puppes,
disiectasque rates, Turcarum milia capta.
Ut iam Turca phalanx instructis navibus ibat
per Graias urbes captivam ducere praedam
95 coeperat et portus verrens per litora latos;
saepe Corinthiaci spumas salis aere secabat.
Tercentum longae rostris stridentibus agmen
implerant magnum scindentes aequora naves,
quot prius in portu Byzantum viderat ingens
100 Bosphorus angusto quas misit fervidus aestu.
In caelum pini surgebant; marmore silva,
arboribusque frequens fluctus percurrere visa est
Hispanam versus classem; nam iussa Tyranni
urgebant Turcas Hispanos quaerere late,
105 Herculis extremas sequerentur ad usque columnas,
(en tibi quo excellat princeps mens, Deza, superbi)
et traherent toto fugientes aequore puppes,
ni facerent iugulo poenas in morte daturi.
Concussique metu saevi dictisque Tyranni,
110 vela dabant Turcae iam pulsis ordine remis.
Ut mare vel Siculum lustrarant Cycladas olim,
sic Peloponnesi percurrunt litora fluctu,
Naupactum tendunt Epiri classe per isthmum.
Cum subito nostras cernunt adnare carinas,
115 regalem remis ingenti mole sequentes
vexillumque crucis celsas volitare sub auras,
et niveum spargi, fulgere et ducere cursus.
Salvator mundi tendebat bracchia fixus
monstrabatque latus cunctis adapertile ferro.

come to our lives in answer to our prayers; that John, born from 90
the House of Austria, brilliant in his virtue, had vanquished war-
riors skilled in naval combat and once proud in war, and had scat-
tered the Parthian leaders and plunged their galleys into the waves,
destroyed their vessels and seized thousands of Turkish prisoners.

As the Turkish attack force traveled in a fleet of galleys, it had
begun seizing spoils from the Greek cities and sweeping the spa- 95
cious seaports that lay along the shores, often cleaving the foam of
the Corinthian Sea with bronze. Three hundred warships with
screeching prows filled out the great flotilla as it sliced the waves,
the same number mighty Byzantium had seen in the harbor, when
the choppy Bosphorus conveyed them through its narrow passage. 100
The masts rose to the sky: a forest on the marble surface of the
sea, crowded with trees, seemed to race across the waves toward
the Spanish fleet. For the Tyrant ordered the Turks to follow the
Spaniards as far as the Pillars of Hercules, (look, Deza, how your 105
noble plan surpasses the sultan's strategy), and to pursue our
speeding ships across the entire sea; if they failed, they would pay
with their heads. Driven by fear and the savage Tyrant's com-
mands, the Turks set sail, their oars now beating in turn. Just as 110
they had once traversed the Cyclades or the Sea of Sicily, so now
they fly over the waves along the Peloponnesian shores, advancing
with their fleet through the Isthmus of Epirus toward Naupactus.

Suddenly they see our galleys sailing under oars following be- 115
hind the royal flagship in a giant mass. Then they see the standard
of the cross flying in the air, glimmering like fallen snow to
brighten and guide the way. The crucified Savior of the world
hung with his outstretched arms, showing to all his spear-pierced

120   Fert titulus felix inscriptum nomen Iesus,
      Hebraice ut Graece scripsit tunc ille Latine.
      Romanae Ecclesae mirantur terna per altum
      vexilla, in caelumque undis albescere Matris
      Virginis, ut lunae, pulchram radiare figuram.
125   Arma, duces, rictus aquilarum, signa Philippi
      erectosque viros, his dantem iura Ioannem
      conspiciunt, fratrem cognoscunt esse Philippi.
      Bassani missus, Luchalli regulus Alger,
      dixerat Hispanas fratrem vectare carinas.
130   Turcarum proceres, Bassan regnique phalanges,
      Phoebus cum primo spargebat lumine fluctus
      et radiis longe terras lustrabat apertas,
      ut videre virum fulgenti classe per undas,
      Illyricos ausumque duces ductare sequendo,
135   urbes Argolicas, portus cognoscere saevos.
      Quid struat his coeptis miratur Turca Ioannem,
      qui pelagi dominus Neptunus visus adesse,
      Hispanisque deus, manibus cui fuscina sceptrum
      esse videbatur, per fluctus rector aquarum
140   ire in conspectum nulla formidine captus.
      Stans celsa in puppi classem deducere felix,
      ausus qui Turcas Parthosque lacessere Marte,
      despiciens nomen magni dominique Selini.
      Obstupuere animis, confusi et mente superbi,
145   qui fragilem nostram sperarant fundere classem
      facturasque fugam, ut quondam fecere, carinas.
      Sors mutata viris, movit quae adversa timorem,
      aequa tuo Austriadae—Turcis contraria—princeps,
      concussit Parthos referentes omnia Parcis,
150   quos iuvenis fatum reddebat ab agmine tristes,
      regia progenies Quinti patrisque figura,

side. An auspicious inscription bore the name of Jesus, as Pilate 120
had written in Hebrew, Greek, and Latin. They are amazed to see
the triple banner of the Roman Church glistening white across the
waters and the pure image of the Virgin Mother shining like the
moon on the waves. They see artillery, commanders, menacing ea- 125
gle beaks — Philip's banners — men standing at attention, and John
— whom they recognize to be Philip's brother — giving them or-
ders. Uluj Ali, the governor of Algiers sent ahead by the Pasha,
had reported that the king's brother led the Spanish galleys. Phoe-
bus was scattering morning light on the waves, and lighting swaths 130
of land from afar with his rays when the Turkish commanders, the
Pasha, and the sultan's armies caught sight of the brave leader with
his dazzling navy across the waves. They saw that he dared to lead 135
the Illyrian leaders in pursuit, to reconnoiter the Greek cities and
hostile ports. The Turks wonder what John is planning with these
endeavors. He seemed to stand before them like Neptune, lord of
the sea, the Spaniards' god, his scepter like a trident in his hand as
he passed through the waves, the ruler of the waters. On his face, 140
he shows no fear; he stands joyfully on the lofty stern and guides
the fleet. He defies the Turks and Parthians to take him on in
battle, scorning the name of their mighty ruler Selim. They were
struck dumb in their hearts, their minds alternately perplexed and
disdainful. They had expected to sink our feeble fleet, as they did 145
before, with our galleys in retreat. Yet Fortune had turned on these
men, Fortune who incites fear when she is hostile; but now, favor-
ing your John and turning against the Turks, first she struck the
Parthians, who blamed their setbacks on the Fates. Indeed, the 150
young man's destiny sent them back from the battle line in despair,
the royal son of Charles V, in the manner of his father, a terrifying

Carolus ostensus terrens, quae concutit orbem,
nomine maiestas superantis regna Philippi
et classis coniuncta Deo terrebat in undis.

155   Compressoque gradu lunae curvantur in arcum
cornibus adversis, referentes fronte Dianam
lucentem, primo visam tunc surgere mense,
adverso faciem niveam se ostendere sole.
Extensi pelago tendebant cornua late,

160   ordinibus raris pergebat classis in altum,
pluribus ut visi terrerent puppibus agmen,
Hispanaeque procul trepidarent undique naves,
paulatimque ducem Turcae de more secuti.

      Regia puppis erat praestanti milite plena,

165   foeta armis. Senae puppes quam mole tegebant
atque latus geminum servabant agmine tutum,
ad pugnam Turcas reddebant tempore promptae.
Si quando in bello miles succumberet, illinc
adiutor praesto saliebat Turca satelles,

170   auxiliumque recens capiebat regia bello,
qua Bassan vectus ductabat fortia secum
pectora, magnanimos Turcas in bella paratos,
arma, duces, robur populorum, munera, pondus,
argenti saccos, auri tot ferre talenta.

175   Spes rerum tantas mittebat classe Tyrannus,
ut Graecos Venetos prorsus deleret in undis,
quosque rebellantes sensit virtute Philippi
et patris sancti monitis contemnere Turcas.
Stabat in arma phalanx expectans iussa regentis.

180   Cornua iam verti mandat classemque parari,
et rostra in nostros conversus rector agebat;
Hispanas naves tendit submergere primas,
instruxit puppes, quae terga et milite forti
servarent tuta, et promptos dedit ire maniplos.

apparition of Charles; John of Austria's majesty stuns the world in
the name of Philip, conqueror of kingdoms. Thus, the fleet joined
by God spread fear on the waves.

   With measured pace, the galleys bend into the shape of a cres-   155
cent moon with parallel horns, like gleaming Diana when she rises
at the start of each month and shows her snow-white face to the
sun. In this formation, they spread their wings wide over the sea.
The fleet advanced across the deep in thinly scattered lines to   160
strike fear in the enemy column at the sight of so many galleys and
to terrify the Spanish ships from afar. Keeping to their custom,
the Turks follow a few at a time behind their leader.

   The flagship was packed with high-ranking soldiers, brimming   165
with weaponry. A group of six galleys gave it cover and guarded
the twin flanks, ferrying Turks quickly to the front lines. If a sol-
dier fell in battle, a Turkish escort boat rushed in and the flagship   170
received immediate support in the fight. On it sailed the Pasha,
bringing with him strong warriors, brave, battle-tested Turks,
along with arms, officers, the strongest of foot soldiers, provisions,
heavy sacks of silver, and almost as many gold bars. The Tyrant   175
held out great hope that his fleet would quickly crush the Greeks
and Venetians in the waves, and he was convinced that some of
those returning to battle underestimated the Turks because of
Philip's power and the Holy Father's prophecies. The fighting
force awaited commands from the flagship. The order now comes   180
to turn the flanks and prepare the fleet, and the pilot maneuvers to
position the rams against our men, striving to sink the Spanish
galleys in the front line. He deployed some ships to protect the
rearguard with strong fighters and instructed the readied infantry

185   In frontem Bassan, quem vexit regia puppis,
    conversus stabat medius pugnamque regebat.
       Hoc habitu Parthus visusque hac, Deza, figura;
    cui pharetra ex humero pendebatque aureus arcus
    isque caput nivea cingens et tempora vitta.
190   Pileus inde ruber surgebat vertice cano,
    regia cui vestis talos defluxit ad imos,
    ensem fulmineum dextra versabat in auras,
    exemplum praestans Turcis Parthisque virile,
    bellator summus veniens, quem Turca superbus
195   praefecit classi gestorum nomine clarum.
       Nam princeps mirus deducere in arma triremes,
    qui missus felix ductarat saepe triumphos
    et bellum ductor multos iam gesserat annos
    isque Ali Bassan ferebatur nomine Turcis,
200   praeposito cunctis piratis iure Selinus
    cognatam nuptum dederat. Geminique nepotes
    ardentes iuvenes comitati ad bella parentem,
    qui patris vultus referebant ore minaci,
    monstrabant facies, ardentia lumina gentis.
205   Spem classis Bassan, geminos in bella leones,
    instituitque feros adversus regna Philippi,
    assuetos fluctus teneris contemnere ab annis,
    proelia dura pati, possent ut vulnera ferre.
       Nescia mens hominum fati delusit amantem
210   disiunxitque duos natos et Parca parentem.
    Felix morte pater, captivos cernere quando,
    nec valuit tantum vivus tunc ferre dolorem;
    quamvis saeva diu passus cum classica ductat,
    quis fratres patri rapiendos diceret undis?

to advance. In the middle, the Pasha, carried atop the royal flag-   185
ship, stood facing the front and directed the attack.

This Parthian, Deza, appeared in the following costume and
demeanor: from his shoulder hung a quiver and gilded bow. He
wrapped a white turban around his head and temples. A red Phry-   190
gian cap rose from his gray hair. A royal robe billowed down to his
heels, while his right hand brandished a flashing sword in the air.
He was an outstanding example of strength for the Turks and
Parthians. This was the consummate warrior to whom the proud
Turk entrusted the command of the fleet, known by reputation for   195
his military exploits.

Indeed, this wondrous prince who now guided the warships
into battle had often led triumphant campaigns. He had already
waged war as a commander for many years, and he was known to
the Turks as Ali Pasha. Following the custom observed by all pi-   200
rates, Selim had given his sister to him in marriage. His two sons,
passionate youths, followed their father into battle. They resem-
bled their father with their menacing faces, showing the complex-
ions and fiery eyes of their race. The Pasha raised them to be twin   205
lions in war, the hope of the fleet, hostile to Philip's realms, inured
to the sea's waves from earliest youth, so they could endure harsh
battles and blows.

The human mind, ignorant of fate, deceived him, and Destiny
divided the two sons from their loving father. Blessed in his death,   210
he never saw them taken captive: he never could have borne such
sorrow alive. He suffered terrible things while he led the fleet, but
who could speak of brothers taken from their father by the waves?

215   At fatis cedens vivet dum fama Philippi,
       nec spem Turcarum tolli ducique triumpho,
       nec vidit classem nomenque perisse Tyranni.
       Indulsit fortuna duci patrique pepercit.
          Ductores seni tutelam classis agebant,
220   fidos rectores dederat per regna Tyrannus,
       horum consiliis ductabat classica Bassan,
       qui puppes nostras angustis faucibus isthmi
       opprimere optabat cautusque extinguere cunctas,
       dum cohibent proras duro retinacula ferro.
225   Interea sortes urna bis ducere tentat,
       venerat in dubium sors ipsa, et calculus idem.
       Volveret ipse ducum Bassan monumenta priorum,
       orabant proceres Turcarum et multa superbi
       exempla ingentes repetebant facta per undas
230   et classis nostrae ductorem temnere visi.
       Rursus fata timent Parthi rerumque recursus
       fortunaeque vices, sors iam mutabilis angit.
       Quod iuvenis tantam tendat contingere laudem,
       contigerit simile exemplum ductoribus olim,
235   si forte in terris orant pelagove fuisset,
       qui iuvenis gentem superasset in agmine Turcam?
       'O demens,' dixit, 'gestorum ignara iuventus!'
       Inter currendum narrabat ductor acerbus,
       adversum fatum, quod iam sibi forte timebat.
240   'Succurrat gestum iuveni memorabile bellum,
       Hannibal ut quondam Romano victus ab hoste,
       postquam Romanas vicit domuitque phalanges,
       post tot res Italas, viduatam et civibus urbem,
       succubuit Poenus iuvenili sorte repulsus.
245   Scipio quem felix superavit Marte superbum,
       Poeno congressus rupit Cornelius Afros,
       Africa cui nomen peperit virtute paratum.

But yielding to his fate, he will live as long as Philip's fame. He did   215
not watch his two sons, the hope of the Turks, carried away and
paraded in triumph, nor did he see the destruction of the fleet and
the Tyrant's name. Fortune looked kindly on the admiral and
spared the father.

Six commanders guided the fleet's course: trustworthy leaders   220
from across the kingdom, each appointed by the Tyrant. The Pa-
sha led the navy with their advice, aiming to pinch our prows in
the narrow straits of the isthmus and safely destroy them all while
cables of hard iron kept the ships at bay. Meanwhile, he twice   225
pulls lots from an urn, but each draw and each stone comes out
uncertain. The haughty Turkish officers begged the Pasha to think
on the exploits of past admirals, remembering their many praise-
worthy feats at sea, and seemed to scorn the commander of our   230
fleet. But still the Parthians fear the Fates, the twists of destiny,
and Fortune's vagaries; now fickle luck torments them. Could this
young leader win such fame as those exemplary commanders once
did? What young man, they ask, could possibly defeat the Turkish   235
nation on land or sea? "Oh foolish youth," he said, "ignorant of
past events!" The stern leader addressed them as they advanced,
perhaps because he feared fate had already turned against him:
"Another famous battle waged by a young man comes to mind,   240
when Hannibal was defeated by his Roman opponent. After the
Carthaginian had routed and subdued entire Roman legions, after
he had waged so many campaigns in Italy, after the city itself was
widowed of its people, he was forced to surrender to a young
man's destiny. Cornelius Scipio destroyed the Carthaginian's Afri-   245
can army and had the good fortune to defeat that proud man in
war, for which Africa gave him a name to match his achievement.

Scipio sic Turcas poterit terrere Philippi
alter ut Actiacas bello rapuisse carinas,
250   Augustus fertur Romamque tulisse triumphum.
Vos tandem iuvenis fatali nomine Turcas
concutiat, Caroli natus fraterque Philippi est,
quos orbis reges exhorrent; barbara regna his
imperio superanda manent, si vincimur ipsi.
255   Quare agite et fortes rapiendam fundite classem,
audacem iuvenem subvertat Turca virilis.'

Iniecit quamquam scrupulum ductoribus altum,
addidit haec dicens stimulos rectoribus acres,
hinc timor ipse viros tangit, sors inde revolvit
260   (ut te, Deza, diu torquebant fata Ioannis,
plurima per noctem volventem incommoda ponti),
magnanimosque duces tentat victoria classis:
'Aut vinci aut victos Hispanos sternere late,'
decrevit Bassan ductor cunctique sequuntur.

265   Austriades longas animosus currere naves
iusserat in Turcas iam fuso sole per altum;
regalis puppis cernens custodia longe,
ecce duo adverso vidisse in marmore vela,
nuntiat Austriadae, classem sic ordine totam.
270   Parthos Austriades bello ductare triremes,
ordine quasque suum Bassanem rite secutas,
Turcarumque procul celsas fulgere carinas
ut vidit puppes aequatis pergere velis
Hispanosque suos gaudentes cernere Turcas,
275   iam cupidos pugnae, meditantes proelia telis.
Concipit audaces animos iam vincere gestit
incenditque virum patris nunc aemula virtus,
regia fama ducis gestis vulganda per orbem,
concussit iuveni generosum pectus in armis.

304

So Philip's new Scipio will wreak havoc on the Turks, just as they   250
say Augustus seized warships at Actium and led them in triumph
to Rome. This youth will smite you Turks with his fateful name,
for he is the son of Charles and brother of Philip, before whom
the kings of the world shudder; if we are defeated, the barbarian
realms lie open to be brought under their sway. Therefore go,   255
bravely sink the fleet and take its spoils. May the mighty Turk
overcome the bold youth."

Although he inspired deep dread in the commanders, he added
these words as a sharp prod for the officers. This fear then reaches
the soldiers, their luck turns (just as John's fortune troubled you,   260
Deza, as you pondered through the night the many dangers at
sea), and victory rouses the fleet's brave leaders: "Either be van-
quished or utterly crush the vanquished Spaniards," the Pasha
cried out, and all the men follow.

John of Austria, undaunted, had ordered the long warships to   265
charge the Turks when the sunlight spilled over the sea. The flag-
ship's watchman gazes out into the distance: look, he tells John
that he has seen two sails in the sea ahead, and then the full navy
in formation. John of Austria saw the Parthians readying their gal-   270
leys for battle, each duly following his Pasha; the towering Turkish
warships shining from afar; and their galleys advancing with open
sails. He saw his Spaniards rejoice as they caught sight of the
Turks, so eager for combat, testing their weapons for battle. Seeing   275
their bold spirits, John now yearns to conquer. A valor akin to his
father's rouses him; royal fame, to be spread the world over by
his deeds as commander, stirs the youth's noble heart for battle.

280 Gloria nunc fratris, regni fortuna, potestas,
unius in sortem commissa Hispania tangit.
In se conversos oculos atque ora videbat
(en curas hominum, regumque en dura potestas,
queis regni cupidis numquam dat cura quietem).
285 Italiae facies, Romae trepidantis imago,
attentus Gallus, visa est Germania mota,
Graecia capta suos extendere vertice canos,
Oceanusque procul, peregrini litora mundi,
haeretici Maurique arrectis auribus Arctos;
290 expectant reges, cui iam victoria cedat.
Terribilis classis, Parthorum fama per orbem,
eventus belli varius, res unica, miles,
degener Hispanus Turcis, iam visus ab armis
et toties victus. Torquent Bassanque Pialli et—
295 hic victor nuper Getulis Syrtibus, ille
assuetus pelago captas deducere classes,
Hispanae gentis Parthis suspensa trophaea—
volvebant mentem iuvenili in pectore grandem.
        Sed Christi auspiciis et Matris Virginis audax
300 divinis avibus vincendum tendit in hostem,
ostendens vultum placidum faciemque virilem
(qua tibi saepe volens arrisit regia proles,
si quid, Deza, piis monitis evenerat apte,
consiliisque tuis non usus saepe dolebat)
305 et frons laeta suis iam spem faciebat amicis.
Quamvis consiliis nondum maturus ab annis,
excelsam generis mentem natura movebat,
prudentesque viros superabat regia virtus.
        Nam multi patres summis de rebus agebant
310 consilio et quantum posset nova fama regentis,
quo praedulce decus iuvenem compellat et ardor
vincendi Turcas reddendaque gloria soli. Haec

His brother's glory, the kingdom's fate and power, and Spain — en- 280
trusted to his fate alone — now move him. He saw that all eyes and
faces turned toward him (alas, the cares of men, the onerous
power of kings; duty never grants respite to those who long for
royal rule). He could see Italian faces, the likeness of fearful Rome; 285
the alert Gaul; unsettled Germany; captive Greece spreading her
long white hair from her head; and far away, the ocean, the shores
of an exotic world, the heretics and Moors, and the Greater and
Lesser Bear with ears pricked; kings wait to see to which side vic- 290
tory will fall. There was the formidable fleet, and the Parthian's
reputation throughout the world; war's uncertain outcome; the
singularity of the event; the Spanish soldier's inferiority to the
Turks, already demonstrated in as many defeats as battles waged.
For their part, the Pasha and Piali were anxious — the latter re- 295
cently victorious over the Getulian Syrtes, the former accustomed
to bring home scores of ships captured at sea, Spanish trophies
hung for the Parthians — and they both worried about the bold
plan within that young heart.

   But the youth, emboldened by Christ's good omens and the
Virgin Mother's sacred signs, advances to conquer the enemy with 300
a calm expression and brave face (the king's son so often smiled at
you in this way, Deza, if something turned out well because of
your pious counsel, and he would often regret not heeding your
advice). His joyful face spread hope among his allies. Though John 305
was not yet mature in counsel because of his years, nature had in-
stilled in him his family's superior intellect, and his royal virtue
surpassed even prudent men. Now many elders were debating the
most critical issues: even with their advice, how much could this 310
ruler's newfound fame accomplish? Where would sweet honor and
his zeal for defeating the Turks drive the youth? What glory
would he claim for himself alone? With their cautious minds and

noverat ingenium prudens et grandior aetas,
experta et quo fata trahant retrahantque sequendum.
315 Hi rerum summae cauti per cuncta timebant
in tempus praesens pugnam differre volentes,
cum maior posset nullo discrimine classis
vincere captivam ferro et superare minorem.
Ambabus virtus summa est nam classibus, illi
320 ultima mors referunt congressas dividet ambas:
'Praestat nunc tempus nostris exquirere rebus
cum faveat classi ventura occasio tantae,
omniaque ad votum facili ratione recurrant.'
Hi 'nihil invita faciamus sorte per undas,
325 cuius paeniteat fecisse,' adversa petebant,
'dicere nam stultum est terris undisve "putaram."
At si fortunam volumus tentare,' fremebant,
'victores victique duces rumpemur et arma,
ibunt in dubium classes ductorque Ioannes,
330 in quo — post Christum — spem nostra Hispania sistit.
Aequabit luctus Mars ipse et funus utrisque
Europa atque Asia hic vires iam perdet in aevum.
Nam quae gens ibit tanto certamine laeta?
Si victis Turcis Hispani forte dolemus?'
335 Talia grandaevi memorantes dicta viritim,
spes tantas horae momento tradere nollent.
Quo magis Austriadae mentem discrimina tentant,
hoc minus ille silex cautesve ut dura movetur,
grandibus et constans incendit pectora dictis:
340 'Alea iacta est haec, vincendum, estote parati,'
Austriades cunctis respondens addit, 'in hostem
sumite tela manu fortes, impellite remos.
Quis Christi miles dubitat nunc tendere in hostes,
qui videat Turcas, inimicae et nomina sectae?
345 Rumpite iamque moras, omnes iam tollite causas.'

advanced age they understood all this: they knew a man must fol-
low wherever the Fates led him. With utmost caution, they were   315
fearful in all respects, wishing to delay battle until a more favorable
time, when a larger fleet could, without risk, vanquish the cor-
nered navy with its rams and overpower the smaller force. The
strength of both fleets is great, and some insist that in the end   320
death will decide between the clashing navies: "Now is the time to
press on in our efforts, when the coming event favors a mighty
fleet, and all things come about with ease as we desire." Others
presented contrary arguments: "Let us do nothing we might regret
to have done when the Fates are against us on the sea." "On land   325
or sea, it is foolish to say 'I had assumed so'; but if we wish to
tempt fortune," they muttered, "we will all be crushed: both the
victors and the vanquished leaders, along with our arsenal; the
fleets will be in danger, along with the commander, John, in
whom, after Christ, our Spain places its hope. Mars himself will   330
distribute grief and death evenly to both sides; Europe, like Asia,
will lose soldiers in their prime. What nation will go with joy into
so great a battle? For won't we Spaniards suffer even if the Turks
are conquered?"

  Speaking these words each in turn, the senior commanders   335
might not have wished to betray great hopes at this critical mo-
ment. But the more dangers test John's resolve, the less he — like a
rock or an unyielding cliff — is shaken, and he steadfastly fires his
heart with brave words: "This die is cast; we must conquer, ready   340
yourselves." Speaking to all, he adds: "Brave men, brandish your
weapons against the enemy, strike the oars. What soldier of Christ
who looks on the Turks and the names of their hateful sect now
hesitates to charge the enemy? So now break off your delay; end   345

(Incensusque tuus referebat, Deza, Ioannes,
quid valeat belli rapienda occasio rebus.)
'En volvenda dies votum nunc attulit ultro,
quod nostri numquam valuerunt cernere reges.
350 Hispanae an pelago poterant sperare cohortes?
Quod ne aliud tempus? Quae sors? An gratior ulla
esse potest Christo ductore et auspice Christo,
quem ferimus ligno pendentem hic agmine vero?
Quis coluber feriet viroso dente cohortem?
355 Cernentesque crucem poterunt sperare salutem,
victores nautae salvasque videre carinas;
Turcarum pestis fugiet, pelagoque retrorsum
adversus Bassan, serpens iam fusus, abibit.
Diripiet pugnax aurum vestemque iuventus,
360 arma, rates Turcas, tormenta et ferrea, signa;
e pelago veniet classis iam victa Philippo.
Audere est opus in Turcas, fert cetera Christus:
ille dabit cursum, cui parent aequora, venti;
ille reget classem, Turcas submerget et arma;
365 ille et per fluctus Bassanem fundet iniquum,
Aegypti ut quondam Pharaones mersit in undas.
Omnipotensque suo coniunctis nomine vincet.'

Dicentis vocem tollunt ad sidera patres,
regia dicta notant, pietatis plena verentur,
370 concipiunt vires longaevo in pectore grandes,
exortis lacrimis Dominum laudare frequentes
non cessant, classi qui tantum reddere summae
ductorem voluit natum felicibus annis.
Assensere duces, Andres, Marcusque Colonna,
375 Marchio Bazanus, commotus honore Philippi,
consensit pelago Turcis concurrere pulchrum.
Ex animo cuncti iam fassi crimina rite
orant servari manibus genibusque Ioannem:

all debating. (All ablaze, your John was repeating your advice, Deza, that what matters in war is to seize the moment.) Look, the revolving day has fulfilled of its own accord the promise which our kings were never able to witness. Have not the Spanish legions been able to sustain their hopes at sea? What better moment? What other chance? Could any occasion be more favorable, if Christ is our leader and safeguard, whom we carry, hanging on the true cross, here in the battle line? What snake will strike this fleet with its poison fang? As they look at the cross, our triumphant sailors will be able to hope for safety and see their ships saved. The plague of the Turks will flee, and our enemy, the Pasha, will shrink back on the sea, a serpent now routed. Our fighting youth will seize gold, garments, arms, Turkish vessels, catapults, weaponry, and banners; their fleet will withdraw from the sea, duly defeated for Philip. We must dare to face the Turks; Christ will do the rest. He, whom the water and the winds obey, will guide our course; he will lead the fleet, sink the Turks and their weapons. He will submerge the wicked Pasha in the swells of the sea, as he once submerged Pharaoh in the waves of Egypt. And the Almighty will prevail for those allied in his name."

The elders praise the speaker's words to the stars, acknowledging his kingly words and honoring his piety. Noble courage stirs in their aged hearts: with tears welling forth, they praise the Lord without ceasing because he was pleased to bestow on the great fleet so mighty a leader born in auspicious times. The commanders Andrea Doria and Marco Colonna assent; Marquis Bazán, moved by Philip's honor, agrees that it is glorious to attack the Turks at sea. Having all duly confessed their sins from the heart, they pray—hands clasped, on bended knee—for John's safety:

350

355

360

365

370

375

'Sis memor ipse Deus nostri, iuvenemque gubernes,'
380   redditur alta viris, 'Vivat,' vox omnibus una
insequitur clamor nautis clangorque tubarum,
hostem iam quaerunt animis et corpore toto.
    Audivere rates ductoris classica longe
remigium cunctis aptatur navibus ingens,
385   nudatosque humeros ostentat rara iuventus.
Haec classis virtus, haec vis, haec, Deza, potestas,
qua naves currunt, fugiunt pedibusque sequuntur
et remis vincit, remis dux regnat in undis,
nautarumque animis spes ponto haec altera fertur.
390   In transtrisque pares intendunt bracchia remis,
auribus arrectis signum expectare videres,
corda pavor pulsat mentesque incendit in hostem,
ira furorque novus consurgit perdere Turcas.
    Ductores animosa cohors — in puppibus altis
395   fulgentes armis — trepidos incendere nautas
incipiunt dictis: 'Vexillum ut quisque sequatur,
pugnet victurus, nam Christi nomine vincet.'
Terque quaterque viri referentes verba Ioannis,
ductoris similes cuncti de more regebant.
400   Sed remex Maurus captus vinctusque catenis,
inter spem timidus Turcas dum cernit amicos,
iratis ducibus mortem sibi quisque timere.
Quos cautus ductor verbis terrere superbis
incipit et gladio fulgenti magna minatur:
405   'Prospice, Maure, tuae remex en consule vitae,
remigii numerum ni turbas arte maligna
atque fidem nostris servas ductoribus unam,
victore Austriada tu liber sorte futurus.
Quod si mendosus remum nunc pellere tentas

"God be mindful of us and guide our young commander." One   380
deep voice rang out from all the men: "Long may he live!" Then
follows a shout from the sailors and the blast of trumpets. Now
they pursue the enemy with their whole hearts and all their
strength.

The fleet heard the commander's trumpet call from afar. A vast
rowing deck is fitted to all the galleys, and here and there the   385
young men reveal bare shoulders. This is the fleet's power, Deza.
This is its strength, the force by which the galleys run, flee, and
follow with foot soldiers. A commander conquers with oars, and
with oars he rules the waves: this is said to be the other source of
hope in the minds of all sailors at sea. On the thwarts, pairs of   390
rowers set their arms to the oars. You would have seen them wait
for the signal with ears perked. Fear beats in their hearts and fires
their minds against the enemy; a new wrath, a new fury rises to
destroy the Turks.

The commanders — a brave group — up high on the sterns and
resplendent in arms begin to rouse the fearful sailors with their   395
words: "Let each follow the standard, and fight to conquer, for he
will vanquish in Christ's name." Three and four times, the men
repeat John's words, all giving their commands in the same manner
as their commander.

Yet each Moorish rower, captured and bound in chains, is ap-   400
prehensive even in the midst of his hope when he sees his Turkish
comrades, and fears his own death if the commanders are angered.
A vigilant captain begins to frighten them with menacing words,
and sword flashing, snarls: "Eyes forward, Moor, think of your   405
own life. If you do not disrupt our oar strokes with evil tricks, and
if you keep faith with our leaders, when John of Austria prevails,
perhaps you will be free. But if you treacherously strive to row the

410 ut Turcis operam des iam victoribus, ipse
tardanti stricto hoc iugulum mucrone resolvam.
Proditor et salsas ibis iam truncus in undas.'
    Invitus quamvis remum pellebat acerbe
et limis oculis Turcas spectabat ovantes,
415 nota nimis miseris lunam referentia signa,
Parthorum seriem regum monstrantia Turcis;
impellens dulcis patriae reminiscitur agros,
cui mors aut summo libertas danda periclo.
    Austriades, cernens in Turcas arma parari
420 praecinctosque duces, naves et robora belli,
emicat e puppi per proram regia proles.
Inspicit armatam telis fulgere cohortem.
Incedens navis rectores consulit omnes
et galea tectusque caput cristisque decorus,
425 exultat ductor praecinctus flore iuventae,
armatus pectus lorica et fortibus hamis.
Arripit inde manu telum, quod vibret in hostem.
Tunc cymba vectus summas perlabitur undas,
visurus puppes agiles structosque magistros.
430 (Regum nunc animo surgant tibi, Deza, labores)
Austriades visus sic lintre occurrere Caesar
Iulius, hunc remex comitatus gurgite quondam
Hellespontiaco captus ubi Cassius uni.
    Lenisiusque comes ibat vir fidus Achates,
435 advectus bello generosa a stirpe parentum,
non opibus parcens cognati Martis amore.
Corduba nam genuit bellantum prodiga mater,
quae Mariscallos victores attulit orbi
et solita est quondam Gonsalvos edere magnos
440 felicesque duces bello non aere Suessas,
pauperie et claros referentes Marte Camillos.

314

oars to assist the Turkish conquerors, I myself will sever your lag- 410
gard's neck with this drawn sword. Then your body, traitor, will
fall headless into the salty waves."

Though unwilling, the Moor rowed on bitterly, casting sidelong
glances at the cheering Turks. He sees the standards — known so
well to those wretches — emblazoned with the image of the moon, 415
displaying the succession of Parthian kings. As he rows, poised
between death and liberty in the gravest danger, he remembers the
fields of his sweet fatherland.

John of Austria, the king's son, surveys the artillery aimed at
the Turks, his commanders ready in arms, his ships, and their 420
fighting force, dashing from stern to prow. He inspects the armed
troops flashing with weapons. As he goes, he confers with all the
ships' pilots. Then donning a helmet embellished with feathers,
the leader rejoices, girded with the bloom of youth, his chest 425
shielded by a cuirass with strong clasps. Then, he snatches a
weapon in his hand and brandishes it against the enemy. Borne in
a skiff, he skims the high waves to inspect the agile ships and the
ready commanders. (The toil of kings should now come to mind, 430
Deza.) John seemed to cross in his boat like Julius Caesar, whom
a rower once accompanied on the straits of the Hellespont, where
he alone took Cassius captive.

Then came Luis, his faithful Achates, drawn to battle by his 435
parents' noble lineage, sparing no expense in his inherited love of
war. For Cordova bore him, prodigious mother of warriors, who
gave the world victorious field marshals and engendered the line
of mighty Gonzalos. The Dukes of Sessa, blessed in war if not 440
in wealth, brought to mind the famous family of the Camilli in

Consiliis ibatque Soto rebusque gerendis,
quem fratri dederat meditans Augusta Philippus.
Hoc comite Austriades visebat classica laetus,
445 nunc has, nunc illas, perlustrans aequore naves;
orabat memores pugnarent nomine Christi,
ne magni faciant Turcas sed Marte resistant.
Nam si Hispana cohors quaesisset proelia prima,
si noster miles si dux ivisset in hostem,
450 Ausoniae hinc numquam vastaret litora Bassan,
nec Graeci aut Veneti Parthos Turcasve timerent.
Hispanus semper remeasset victor ad arces,
victrices naves vidisset et arma Philippus,
Hispana in Turcas felicia signa redissent
455 et nostros numquam trepidantes Turca videret.
'Audere est opus in Turcas, fert cetera Christus.
Diximus et repetens iterum per cuncta monebo.
Spiritus arma dabit Sanctus, mortalia vincet,
principium pugnae cum Christo in proelia curro.
460 Per Christum nostris veniet victoria laeta.
Quare agite et primi Martem committite mecum,
vincimus, en Christus pro nobis astat in armis.'
Catholicus Christi repetebat nomen amicis
Austriades, nostros victores saepe vocabat,
465 magnanimus Turcas perituros nomine tanto
dictabat prudens ductor, ventura canendo.
Ad navem versus fidos affatur amicos,
commendatarium maiorem amplectitur, orat:
'Huc, huc bellator, iam nostra, huc respice fata;
470 felix Marte sequi gentemque incendere ductu,
gloria nostra tibi commissa et vita Philippo,
tu belli mecum sortitus magna pericla,
nunc maiora feres, quae Mars non novit et ipse.
Certatur pelago, concurrit viribus orbis.

poverty and arms. Also present for the planning and preparations
was Juan de Soto, whom Philip, as befitting an emperor, had as-
signed to his brother. With this man as his companion, John was
cheerfully reviewing the fleet, scanning the ships on the water, first   445
these, now those. He prayed they would fight mindful of Christ's
name; that they would not overestimate the Turks, but resist them
in battle. For if the Spanish army had sought battle earlier, if our
soldiers, our leader had charged the enemy, then the Pasha would   450
never have sacked the shores of Ausonia; the Greeks and Vene-
tians would not fear the Parthians or the Turks; the Spaniard
would have always returned victorious to his castle; Philip would
have seen triumphant ships and weapons; the blessed Spanish
standard would have marched against the Turks; and the Turk   455
would never have seen fear in our troops. "We must dare to attack
the Turks; Christ does the rest. So I have said, and so I will advise
again in any situation: the Holy Spirit will take up arms and tri-
umph over mortal concerns. At the start of the fight, with Christ
at my side I run into battle. Through Christ, joyful victory will   460
come to our troops. So go, and with me be the first to engage in
battle. Then we shall conquer, for look, Christ stands with us in
arms." Catholic John of Austria invoked Christ's name for his
comrades, often recalling our victories; courageous and prudent as
a leader, he proclaimed that the Turks would perish along with   465
their great name, heralding things to come. Back in his galley, he
speaks to his faithful companions, and embraces the senior com-
mander, beseeching: "Here, here warrior, look now at our destiny:
you are blessed to follow Mars and inspire the nation with leader-   470
ship. Our glory and our life are entrusted to you and to Philip.
You chose to endure the grave perils of war with me; now you will
endure dangers still greater, that even Mars himself has not known.
The battle is waged on the sea, and the whole world clashes with

475 Hinc Christus pugnat, illinc Mahumeta superbus.
Ille pius nostra dux fundet classe Tyrannum.
Regali, ductor, me semper respice, puppi
si quid defuerit, praesto sis, prospice classi,
vincamus fortes; en Christus vota secundat.'

480 Ad quem magnanimus Requesenes reddidit heros,
Augustis iuveni dictis exaggerat iras:
'Tu Caroli vinces hodie virtute parentis,
vincere iam poteris Turcas, quia posse videris.
Sors concessa tibi hos nunc debellare superbos,

485 ut pelago regnans consurgat ad astra Philippus.
Bassani iugulum victor mucrone resolves,
iam rerum Dominus felici hac sorte futurus,
disiectos Parthos, captivos Marte videbis.'
Annuit omnipotens, qui nutu fata gubernat.

490 Spem iuvenis magnam vincendi concipit hostem,
et saepe in Turcas conversus plurima mandat,
qui mira proras aptavit et arte carinas,
scindere praecepit rostratas ordine naves,
congressus facili miles concurrere Turcis

495 ut posset plano et Parthos invadere saltu,
ne in fluctus iret, pugnae si intenta iuventus,
nec caderet subito miles, dum pugnat, in undas.
Amplexusque iterum lacrimis instillat amicis
commendatque viro classem nomenque Philippi.

500 Tunc sese ad reliquos conversus concitat omnes,
Tuscos Germanos Venetos Italosque Liburnos
Hispanosque suos dictis incendit honestis:
'Eia, estote viri memores ad cuncta Philippi,
qui manibus vestris fratrem commisit et armis,

505 vos pater ut quondam victores vidit in orbe.
Per vos res Italas vicit duxitque triumphos;

all its strength. Here, Christ fights; there, proud Muhammad. 475
That pious leader will rout the Tyrant with our fleet. Helmsman,
watch me constantly. If the flagship should falter, stand ready, be
on the watch for the fleet. Let us be strong and conquer. Christ
favors our prayers." To whom the noble hero Requesens replied, 480
stoking the young man's rage with regal words: "Today you will
conquer with virtue worthy of your father Charles. You will be
able to defeat the Turks because you seem to be able. It has fallen
to your lot to subdue these proud men, so that Philip may reach 485
the stars by ruling the waves. In victory, you will sever the Pasha's
throat with your sword. By this blessed fate, you will be lord of all,
you will see vanquished Parthians taken captive in war." The Al-
mighty, who governs the Fates with a nod, gave his assent.

   The youth remains hopeful about defeating the enemy, and 490
looking often toward the Turks, he issues many orders. With stun-
ning skill, he had the prows and keels fitted out, and ordered that
they divide the beaked warships in a line, one after another, so
that when the soldiers engage the Turks, they can fight from an 495
easy angle and overtake the Parthians with a leap; otherwise the
young men, focused on the fight, might slip into the seawater or
suddenly fall overboard while they do battle. In tears John again
embraces his comrades and entrusts the fleet and Philip's honor to
the soldiers. Then he turns to exhort the rest—Tuscans, Ger- 500
mans, Venetians, Italians, and Liburnians—and to inspire his
Spaniards with stirring words: "Comrades, be mindful of Philip
in all things, for he has put his brother in charge of your armies
and weapons, much as my father saw you triumphant around the 505
world. It was because of you that he won his Italian campaigns

haereticos vobis superavit fretus ad Albim.
Filius Hispanos vos ducto in bella leones;
imperium pelagi vobis en traditur unum,
510   vobis spes grandes, vobis sua regna Philippus,
fortunamque meam, classem tot milia gentis,
vobis — lecta phalanx — commisit. Spargite tela,
discinctos Mauros, imbelles temnite Parthos,
pro Christique fide pugnantes promite vires
515   dignas Hispanis rigidasque ad proelia natas,
quae magno quondam Solimanum Marte fugarunt,
tunc quas Danubius novit fortisque Vienna,
quae adversus Turcas propugnat nomine Christi.
Hac urbe est solitus pelli vincique Tyrannus.
520   Tales vos opto, sensit quos Turca superbus,
et quibus ipse pater Tunetem cepit ab hoste,
et Barbarrossam Turcam deterruit armis.
Hos ego victurus vobis nunc expeto nervos,
quos frater victor Quintini ad moenia duxit.
525   Adversus Turcas et Christi nominis hostes,
nunc animi crescant, irae, nunc pectora, vires.
Sollertesque duces, generosi in bella furores,
Hispanae partes antiquae in bella resurgant.
Victoresque duces Turcae experiantur in undis,
530   Hispanum robur pugnasse intelligat orbis.
An non spes nostrae vertuntur? Gloria gentis
hic agitur, nomen vestrum per saecula magnum?
Crescat in arma diu gestorum fama per orbem,
Romani et Veneti rerum potiantur amici.'
535   Ingeminans Christum referebat verba salutis,
pontificis sancti fatum, quod dixerat ingens:
'Spiritus en Sanctus promisit prospera classi
ventura et victrix rerum dominabitur undis.
Pugna, nam vinces; victorem numina poscunt.

and led his triumphs. With your help he overcame the heretics at
the River Elbe. As his son, I lead you Spanish lions into war. Be-
hold, the dominion of the sea is granted to you. To you, chosen
few, Philip has entrusted his great hopes, his realms, my fortune,   510
and a fleet of many thousands of men. Let your weapons fly; scorn
these slovenly Moors, these spineless Parthians. As you fight for
the faith of Christ, show the strength born for war that is worthy   515
of Spaniards, which once routed Suleiman in a great battle; the
Danube felt your power and mighty Vienna, which fights against
the Turks in Christ's name, the city where the Tyrant came to
know setbacks and defeat. I pray that you be like past foes the   520
haughty Turk has known: those with whom my father himself
seized Tunis from the enemy and frightened away the Turk Bar-
barossa in battle. As I prepare for victory, I ask you for the resolve
my victorious brother brought to the walls of St. Quentin. Now   525
let your spirits swell against the Turks and the enemies of Christ's
name, with your fury, your hearts, and your strength; and let
shrewd leaders rise up again with a righteous rage for battle. Let
the lands of ancient Spain again take up arms. Let the Turks feel
the might of our conquering leaders at sea. Let the world know   530
that the raw strength of Spain has done battle. Are our prospects
not changed? Is not our nation's honor at stake, your reputation
for all time? Let the fame of our deeds in arms extend throughout
the world. Let our Roman and Venetian allies prevail." Invoking   535
Christ, he relayed the words of salvation that the Holy Pontiff had
spoken: "The Holy Spirit has foretold the fleet's coming victory,
and it will rule victorious over the waves. Fight, for you will win;

540 Auxiliumque Deus referet tibi caelitus ipse.'
Dixerat atque oculis classem circumspicit amplam,
regius Austriades miratus robur et arma,
flet memor et sancti patris iunctique Philippi
principibus curae queis Christi gloria solis.

545 Alter Christicolas regnans defendat ut armis
Ecclesaeque caput precibus nos servet ut alter;
praesentes vultus amborumque ora veretur,
qui classem iuveni divino iure ligatam
ducendam dederant, Venetis Italisque timebat,

550 Hispanisque suis, Romanis puppibus unus
velivolum pontum cernens implere carinas,
innantes populos fluctu decurrere visas.
Longa vehi ut campis ferrique magalia puppes,
non similes undis, Romana potentia vidit,

555 aeratas proras verrentes aequora remis,
extensas pelago longe lateque moveri,
tot celsas naves turritis puppibus ire,
tanta mole ducum spargentia signa colores.
Fervebat pelagus scaphulis cymbisque Liburnis

560 servitioque leves serpebant undique lintres;
remorum sonitu renovantes commoda bello
augebantque globos colubris et lintea velis.
Huc illuc celeres videas occurrere classi.
Illis arma dabant, Bacchum his, Vulcania, sulfur,

565 atque pilas plumbo liquefacto ferre rotundas.
Puppibus inde cibos, collecta viatica reddunt.
Accipiunt Venetos, exponunt litore quosdam,
nunc vestem revehunt, nunc vectam classe ministrant,

Providence demands your triumph. God himself in heaven will   540
assist you." When he had spoken these words, the royal Austrian
looked out over the massive flotilla, admiring the raw strength and
weaponry. He weeps, thinking of the Holy Father and Philip, the
allied princes on whom Christ's glory depends. The one, a king, to   545
defend Christians in battle, and the other, head of the Church, to
protect us with his prayers. He reveres both men as if their faces
were before him; for they had appointed him, though young, to
lead the navy united by holy decree. He alone feared for the Vene-
tians, the Italians, and his own Spanish and Roman galleys, as he   550
watched the ships fill the sail-strewn sea, like swimmers floating
on the waves. He saw ships like broad tents being dragged and
carried as if over fields, not waves: the Roman contingent. Their   555
bronze prows were sweeping the water with oars, stretching far
and wide over the sea, so many tall galleys with towering sterns,
the commanders' banners showing their colors in the huge array.
The sea seethed with skiffs, small boats, and Liburnian galleys,
and nimble support vessels were snaking in all directions. Replen-   560
ishing battle provisions amid the sound of the oars, they added
cannonballs to the culverins and linen for the sails. Now here and
now there, you see them bustling around the armada. To some
they bring weapons, to others, wine, gunpowder, sulfur, and round   565
balls of molten lead. Then the supply ships distribute gathered
provisions, food for the galleys. They welcome the Venetians and
station some on shore. Now they pick up and deliver clothing for
the fleet, like crowds rushing through the streets: for the turreted

visi per calles populi decurrere cives,
570 urbem nam classis referebat turribus altam,
quae Venetos nutrit medio circumdata ponto.
Dux Venetumque sua cum puppi vectus ad arces,
consulibus populi comitatus regia mandat,
accipit atque sinu resonans tunc Adria patrem
575 sic patriae; Veneti iuncti sparsique per undas
navigiis parvis dextra laevaque sequuntur,
templaque per fluctus in caelum celsa minantur.
Ast urbs ipsa frequens pelago consurgit aperto,
ad quam visurus vector decurrit ab alto
580 et varias merces cymba comportat onusta,
impositas fluctu turres, nantesque Liburnas,
dum mediam remis perstringit nauta, subinde
miraturque domos cernentes fluctibus agros;
haud aliter lintres naves lustrare videres,
585 currentes pelago ad naves deferre magistros,
puppibus et praesto quacumque est copia subsunt.
Navigia haec iussit tutari puppibus altis
Austriades, lintrem ne parvam perderet ullam,
a tergo classi coniunctas clauserat omnes.
590 Tum celsae naves pergebant milite plenae,
armaque vectabant, hastas, venabula, pila,
subsidio belli, classi, gentique futurae.
Annonam longo reddentes ordine promptam,
ut ferrent aegros, portentque obsonia cunctis,
595 tempore si quando penuria cogat edendi.
    Ibat longaevus Venetum dux vectus in hostem,
consultus iuris, bellator fervidus armis,
militiae expertus, vir qui ad utrumque paratus,
seu regere imperio populos, seu ducere castra,
600 navali instructas bello et ductare carinas.
Non ille exhorrens Turcas, non arma, procellas;

fleet looked like the lofty city that sustains the Venetians on the   570
encircling sea. The Venetian commander sails to these towers
aboard his flagship, accompanied by the consuls of the people, and
he delivers the royal commission. Then the Adriatic, echoing in
this harbor, receives this nation's protector, and the Venetians,   575
united and arrayed across the water, follow in small ships to the
left and right, and the towers soaring to the sky loom over the
waves. So a bustling city rises on the open sea, to which the sup-
plier sails on the deep, carrying numerous wares in his loaded   580
skiff, soon to see the fortresses perched on the waves and the
Liburnian galleys all afloat. Meanwhile, with strokes of the oar,
the sailor keeps to the middle. Suddenly he marvels at the sight of
houses separating fields on the waves. In the same way, you could
see light ships rushing on the sea to ferry commanders between   585
galleys: they approach the ships and stand ready wherever the
troops may be. John of Austria, lest he lose a single small ship,
ordered the large warships to protect them; he had enclosed all the
armada's converging galleys with a rearguard. Then the towering   590
warships began to advance, filled with soldiers, bearing weapons,
spears, pikes, and cannonballs as protection in the war for the fleet
and the future of the nation. In a long line, they carry provisions
ready at hand so that they can transport the wounded and bring   595
food to all, should hunger beset them in the time ahead.

The aged commander of the Venetians advanced, sailing toward
the enemy. Learned in the law, a warrior eager for arms, skilled in
war craft, he was a man truly ready for anything, whether to rule
citizens with authority, direct encampments, or organize galleys   600
equipped for naval combat. He was not afraid of Turks or artillery

ventorum flatus norat maturus et alto,
murmura silvarum nautis quid prodere pergant,
ortus, occasus, tacito surgentia caelo
605   sidera cuncta, polos geminos, qui in vertice mundi.
Qui pietate gravis meritisque incenderat omnes,
adversus Parthos viridis pugnare senectus.
Oderat infensus Mauros Turcasque tyrannos.
In frontem senas oblongas iusserat ire,
610   quae Venetos fortes instructa in bella vehebant,
claudit utrimque latus Venetus, Romanus amicum.
Marchio Bazanus servabat terga Ioanni.
In fronte Austriadae fulgens victoria laeta,
addebat cunctis miras in proelia vires,
615   qui imperii speciem prae se vultuque ferebat.
Atque ducis magni reddebat signa Ioannes,
qui medius pugnam felici Marte regebat
et saepe in classem vertebat lumina ductor,
respiciens ponto tot celsas ire figuras,
620   stemmata ductorum depicta et nomina gentis.
Commorat mentem tendentes bracchia remis,
nudatis tergis undas superare gigantes,
in numerum largo pellentes ordine puppes.
Laetitia motus subrisit ductor honeste,
625   dum tacitum iuveni tentabant gaudia pectus.
Inter spem curasque graves, memor ille salutis
qua pater ingentes pugnando vicerat hostes,
Carolus ille potens pietatis cultor in armis:
'Ducat vos Christus,' dixit, 'servetque per altum,
630   pugnet pro vobis, qui solus vincere scivit.'
Tunc genibus flexis sic Christi numen adorat:
'Da, Pater, infandas Turcarum perdere naves,
vincamus Turcas virtute atque omine vero,

or tempests; experienced on the sea, he understood the blasts of
the winds, how murmurs of forests can mislead sailors, sunrise,
sunset, all the stars that rise in the silent sky, and the twin poles   605
that crown the world. Renowned for his piety and accomplish-
ments, his vigorous old age had incited all to fight against the
Parthians, for he fiercely hated the Moors and despotic Turks. He
had ordered six oversized galleons to the vanguard, which, readied   610
for combat, were bearing brave Venetians. The Venetian contin-
gent covers either flank; the Roman, that of its ally; and Marquis
Bazán guarded John's rear flank. Radiant hope shining on the face
of the Austrian gave miraculous strength to everyone in the battle:
in face and bearing, he bore the very image of power. Indeed, John   615
showed the traits of a great military leader, and he led the battle in
the center with Mars on his side. Repeatedly, the commander
glanced at the flotilla, looking back at so many towering shapes
advancing on the sea and the colorful blazons of generals and   620
names of their families. His thoughts then turn to those giants
stretching their arms at the oars, as they master the waves with
bare backs, rhythmically propelling the galleys in a broad swath.
Stirred with happiness, the leader smiled nobly, while joy was   625
pricking his quiet young heart. Amid apprehension and grave
cares, he recalled the promise of eternal salvation with which his
father had vanquished powerful foes in battle. Mighty Charles
himself, powerful champion of piety in arms, had declared: "Let
Christ guide you, let him protect you at sea; let him, who alone   630
knows how to conquer, fight on your side." Then on bended knee,
he worships Christ's godhead: "Bring destruction, Father, on the
unspeakable ships of the Turks. With courage and this true sign,

nomine namque tuo pugnat Hispania sancto,
635 cui genua et flectunt Orcus barathrumque profundum,
terrarumque globus, parent cui sidera caeli.
Hoc vincat miles, quem crux tua vera per altum
deduxit fretum fuso tibi sanguine. Parthos
fundat nostra manus; Turcas Hispania victrix
640 arma, viros rapiatque duces referatque triumphum.'
Concipit hic subito mira virtute vigorem,
regia vis animo iuvenili surgit in hostem.
Ut si sensisset praesentia numina caeli,
impulsam classem iussit concurrere Turcis.
645 Consulto Hispanis Venetos adiungit in hostem,
virtus amborum geminata ut fortior iret.
Adversus Parthos fertur cita gurgite navis.
Remigium dictis incendit tendere nervos,
libertas cunctis mandatur voce regentis.
650 Iam fratres comitesque vocat, iam munera donat,
insurgunt rursusque sedent, fera bracchia tendunt,
sudantes rivis non cessant pergere contra,
annixi remis incumbunt, ictibus undas
tum quatiunt vastis, gemuit sub pondere puppis,
655 et tabulata virum crepuerunt mota labore.
Ductrici ante alias certat concurrere princeps,
hanc petere et pugnans decrevit vincere (si fas)
consilio ductus patrum procerumque Ioannes,
nam si Marte Deus concedat rumpere nostro,
660 Bassanemque suum videat gens barbara fractum,
atque caput victum, Parthum sine nomine truncum,
succumbet classis nobis viresque remittet,
dispersas nostrae rapient fundentque carinas.
Victores Venetos, Hispanos Marte Philippi,
665 Catholicam classem victricem Roma videbit,
et victos Turcas orbis mirabitur omnis.

let us defeat them, for Spain fights in your holy name, before
which Orcus and the deep abyss kneel prostrate, and which the 635
earthly globe and heavenly stars obey. In your name, let the soldier
prevail who is guided on the sea by your true cross, strengthened
by your spilled blood. Let our forces rout the Parthians; let victo-
rious Spain seize the Turks — arms, men, and leaders — and bring 640
them back in triumph."

Suddenly by miraculous virtue he feels a surge of strength. A
kingly power rises in his youthful heart against the enemy. As if
heeding a divine presence, he ordered the fleet to press forward to
engage the Turks. As planned, he unites the Venetians with the 645
Spaniards against the enemy, so that their combined strength
might advance more powerfully. His nimble galley sails over the
surf toward the Parthians. With his words, he incites the rowers
to exert their muscles; freedom is offered to all who follow his
command. Now he calls them brothers and comrades, now prom- 650
ises rewards. Rising and sitting back down, they extend their fierce
arms. Sweating in streams, they do not stop their advance; press-
ing upon the oars, they lean in; they churn the waves with power-
ful strokes as the stern groans under their weight. The floorboards 655
shook, rattled by the men's toil. John vies to engage with the en-
emy flagship before the others. He vowed to pursue and fight to
capture it (if it is possible), guided by the counsel of elders and
captains. For should God allow us to bring destruction in the
battle, should the barbarous nation see its Pasha undone — its van- 660
quished leader a headless, nameless Parthian trunk — their fleet
would succumb to us, yielding its power as our ships snatch and
sink their dispersed galleys. Rome will see the victorious Vene-
tians, Philip's triumphant Spaniards, and the conquering Catholic 665
fleet, and the entire world will marvel at the vanquished Turks.

Felici currit iam fato regia puppis,
in Turcasque levem fert pontus et impetus illam
impulit in fluctus remis pelagoque volantem.

670 Tunc prohibet princeps velocem currere puppim,
expectans comitum naves tardasque triremes.
Consulto ductor spatioso pergere cursu
et paribus remis sulcos scindebat aquarum
ostentansque crucis fulgentia signa per undas,

675 pontificis munus, quod nuper miserat almum.
Illo fretus aquas spumosas aere secabat;
illius impulsu Turcarum tempserat arma.
Illud, dum currit, volvebat mente subinde.

It pariter Marcus Romana a stirpe Colona,

680 an gens illa virum memorentur voce Coloni,
quae Romae positis dicta est de gente columnis,
ex Agrippina an lata haec cognomina Romam,
vulnere crudelis nati quae occisa Neronis,
hinc nomen Marco an permansit in urbe Colona?

685 Suspice ductorem pietatis lumine, princeps.
qui sancti patris coniunctus munere venit
consilio ut classem, Romana et duceret arma.
Vir magnus bello, tollit quem gloria Romae.

Dum Bassan nostram venientem tendere classem

690 in se conversam cernit totamque moveri,
intrepidam Turcam petere et iam temnere Parthos;
Austriadae inceptum laudabat Turca virile,
quod prudens fauces angustaque litora liquit,
Catholicam temnens classem pirata superbus

695 ad rem collatum bellum non credidit iri.
Multa movens avidum reputarat saepe Ioannem
excelsae famae, dixit cupidumque per undas
audacis cursus, animumque ad regia natum,

With the blessing of destiny, the flagship now advances, and the sea carries it lightly against the Turks. Oars drive it over the waves, flying over the sea. Then the commander restrains the swift galley 670 from its course, as he waits for the ships and slower galleys of his allies. As planned, the helmsman was plowing furrows of water with even strokes to advance across a broad reach. Atop the waves, they displayed the resplendent flags marked with the cross, a gift 675 from the pope, which he had sent for protection. Relying on this cross, he cuts the foamy waves with the bronze prows; by its force, he had scorned the weapons of the Turks; while he advances, he trains his mind on it.

Marco Antonio Colonna, from Roman lineage, moves forward apace. Is that family of men known as "Coloni" from the columns 680 that stood in Rome? Or was this name brought to Rome by Agrippina, mortally wounded by her cruel son Nero? Could it be that the name of Marco Colonna has survived in the city from that time? Take note, great prince, of the commander with the 685 aura of piety. He was entrusted with the Holy Father's commission, and came as an advisor to lead the fleet and the Roman forces. A man mighty in war, Rome's glory exalts him.

Meanwhile, the Pasha sees that our approaching navy is advanc- 690 ing against him, moving as one, to engage the bold Turk and defy the Parthians. The Turk admired John's bold maneuver, as he wisely left the straits and the confining shore. Still, the haughty pirate, disdaining the Catholic fleet, did not believe that the battle 695 would come about as planned. As he considered the matter, he had often concluded that John was eager for great fame, noting that he hungered for a bold advance on the waves and that his spirit was born for royal pursuits, burned for battle, was seized by

flagrantem bello, Martisque cupidine captum,
700 ignarumque maris iuvenem dum iudicat, inquit:
'Credebam impubem visenda per aequora vectum,
ad pompamque ducem meditari in proelia vires,
ductorem iuvenem cristatam ducere gentem;
scilicet audacem regali a stirpe, decorum est,
705 instructosque duces, orbes et ducere classes
gaudentes. Telis vanas dum verberat auras
ostentatque suas sectando per aequora naves;
dum fugiunt cymbae et quaerunt se abscondere parvae,
tunc victor iuvenis nunc has, nunc arripit illas,
710 principium pugnae, quaerens maiora per altum.
Armiger ipse Iovis volucres ut captat ineptas,
et reliquas caelo princeps disturbat aperto;
consurgitque novus ductor gaudetque iuventa
utque iubas spargunt lascivi in terga leones
715 erecti ad praedam cum primum proelia tentant.
Sic iuveni primo quaerenda est gloria bello,
quod nos in pelago tirones fecimus. Esto.
At post bella, duces, exhausta et parta trophaea,
sectari Parthos Turcasque invadere saevos,
720 navalis pugnae expertos animosque viriles,
hunc iuvenem bello telisque instare per undas,
ausum tironem veterano occurrere Turcae,
non vanum credo.' Non iam sine numine divo
esse putat Bassan, fortunae incommoda sensit.
725 Paenituit coepti magni classique timere
coepit et ad proceres conversus respicit agmen,
maerentesque videns rectores, tristia fata,
praesagusque mali concepit mente furorem,
grandibus et revocat maerentia pectora dictis:
730 'Quis metus audaces animos ad proelia tentat?
An dubitamus adhuc Hispanos vincere Parthi?

a passion for war. Though he judges the youth to be untested in 700
naval battle, he declares: "I thought this youth sailed to see the
ocean, and was considering his strength as a leader in battle for
show: a young commander leading a plumed people. Granted, his
royal lineage makes him bold, and it is only right that he leads 705
readied commanders, formations, and prosperous fleets. While he
lashes the insubstantial winds with his weapons and parades his
galleys as they slice through the waves; while small boats flee and
seek shelter: then the young leader, at the head of the battle,
snatches now these skiffs and now those, seeking greater glory at 710
sea. Just as when Jove's arm-bearer seizes unsuspecting birds and
then scatters the survivors across the open sky, this new leader
rises and flaunts his youth, just as ravenous lions display their
manes and toy with their prey just before they attack. So a young 715
man needs to seek glory at the onset of battle, the way we did as
young Turks at sea. So be it. Yet, commanders, when the battle
has ended and the spoils are doled out, I have no doubt that this
youth will still come after the Parthians and attack the ferocious
Turks, despite their long years in naval combat and their brave 720
spirits; this bold novice, who dares to engage the veteran Turk, will
threaten us with war and weapons on the waves." Already, the Pa-
sha believes that the youth is not without divine guidance and
feels an unkind turn of fate. He regretted this massive undertaking 725
and began to fear for his navy. Turning back toward the command-
ers, he looks over the front line. He sees the grim pilots and their
gloomy fates. Envisioning a bad end, his mind burns with rage,
and he rouses their sorrowing hearts with stirring words: "What is 730
this fear that troubles your courageous hearts on the eve of battle?
Do we Parthians still hesitate to vanquish the Spaniards? Are we

Victores semper Turcae pelagoque potentes?
An fuga commovit ductorum fortia corda?
Audite ergo, animis Turcarum haec figite dicta,
735 quae discedenti mandavit rite Selinus
servanda ad votum; vincendum protinus undis,
ni mortem vultis patiamur more ferarum.'
Tunc fera coniunctis ostendit verba Tyranni
grandia, quae gemmis venerans depinxit et auro,
740 quae numquam Parthis ausus monstrare per altum,
donec et ad puppes Hispanas Turca sequendo
venisset pelago rapturus viribus ipsas:
'Hispanam classem fugientem nave secutus,
ad me captivam Byzantum, Turca, reportes,
745 fluctibus inventam curabis mergere Bassan,
si non adnutus, sese demiserit omnis.
Haec sunt quae nobis facienda hic tradidit ille.
Quis nunc audebit mandatum temnere tantum?'
Respondent cuncti summissa mente superbo:
750 'Adsumus, ecce tuis manibus victoria parta est.
Prospice iam classem conversam tendere retro.
Ni longe fallunt revoluti marmore fluctus,
dona ferunt Veneti domino, ut de more, Selino.'
(Deceptus Maurus classis tunc ordine nostrae
755 commorat Turcas magno clamore sequendum).
'En fugiunt timidi victricia signa videntes.
En classi cedunt nostrae trepidique recurrunt.
Ecce et terga tibi Hispani iam vertere coeptant,
sexaginta puppes iam mihi dentur in ipsos,
760 Bassan,' Luchalli conclamat regulus Alger,
'captivam classem convertam protinus omnem.'
    Nam sex praemissae naves praecurrere visae
et classis moles Austridae coepta moveri.

not Turks, victorious always and mighty at sea? Does retreat
tempt the steadfast hearts of our leaders? Listen now; impress
upon the minds of the Turks these words, which Selim rightly   735
imparted to me when I left. Guard them as sacred. We must con-
quer here and now on the waves or suffer death like wild beasts."
Then he revealed to those gathered the Tyrant's fierce words,
which he revered as if they were made of gems and gold, words he   740
had not dared to reveal to the Parthians at sea until the Turk had
reached the Spanish galleys and was soon to capture them by force
in the waves: "'When you have chased the fleeing Spanish fleet by
ship, Turk, bring it captive to me in Byzantium. Pasha, you will   745
take care to find the fleet and sink it in the waves. Every man who
fails to heed me condemns himself.' With these words, he told us
what we must do. Who now will dare ignore such an order?" All
reply, their minds obedient to the proud one: "We stand with you.   750
Look, victory is in your hands: see how the enemy fleet already
turns back. Unless the churning white waves deceive us, the Vene-
tians are again bringing gifts, as before, to their master Selim."
The Moor, fooled by our fleet's alignment, incited the Turks to   755
give chase with a loud shout. "Look how they flee, terrified at see-
ing our conquering flags. Look how they back down before our
fleet and retreat in fright. And look, even the Spaniards already
begin to turn their backs to you, Pasha. Give me my share of sixty
captured galleys," shouts Uluj Ali, governor of Algiers. "I will soon   760
tow back the whole fleet captive."

For just then, the six leading galleons could be seen approach-
ing. The Austrian's giant flotilla, set in motion, was advancing into
battle.

[END OF BOOK 1]

335

Liber Secundus

Iam Deus omnipotens miseratus ab arce ministros
765 Adriacosque sinus, Cephalenes litora versus
despexit, pontum, terras classemque suorum,
sollicitos nautas, instructas Marte carinas
viribus humanis, quas mens valet arte parare,
Austriadae curas, ductorum corda videbat.
770 Omnia nota sibi. Cernens qua mente profecti
optarentque duces ut Christi extendere nomen,
quos pater ipse suo coniunctos foedere norat.
Promissique memor, quod natus dixerat olim
veridicus Christusque volens coniungere in unum
775 discipulos, servos, quos crux pietate ligarat:
'Si duo tresve meo coniuncti in nomine subsunt,
illic sum medius, vobis ad cuncta benignus.'
    Hinc Deus in nostros defixit lumina clemens
inspiciensque oculis, queis munera viderat Abel,
780 Austriadae classem Christi iam nomine iunctam.
Ad mundi metas numen mansurus ubique
nobiscum Dominus vivet. Christusque futurus
altari in summo pro cunctis hostia viva;
qui Deus in caelis colitur divina potestas
785 puppibus Ecclesae Romanae in proelia summus
virtutem misit victricem a vertice caeli,
auxilio ut nostri Turcas iam vincere possent.
Hispani hinc animos sumuntque ferocia corda,
imprimisque Deo Veneti iam fausta ferenti.
790 Felix ille dedit cursum ventosque secundos
direxitque rates, vertit virtute procellas,
pelleret ut classem minimo luctamine remex.
Sternitur aequor aquis Christo, crispantur et undae.
Sic facies pelagi visa est gratissima nostris.

Book Two

Now almighty God, taking pity on his servants, looked down   765
from the heavenly citadel. He saw the Adriatic Gulf, the Cephalo-
nian shores opposite, the sea and land, and the fleet of his men,
dutiful sailors, and galleys manned for war with all the human
strength that the mind is able to make ready by tactical skill. He   770
perceived John of Austria's worries and the commanders' inner-
most thoughts. All things were known to him. The Father under-
stood the intention with which the commanders had set out, that
they hoped to spread the name of Christ, and he knew that they
were joined in alliance. He remembered the promise that Christ,
his truthful son, had once spoken, wishing to unite his disciples   775
and followers as one, bound together by reverence for the cross:
"When two or three are gathered in my name, I am in their midst.
I look kindly on you in all things."

    So God in his mercy fixed his eyes on our forces; the same eyes
that looked on Abel's gifts now inspect the Austrian's fleet united   780
in Christ's name. The Lord will live with us forever; his power will
endure to the ends of the earth. On the high altar, Christ will be
the living sacrifice for us all. In heaven, he is worshiped as God,
pure divine power; supreme in battle, he sent his conquering   785
strength from the heights of heaven to the fleet of the Roman
Church, so that with his protection, our side could now defeat the
Turks. From him, the Spaniards draw their courage and fierce
hearts, and so too do the Venetians as God brings them good
fortune. In his benevolence, he granted them safe passage and fa-   790
vorable winds. He guided the ships and turned away storms with
his power, so that the rowers could propel the fleet with the least
exertion. Through Christ, the sea is smoothed and the waves are
curled. So it was that the sea's surface seemed most favorable to
our forces.

795   Dum cernunt classem propius iam tendere nautae
monstrantes digito Turcas et signa Tyranni;
una salus visa est manibus sperare salutem,
dixerat Austriades. Ductores ore frementes
vincere decernunt, aut fatis cedere fortes,
800   pro Christique fide morientes visere caelum.
Hic se mortales noscunt cunctique frequentes
ad Christum Dominum mentes attollere visi.
Quisque sacerdotem cepit tum crimina fassi,
quae quis bellando fratri commissa malignus
805   fecerat, oblitus legis, quae parcere suadet.
Militibus veniam ut possis iam reddere, rursus
ignoscenda tibi poscenti culpa vicissim.
Lustrarunt animas peccatis ore repulsis.
Paenituit peccasse viros rituque sacerdos
810   absolvit falsos, cui Christi est iure potestas,
sanguine qui fuso nos tristi a morte redemit.
Austriades primum Patri de nomine Iesu
tunc genibus flexis humilis delicta iuventae
dictabat princeps lacrimosa mente, subinde
815   pectora percutiens exemplum reddidit almum,
ex animo classis ductorem prona secuta est.
Inspiceres digitis signari pectora, frontes,
deiecere in ventres ulnas vertique deorsum,
in dextrumque latus mutari atque inde sinistrum,
820   nomine dum Sanctae Triadis se fortius armant.
Tot crucibus variis, sublata et bracchia versant
ad Christum versos oculos atque ora tenebant.
    Audires duris crepitantia pectora pugnis,
percussos lapides referentia tempore quando
825   salvator mundi pendebat in arbore fixus,

Meanwhile the sailors see the fleet approaching, drawing nearer,   795
and they point out the Turks and the Tyrant's standards. John of
Austria had said, "The only safety is to hope for salvation from
your hands." The commanders rage and resolve to win or yield
bravely to destiny, and, dying for their faith in Christ, to reach   800
heaven. Here they acknowledge they are mortal, and all in unison
seem to lift their thoughts to Christ the Lord. Each found a priest
and confessed the sins he committed wickedly against his brother   805
in war, forgetting the law that demands forbearance. In order to
grant pardon to the soldiers, you must first ask forgiveness in turn
for your own sins. By confessing their sins through their words,
they purified their souls. The men repented their transgressions,   810
and the priest, through the sacrament, absolved their wrongdoing,
for he is vested with the power of Christ, who redeemed us from
woeful death with the blood he shed. First the Austrian knelt
humbly in Christ's name before the priest; the prince tearfully
confessed the sins of his youth, and beating his breast, offered an   815
edifying example. The fleet followed their leader on their knees in
heartfelt prayer. You would have seen them make the sign of the
cross on their chests and foreheads, hands drawn down to their
waists, then brought from right to left, as they arm themselves
bravely in the name of the Holy Trinity. They also turn their up-   820
raised arms toward so many different crosses, keeping their eyes
and faces turned toward Christ.

You could have heard them pounding their breasts with firm
fists, recalling the stones that crashed when the Savior of the   825
world hung nailed to the tree. In his name the watchful Austrian

nomine quo Austriades currebat tutus in hostem.
Lenisius cui dicta dabat generosa salutis:
'Armis instructus princeps mihi pergis ut istis,
sic manibus victor nudandus regia proles,
830   haec tibi dicta dies, Dominus quam fecit, ut illa
gaudeat Austriades, victrici et classe Philippus.'
Tunc pariter mentes commoti his vocibus ambo;
Austriades humeris deponit bracchia, faustam
Lenisii faciem miratus lumine laeto.
835   Ibat per pelagus decurrens ordine classis.
Neptunusque caput visus submittere remis,
nympharumque choros curru deducere laetos,
Tethys ipsa suo fluctus sternebat Achilli.
Currenti Austriadae spumosum temperat aequor
840   caeruleus Triton, Austriadae et carmine conchae
victuro cantat Turcae praesagia gentis,
tristia fata ducum Parthis classique Tyranni,
filaque Bassani revoluta abscindere Parcas,
Austriadae captas victoris honore sorores.
845   Tresque deos orant Syrtes aperire marinos,
vitet ut Austriades vi saxa latentia ponto,
cui risit Scylla et stetit implacata Charybdis.
Saltant delphines verrentes aequora caudis,
grandaevus Nereus natas clamore vocabat,
850   Nereides currunt Austriadae ad classica laetae.
Respicit hinc fluctus Bassan classemque suorum,
contemplans cursus exhorret numina ponti,
mutatosque deos, in se Neptunia verti.
Defixis oculis sortem miseratus iniquam
855   Turcarum et tantos ductoribus esse labores,
cum fratre et tandem pugnandum Marte Philippi,

was moving carefully against the enemy. Luis offered him these noble words of salvation: "As you charge ahead, Prince — remember, I trained you for military command — a king's son must be visible to your men as a conqueror. This is the day that was fore-   830 told to you, which the Lord made, so that Austria's son and Philip might rejoice in their victorious fleet." Then, the minds of both men were moved equally by these words; John of Austria places his arms on Luis's shoulders, marveling with joyful eyes at his friendly countenance.

The fleet was advancing over the sea in formation. Neptune   835 seemed to bow his head to the oars and lead forth joyful bands of nymphs on their course, while Tethys herself was taming the waves for her Achilles. Blue Triton calms the foamy waters for the   840 charging Austrian, and, to the tune of his conch, sings prophecies about the Turkish nation to John, poised to conquer them. To the Parthians and the Tyrant's fleet, he sings the dire doom of their leaders; and to the Pasha, he tells how the Fates, sisters enthralled by the honor of the victorious Austrian, have cut his unspooled thread; these three pray that the sea gods will open the Syrtes, so   845 that John of Austria might deftly avoid the rocks hiding in the sea. For him, Scylla smiled and insatiable Charybdis stood still; dolphins leap, sweeping the waves with their tails. Old Nereus called to his daughters with a great cry, and the joyful Nereids rush to   850 the Austrian's fleet.

Then the Pasha looks over the waves and his people's fleet. Scanning the route, he shudders at the powers of the sea, the fickle deities, Neptune's realm turned against him. With his eyes cast   855 down, he laments the unfair lot of the Turks: that there were such daunting trials for his commanders, that in the end battle must be waged with Philip's brother. He feared the strength of

regnorum vires iunctas ductasse timebat.
Quippe suis classem cernebat currere remis
Hispanosque duces animosos tendere contra.
860 Sex illas longas pergentes agmine tuto,
armis instructas scindentes aequora rostris,
quae primae ante alias fuderunt agmina, Parthos
turbarunt, nostris animos viresque dedere.
Tot capita in caelum, fulgentia tela per undas
865 et Venetos furere, et iam fortes temnere Parthos.
Illyricos Italosque audaces currere remis,
qui prius et morem Turcis Parthisque gerebant,
et timidi portus trepidanti milite curvos
servabantque domos, natos castasque puellas,
870 hostes ne saevi vastarent litora late.
Mutatis animis optantes proelia, mirum,
visi Myrmidones Dolopesve, Argiva iuventus
in Teucros iterum venisse et Pergama contra.
    Incusat sortem, quae iam mutabilis esse,
875 adversa, inconstans Turcis videatur in undis:
'O sors laeta, meis quae tot discrimina bellis
vicisti et casus felix capitisque pericla?
Fulmina missa, polos caelo fulgente tonantes,
stridentes fluctus, varias Aquilone procellas
880 vitasti indulgens Turcis in bella benigne?
Quorsum pertinuit regnasse per aequora Turcas?
Quid retulit pelago gentes vicisse superbas?
Sensimus haec, princeps animis et navibus olim.
Italiae portus Venusinaque litora classe
885 vastasse? Et praedas ponto rapuisse quotannis?
Si nunc in dubiam versa est victoria laudem,
si tandem vanos ad metam reddis honores
principibus duros magno discrimine partos?

the kingdoms that had gathered together. Indeed, he watched the
fleet flying on its oars and the brave Spanish leaders training
their weapons on him. He watched those six long galleons advance 860
in a secure formation, readied with arms, slicing the water with
their prows; these, charging in advance of the others, devastated
the Turkish column, threw the Parthians into disarray, and gave
strength and courage to our men. So many heads rose into the air,
weapons gleaming atop the waves; the Venetians stoke their rage 865
and already scorn the mighty Parthians. He sees the Illyrians and
brave Italians advancing with their oars, who once obeyed the
Turks and Parthians and cautiously guarded their curved ports,
their homes, children, and chaste daughters with fearful sentries,
so that the brutal enemy would not ravage their coast. Now their 870
hearts have changed, and—amazingly—they seek combat, as if
the young Myrmidons, Dolopes, and Argives returned to lay siege
against the Teucrians and great Troy.

   The Pasha blames their lot, which now seems so uncertain, 875
contrary, and fickle for the Turks at sea: "Good Fortune, did you
not overcome many dangers in my battles, both in good times and
amid mortal threats? Did you not avert hurled lightning bolts,
thundering poles in the flashing sky, the crashing waves, and fierce 880
northern storms—always generous to the Turks in war? To what
end have the Turks ruled the waters? What did it matter that this
proud nation has triumphed at sea? I myself experienced these
things, once first in courage and galleys. Why did our fleet ravage 885
the ports of Italy and the Venusian shores? And what of the spoils
carried away at sea for so many years? Is victory now to be turned
into doubtful praise? Are our honors to be rendered meaningless
at this turning point—honors won by our leaders at great risk?

At si Parca mihi non scindit fila maligne,
890 si iam summa meae non instant tempora vitae,
contingat nostris Byzantum visere fato,
puppibus ad caros detur remeare penates,
incolumisque lares cernam regnumque Selini;
si dux aut Bassan contendam vivere posthac,
895 in rupes, in saxa meas, Neptune, carinas
subvertasque vadis, illisus fluctibus, oro,
funditus ut pere021 revolutus Syrtibus illic.
Scyllaque me frangat, vivum implacata Charybdis
sorbeat ipsa lacu vastaque voragine mergat,
900 quo neque me Turcae videant, nec fama sequatur,
quae gestis pelago nostris vulgata per orbem.
Iamque leves hamos nodosaque retia ponto —
quam mallem — tremula captasse et harundine pisces,
piscator visus victum perquirere cymba,
905 quam molem tantam ductando perdere nomen,
obscuras generi tenebrasque offundere Bassan.'
     Haec secum reputans volvebat grandia dictu:
'Quid faciet noster crudeli mente Selinus?
Impatiens vinci semper victorque superbus?
910 Qui Venetos numquam bello fuit ille moratus,
quos parere iubet Turcis et lege teneri,
illorum victas quas cepit classe triremes,
Illyricos temnens superarat saepe Liburnos.
Dixerat Hispanam non magnum vincere classem
915 abreptamque trahi Byzantum scilicet usque
iusserat.' Heu demens, qui invito numine turget
et genus humanum contemnit mente superbus,
oblitusque sui non haec mortalia curat,
ut Deus hos tollat iustus, iam deprimat illos.

But if Fate does not spitefully sever my thread, if my time has not
yet come; should destiny allow me to lead my forces back to By-   890
zantium, to sail in my ship to my cherished home and gaze un-
harmed on the gods of my hearth and Selim's domain; if as leader
and Pasha, I survive the battle, I pray, Neptune, crash my ships on   895
crags, on rocks, in shoals. Bashed by the waves, let me utterly per-
ish, washed up there on the Syrtian banks. Let Scylla crush me, let
merciless Charybdis herself swallow me alive in her whirlpool, and
drown me in her massive vortex, where the Turks will not see me;   900
nor let Fama follow me, bandied about the world over because of
our exploits at sea. I would have much rather been a fisherman
hunting food in his skiff—with light hooks and a loose net at sea,
snaring fish on a trembling rod—than a Pasha who destroyed his
reputation or cast dark shadows on his family by leading a doomed   905
enterprise."

    Considering all this, he pondered weighty things in his speech:
"What will our Selim devise in his cruel mind, disdainful of de-
feat and proud of his conquests? He never thought highly of the   910
Venetians in war. He demands that all whose ships he captured
in battle bow to the Turks and keep their laws; and he always
scorned the Liburnian galleys of Illyria. He had declared that it
would be no great task to conquer the Spanish fleet, and ordered   915
me to tow its tattered remnants back to Byzantium." Alas, the
fool: he swells with pride against the will of God, disdaining the
human race in his proud mind; and oblivious to his own state,
cares little for mortal duties: that a just God elevates some and   920
humbles others.

920　　　Longe aliter Graia haec penetravit litora classis,
　　　　non haec quae Epiri congressa est fluctibus olim,
　　　　quae Barbarrossam non ausa est currere contra,
　　　　nec quam nos nuper ductorum nomine verti
　　　　vidimus errantem Getulis Syrtibus ipsi,
925　　　Hispanosque duces oblitos nominis alti
　　　　in varias pelagi partes discurrere classe.
　　　　An putat ut quondam dispersam forte videre?
　　　　Desipit. Ipsa dies aliter rem postulat esse,
　　　　non iam discordes animos, non iurgia servat,
930　　　ductorumque dolos, non iam certamina portat.
　　　　Iamque duces alios classis vehit atque magistros.
　　　　Unanimes tendunt miles nautaeque per altum
　　　　ducit Caesareus ductor fraterque Philippi,
　　　　nam quamvis Venetos ductet variosque Liburnos,
935　　　Hispanosque simul, sapiens coniunxit in unum.
　　　　Appellat populos Hispanos nomine ab uno,
　　　　una et iura viris dat frater lege Philippi.
　　　　　'Quid si forte meas subvertunt fata carinas?
　　　　Atque fugam naves video fecisse per undas
940　　　impulsas virtute nova iuvenisque labore?
　　　　Victores Venetos pugnantes ire sequendo?
　　　　Quis dux iam Turcas Hispanis terga dedisse
　　　　nuntiet? An vivus referet fera dicta Selino?
　　　　Ecquis ad aspectum veniet? Quis re male gesta
945　　　excuset Turcas narretve incommoda belli?
　　　　Qui non exoptet submergi fluctibus ante
　　　　quam faciem vultumque ferum vidisse, superbi
　　　　ardentes oculos mortem spectasse minantis?'
　　　　Conversus Bassan puppim sic fatur ad altam,
950　　　qua classes varias pugnando merserat unus,
　　　　ingentes praedas pirata averterat undis
　　　　Byzantum versus: 'Puppis pergrata Tyranno,

This fleet that has reached Greek shores is vastly different. It is not like the one that once gathered in the waters off Epirus, but did not dare confront Barbarossa in battle; nor is it like the one we ourselves recently saw turned in flight at the name of the commanders, as it wandered along the Getulian banks of Syrtis. The Spanish commanders forgot their honor, and fled to different parts 925 of the sea with the fleet. Does the Pasha expect, by chance, to see the fleet dispersed again? He is a fool. This day demands a different outcome. It brooks neither divisive spirits nor the treachery 930 and wiles of leaders. Quarrels find no quarter. Now the flotilla carries different leaders and pilots. The soldiers and sailors advance together over the sea; Philip's brother, a leader like Caesar, directs them: for although he commands Venetians, diverse Liburnians, and Spaniards alike, he has wisely joined them as one. He 935 calls these people by one name, Spanish, and commands his men as Philip's lawful brother.

"What if the Fates should happen to overturn my galleys? Or I should see my ships take flight, driven across the waves by the 940 young man's fresh strength and effort? Or what if I see the conquering Venetians chasing after me, still intent on fighting? What commander could report that the Turks had fled the Spaniards and live to tell of Selim's savage response? Who will go to face him? Who could justify the failure of the mission or recount our 945 misfortunes in combat? Who would not rather choose to sink beneath the waves than see the sultan's face and savage expression, or gaze into the burning eyes of that proud man as he threatens death?" The Pasha speaks turning to the lofty galley, with which he had sunk many fleets in combat singlehanded; as a pirate, he 950 had carried abundant spoils across the sea toward Byzantium. "This ship has greatly pleased the Tyrant, a glory in war whenever

haec decus in bellis, si quando hac victor abibat,
haec solamen erat ductori, haec gloria fausto.'
955 Suspiciens oculis vexillum grande Selini,
inscripta et circum Mahumeti et carmina sectae
portabant orbes rectorum nomina seni.
'Navis cara mihi, fatalis regia Turcis,
Illyricos, Venetos, Hispanos, regna, Liburnos,
960 quot sola in pelago retulisti invicta triumphos?
Quas gentes Italum vectas videre Tyranni?
Per te quas classes submersas novimus ipsi?
Aut hodie victrix Hispanos ire videbis
Byzantum versus captivos, celsa trophaea.
965 Aut si adversa tuis rebus fortuna minatur,
occumbas pariter per fluctus obruta, quando
Hispanos portus nequeas captiva subire,
nec grandem poterunt aliena et iura domare,
nec poteris Dominum vel fratrem ferre Philippi.'
970 Tunc se fortunae mandat classemque virosque,
dans signum pugnae, moriturus tendit in arma,
quem rector navis monuit, huc regia pergit,
qua vectus frater regis decurrit in hostem:
'Torquebo clavum, si vis vitare periclum.
975 Puppis nam validis remis impellitur ingens.'
'Quo diversus agis? Fratri concurre Philippi,
o turpis,' dixit, 'cur non discrimina quaeram?
Cum quo certamen peperit mea gloria ponto?
Quo mecumque rapit fortuna hic pulchra sub armis.'
980 Pandite, Musae faciles, Helicona virentem.
Tu cantus resona divino a vertice, Apollo.
Et tu prosper ades, Maecenas Deza, cruentos

he set sail in her as conqueror. She gave comfort and brought renown to her commander while he was so fortunate." Then, turning his eyes on Selim's great banner, inscribed with Muhammad's 955 words and the verses of his followers, with six circles bearing the commanders' lineage: "O my beloved galley, doomed flagship of the Turks! How many Illyrians, Venetians, Spaniards, Liburnians—entire kingdoms—did you seize as trophies at sea, alone and 960 unbeaten? What peoples of Italy did the tyrants see captured? What fleets did we learn were submerged by you? Today, you will either conquer and watch the Spanish come to Byzantium as prisoners and coveted spoils; or if fortune threatens to turn against 965 your enterprise, may you perish as well, broken to pieces beneath the waves. May you never be taken captive to Spanish ports, may you never let foreign laws tame your grandeur, and may you never be forced to carry their Lord or the brother of Philip."

Then he consigns himself, the fleet, and his soldiers to fortune. 970 Giving the signal for attack, he advances—doomed—into battle. The ship's pilot advises him, as the flagship approaches, bearing the king's brother as he charges at the enemy. "I'll turn the tiller," he says, "if you want to avert danger, for the massive galley is being 975 propelled by strong rowers." "Why change course? Go meet Philip's brother, you coward," the Pasha declared. "Why would I not seek danger? Has my glory brought about this battle with him on the sea? I am here, ready for battle, wherever noble Fortune takes me."

Now gentle Muses, open verdant Helicon. You, Apollo, intone 980 your songs from the holy peak. Deza, my generous Maecenas, be present with your favor; you will see courageous and blood-soaked

magnanimosque duces cernes, et proelia numquam
sic Martem visum pugnas accendere ponto,
985   queis, neque in Actiaco vicino hic litore Marcum
Augustus vicit, Cleopatram aut mille carinis,
nec gentes umquam pugnarunt puppibus aequis,
nec magis infestis animis ad bella paratae,
quam tunc Naupacto pugnatum est fluctibus, illic
990   saxa ubi consurgunt Acheloia flumina contra.
    Ad teli iactum dum classis nostra subiret.
Erectis signis aquilarum expanderat alas.
Inclinansque caput Christus vocat agmina ligno
in medio fixus, classem ductabat in hostem.
995   Classica nostra suum resonabant pulsa Philippum,
Hispani divum iam clamant voce Iacobum,
at sanctum Veneti reddebant nomine Marcum.
Clamorem toto tunc fundunt aequore Turcae,
utque grues caelo crepitantes, Thracius orbis
1000   littera quas mire depinxit nubibus actas,
altivolans oculis agmen scribuntur. At illae
oceani tranant fluctus volucresque sonorae
clangentes pergunt. Nostras invadere puppes
tres tunc ardentes immisit Turca phalanges.
1005   Irrumpunt omnes Parthi Turcaeque furentes,
quos iussit Bassan puppes impellere ad unam.
Concurrunt magno ductrices pondere naves,
congressu utrimque et visum se abrumpere caelum.
Tunc pariter rostris feriunt se fortibus ambae,
1010   et ferro proras collidunt quaeque fatiscit.
Dum sex praemissae submersas aequore puppes
turbarantque duces tormentis sulfure iactis.
Et tabulata graves quassant; compagine laxa
accipiunt undam rimis fluctuque laborant.

350

leaders and battles, on a scale, it seems, that Mars has never kin-
dled on the sea; which not even Augustus surpassed, when he   985
conquered Mark Antony on the nearby shore at Actium or Cleo-
patra, with her thousand ships. Nations have never fought with so
many ships, nor were they more fired up for battle than in the
clash on the waves at Naupactus, where rocks rise up beside the   990
Achelous River.

Meanwhile, our fleet advanced to firing range. Wings of eagles
stretched wide on the high-hoisted standards. Christ, head bowed,
rallies the troops. Nailed to the wooden cross, he led the fleet to
face the enemy. Our trumpets sounded the battle cry for King   995
Philip. Spaniards shout the name of Saint James. The Venetians
respond calling Saint Mark by name. Then the Turks unleash a
cacophony over the whole sea, like cranes screeching in the sky,
which, driven from the clouds, a Thracian arc miraculously por-   1000
trayed as a letter; the high-flying flock is written on the eyes. The
noisy birds cross the ocean waves and press on, squawking. Then
the Turk sent ahead three units burning to attack our galleys. All   1005
the raging Parthians and Turks—though Ali Pasha ordered his
ships to strike as one—break formation: the lead galleys attack
with great momentum. As they struck from both sides, the sky
seemed to split open. They hit one another with their mighty   1010
rams and smash prows with iron. Each gapes open. Meanwhile,
the six galleons sent ahead had smashed the ships already sunk
in the sea, and their commanders, with sulfur-driven missiles.
Heavy blows rattle the decks; once their joints are loosened, the
ships take in water through the cracks and struggle in the waves.

1015 Sed fabri praesto tabulis et claudere ferro,
Sulfura iamque globos spargebant picea fumo
permixtos, crebris aether micat ignibus ingens.
Tunc sonitu curva et resonabant litora late,
fluctibus in mediis geminantia saepe fragorem.
1020 Non lapides iactos Turcae perferre valebant.
Saxis nam crebris repetebat saepe procella;
queis capita et dentes, oculos cerebrumque refringi,
malas, mandibulas, resoluta et pectora cernas.
Rupibus et nubes iam terque quaterque cadebat
1025 machina, nec colubri poterant, nec sulfura pelli.
    Confusus Bassan mira haec de pectore dixit:
'Non pilae humanis mittuntur viribus in nos,
omnipotens Turcas iratus dissipat armis.
Si Deus hic pugnat poterit quis tendere contra?
1030 Nil fabri audaces, nil prosunt arte magistri.'
Tanta mole petris instabat ab agmine remex,
quae vis turbavit Turcas Parthosque repressit,
copia nam lapidum solita est disrumpere Turcas,
quondam, cum Caramat vicit Mendozius heros,
1035 piratasque duos victores Hallihametos,
missilibus ductor vastisque molaribus ipsos
disiecit saxis, qui Parthos, arma, carinas.
Caelitus ut missa crepitabant grandine puppes.
    Dum pugnant geminae naves iunctaeque catenis,
1040 alterni saliunt Hispani et Turca subinde,
regius Austriades dictis hortatur in hostes:
'Hispani, Hispani,' geminabat saepe, 'leones!'
Congrediturque ferox Parthusque Italusque resultat,
excutitur miles Romanus pronus in hostem.
1045 Hispanosque iterum repetens, Hispana vocando
arma, viris flammas iterum sic spargere visus.
Tunc Veneti fortes rabiosi in proelia tendunt,

But the carpenters are quick to seal the leaks with lumber and 1015
iron. And now the pitch-black sulfur discharges clouds mixed with
smoke, as the mighty ether flashes with repeated fire. Then the
curved shoreline resounds far and wide, sometimes echoing the
din in the middle of the waves. The Turks are unable to endure 1020
the volley of stones. The storm is relentless, dense with rocks: you
could see heads, teeth, eyes, and brains shattered by them, cheeks,
jaws, and torsos gone limp. Three and four times the war engine
dropped clouds of rock. Neither culverins nor artillery fire could 1025
be repelled.

Bewildered, Ali Pasha spoke these stunned words from his
heart: "These mortar shells are not sent against us by human
strength: an angry god destroys the Turks with gunfire. If God
himself fights here, who can withstand him? Neither deft carpen- 1030
ters nor master strategists can prevail." An oarsman from the op-
posing battle line was attacking with a large pile of cannonballs.
These munitions startled and checked the Turks and Parthians,
for a similar onslaught of stone had shattered their forces when
the famed Mendoza vanquished two fearsome pirates, Al Borani 1035
and Ali Hamet: the commander devastated them with missiles
and huge projectiles, laying low Parthian soldiers, their artillery,
and their galleys. Their warships shook as if hail had been sent
from above.

While the vessels pair off and fight, grappled together with
chains, first Spaniards, then Turks leap forth. The Austrian prince 1040
exhorts his men to attack, repeating time and again, "Spaniards!
Spanish lions!" Both the fierce Parthian and the Italian attack and
retreat; the Roman soldier throws himself headlong at the enemy.
"Fight on, Spaniards!" John cries again; by calling "Spanish arms" 1045
he seems to ignite his men. Then the powerful Venetians charge,

nam latus Austriadae praereptum forte tegebant.
pontificis ductrix dextrum claudebat amica.

1050   Nunc Bassan gladio pugnat nunc flectit et arcum,
bracchiaque extendens nunc mittit ab aure sagittas.
Nomine quemque vocans repetebat verba Tyranni,
et classes victas, submersas aequore puppes,
Hispanos captos Byzantum Marte trahendos,

1055 imperium pelagi, terris direpta trophaea,
regnatorem Asiae Turcam dominumque potentem,
vociferans, Turcas dictis incendit in hostem.

    Ipsae se impellunt puppes et mutua virtus,
ferratae nulla poterant discedere parte.

1060 Virque viro certans infense. Pesque pedi stat.
Haerens sic Turcas feriebat comminus ense.
Austriades cernens flagrabat Martis amore,
ast vi custodes coeptis audacibus obstant.
Ter penetrant nostri pugnando vulnera passi,

1065 arboris ad partem mali, Turcasque repellunt.
Ter Parthi instando conversos caede fugarunt,
Hispanus quarto puppim pervenit ad ipsam.
Turbantur Turcae subita formidine mortis,
transtra per et remos trepidabant undique fortes,

1070 deseruere suum Bassanem, regia cuncta,
ductores, Parthos, rectores classis in undis,
regali puppi, signis armisque relictis.
Delphinum similes iuvenes immania cete,
per fluctus videas timidos optare salutem.

1075   Hic Bassan caesus fertur gladioque perisse,
atque humilis miles truncum liquisse superbum.
Victrici hic tandem cessit gens perfida nostrae.
Hispanus miles bellator spargere tela

raging for combat, for they were covering the Austrian's flank, which had been exposed by chance. The allied command ship of the Papal forces gave cover on the right flank.

Now the Pasha wields the sword, now he bends the bow, and extending his arms he launches arrows from ear level. He calls each fighter by name and echoes the Tyrant's demand that the ships be vanquished, that galleys be sunk under water, and that the captive Spaniards be brought to Byzantium. He recalls their dominion of the sea, the booty they had captured on land, and the Turk as the mighty lord and ruler of Asia; he fires up Turkish forces against the enemy with his words.

The galleys and well-matched forces ram one another, with no gap where the iron prows can pull apart. Man vied fiercely against man. Foot treads on foot. Closing in, the fighters struck the Turks at close range with the sword. As he watches, John of Austria burns with zeal for battle. But his advisors check his bold ardor with force. Three times our men—despite the wounds they suffer in the fight—breach the enemy's mainmast and drive the Turks back. Three times, the Parthians repel them in bloody combat. On the fourth charge, the Spanish force takes control of the enemy flagship. A sudden fear of death unnerves the Turks. Everywhere amid the thwarts and strong oars, they shuddered, leaving their Pasha, the entire royal navy, its commanders, Parthians, and ships' pilots in the waves, with artillery, their flagship, and their standards left behind. You could see scared youths struggling for safety in the waves like dolphins alongside huge whales.

At this moment, Ali Pasha is said to have been struck and to have perished by the sword. Some lowly foot soldier reportedly left nothing but a proud torso. Then at last, the evil nation succumbed to our vanquishing army. The Spanish infantryman strives

1050

1055

1060

1065

1070

1075

contendit vires natas ostendere bello.

1080 Austriadae in Parthos urget praesentia, quando
tunc memor ipse sui veterani roboris artus
iratusque sibi generosas suscitat iras.
Illyrici fortes pugnant mixtique Liburni,
at Venetus patrias defendens agmine naves

1085 ostendit pulchrum vitam iam perdere in armis.
Iamque Italus, Tuscus, Germanus miles ad unum
aequo certabant in Turcas Marte feroces.
Instant ardentes telis et robore Turcae,
quos Ligures pilisque globis, ignique fatigant.

1090 Nam fulmen belli radiabat fluctibus Andres
Horia, qui nomen traxit de nave per undas.
Sed crebras Parthi mittunt de more sagittas.
Agmina telorumque seges figebat abunde,
arcus in nostram lunantes saepe cohortem,

1095 saepe et remigium feriebant undique saevi.
Pectora confossus non cessat pellere remex,
fortius adductis volvit freta versa lacertis.
Innumeras colubri mergebant sulfure naves,
machina dum crebro torquet nitraria plumbum.

1100 Puppibus ex altis rapiebant transtra virosque,
glandibus immissis verrebant agmina late.
Stuppea flamma volans Vulcani ex arte remissa
spargitur in Turcas ignis comburere naves.
Patrona, instando, iaciebat corpora ponto,

1105 commendatari virtute ac viribus acta,
quem proceres fortem comitati in proelia clari.
Turba Faventini Barcino in bella secuta est.
Iamque duces nostros pugnantes inspice, princeps:
Bazanus ductor claris pugnabat in armis

1110 Alvarus, in ponto teneris nutritus ab annis,
gloria cui pelago patris cognomine crescit.

356

to scatter bullets and display his natural talent for war. The presence of the Austrian adds unrelenting pressure against the Parthians; now mindful of the war-tested strength in his limbs, he grows angry and stokes the noble fighting spirit within him. Strong Illyrians and Liburnians fight side by side. The Venetian, defending his nation's ships in a line, proves that it is honorable to lose one's life in battle. And now the Italian, Tuscan, and German infantry vie as one against the ferocious Turks in matched battle. Raging, the Turks resist with arrows and raw strength: Ligurians batter them with bullets, cannonballs, and artillery. 1080

1085

Now Andrea Doria — lightning bolt of war — flashed across the waves. He won his fame on his ship at sea. But the Parthians launch their accustomed volleys of arrows. While they set up lines and rows of weapons in quick succession, the moon-shaped bows strike our forces time and again, and time and again savagely attack our oarsmen from all sides. Pierced in the chest, the oarsman keeps rowing. Still more bravely he churns the waves, plying them with tensed forearms. Culverins sank countless ships with sulfurous fire while the harquebus issues a stream of bullets: from the tall galleys they were picking off thwarts and men, sweeping clean a line of fighters with a hailstorm of bullets. Volleys of flaming tow launched with Vulcan's art scatter sparks at the Turks to ignite their ships. The *Patrona* pressed on, hurling enemy bodies into the sea driven by the power and strength of its commander; storied noblemen accompanied that brave man into battle, and a throng from Faventian Barcelona follows their charge. 1090

1095

1100

1105

Look at our commanders battling, prince: Admiral Álvaro Bazán fought in gleaming armor, having trained at sea from his earliest youth; his glory on the water sprung from his illustrious family. 1110

Si quae tunc longis scindebant aequora remis
Hispanae hinc puppes certabant vincere naves
Turcarum; at ductu Bazani, et fortibus ausis
1115   Parthenopes classes Cumano milite surgunt,
corpore Parthenopes dictae quae rite sepulto.
Gens Campana virum bellatrix viribus agmen
Turcarum fractis vertebat puppibus ingens.
      Iam Marcus ductor Romano milite plenam
1120   impulerat classem Turcas submergere naves;
agmine remorum telisque volantibus acto,
pugnabat Parthos ducibus superare Latinis.
Iamque graves luctus auditi et mutua Martis
funera, perque rates geminari tristia fata,
1125   hi quibus invisi Turcae Parthique superbi,
et qui nostra suis experti viribus arma.
Iam cedunt pariterque ruunt, ferroque petuntur.
Vincere contendunt nostri, Turcaeque resistunt.
Eventusque diu dubia et victoria perstat;
1130   non his, non illis Mars se ostendebat amicum.
Tunc fluctus pelagi morientum caede rubescunt.
Inspiceres undis revoluta et corpora ferri,
fluctibus in mediis pugnam geminosque revolvi,
et pedibus nexis arrectos pectora ab undis,
1135   pube tenus. Videas pugnis contendere saevis,
unguibus et nares scindentes more ferarum.
Atque alios vivos innantes gurgite vasto,
complexos alios sese dimittere in undas,
et sparsos fluctu rursus committere pugnam;
1140   praecipiti saltu quosdam fera vulnera passos,
abscissis manibus dum certant prendere proras,
dentibus et morsu (si fas est) tangere puppes.

As they were plowing waves with long oars, Spanish galleys were
striving to overcome the Turkish warships; guided by Bazán's lead-
ership and great daring, the Parthenopean galleys attack with sol-   1115
diers from Cuma, so named for the body of Parthenope given
rightful burial there. With raw strength, the Campanians—a war-
like people—were devastating a huge column of Turks, their sterns
shattered.

By now, the commander Marco Colonna had ordered the fleet   1120
full of Roman soldiers to sink the Turkish galleys: while the battle
line of oarsmen drew up and weapons were flying, he fought
alongside the Latin leaders to overcome the Parthians. And now,
dire laments are heard and the death moans of those fallen in
battle; cruel ends ring out on both sides throughout the galleys,
whether from our men, who despise the Turks and haughty Par-   1125
thians, or theirs, who test our weapons with their strength. Now
they withdraw, then push back with equal force, then they are at-
tacked with the sword. Our men strive to conquer, but the Turks
stand firm. Both the outcome and victory hang in the balance;
Mars was showing himself a friend to neither side. The seawater   1130
grows red with the blood of the dying. You would have seen bod-
ies—overturned and borne by the waves—do battle amid the
surge, pairs intertwined, with feet bound together and chests pro-
truding from the waters all the way to the groin. You would see   1135
them fighting in vicious combat, clawing at noses like wild ani-
mals. Some still alive flail in the gaping vortex, while others,
grappled together, dive overboard, where spread out in the waves,
they continue their fighting; soldiers with fierce wounds leap head-   1140
long, while ones with severed hands try to reach the prows and (if
possible) grasp the galleys with tooth and jaw.

'Quis furor ille virum?' miratur in agmine ductor.
'Quae ne seges ferri, telorum qua ingruit horror?
1145   Impetus ille ducum quo nunc certamine pergit?
Fulgura quae in fluctus armis immissa coruscant?'
Austriades undis extendens lumina quaerit:
'Quae moles Turcas iunxit? Quis clamor ad undas?'
Iamque faces, flammas, volitantia tela videbat.
1150   Inspiciens pelago Christi videt esse cohortem.
Nam qui iam crucibus candentes pectora sacris,
commendatari sacra de classe Ioannis —
virtute antiqua, nervis, et robore belli —
telorum segetem mittentes viribus alte,
1155   (imbrem de caelo spissam cecidisse putares)
irruerant Turcas remis et nave sequendo.
In puppes telis salientes vincere captant
Turcas iam notos, lacerantes undique ferro.
Certabant animosa cohors. Huc impetus omnis
1160   Turcarum versus luctatur rumpere gentem
infensam Mauris, Parthis regique Tyranno.
    Ecce furens animis hos cernit regulus Alger
Luchalli, Mauro dictus de nomine Turcis,
quique fidem Christi Mahumeti peste negarat,
1165   oblitusque crucis vivae quam fronte gerebat.
Agnovit puppim ductricem et signa Ioannis.
Nam ductor discors ira commotus iniqua,
quod latus Austriadae non posset claudere classis,
Luchalli saevis occurrit navibus unus.
1170   Protinus in sanctam fertur vi ac robore navem,
quinis armatis invasit puppibus unam.

"What is this rage among the men?" the leader wonders from the battle line. "What are these fields of iron, where bristling weapons crash down? With what hostility does the charge of our leaders now proceed? What of the lightning that bursts from the cannons and flashes across the water?" Casting his eyes over the sea, John of Austria continues: "What enterprise has united the Turks? What is this uproar on the waves?" Now he saw the torches, firestorms, and flying spears. Looking around the water, he recognizes Christ's regiment. Their chests gleaming with the holy cross, the officers of John's own holy fleet — with their ancestral virtue, muscle, and military resilience — launch a hail of gunfire far ahead (you would have thought a thick rain fell from the sky), and they had charged at the Turks with oar power and ships in pursuit. Boarding the galleys with their weapons, now they strive to capture the prominent Turks, slashing every which way with sword blows. The brave unit fought on. Here the full strength of the Turks toils to break the nation that loathes Moors, Parthians, and the tyrant king.

Look, the governor of Algiers, his spirit raging, catches sight of the enemy. Uluj Ali was known to the Turks by his Moorish name, for he had renounced the Christian faith for the Muhammadan plague, forgetting the living cross he once wore on his forehead. He recognized the command ship and standard of John of Austria. The dissident leader is overcome by blinding anger; since the central flank could not trap the Austrian's fleet, Uluj Ali alone attacks with his fierce galleys. Straightaway, he is borne against the holy ship by brute force and strength, attacking the one boat with five armed galleys.

Exoritur clamor surgitque miserrima caedes.
Incenditque viros Mars ipse et robur utrimque.
Tisiphone telis media inter funera saevit.
1175 Commendatari memores virtutis avitae; hos
conscia, dum pugnant, stimulabat gloria ponto.
Infensos Turcas, inimica et nomina gentis,
et Melite quondam commorat — sanguine rubra
ac tunc ipsa madens, Parthorum plena cruore —
1180 insula Bassanes geminos quae vicerat olim,
terruerat bello dispersos aequore toto,
irrisos fecit patriam remeare fugaces.
Sic stragem magnam Turcarum Marte dedere,
monstrantesque cruces divique insigne Ioannis,
1185 pro Christique fide dum pugnant sanguine fuso.
Ad votum cuncti caelum petiere beati.
Quos Deus omnipotens cepisse hinc creditur, illis
Spiritus et Sanctus mentes afflasse piorum —
vivorum iudex, defunctis gloria sanctis —
1190 Christus venturus iustam dabit ipse coronam.
Barbarigo Venetus, perfosso lumine telo —
Hannibalem referens — postquam victoria parta est
magnanimus dixit: 'Placida nunc morte quiescam.'
Iam Bassan truncus summas volitare per undas,
1195 atque caput magnum praefixum cuspide acuta,
praelongo in pilo, magno clamore videntum.
Terribiles oculos nequeas adversa tueri,
ora viri tristi nigroque fluentia tabo.
Semiferi facies terret prolixaque barba,
1200 turgentis vultus (ut vivens, fronte minari
visus) nam Turcis ostendit cautius ipsis
dux quidam. Victor voluit vectare trophaeum

A shout rises as horrific slaughter ensues. Mars himself incites the soldiers and fighting strength on each side. Tisiphone rages with missiles amid the carnage. The officers recall their ancestral 1175 courage; conscious glory drives them on as they fight. Malta too had once checked the savage Turks and the nation's fearsome reputation; the island — red and dripping with blood, overrun with Parthian gore — had once vanquished both Pashas, terrorized enemies 1180 scattered over the whole sea, and made the fleeing invaders return home, humiliated. Thus they inflicted a massive slaughter of Turks in the fray, wearing Saint John's crosses and emblem, while they battle with much bloodshed for the Christian faith. Blessed 1185 souls all, they reached heaven in answer to their prayers. Here God almighty is believed to have claimed them, and the Holy Spirit inspired them with the thoughts of the blessed. Christ himself — judge of the living, glory for the sainted dead — will return 1190 to bestow on them their deserved crowns. Barbarigo the Venetian, his eye pierced by an arrow — bringing to mind Hannibal — declared heroically after victory was assured, "I will now rest in a peaceful death."

Now the mutilated Pasha drifts atop the waves, and his great head is displayed up high on the sharp tip of a long pike, with a 1195 great cry from those watching. You could hardly look at the fighter's terrifying eyes, his hostile face, oozing with miserable black gore. The expression and full beard of the animal-like face frightens as it swells (it seemed to threaten with its brow as when alive); for one of the officers showed it in warning to the Turks. The 1200

ductricem navem pelago, quo terreat hostes
de more ut faciunt victore classis ovantes.
1205 Qui gladio pugnans fatis concessit honestis,
nec potuit patriam Turcamque videre superbum.
    Quod si inter pugnam captus vir forte fuisset,
ille fidem mira Christi virtute bibisset,
quem remex noster captivus semper amarat
1210 optaratque crucem Bassani in fronte videre.
Sunt etiam Turcis quamvis sua praemia laudi.
Infelix, mortem fato solabitur unam,
tunc dextra fratris cecidisse et Marte Philippi.
    'Victori' auditur. Victoria et incipit ire
1215 redditur et victos clamat victoria Turcas.
'Victori Austriadae, victori Augusta Philippo.'
Cantatur patri Romae victoria sancto.
Clamorem excipiunt Mauri Parthique fugaces.
Franguntur vires. Bellantum concidit ardor.
1220 Inclinat classis, dimittunt signa phalanges.
Turcarum proceres nati — par nobile fratrum —
ut videre caput perfossum cuspide pili,
haerent, ingenti trepidant formidine classes.
Sed fratres lacrimas perculsa mente dedere,
1225 tunc gemini tristem rumpunt de pectore vocem:
    'An tu, magne pater, dederas promissa parenti?
Ut te per fluctus crudeli morte peremptum
cernentes animis rumpamur tristibus ambo?
Captivos moriens potuisti linquere natos,
1230 invisos Graecis, Italis, Venetisque, Liburnis,
patribus ob natas raptasque ex litore matres?
Non capita amborum comitata in morte parentem,
praefixa in pilo classis pontusque videret?

winner wished to tow the flagship over the sea as a trophy, to ter-
rify the enemy as ships rejoicing in victory often do. Wielding a   1205
sword in combat, the Pasha yielded to a just destiny, never to see
his homeland and the proud Turk again.

Yet if by chance the man had been captured while fighting, he
would have imbibed the Christian faith because of his wondrous
virtue. Our captive rowers had always revered the Pasha and
hoped to see him wear the cross on his forehead. Even among   1210
Turks honor has its rewards. Unhappy man, he will take comfort
in a singular death: to have fallen by the hand and the military
might of Philip's brother.

"Hail Victor!" rings out. Victory cries spread, echo, and pro-   1215
claim the Turks defeated. "Hail conquering Austrian," "Hail,
Philip, emperor!" A victory cry rings out for the Holy Father in
Rome. The fugitive Moors and Parthians hear the shout, and their
strength is broken. The fighters' zeal dies away. The navy surren-   1220
ders, and the battalions abandon their standards. The Pasha's
sons, Turkish lords — two noble brothers — cringe when they see
the impaled head on the tip of a pike, and the fleets shudder
with overpowering fear. Then the brothers pour forth tears from
stricken minds, and then they both utter a sad, heartfelt lament: 1225

"Are these the parent's vows you made, mighty father: that we
both would be broken with sad spirits seeing you amid the waves,
taken from us by cruel death? Even in death, could you leave your
sons as prisoners, hateful to the Greeks, Italians, Venetians, and   1230
Liburnians, for daughters taken from fathers and mothers kid-
napped from their shores? Why should the navy and the sea not
find both our heads likewise impaled on a pike, accompanying our

Hae iam spes nostrae, bella haec exhausta per undas,
1235   gloria Turcarum, felicis gesta Tyranni. En
sub iuga venturae gentes rerumque potestas;
Bassani en classis Byzantum haec usque trahenda;
scilicet ut Veneti nostri potirentur et arma,
tot reges victos disiectaque corpora ponto,
1240   captivam classem cernant? Fraterque Philippi
ut geminos ductet puppi vinctosque triumpho?
Sordidus ut miles iugulum regale feriret?
Regnatorque pater truncus videaris in undis?
Quo ferimur miseri servi ad fastidia regum?
1245   Non iterum campos Byzanti, et regia castra
visuri, et caros materna in sede penates?
At vos Hispani nostri miserescite duri:
spargite nos fluctu, vasto hoc immergite ponto.
Iam Venetus crudum per costas exigat ensem,
1250   crudeles sumat nunc patris nomine poenas.
Gaudeat Illyricus Turcarum sorte repulsa.
In nos ardenter mites convertite ferrum.
Porrectum iugulum mucrone en solvite nostrum.
Figite iamque caput geminum sic puppibus altis.
1255   At patris digno nostri mandate sepulchro.'
     Et iam lecta manus Parthique abiere retrorsum.
Atque fugam versae ad ripas fecere carinae;
permultae Turcas exponunt litore late.
Insequitur nostra et puppes rapit inde fugaces.
1260   Austriades alias pugnantes aequore naves
cernit adhuc nostras Turcasque resistere fortes.
Rursus et arma parat. Proram tum regia puppis
convertit, cursu cita gurgite devolat illuc
auxilioque levat certantes. Turca subactus
1265   agnovit puppim ductricem cedere coepit

father in death? As this battle on the waves has come to end, now
too have our hopes, and the glory of the Turks, and the deeds of   1235
the once fortunate Tyrant. Behold, our people and the power of
our empire are to come under the yoke. Behold, the Pasha's fleet is
to be towed all the way to Byzantium. Can it really be that Vene-
tians have gotten the better of us, and now look on our artillery,
scores of conquered rulers, sea-strewn corpses, and our captive   1240
fleet? That Philip's brother leads your two bound sons on his ship
in triumph? That a vile soldier has slit a royal throat? And that
you, admiral and father, are seen as a trunk on the waves? Where
are we bound, miserable slaves to endure the scorn of kings? Will   1245
we ever again see the fields and royal fortresses of Byzantium, or
the cherished hearths of our maternal home? Fierce Spaniards,
have mercy on us! Scatter us over the water, submerge us in the
deep sea. Let a Venetian now thrust a merciless sword through
our ribs and exact harsh punishment in the name of our father.   1250
Let the Illyrian rejoice at the ill fortune of the Turks. Be kind,
and turn your sword zealously against us. Come now, sever our
exposed necks with your sharp blade. Display our twin heads up
high on your stern. But then grant us a burial worthy of our   1255
father."

By now the Parthians and their forces have fled. The retreating
ships withdrew to the shores: many deposit Turks on the coast far
and wide. Our contingent gives chase and seizes the fleeing gal-
leys. John of Austria observes our other ships still fighting on the   1260
water and the brave Turks resisting, and he readies the artillery
once more. The flagship turns its prow and flies on its course with
the rushing current to relieve the combatants with reinforcements.
The beaten Turk recognizes the flagship and begins to withdraw,   1265

cristatumque videns iuvenem percurrere saeve,
victoremque sequi Turcas Parthosque, superbum
diripere et naves obiter quascumque videret,
praecipitesque viros cursu detrudere ad undas,
1270 arma, rates, puppes spumoso immergere ponto;
a dextra laevaque frequentes vincere naves
victoresque duces. Inimica venire per altum
tela, neque adversos Turcas, nec currere Parthos,
cernit, nec reliquos ullam sperare salutem.
1275   Iam summo in fluctu victricia signa Philippi
conspicit, Hispanos raptores tendere contra,
in naves subito salientes spargere praedam,
oblitosque sui, pestis sociumque salutis,
de rapto solum pugnantes saepe videbat.
1280 Cornua rauca, tubae crepitantes, classica, victos
(ut se iam Turcae tradentes arma relinquant,
ne mortem hoc miseri patiantur nomine saevam);
terrebant sonitu, clangentes aere canoro.
His visis Parthus desperat, Turca refugit.
1285 Tunc multi iunguntque manus vinctique feruntur
et sua victori commitunt arma benigno.
Caesareo princeps subiectis more pepercit,
militibus tradit rapiendas undique praedas,
captivosque trahi Turcas gentemque superbam.
1290 Ad proras multi properabant ire natantes,
tunc miseros videas revomentes pectore fluctus.
Iam captam miles posset divendere praedam,
quamcumque et Parthus pelago deduxerit audax.
Imperat, heu miseri, qui se sine nomine nollent
1295 dedere victori et sortem vitamque tueri.

seeing that the young man in his plumed helmet fiercely charges
on and in his triumph chases Turks and Parthians, proudly seizing
any galleys he sees along the way. He pushes men headlong from
his path into the waves, submerging arms, skiffs, and galleys in the   1270
foamy sea. On his right and left, he conquers swarming ships and
victorious commanders; enemy arrows fly overhead. Neither en-
emy Turks nor Parthians escape, and the survivors hold out no
hope for a rescue.

   Now he sees Philip's victorious standard atop the waves, and   1275
Spanish raiders turning back toward the enemy, boarding their
galleys quickly to disperse the spoils, forgetting themselves, the
plague, and the safety of their comrades. He saw them fight-
ing — as so often — solely for plunder. Deafening horns, screaming   1280
clarions, and trumpets frightened the vanquished with screeching
brass, so that the Turks surrender and drop their arms, miserable
wretches, to avoid suffering a harsh death for their name. Seeing
these things, the Parthian despairs, the Turk takes flight. Then   1285
many, surrendering their arms to the merciful winner, clasp hands
and are carried off bound together. Following Caesar's example,
the prince spares the suppliants and distributes all the plunder to
be carried off by the soldiers, and hands over the captive Turks
and the proud nation to be dragged away. Many others were swim-   1290
ming to try to reach the prows; you could see these sad men spew-
ing seawater from their chests. Now the soldier was able to sell off
captured spoils, anything at all that the bold Parthian had borne
away at sea. Alas, miserable wretches, he orders those reluctant to
surrender without honor, to look to their lives and fate.   1295

Certabat miles praedam cognoscere captam,
atque suas iuste partes sibi tradier inde,
qui pro rege suo Turcas invaserat hostes
pectoreque adverso monstrabat vulnera passus.
1300 Ductores avidi totam de more volebant.
Incertum vulgus studia in contraria fertur;
seditione levis populus consurgere visus.
Iamque furor gentis commotis arma ferebat.
Ac ne forte viros fortuna adversa sequatur
1305 victoresque duces casus contristet acerbus,
Austriades animos dictis et pectora mulcet.
Imperio iustum munus sibi quisque recepit,
nam bonus auditor factis tunc partibus aequis,
iussus sic Nabbas lites disiunxit iniquas,
1310 quem classi cunctae praefecit lege Philippus.
Pars maior rerum Turcarum est obruta fluctu,
quippe inter pugnam mergebant multa ministri,
multaque praeterea restabant capta per hostem.
Dilapsae et naves fugientum multa tulere.
1315 Direpta est ducibus regis captiva supellex,
ingens argentum, vestes pulchrique tapetes.
Ostro iam regum vario radiantia signa
abstulerant Turcae memores vel morte Tyranni.
Quos studio patriae videas ardere ferentes
1320 stemmata, ne nostri reges captiva viderent,
gauderet vultus cernens atque ora Philippus.
Et quibus ad mensas lautas accumbere sueti
portaruntque toros et lato margine lances;
Turcarum seriem longam regumque superbas
1325 auratos calices referentes orbe figuras,
victorem Turcam cum gente atque agmine pictum,

Each soldier, striving to assess the captured loot and ensure that his share of it was fairly handed over to him, displayed the wounds he suffered on his exposed chest when he had attacked the Turkish enemy for his king. Greedy commanders, as usual, wanted every- 1300 thing. The unsettled crowd is drawn into conflict; the fickle throng seems on the verge of mutiny. Now the men's wrath brought weapons into the heated disputes. Lest a dire turn of fate befall the men and bitter disaster grieve the exultant commanders, John of 1305 Austria calms their minds and hearts with his words. By his command each receives a just reward; for Nabbas—the wise judge Philip had appointed to guide the entire navy in legal matters— 1310 tallies shares befitting deeds and resolves unjust quarrels.

The greater part of the Turkish cargo sank in the waves when attendants tossed much of it overboard in the midst of the battle, but many other purloined treasures remained in the hands of the enemy. The tattered galleys of those who fled bore away many 1315 other items. The commanders plundered the captured furnishings of the king: piles of silver, garments, and beautiful tapestries. The Turks had secreted away the royal standards dazzling in purple hues, mindful of the Tyrant even in death. You could see them burning with patriotic zeal, as they tucked away the royal insignia, 1320 lest our kings lay eyes on them as loot, or Philip's face and expression brighten at the sight. As they are wont to recline at sumptuous tables, they had brought cushions and wide-rimmed platters, and golden goblets whose round surfaces revealed in proud figures 1325 the long lineage of Turkish kings; the victorious Turk was depicted with his people and army, with scores of vanquished fleets, nations,

tot classes victas gentesque et barbara regna,
caelata ex auro Persarum nomina regum
captorum, ductos pelago terrisque triumphos,
1330   quos bello vincens depinxit Turca superbus,
ut potans et iam Turcas incenderet armis
vel memores animos renovaret Martis amore.
     Quid referam Venetos, rapientes magna Liburnos,
Illyrici captos Turcas quos inde tulerunt?
1335   Atque Italus, Tuscus redeuntes, nauta redemptor
advectasque sibi merces quas emerit illinc?
Captivosque duces, dandos puerosque parenti,
ingenti pretio redimendos undique Turcis?
     Regulus aufugit timidis inglorius armis,
1340   non ausus nostris pelago concurrere, caute,
quos iam victores cernebat sorte superbos,
Andres quas toto fugientes aequore naves
Horia tunc sequitur, frustra tamen ire Ioannes
contendit, remex animo quia linquitur ipse.
1345   Perfidus evasit dilapsus regulus undis;
hic partem classis duxit puppesque sequentes,
piratasque suos, arces et claustra revisit.
Puppibus et tacitis nocturnus venit ad Alger,
quam Saldem quondam veteres dixere coloni.
1350   Tristia custodes non ausi inquirere fata,
ne qua in captivos saeviret perfidus ira.
Res gestas pelago narrarat nuntia veri
Famaque vulgarat Turcas cessisse Philippo.
     Iam fusos Turcas, dispersas aequore naves,
1355   Austriades classem miratur et agmina capta.
Iam fractas puppes, revoluta per aequora transtra,
cymbas, antennas, malos tabulasque revolvi
sulfure quas colubri flammis dispersa.rat ignis.
Nec se victores Hispani credere possunt,

and barbarous realms. Etched in gold were the names of captured
Persian kings, and triumphs celebrated on sea and land, commis-
sioned by the proud Turk when he won in battle, so he could in-   1330
cite Turks for combat while he drinks, or stir mindful spirits with
the love of war.

Why should I speak of the Venetians and Liburnians as they
seized great spoils? Or the captive Turks that the Illyrians carried
away? And what of the goods that the Italian or Tuscan merchant   1335
seaman acquired from there and took for himself as he returned?
Or the captive leaders and youths that will be returned to their
family after being ransomed at a great price from the Turks?

The pirate king Uluj Ali flees in dishonor with his cowardly
forces, not daring in his caution to confront our men at sea, having   1340
already determined that the victors were exultant in their fate.
Andrea Doria gives chase to his escaping galleys on open sea. John
of Austria tries to pursue, but in vain since his rowers are sapped
of strength. The treacherous king escaped in retreat over the   1345
waves. He led part of the navy along with trailing galleys and pi-
rate allies to reach his fortresses and strongholds. With his ships
sailing stealthily in the night, he reaches Algiers, the place ancient
colonists once called Saldae. The sentries dared not ask about   1350
the grim outcome, lest their treacherous king, in his wrath, rage
against his captives. For Fama, messenger of truth, had reported
the deeds wrought at sea and spread word that the Turks had suc-
cumbed to Philip.

Now John of Austria marvels at the routed Turks, the boats
scattered on the water, the fleet and captured troops. Now too he   1355
sees the crippled galleys, thwarts overturned on the water, capsized
skiffs, sails, masts, and planks, which the gunfire had scattered
with flames from the sulfur of the culverins. The Spaniards can

1360   nec Turcae victos patiuntur classe vocari.
           Haerentesque duces videas caelumque tuentes.
           Luminibus tacitis contemnunt undique vires
           mortalesque hominum nervos, sine numine vanos.
1365   Victoremque Deum nostri Turcaeque fatentur.
           Corporibus plenae Turcarum stare carinae
           et remex visus pendens — miserabile dictu.
           Intrabantque duces milesque et vulgus inerme
           ut raperent avidi Turcarum regia furtim.
1370   Viscera perque foros calcabant, membra virorum
           et sparsos oculos, rorantes sanguine remos.
           Haec dum Caesareo iuveni miranda videntur,
           dum stupet et fratrem Turcas vicisse Philippum
           congaudet ductor cunctos optabat adesse
1375   Hispanosque duces grandes regnoque potentes,
           ut Spinosa caput populorum fratris in orbe,
           consilium regale, viri clarissima gesta,
           et faustos belli eventus sortemque Philippi,
           Hispanae gentis non enarrabile fatum
1380   suspicerent, summasque Deo persolvere grates,
           curarent dictis, ferrent donaria templis.
           Imprimis te, Deza, suum dum laudat amicum,
           quae tibi vitarit narrare pericula gestit.
             Ad proceres versus repetebat, Deza, subinde:
1385   'quid nunc noster,' ait, 'faceret, iam Deza per urbem,
           si nunc Hispanos victores crederet unus?
           Obvius, ut ridens nobis occurreret ille
           fortunasque meas, fratris nomenque Philippi
           aequaret caelo, vultu acceptissimus omni.
1390   "Iam iam Byzantum, et Christi expugnare sepulchrum,
           tu fratri poteris," vates cantaret in ora,
           illustre ut pectus dictis aperiret amicis.
           Qui si forte mihi bellanti prospera scisset

hardly believe that they have won, nor can the Turks bear to be   1360
declared vanquished by the enemy fleet. You could see officers
perplexed and looking to heaven. With their silent eyes, they dis-
miss the power and mortal strength of men as nothing without
divine protection. Both our men and the Turks pronounce God
the vanquisher. Galleys full of Turkish corpses stand upright,   1365
and a rower is seen hanging, a sight pitiful to describe. Command-
ers, soldiers, and unarmed commoners boarded, eager to plunder
the Turkish royal treasure in secret. On the decks they trampled
the guts, limbs, dislodged eyeballs of soldiers, and oars dripping   1370
with blood. While these wondrous events are surveyed by the
young Caesar, while he stands speechless, rejoicing that his brother
Philip has conquered the Turks, he wished that all the Spanish
commanders and powerful lords from the realm had been there, so   1375
that along with Espinosa, the head of state and royal counselor in
his brother's kingdom, they could have witnessed his astounding
deeds, the battle's happy outcome, Philip's good fortune, the Span-
ish nation's ineffable destiny, and render great thanks to God, offer   1380
prayers, and carry gifts to the temples. He praises you especially,
Deza, as his longtime friend, and he longs to recount to you the
dangers he narrowly avoided.

 Just then, Deza, John turned to the leaders: "What," he asks,
"would our Deza do now in the city, were he the first to know that   1385
the Spaniards are victorious? He would run joyfully to greet us; he
would praise to heaven my successes and the name of my brother
Philip, clearly delighted in his whole expression. 'Even now you
will have the power to capture Byzantium and Christ's tomb for   1390
your brother,' he would prophesy in song, to incite my noble heart
with encouraging words. If by chance he learned that success had

venisse haec, nullus celebraret laetior illo.
Est famulus regi fidus promptusque Philippo.
1395 Argumentum ingens mentis, quae ad regia nata est:
"Pellebam haereticos, Mahumeti et crimina sectae,
scindere dum propero non iam medicabile vulnus,
sinceras partes purgataque oppida peste,
dumque scelus linquo Garnata ex urbe revulsum,
1400 supplicio affectos Mauros civesque rebelles
exactosque mihi Castellae ad moenia regis,
invisasque procul terras habitare malignos,
dum facio iussu moderantis cuncta Philippi.'"
(Extollens ductos laudabat, Deza, triumphos,
1405 molem Romanos tantam vertisse negabat).
'Quid si nostra Deo ducente haec proelia summo
inspiceret? Classem coniunctam temnere Parthos,
obruere infestos hostes? Puppesque superbas,
et fractas proras? Dispersos aequore Turcas?
1410 Victorem Hispanos resonantes classe Philippum?
Quid si Bassanem truncum? Victumque Tyrannum?
Captivos Turcas? Raptas ex hoste carinas
vidisset praeses? (Generoso est nomine Deza)
quam vellet pars esse mei vel prima pericli.'
1415 Ex animo Austriades repetebat nomen amici
principibus classis, Venetis Italisque viritim,
multa super Deza referens ductoribus, idem
ut de more duces laudat regisque ministros.
      Iamque omnis fluctu classis currebat ab omni
1420 visuri Austriadam victorem classe Philippi.
Nostrates cuncti veniunt, regisque cohortes,
ordine laetanturque duces nautaeque magistri.
Hinc primus Venetum dux, tunc laetissimus armis,
accessit senior comitatus gente suorum.
1425 Regius Austriades venienti occurrit honore,

come to me in battle, no one would rejoice more gladly than he.
He is a faithful servant to the king, ever at the ready for Philip.
His is the best proof of a mind born for royal affairs: 'I drove out   1395
the heretics and the crimes of Muhammad's sect, as I rushed to
cut away the wound that could not be healed from healthy places
and towns purged of the plague; I isolated the evil removed from
the city of Granada. I drove the Moriscos after they suffered pun-   1400
ishment and the rebellious citizens to the king's walls of Castile,
forcing those dangerous people to inhabit distant, hostile lands. I
do all these things by order of Philip in his temperance.'" (He was
celebrating and praising the triumphs you accomplished, Deza,   1405
insisting that even the Romans had not overcome such obstacles).
"What if Deza had seen these battles we fought with God as our
guide? Our allied fleet defying the Parthians, destroying the hos-
tile enemy? Their proud galleys and shattered prows? The Turks
scattered at sea? Spaniards celebrating Philip's naval victory? What   1410
if he had been the commander (Deza is from a wellborn family)
and seen the Pasha's headless body, the vanquished Tyrant, captive
Turks, and galleys seized from the enemy. How he would have
wished to be right at the forefront of danger with me!" The Aus-   1415
trian spoke his friend's name to the fleet's commanders with his
whole heart: to the Venetian and Italian captains, man by man,
John relates many things about Deza just as he, according to his
custom, praises leaders and royal ministers.

Now the entire fleet was gathering from all parts of the waters
to see the triumphant Austrian with Philip's navy. All our com-   1420
patriots and royal regiments come forth: commanders, sailors,
and pilots celebrate in procession. The aged admiral of the Vene-
tians, so fortunate in war, has come here first with a retinue of
his men. Royal John greets him with honor, and then the leaders   1425

et tunc se solito ductores more salutant.
Et Marcus venit, clarus virtute Colonna,
Marchio Bazanus bello et clarissimus illo
bellatorque mari. Nautarum gloria summus
1430   Horia, qui Hispanos semper dilexit amicos.
Omnes victori gratantur iure Philippo,
qui fratrem Hispanis sortitus caelitus armis,
felix, qui in Parthos natus quos nulla subegit
regnantum virtus, Crassum Romanaque signa
1435   fregerunt olim, terris pontoque superbi.
Ut Babylon quondam Romanis nota per orbem,
sic nunc Byzantium Latiis Graecisque trophaeis.
Arma tamen pelago Turcarum, signa Tyranni
Austriadae magnis non responsura triumphis.
1440   En novit victor fratris virtute Philippus.
Hinc fera Turcarum vis fluctu effracta peribit,
si classis regis Venetumque ligata, Philippi,
Romani ductu pastoris, pergit in hostem.
Haec tunc Austriadae ductores fata canebant.
1445   Iam longe tuto fugientes remige Parthi
fluctibus in mediis procul evanescere visi,
excelsas naves velis albescere ponto,
atque mari summo tenues vix currere puppes,
conspicit, hic Christum pelago vicisse potentem,
1450   cui virtus, nomen reddendaque gloria soli.
Narrabat ductor Caroli de more parentis,
qui cuncta ad Christum referebat parta labore,
haereticos postquam vicit fuditque malignos
Saxoniumque ducem cepitque ex hoste trophaeum.
1455   Sollicitus nostros proceres dum quaeritat inde,
omnes in tuto cernit, duo fortia bello
pectora de numero Martem rapuisse furore,

salute one another in the accustomed fashion. Next came Marco
Antonio Colonna, famous for his virtue, then Marquis Bazán, a
warrior on the sea so brilliant in this battle. Then comes great
Doria, glory of seafarers, who always cherished his Spanish allies.   1430
All rightly congratulate the triumphant Philip, who with divine
inspiration entrusted the Spanish forces to his brother, destined at
birth to fight the Parthians whom the power of kings had never
beaten; once they destroyed Crassus and the Roman standards,   1435
ruling supreme on land and at sea. As Babylon was once known
throughout the world for its Roman trophies, so now Byzantium
is known for Latin and Greek ones. Yet Turkish arms and the
Tyrant's standards will not be a match for the Austrian's great tri-
umphs on the sea. Indeed, Philip recognizes that he is a conqueror   1440
through his brother's virtue. The savage might of the Turks—
shattered at sea—will perish forever if the allied fleet of Venice
and King Philip, with the guidance of the Roman bishop, contin-
ues to advance against the enemy. So the commanders heralded
John of Austria's destiny.

By now the Parthians seem to fade from view far across the   1445
waves as they flee on safe oars: the commander sees tall ships
whitening the sea's surface with their sails and fragile galleys hardly
moving on the tops of waves. He sees that mighty Christ con-
quered here on the sea, and that the virtue, honor, and glory be-   1450
long to him alone. The commander spoke in the manner of his
father Charles, who attributed all things won by his own effort to
Christ, when he vanquished heretics, laid low criminals and the
Saxon leader, and then claimed enemy spoils. John is anxious to   1455
ask about our leaders: he sees that all are safe, but learns that rag-
ing Mars had seized two brave hearts from their number. Though

comperit, inferias quae iam daret ille sepultis.
Bernardinus abest — Macquedae Martius heros —
1460   Cardenas fato navali hoc vectus in hostem,
qui Christi miles vitam in certamine fudit.
Ingemit Austriades, generoso haec pectore dixit:
'Non constant parvo memoranda et grandia bello,
magnaque mortales subeunt discrimina vitae.
1465   Gloria queis curae est properant per vulnera morti.
Sic nihil ex omni cernas iam parte beatum.
Bernardine vale, longum vale, ipse resurges.
Invidit fortuna mihi, ne clara per altum
gesta meis ducibus felici Marte videres.
1470   At tu iam regnas pro Christo sanguine fuso,
cum sanctis felix caelo victurus in aevum.'

    Victores praedae cuncti rerumque potiti,
iam portus alios urbesque invadere tentant.
Sed quassae puppes, non iam tractabile caelum
1475   et saevum pelagus, cogebat quaerere portum.
Gaudentesque mari Siculas vertuntur ad oras,
ingentesque Deo grates iam solvere certant,
dum cursus pelago Siculorum litora monstrat;
angustique procul rarescunt claustra Pelori.
1480   Hinc iam Fama volans, successu laetior ipso,
quam vulgi primam movisse et vocibus aures
diximus et cives dictis turbasse loquendo.
Gestorum classis, tanti praenuntia cursus,
Italiae portus Venetum turresque marinas
1485   commorat, celso victoris ducta triumpho.
Expandit gaudens horrendo in pectore plumas,
mille oculos, linguas aperit, tot subrigit aures,

they were already buried in the sea, he would give them their last
rites. Bernardino Cárdenas is lost, war hero of Maqueda, carried   1460
by his sailor's fate against the enemy. A soldier of Christ, he
poured out his life in the conflict. The Austrian sighed, then
speaks these words from his noble heart: "Memorable and grand
acts in war come at no small price, and mortal lives encounter
great tribulations. Those concerned with glory rush to death with   1465
mortal wounds. Thus, you will find nothing is blessed in every
respect. Farewell, Bernadino, forever farewell. You will rise again.
Fortune begrudged me this: that you did not see the great exploits
of my officers in this successful battle on the sea. But now you are   1470
supreme, having shed your blood for Christ, and you will live for-
ever happy in heaven among the saints."

Now the victors, having acquired plunder and goods, attempt
to make raids on other ports and cities. But the battered galleys,
turbulent skies, and a savage sea drove them to seek harbor. Re-   1475
joicing on the water, they turn toward Sicilian shores. Catching
sight of the land of Sicily from afar, they vie to give great thanks
to God. From a distance, the straits of narrow Pelorus close in.

Then Fama takes wing, rejoicing in this outcome; she was the   1480
first, we said, to have moved the people's ears with her voice, to
have stirred up citizens with her words as she speaks. She pro-
claims the navy's deeds and its great voyage. Set in motion by the
winner's exalted triumph, she rouses the ports of Italy and the   1485
Venetian towers on the sea. Rejoicing, she spreads her wings
on her bristling chest; she opens a thousand eyes, a thousand
tongues, perks up as many ears, striving to spread news of this

spargere contendit peregrino haec proelia mundo,
gentibus occultis Austridam pandere magnum.
1490 Sed quia dignus erat felicia noscere gesta
primus, qui classem coniunxit foedere divo,
ad patrem sanctum pennis sublata per auras
convertit cursum Romana palatia versus.
Clavigerumque petit caeli, cui summa potestas
1495 concessa, hac animas solvitque ligatque resolvit,
atque alias iuste tenebrosa in Tartara mittit.
　　Sollicitus mentem volvebat nocte, per undas
currentem Austriadam repetens Turcamque superbum
Romanosque duces Venetos classemque piorum.
1500 Ante oculos pugnam, crudelia funera fratrum
cernebat, gemitus morientum, proelia, luctus,
tangebant animum patris mortalia sancti,
qui genibus flexis manibusque orare supinis,
non cessans Dominum noctesque diesque, precatur.
1505 Perpetuo grandis Christum sermone vocabat:
'Da, Pater, his cursum, ventos et puppibus aptos,
da dextram famulis, tecum nunc aequora verrant,
qui Petrum summas direxti, sancte, per undas,
quique rotas, currus Pharaonis, classica ponto
1510 sparsisti quondam dextra virgaque potenti,
qui pedibus siccis mediis tunc fluctibus illam
duxisti gentem populumque et barbara castra.
Fugerunt undae, tenuerunt flumina cursus,
cum geminos montes murus scindebat aquarum
1515 a dextra laevaque fretum peditesque subire
mortales longe mirati e rupibus agmen,
pyramides fluctus caelo consurgere visi,
Aegyptusque Dei mersas virtute phalanges—
in mare proiectum vidit cum gente Tyrannum.

382

battle around the world abroad, and to broadcast the mighty Austrian even to remote people. But since it was right that he who 1490
joined the fleet in holy treaty should be the first to know the happy news, she turns her course, borne on the wind by her wings toward the Holy Father and Roman palaces. There she seeks heaven's gatekeeper, to whom was given the greatest power: to absolve some souls, bind and release others, and send still others to 1495
the depths of hell.

He was anxiously meditating in the night, thinking of John of Austria racing through the waves, the proud Turk, the Roman and Venetian commanders, and the holy fleet. In his mind's eye he saw 1500
the battle, the merciless deaths of brothers, cries of the dying, combat, and grief. Such mortal concerns moved the Holy Father's spirit; on bended knee with hands outstretched in prayer, he never ceased to entreat the Lord, night and day. The majestic old man 1505
invoked Christ with continuous words: "Grant them, Father, favorable winds for their ships; give strength to your servants so that with you they may now sweep over the waves. You guided Peter — O holy one — over high waves. You once scattered Pharaoh's 1510
wheels, chariots, and war trumpets on the sea with your right hand and powerful staff. You then led that tribe with dry feet amid the waves, the people, and their foreign camps. Seas parted, the currents stemmed their flow. A wall on the right and left sides cut 1515
through twin mountains of water; men marveled that the foot soldiers and battle line crossed the strait far from the rocks. The waves seemed to rise to the sky like pyramids, and Egypt saw its armies submerged by the power of God, and the Tyrant hurled

383

1520 Turcae sic pereant et Christi nominis hostes,
Christicolae reges vincant, quos vincere mavis.
Lex tua sancta, fides, crux nunc, Ecclesia victrix
per pelagusque tuo haec dominetur regia sceptro.'
Devotusque senex numquam ieiunia fregit,
1525 sulcarat rugis corpus duroque cubili,
verberibus carnem pro nobis urere sanctam.
Isque gregem pastor, legis doctissimus almae,
assiduo Christi vitam sermone docebat,
Spiritus et Sanctus vivo resonabat ab ore.
1530 Auxilio Christum, sanctorum nomina caeli
implorans, nostros victuros iure ferebat.
Ad quem Fama suis gaudens sermonibus usa est.
'Sancte, quod optaras, vidit longaeva senectus,
ecce tibi ad votum venit victoria laeta.
1535 Austriades vicit, stant tutae in litore puppes,
volvitur in fluctu Bassan sine nomine corpus,
rectores, capta est classis geminique nepotes,
machina, tot colubri, captiva et signa Tyranni.'
Auditis princeps Ecclesae his vocibus almus
1540 direxit mentem, quo semper cuncta solebat.
'Optavi omnipotens non frustra haec saecula,' dixit,
'ut tandem vivens devictum Marte Tyrannum
nunc oculis cernam, victorem classe dedisti
natum, quem vellem rerum dominumque Philippum.
1545 Servasti Austriadam, classem te auctore ligatam.'
Caelestemque iterum traxit de pectore vocem.
Ad Patrem et Natum procedit Spiritus unde:
'O sanctus, sanctus, sanctus, cui gloria soli
debetur, caeli ac terrae Pater unicus adsis.
1550 Non nobis, Domine, haud nostris victoria gestis

into the sea with his people. Thus may the Turks and enemies of   1520
Christ's name perish. Let Christian kings vanquish those whom
you wish to conquer: may your holy law, your faith, the cross, and
the Church now triumphant overseas bring these kingdoms under
your scepter."

The devout old man never broke his fast; his body was fur-   1525
rowed with lines, and he tormented his holy flesh for us with a
hard bed and whips. This shepherd, so learned in nurturing law,
was teaching his flock about the Christian life with continuous
preaching, and the Holy Spirit resounded from his lips. Imploring
Christ for help, and the names of heaven's saints, he rightly pro-   1530
claimed that our forces would be victorious. To him joyful Fama
directed her words. "Holy one, your great old age has granted what
you wished for: look, a blessed victory comes in answer to your
prayers. John of Austria has won, the galleys are safe on shore, and   1535
Ali Pasha's nameless body drifts in the waves. His fleet and officers
have been captured, along with his two sons, his artillery, as many
culverins, and the Tyrant's standards." Having heard these words,
the benevolent prince of the Church turned his thoughts where he   1540
was accustomed in all things. "Almighty God," he said, "not in vain
have I hoped for this age. You granted that I live to see with
my own eyes the Tyrant conquered in war, and your son Philip,
whom I wished to be lord of the world, victorious with his fleet.   1545
You watched over the Austrian and the fleet bound by your au-
thority." Again, he drew heavenly words from his breast. His spirit
turns to the Father and the Son: "O holy, holy, holy one, to whom
alone belongs all glory. Only Father of heaven and earth, stand   1550
with us. Not by us and not by our deeds is this victory delivered,

haec parta est. Nomen Nati dedit auctor Iesus.
Austriada hoc tandem vicisti nomine Christi,
ad Christum Dominum referantur cuncta, Philippe.
Caelitus omne bonum misit mortalibus ille,
1555   de caelo iunxit ductores classis in unum,
de caelo Turcas mersit fuditque triremes,
de caelo cursum, de caelo haec grandia gessit.
Bassanem truncum caelesti Marte videmus,
orbem de caelo vinces iam, nate Philippe.'
1560   Dixerat haec summus divina mente sacerdos.
Circumstant patres dextra laevaque frequentes;
purpureis adsunt induti vestibus omnes,
gratantur Petri Romana in sede locato.
Oscula dantque pedi sancto pia nomine Christi.
1565   Hinc iam persolvi votum quodcumque pararat,
imperat et Romae celebrantur sacra piorum.
Hostia viva Deo offertur. Iustusque sacerdos
rem facit in templis divinam carmine sacro.
Ducuntur pompae Romano more per urbem.
1570   Defunctos iussit decorari in classe supremis
muneribusque duces. Fuso qui sanguine Christum
confessi in Turcas pugnarunt Marte viriles.
Egregias animas, absolvens sanctus in aevum,
exortis lacrimis requiem poscebat amicis
1575   sedibus aeternam, ut placidis a morte quiescant.
      Hinc se Fama suis convertit protinus alis.
Alpinos saltusque nivosa cacumina turbat
et praeceps veris Gallos rumoribus implet:
vicisse Austriadam Turcas iam classe Philippi,
1580   Parthos, Bassanes, inimica et signa Tyranni.
Obstupuit gens illa, diu vix credere factum.

Lord. God gave to Jesus the name of Son. You, John of Austria, conquered in Christ's name; let all things, Philip, be referred to Christ the Lord. He sent all good things to mortals from above: from heaven he joined the navy's leaders as one, from heaven he 1555 sank the Turks and routed their galleys, from heaven he gave passage, and from heaven he performed these great deeds. Because of his heavenly combat, we see the Pasha's corpse. From heaven, Philip, my son, you will conquer the world."

The pope uttered these words from his holy mind. Priests gath- 1560 ered around, crowding in on the right and left; they are all there dressed in crimson robes, giving thanks to the one seated on Peter's Roman throne. They bestow reverent kisses on his holy feet in Christ's name. Now he orders that whatever vows he made 1565 must be fulfilled, and the sacred rites are celebrated in Rome. The living sacrifice is offered for God. In churches, the righteous priest carries out the holy rites with sacred songs. Processions are led throughout the city in the Roman custom. He ordered the fleet's 1570 dead be honored with obsequies and its commanders, with gifts. Having professed Christ with the blood they shed, they fought vigorously against the mighty Turks. The holy man, absolving the great souls for all time, tearfully sought eternal rest for his be- 1575 loved, so that after death they might rest in the peaceful seats of heaven.

Then Fama turns herself straightaway on her wings. She speeds over Alpine passes and snowy peaks, and headlong, she fills the Gauls with truthful reports: that John of Austria, with Philip's fleet, has conquered the Turks, the Parthians, the Pashas, and the 1580 Tyrant's hated standards. This nation was dumbstruck, for a long time hardly able to believe the news.

Iam iuga monstrabat flammis combusta Pyrenne,
Hispanos Gallis medius qui terminat unus —
Vasconesque fame invictos tunc Marte Metelli,
1585   humanas ausos carnes violare voraces,
corporibus vesci solitos discrimine belli —
concitat Austriadae fato victoris in undis.
Cantaber occurrit gaudens felicibus armis,
Astur vicinus consurgit ad arma Philippi.
1590   Protinus Hispanas currit vulgata per urbes.
Invenit regem volventem grandia secum,
insomnem curis, meditantem incommoda classis:
eventus belli dubios pelagique procellas,
quas puppes toties submersas viderit undis,
1595   audacis iuvenis generoso in pectore vires,
torquebant regem per noctem proelia ponti.
Catholicus Christo fratrem commiserat uni,
victurumque Dei sperarat viribus hostes.
Cum subito Augustas victoris nuntius aures
1600   implevit fratris felici Marte Philippo.
Quis pectus, rex magne, tuum depingere vates
contendet tacitum? Vultu ut tranquilla potestas
gaudia dissimulat sanctos mentisque recessus,
vertere quos numquam potuit fortuna laborum
1605   adversa aut rebus mundi sublata secundis.
Victorem fratrem, victos Turcasque superbos,
incolumes portu — dum narrat Fama — carinas,
atque duces salvos vitasse pericula belli.
Maiestate deo referens haec proelia summo
1610   tandem pauca pia dixit de mente Philippus:
'Hispanis frater si tunc Deus astitit armis,
quis Turca aut Bassan poterat concurrere contra?

Already, the Pyrenees — the sole boundary that separates Span-
iards from Gauls — showed their ridges lit up with sunbeams.
Then she came to the Basques, unconquered by hunger in the war   1585
with Metellus; ravenous, they dared defile human flesh, accus-
tomed to consume corpses in the heat of battle. She rouses them
with news of the Austrian's naval triumph. The Cantabrian rushes
forth rejoicing at the happy victory; the neighboring Astur rises up
before Philip's arms. Straightaway, she runs through Spanish cities   1590
spreading the word. She finds the king turning over grave matters
in his mind, sleepless with his cares, considering the fleet's perils:
the uncertain outcome of war, storms at sea, such as he had seen
sink many ships in the waves, the strength in the noble youth's   1595
heart, and the battle at sea — all this tormented the king through
the night. As a Catholic, he had commended his brother to Christ
alone in hopes that he would vanquish God's enemies with his
strength. Suddenly, the victor's messenger brought word of his
brother's blessed battle to Philip's imperial ears.   1600

What bard, great king, could dare describe your silent heart?
For his calm authority hides joy and the deepest thoughts of his
mind from his face, and no turn of fortune — whether contrary or   1605
exalted by favorable world affairs — could alter it. When Fama tells
him that his brother is victorious, the proud Turks are vanquished,
his galleys are safe at port, and the leaders have escaped war's per-
ils, Philip ascribes the battle to God's highest majesty, and at last,   1610
he spoke a few words from his devout mind: "If God stood as a
brother to the Spanish forces, what Turk, what Pasha could have

389

Astitit ille Deus, tecum qui perdidit hostes,
illi acies parent, necnon exercitus omnis
1615 bellorum Dominum terris undisque fatetur.
Cognoscunt nomenque, timent tua classica reges,
teque potestates exhorrent, rector Olympi,
Romanae Ecclesae tutor, defendis ab hoste
servos, in summo positos discrimine servas.
1620 O clemens sanctusque Deus, miserere tuorum.'
Haec pia Catholicus fundebat verba Philippus.
Edocet inde duces dictis regnique cohortem,
quos iam sollicitos norat classique timentes.
Certior ipse viris factum remque ordine pandit.
1625 Consilium regale forum bellique senatus—
Didacus ille suo regi Spinosa beatus,
Ecclesae princeps, rubra cum veste sacerdos
gratatur vultu, quo non praestantior alter,
pontificis facie speciosus regibus una,
1630 canities cui culta gravi monstrabat honore
non temere in regnis decorasse ad magna Philippum.
Ipsa et turba ducum fati stupet inscia tanti.
Mirantur multi classem sortemque Philippi, hi
quos iam captivos Bassan advexerat olim,
1635 quique potestatem norant classemque Tyranni,
haerent Hispanos Turcas vicisse superbos.
Fortunas fratris laudant nomenque Philippi,
queis Deus omnipotens concessit adire triumphum,
quem nec Romani, Graeci aut videre Latini,
1640 nec memorare valent gentes ab origine mundi.
Curia dum proceres, ductores, regia gaudet,
dum currus ludosque parant celebrare per arces;
longaevique senes, dum Christi numen adorant
et pompas ducuntque choros, tunc Fama per orbem

fought against them? God stood with you as he destroyed our
enemies. The troops obey him; the whole army calls him Lord of   1615
Battles on land and sea. Kings heed your name and fear your war
trumpets. Before you, great powers tremble, ruler of Olympus,
savior of the Roman Church. You defend your servants from the
enemy, you watch over those placed in the greatest danger. O mer-   1620
ciful and holy God, have pity on your people."

Catholic Philip was pouring forth these reverent words.
Through dispatches he then informs the realm's governors and
advisors, whom he knew to be anxious and fearful for the fleet.
Now fully informed, he recounts the event and the outcome as it
happened to the royal council, the forum, and the war senate. Di-   1625
ego Espinosa, blessed by his king, prince of the church, a priest in
a cardinal's red robe, rejoices, with a countenance more distin-
guished than any other, his bishop's face impressive as well to
kings. His advanced age, graced with the elegance of utmost honor,   1630
proved that Philip had not without reason promoted him to high
rank in his kingdom. Even this assembly of leaders is struck dumb,
never having heard of such a great turn of events. Many marvel at
the fleet and Philip's good fortune; some, whom the Pasha had
once taken captive and who had known the power and the fleet of   1635
the Tyrant, are stunned that the Spanish had conquered the proud
Turks. They praise Philip's name and his brother's fortunes; God
almighty granted them this triumph, the likes of which the Ro-
mans, Greeks, or Latins have never seen, nor other nations can   1640
recall from the world's beginning.

While the royal council, leaders, and commanders rejoice, they
plan to hold races and games in the cities. While long-lived el-
ders worship Christ's divine power and lead celebrations and
dances, talkative Fama herself skims across the world and the

1645   ipsa et Niliacas urbes dum garrula lustrat.
          Invictum spargit terris pontoque Philippum.
          Hispani regis miratur regia Memphis,
          nomen iam Meroe. Celebrant iam moenia Cadmi,
          et Thebae extollunt Hispanae gentis alumnos.
1650   Umbris ipsa suis laudat viduata Syene.
          Extremi Aethiopes fugiunt orbisque remotus —
          omnis Arabs felix, Aegyptus territus, Indus —
          armorum sonitum classis certamina fingunt
          et patrio ritu simulant pugnare carinas.
1655   Aurorae tandem qua sol decurrere visus
          aureus et mergi Boreas qua immurmurat — omnes
          convertens gentes populosque et barbara regna —
          victorem regem docuit victumque Tyrannum.
             Interea princeps praedam partitur in omnes,
1660   Romani partes, Veneti nostrique tulerunt.
          Octoginta autem cepit centumque carinas
          et septem longas omnes, simul arma, Ioannes.
          Innumeros colubros, longos curtosque recepit;
          milia sena virum cesserunt fortia pugnae.
1665   Octoginta ardens iussit deducere regi
          perlongos colubros fratri, quos legerat ipse,
          ductores regni senos, par nobile fratrum;
          quam vellet patrem vivum duxisse triumpho
          et captum frater pelago misisse Philippo.
1670   Ingens nam virtus Mauro prudentia bello,
          Hispanos captos Bassan tractabat amice
          et dabat his vestem, frigus ne laedere posset.
          Atque famem miseris generosus saepe levabat,
          qui semper visus pugnare et ducere classem,
1675   et miles sollers dux fortis gesserat agmen.

cities of the Nile. She spreads news of Philip, undefeated on land 1645
and sea. Royal Memphis — now Meroë — marvels at the Spanish
king's fame. The walls of Cadmus rejoice, and those of Thebes
honor the sons of the Spanish nation. Syene, robbed of her shad- 1650
ows, sings praise. The distant Ethiopians flee, and those at the
ends of the earth — every prosperous Arab, terrified Egyptian, In-
dian — imagine the sound of artillery and naval combat, and in
their ancestral rituals they pretend to fight the ships. Finally, in the 1655
East, where the golden sun seems to melt and dissolve, where
Boreas murmurs, Fama — calling the attention of all nations, peo-
ple, and barbarous realms — reported the king as vanquisher, the
Tyrant as vanquished.

Meanwhile, the prince distributes spoils to all: Romans, Vene- 1660
tians, and our forces took their share. John took 180 galleys, and
seven long ships, with their armaments. He received innumerable
long and short culverins; 6,000 powerful fighters submitted to
him. Zealously he ordered eighty long cannons, which he himself 1665
had selected, to be set aside for the king, his brother, plus six gov-
ernors of the Turkish kingdom and that noble pair of brothers.
How he wished he had brought their father back alive in triumph
and had sent him to Philip as a captive from the sea. For the
Moor's virtue and prudence in war was great, and the Pasha had 1670
treated Spanish captives kindly, giving them clothing so the cold
would not harm them, often mercifully relieving the hunger of suf-
fering prisoners. Always visible fighting and directing the navy, he
led his forces as an accomplished soldier and a mighty leader. 1675

Captorum numerum bis quinque et milia censes,
multaque praeterea, quae Fama obscura relinquit,
longum esset numerum captarum dicere rerum.
Turcarum capta est regni pontique potestas,
nam nautae audaces perierunt fluctibus omnes,
amisit pelago ductores, arma, rudentes
transtraque cum fabris, remex submersus in undis.
Liberaque ex nostris hominum sunt milia sena,
quos Bassan pugna captivos duxerat idem,
servitio longo remos impellere suetos
sub ducibus duris portantes pondera classis.
Septaginta addas quinceno, scriptor, et anno
Virginei partus uno post mille peracto,
nonis Octobris pugnatum, res bene gesta est.
Pontificis dictis cesserunt prospera cuncta.
        Nonis Octobris horisque simillima fato
psallentes summus iussit cantare sacerdos.
Tunc pater, in templo dicto de nomine Petri,
aedibus in sacris responsa haec carmine caeli
cantata, ut mentes pugnamque incenderet ardor,
cordaque flammatus per nervos spiritus iret,
et validos animos impleret vivida virtus
verborum Domini vivi sermonis in hostes.
'Nunc inimicorum vestrorum hunc impetum et arma
ne timeatis,' ait, 'vobis Deus ecce benignus
auxiliabitur in pugna victoribus idem.'
Hisque mares animos dictis in bella sacerdos
exacuit sanctis ut Turcas vincere possent,
mergeret ut ponto classem Parthosque superbos
tunc Caroli natus felix fraterque Philippi.

1680
1685
1690
1695
1700
1705

You would have counted 11,000 captives, and many besides which concealing Fama leaves out: it would be a long task to report the number of captured spoils. Turkish power on land and sea is checked; for along with all the brave sailors who perished in 1680 the waves, the Turks lost leaders at sea, and arms, ropes, thwarts with their carpenters, and oarsmen submerged in the waters. Six thousand of our men, whom the Pasha led into battle as captives, are freed, having rowed in long servitude under harsh overseers, 1685 bearing the fleet's full weight. You would add, chronicler, that the successful battle took place in the year 1571 from when the Virgin gave birth, on the Nones of October. In the pope's words, every- 1690 thing has come to an auspicious end.

On the Nones of October at the exact time of the battle, the pope ordered the choristers to sing songs befitting the fated outcome. Then in the church named for St. Peter, the Holy Father commanded that these responses be chanted with heavenly song in the holy sanctuary, so that zeal would kindle their minds for fight- 1695 ing, a fiery spirit would enter their hearts and sinews, and the hardy strength of God's words would drive their stout hearts against the enemy. "Now do not fear this assault nor your enemy's 1700 weaponry," he said, "behold, merciful God will come to your aid as you triumph in battle." With these holy words, the pope stirred their manly hearts for war, so that they could vanquish the Turks, and so that the blessed son of Charles and brother of Philip might 1705 then sink the fleet and the proud Parthians under the waves.

Iamque ex conspectu Siculae telluris, ab alto
aequatae numero currebant aequore puppes.
Laetitiaque duces, magno certamine rostris
scindebant pelagus, properantes tangere terram.
1710 Iam sale tabentes artus exponere ripis
exoptant avidi nautae classique magistri.
Regiaque Austriadae ductabat celsa carinas,
fatalis puppis victrix Hispana Philippi,
signa vehens proceresque viros regisque cohortem.
1715 Tendebat longo sublatos ordine remos.
Regius Austriades fulgebat victor in armis,
prae se fraternum monstrabant ora vigorem,
victoris Caroli faciem vultusque ferebat.
Aversis proris raptantur ab aequore victae
1720 Turcarum naves, tractae vinctaeque catenis,
vexillis captis verrentes turpiter undas;
Bassanis puppis captiva his turpior ibat.
Mutatisque retro remis humilisque subibat
iam portum, Turcis invisum puppibus ante
1725 signaque versa sui referebat mira Tyranni,
captorum series, fratres regnique potestas,
rectores senique duces Parthique superbi,
demisso vultu fluctus spectare maligne.
Insula consurgit, venientum fama vagatur.
1730 En ruit ad portum Siculorum mira iuventus,
ardentes studio visendi grandia cuncti,
patres atque viri, pueri vulgusque per urbes.
Iam fractas vires, inimica et tela Tyranni
visuri, classem victam, Turcasque subactos,
1735 quos trepidi quondam venientes saepe timebant.
Discurrunt laeti manibusque orare supinis
non cessant Christum Dominum laudare frequentes.

And now, just out of sight of the land of Sicily, ships equal in number raced across the deep water. The leaders were joyfully slicing the waves with their prows in the great contest, hastening to touch land. Eager sailors and naval officers longed to rest their 1710 brine-drenched bodies on the shore.

The Austrian's towering flagship, Philip's victorious Spanish galley of war, was leading the ships, bearing standards and officers, the soldiers and the royal contingent, extending its oars raised in a 1715 long line. A kingly conqueror, he shone in Habsburg regalia, his features manifesting his brother's might; he wore the face and expression of triumphant Charles. With prows reversed, the ships of the Turks vanquished on the sea are dragged, towed, and bound in 1720 chains, shamefully sweeping the waves, their banners captured; more shamefully still, the captive ship of the Pasha was trailing along behind. With backward oars, in humiliation it entered the port long despised by Turkish galleys, displaying the astounding 1725 sight of the Tyrant's inverted standards. Lines of captives, brothers, and magistrates of the realm, pilots, six commanders, and haughty Parthians — faces turned down — look hatefully at the waves. The island rises up as the news of their coming spreads. 1730 Look, the wondrous youth of Sicily rush to the port, all burning with desire to see these great things: fathers, men, young boys, and a crowd from all the cities. They are keen to see the broken forces and dreaded weapons of the Tyrant, the vanquished fleet and captive Turks, whose arrival in times past had brought tremors of fear. 1735 They rush forward joyfully, and with hands uplifted in prayer, they do not stop praising Christ the Lord. Their souls cannot be

Expleri nequeunt animi vultuque subinde
Austriadam repetunt, animis ac mente requirunt.
1740   Et iam turba ducum Siculis advenerat oris
praetoresque loci, custodes, curia regis,
munera cuncta, forum, praefecti ex ordine, iudex,
officii sancti patres — queis impia curae —
et qui ducebat Siculos pro rege marinos,
1745   Marchio nam fuerat Pescarae nomine gentis.
Praeterea templis incedit pompa piorum:
presbyteri, parochi, doctores, rite sacerdos,
in numerumque graves procedunt litora versus,
gloria celsa Deo patri Natoque potenti,
1750   Spiritui Sancto canitur per saecula sacris.
Occurrunt omnes Austriadam nomine patris
et fratris dignum felici voce salutant,
quem Deus incolumem servarit, carmine laudant,
Hispanae gentis ductor per regna futurus,
1755   per pelagus victor fertur, Mars alter in orbe.
Felix qui Turcas subvertat classe superbos
expugnetque domum sanctam virtute parentum;
et nobis Christi iam reddat ab hoste sepulchrum,
extinguat foedam Mahumeti nomine sectam.
1760   Quando haec non Carolo cessit victoria patri,
Austriadae tandem dabitur sub rege Philippo.
    Ipse pater sanctus navale hoc carmine bellum
posteritas mundi, ut teneat ventura legendum,
nunc voluit proprio gentes cognoscere motu,
1765   ut nostros moveat gestorum fama nepotes —
felix eventus classis, victoria, cursus —
ut Romae vigilans custos pastorque piorum,
dux Venetumque simul iunctus nosterque Philippus

quenched, and they strive to again catch sight of the Austrian, searching with heart and mind.

By now a crowd of leaders had convened on the Sicilian shores, 1740 along with officials, guards, the king's council, all office holders, citizens, magistrates, judges, priests of the Inquisition who monitor heresy, and the nobleman who led the Sicilian navy for the king, known as the Marquis of Pescara. Then the procession of 1745 the faithful marches to the churches: deacons, parish priests, canons—all duly ordained churchmen—proceed toward the shore in great numbers. They sing highest glory to God the Father, to the powerful Son, and to the Holy Spirit, blessed for all ages. They 1750 rush to greet John of Austria in his father's name and proclaim him worthy of his brother. With songs, they praise him whom God had preserved; throughout the kingdom he is called the future ruler of the Spanish people, a conqueror at sea, and another 1755 Mars for the world. Blessed is he who destroys the proud Turks with his navy. He shall recapture the Holy Temple through the virtue of his parents; he will rescue Christ's tomb from the enemy and destroy Muhammad's vile sect. Since this triumph was denied 1760 to his father Charles, it will be granted to the Austrian under King Philip.

The Holy Father himself, so that future generations of the world would preserve the memory of the naval battle, a story to be read in this song, wanted the people to understand it of their own accord, so that the fame of these deeds would move our 1765 grandchildren: the happy outcome of the fleet, its triumph, and voyage; how the watchful protector and shepherd in Rome, the allied Venetian leader, and our Philip rightly entrusted the

Austriadae classem committant iure Ioanni.
1770 Proelia qui felix exhausit nomine Christi,
armatusque fide pugnavit vincere Turcas,
sub iuga Bassanes mittet capietque tyrannos,
Parthorum reges ductabit saepe triumphis.
    Sed quia remigium puppes nautasque peritos
1775 perdidit, audaces piratas, arma Tyrannus,
ne possit facili renovare hinc proelia classe,
imperat ipse pater summus, qui sacra gubernat,
ne cupidus quisquam vendat redimatve, remittat,
nec prece, nec pretio, nec vi, nec sorte sub ulla
1780 Turcas captivos, qui capti in navibus extant.
Sed cuncti Hispanis serventur puppibus apti,
compedibus servi teneantur classibus illic,
durat dum Christi miles Venetusque sub armis,
Hispanosque simul Dominus coniungit in unum.
1785 Prospicit inde pater summus nunc numine plenus,
ne saevus Parthus surgat, ne Turca Tyrannus
saeviat hinc iterum in Graecos Italosque per undas,
decisis pennis validas ne sumere vires,
nec valeat fractis iterum concurrere remis.
1790 Haec patri nostro grandis sententia visa est,
gloria cui Christi curae nomenque potentis,
qui caelum terramque regit per saecula vivus.
    Res gestas Garnata ducis per compita narrat,
perque domos civis gaudens et templa sacerdos,
1795 victorem laudant pueri castaeque puellae.
Gaudentes cernas totaque ex urbe canentes
versibus, armatas acies classesque viriles,
proelia victa viri—totum vulganda per orbem—
Austriadae ductu. Cantabant ordine vates:
1800 agmina Persarum perierunt funditus; armis

fleet to John of Austria; and in his good fortune, he carried out   1770
the battles in Christ's name and, armed by faith, fought to defeat
the Turks. He will consign the Pashas to slavery, capture tyrants,
and again bring back Parthian kings in triumph.

The Tyrant has lost oarsmen, galleys, skilled pilots, daring pi-   1775
rates, and artillery, and so that he will be unable to wage new bat-
tles with a readied navy from here on, the Holy Father — who
controls matters of faith — orders that no one be so greedy as to
sell, ransom, or release captive Turks who are held prisoner on the   1780
galleys: not for pity, money, force, or any other reason. Instead, all
should be held in chains on Spanish galleys, to be bound in row-
ers' shackles as long as the soldiers of Christ and the Venetians are
under arms and God unites the Spaniards as one. Therefore, the   1785
Holy Father, filled with divine inspiration, ensures that the savage
Parthian will not rise again, nor the Turkish Tyrant attack Greeks
or Italians at sea, nor revive their fighting strength now that their
wings are clipped, nor muster an attack with broken oars. This   1790
stern decree seemed best to our Holy Father, whose concern is the
glory and name of mighty Christ, who lives and reigns over heaven
and earth for eternity.

Granada spreads news of the commander's deeds through the
crossroads, as the people rejoice in their homes, the priests in the
temples; young boys and chaste girls celebrate the victor. Through   1795
the whole city, you could see them rejoicing and singing of the
readied battle lines and mighty fleets, of the wars won by the Aus-
trian's leadership, worthy of being reported the world over. Bards   1800
were chanting one after another: the battle lines of Persians have

401

Hispanis fracta est rabies insana Tyranni;
victoris cursus felix in bella repressit
progenies Caroli, patris nunc aemula virtus.
Captivosque duces nautas fuditque superbos
1805   rectores gentis vinctos. Praedamque reportat
ingentem miles, pelago fert munera victor,
cum patre et natos rapuit Turcamque potentem
in pugna victum iugulat truncumque relinquit.
      O macte, o virtute valens felixque Ioannes,
1810   cui Deus omnipotens tantum contingere nomen
concessit. Fato consurgis victor in orbe,
Turcarum dominus rerumque futurus ubique,
cuique Asia hoc dives paritura est iure triumphos,
Afros iam victos, Aegyptum, barbara regna,
1815   cernesque ipsa diu venient tibi regia cuncta,
auspiciis subiecta tuis; tunc Indus Arabsque,
sub iuga iam posito mittentur nomine reges.
Oceanusque tibi victori bracchia tendet,
Aethiopesque procul pulsabunt tympana laeti,
1820   victorique sui celebrabunt tura Sabei.
      Haec Garnata ducis dum cantat gesta Ioannis,
ecce tibi rumor sparsus iam moenia complet.
Annam Reginam natum peperisse Philippo,
omnibus est princeps concessus caelitus almus,
1825   haec sors Hispanos victores una manebat,
solamenque viris, multorum causa bonorum
ventura. Hinc pratis fundetur copia rerum,

utterly perished; Spanish forces have crushed the raging fury of
the conquering Tyrant; Charles's blessed son, rivaling his father's
virtue, checked the conqueror's course in war. He has routed cap-   1805
tive leaders, sailors, and the haughty commanders of their nation,
now in chains. And the victorious soldier returns with vast plun-
der, bearing prizes from the sea; for he seized the sons with their
father; he slit the throat of the mighty Turk vanquished in battle
and abandoned the torso.

Hail to you, blessed John, paragon of strength; almighty God
has allowed you to attain great glory. You rise by destiny as a con-   1810
queror over the world. You will be lord among Turks and beyond.
Asia will justly deliver you rich rewards, and you will see the Afri-
cans, Egypt, and the barbarous realms subdued, and all kingdoms   1815
will come to you, subject to your favor; then the Indian and Ara-
bian kings will be sent under the yoke, their glory cast off. Ocean
will stretch out his hands to you as vanquisher. Joyful Ethiopians   1820
from afar will pound drums, and the Sabaeans will offer frankin-
cense to their conqueror.

While Granada sings of the deeds of John of Austria, look, the
news spreads to you and now fills the city walls: Queen Anne has
born a son for Philip—a beloved prince granted from heaven for   1825
all. This singular good fortune awaited the triumphant Spaniards,
a comfort for men, and a promise of abundant blessings ahead.
Now bounty will spring forth from pastures, golden fields will

mollibus hinc flavus gaudebit campus aristis,
militiae spes magna ducum columenque salutis,
1830   gentibus Hispanis virtus et robur avorum.
Iam regnis pax magna tuis, Auguste Philippe,
princeps Fernandus consurgit clarus in orbe.
Hic tibi felici revocabit sorte triumphos,
victrices ducet nostras in bella phalanges.
1835   Hic Christi nomen defendet victor et armis,
ut gentes unum Christum per saecula regem
cognoscant victae Fernandi et Marte Philippi.

LAUS DEO.

rejoice in soft grain, the commanders' great hope for the military, the mainstay of our salvation, a source of strength for the Spanish people, and his forefathers' might. Emperor Philip, great peace is 1830
at hand in your realms, as resplendent Prince Ferdinand comes into the world. It will be his good fortune to win great conquests for you and lead our triumphant troops in battle. He will defend 1835
the name of Christ, a victor in arms, so that the nations, tamed by the military might of Ferdinand and Philip, will come to know Christ, the one and eternal king.

PRAISE BE TO GOD.

Appendix I
Glossary of Names and Places

꽃§?꽃

Below we provide basic biographical information for the most important protagonists of Lepanto, as well as nationalities and places likely to be unfamiliar to many, or whose repeated mention makes them particularly relevant. The poems we feature here draw on classical as well as Renaissance nomenclatures. Though the diversity and variability of Renaissance toponyms make it impractical to include all known variants, we note common alternate nomenclatures in parentheses. In addition, where the translation from classical to early modern or contemporary usage is not obvious, we include Renaissance (Ren.) and contemporary (cont.) toponyms in parentheses. For the former, we limit the entries to usage common in Europe. Readers desiring more detail on the evolution of place-names in the era of Lepanto can now consult crucial primary sources online: Tommaso Porcacchi's 1576 *L'isole più famose del mondo* (hereafter Poracchi; available through the Biblioteca Histórica "Marqués de Valdecilla" of the Universidad Complutense de Madrid (biblioteca.ucm.es/foa); Antonio de Nebrija's *Dictionarium Propiorum Nominum* (hereafter Nebrija; available on Google Books); and Abraham Ortelius's 1578 *Synonymia Geographica* (abbreviated Ort, *Syn*; available on Google Books). Unless otherwise noted our entries below follow these three references, and the *Barrington Atlas*.

For biographical information, we use Capponi's *Victory of the West*, Guilmartin's *Gunpowder and Galleys*, and Bicheno's *Crescent and Cross*. We supplement Ottoman biographies with Lesure's *Lépante: La crise de l'empire ottoman*, and Inalcik's "Lepanto in the Ottoman Documents." Common alternate names — including widely used Italian or Spanish transliterations of Ottoman names — are noted in parentheses, as are noble titles. For titular monarchs, we note their dates of rule (r.).

ACARNANIA. (Acarnia) A region of Epirus, used for the location of the battle.

ACHAEA. (Achaia) A region in the northern Peloponnesus.

ACHELOUS. (Acheloos) A river of western Greece (ancient Acarnania) that empties into the Ionian Sea at the site of the Curzolaris Islands (Echinades), used for the location of the battle.

AETHIOPIA/AETHIOPES. In antiquity, this region refers to Africa and Africans south of Libya. In early modern usage, sub-Saharan Africa and its people.

ALI PASHA, MUEZZINZADE. (Bassan, Halys, Alys) Son of a muezzin (religious official who calls to prayer from a mosque's minaret) and brother-in-law of Selim II, he rose through the Ottoman ranks as a Janissary captain to lead the sultan's fleet at Lepanto. After his death in battle, his two sons, Saïd and Muhammad, were taken captive by the Spaniards.

ALLOBROGES. Gallic tribe living in the Alpine region that roughly coincided with the Duchy of Savoy in the sixteenth century.

AMATHUS. (Amathous; cont. Lemesos) A port of Cyprus.

AMBRACIA. (Ren. Golfo del Arta) The inland sea of the Adriatic and town of the same name in Epirus, site of the Battle of Actium.

ANTARCTICA. The southern pole, used also for Spain's southernmost American realms administered by the viceroyalty of Peru.

AONIA. A region of ancient Boeotia in central Greece.

ARAXES. (cont. Aras or Arax River [Iran]) A river in the Caucasus region, used to refer to the Ottoman Empire.

ARCADIA. A region of the central Peloponnesus.

ARMENIA. Treated generally as part of the East, though in reality, it was on the sixteenth-century frontier between Safavid Persia and the Ottoman Empire.

ASSYRIA. (Sinope) A region of northeastern Asia Minor, used to refer to the Ottoman heartland.

AUSONIA. The Italian peninsula.

AUSTRIA, JOHN OF. *See* John of Austria.

BABYLON. The ancient Mesopotamian city located at the site of Ottoman-controlled Baghdad.

BACTRA/BACTRIA. A province of Parthia, used to convey a generalized East.

BAETIS. Evokes Andalusia overall and Granada in particular, with reference to the Roman province of Hispania Baetica. Also used for the Guadalquivir River.

BARBARIGO, AGOSTINO. Commanded the left wing of the Holy League Fleet for Venice. He died two days after the battle from an arrow wound to his left eye.

BARBAROSSA, KHAIREDDIN. Hizir Re'is, the great Ottoman fleet commander of the era of Suleiman I, became known by his red beard. Renowned for his mastery of galley warfare tactics, he defeated a fleet under Andrea Doria at Preveza in 1538.

BASSA. *See* Pasha.

BAZÁN, ÁLVARO DE. (Marquis of Santa Cruz) As captain general of the Naples Fleet, he commanded the Holy League reserve flank.

BISTONIS (BISTONES). Lake Vistonis in Thracia, presented as part of the Ottoman world.

BITHYNIA. A region of northwest Asia Minor, associated with medieval Byzantium and in the sixteenth century, the Anatolian heartland of the Ottomans.

BONELLI, MICHELE. Nephew of Pope Pius V, he commanded infantry on the pope's flagship.

BOSPHORUS. (Bosporos [Turkey]) The strait that divides Europe and Asia; sixteenth-century European sources often refer to it as the pathway to the "captive" Constantinople ruled by the Ottoman sultan since its fall in 1453.

BRIXIA. Brescia, under Venetian control in the sixteenth century.

BRUNDISIUM. (Ren. Brindisi) A port on the Adriatic Sea.

CAETANI, ONORATO. (Duke of Sermoneta) Led papal infantry at Lepanto and prepared his own epistolary reports of the battle.

CALYDON. A city of ancient Aetolia, just west of the battle site.

CAPHAREUS. (Ren. Negroponte and Leuchime; cont. Kavo Doro) Promontory on the southeast tip of the island of Euboea.

CAPPADOCIA. (cont. Kappadokia [Turkey]) Refers to the Ottoman heartland.

CARACOSSA. *See* Kara Hodja.

CARAS. (Cares) Appears in general terms as part of the Ottoman lands of Asia Minor.

CÁRDENAS, BERNARDINO DE. (Marquis of Beteta) Son of a Spanish grandee, he died fighting to capture the Ottoman flagship.

CARDONA, JUAN DE. A Catalan noble who led a Sicilian contingent at Lepanto.

CARMELAN ROCKS. Mount Carmel of Palestine, in the Holy Land.

CASTRO. A city in Lazio with a strong Farnese connection.

CAYSTER. (cont. Küçük Menderes) A river in Turkey, used for the Ottoman heartland.

CENOMANI. The Gauls who settled in the Cisalpine region corresponding to early modern Brescia and Verona, used generally for the Venetian forces.

CEPHALONIA. (cont. Kephalleia) Largest of the Ionian Islands.

CHABRIANS. (Chabris) People of central France in the region around Tours.

CHARLES V. (King of Spain, as Charles I, r. 1516–56; Holy Roman Emperor, r. 1519–58) Father of John of Austria, often named in poems and chronicles as *Augustus* and *Caesar* in homage to his imperial title.

CILICIA. Roman province in southeast Asia Minor, conceived as part of the Ottoman Empire.

CIRCEAN SHORE. Campania (Naples).

COLONNA, MARCO ANTONIO. (Duke and Prince of Paliano, Duke of Tagliacozzo, and Grand Constable of Naples) The scion of Rome's Colonna dynasty, he served as commander of the papal galleys at Lepanto, after which he organized a lavish triumphal entry into Rome (December 4, 1571).

COLONNA, POMPEO. A cousin of Marco Antonio Colonna, he served under him in the papal fleet at Lepanto.

COLONNA, PROSPERO. Field master of Venetian forces at Lepanto.

CORCYRA. (Corfu) The Ionian island ruled by Venice in the sixteenth century.

CORGNA, ASCANIO DELLA. Nephew of Pope Julius III, he fought in the Siege of Malta and later at Lepanto, where he served as field master general. He died in Rome shortly after the battle (December 3, 1571).

CORINTH, GULF OF. Also called the Gulf of Lepanto, site of the battle itself.

CUMAE. (cont. Cuma) A coastal town of ancient Campania and in Vergil, the entrance to the underworld, used repeatedly to refer to Naples and its forces at Lepanto.

CURZOLARIS ISLANDS. (Echinades) Called the Echinades in antiquity, the precise site of the naval battle.

DACIA. Refers, typically, to the realms north of the Danube and east of the Black Sea (Transylvania, Wallachia, and Moldavia). In sixteenth-century usage, Dacians evoked the Ottoman Empire's northern subjects.

DORIA, GIOVANNI ANDREA. Genoese commander of the Holy League right wing and earlier, commander who led Spanish forces at Djerba. He was the grandnephew and heir of Andrea Doria, who served as Charles V's captain general of the sea.

DORIS/DORIDIAN SEA. The Greek region north of Lepanto, used to denote the gulf itself.

DRAGUT. *See* Turghud Reis.

ECHINADES. *See* Curzolaris Islands.

EMERITA. (cont. Mérida) A city in Spain.

EPIRUS. The district of northwest Greece bordering the Ionian Sea on the west, just north of the site of Lepanto, bearing close associations as well with the site of Actium. It was under Ottoman control in the sixteenth century.

ERIDANUS. The Greek name for the River Po.

EUBOEA. (Euboia; Ren. Negroponte) A Greek island controlled by the Ottomans at the time of the battle.

EVENUS. (Evinos) A river in western Greece, just above the battle site.

FARNESE, ALESSANDRO. (later Duke of Parma) Son of Italian nobleman Ottavio Farnese and Margaret of Austria, the daughter of Charles V and half sister of John of Austria and Philip II. At Lepanto, he commanded the Genoese flagship.

FELSINA. Bologna.

FELTRE. A town in the Veneto.

GADES. The Latin name for the southern Spanish city of Cádiz.

GELONIANS. A Scythian people associated with Ottoman forces.

GETAE. (Geets) A Thracian tribe of the lower Danube, used for the realms of central and eastern Europe under Ottoman control.

GETULIA. (Getullu; Ren. Berberia or Barbaria) Inland Libya, controlled at the time of Lepanto by the corsair state of Tripoli.

GHISLIERI, MICHELE. *See* Pius V.

HAEMUS, MOUNT. A Balkan mountain, today part of Bulgaria.

HEBRUS. (cont. Maritsa [Bulgaria] or Evros [Greece]) A river of Thrace.

HELLESPONT. (Dardanelles or Çanakkale Boğaz) The strait that connects the Aegean Sea to the Sea of Marmara (Propontis), referred to as part of the sultan's realms.

HERMON. Refers to Mount Hermon, a cluster of mountains on the border of modern-day Syria and Lebanon.

HESPERIA. Refers in general terms to the West. Depending on the context, it comprises the diverse regions of Italy or all the western Mediterranean, Spain included.

HISPALIS. Latin name for Seville, used also to refer to Andalusia more generally.

HYDASPES. A tributary of the Indus River.

IBERUS. (cont. Ebro) A river of northern Spain.

IDUMAEA. (Iduma) The Near East, understood in this context as a region under Ottoman control.

ILLYRIA. (Ren. Slavonia) The western Balkans, under Ottoman control at the time of battle.

ILUA. Elba, an island in the Tyrrhenian Sea, under the control of the Grand Duke of Tuscany.

IONIA. (cont. Phocaea-Lebedos [Turkey]) A coastal region in Asia Minor, used to signal the Ottoman heartland.

ISMARIA. (cont. Lake Ismaris [Bulgaria] or Mitricon [Greece]) The Thracian lake and mountain used to refer to hostile Ottoman realms.

ISTRUS/ISTROS. The Greek name for the Danube River.

JOHN OF AUSTRIA. (Don Juan de Austria) Commanded the Holy League coalition fleets at Lepanto. Two years earlier, he led the Spanish troops that suppressed the Morisco revolt in Granada (the Second Revolt of the Alpujarras, 1568–70). As the illegitimate son of Charles V and a commoner, he used the dynastic *Austria* as a surname. His relations with King Philip II of Spain, his half brother, were notoriously troubled.

KARA HODJA. (Caracossa) A convert to Islam—reported to have been a Dominican friar before renouncing Christianity—he rose to become a Janissary commander and the Ottoman governor of Valona. He fought at Lepanto in the Ottoman command, where he was captured and killed by Onorato Caetani.

KNIGHTS OF SAINT JOHN/KNIGHTS OF MALTA/HOSPITALLERS. *See* Saint John, Knights of.

LALA MUSTAFA PASHA. Led the Ottoman siege of Cyprus in 1570–71, gaining notoriety for the torture and execution of Venetian captives.

LEMNOS. (Ren. Stalimene) A northern Aegean island.

LEPANTO. Fortress town at the mouth of the Bay of Corinth (also Lepanto), just east of the actual battle site. In Italian, it is pronounced with the accent on the *e* (as Lépanto), while in Spanish, the accent falls on the *a*.

LEUCAS/LEUCADIA. (Ren. Santa Maura; cont. Lefkada) The Ionian island just north of Ithaca.

LIBANI VALLES. (cont. Kadisha Valley) The land around Mount Libanus.

LIBURNIA. (Ren. Croatia or Slavonia) The Balkan region, where the Ottomans and Venetians competed for influence.

LIBYA. The North African coastal region and also the desert surrounding it; it was a client state of the Ottomans after the 1551 capture of Tripoli by Turghud Reis.

LIBYSSA. (Ren. Diacibyssa; cont. W. Karaburun [Turkey]) A port city on the Sea of Marmara, known as the site of Hannibal's death.

LIGURIA. The Italian coastal region dominated by the Republic of Genoa.

LIRIS. The River Garigliano of Naples.

LOCRENSUS. (Locris Ozolei) A Greek region on the northeastern shore of the Gulf of Corinth, used to situate the battle.

LYCIA. Part of the Anatolia region in Asia Minor bordering the Mediterranean, used to refer to the Ottoman heartland.

MALTA, KNIGHTS OF/KNIGHTS OF SAINT JOHN/HOSPITALLERS. *See* Saint John, Knights of.

MAMERTINOS. *See* Messina.

MARMARA, SEA OF. Known as Propontis in antiquity, the inland sea connects the Aegean Sea to the Black Sea.

MASSYLIANS. A people of ancient Mauritania or Numidia, associated with sixteenth-century Algiers and Uluj Ali, its corsair governor.

MEDES. (Maedi/Maedica) A Thracian people mentioned as part of the Ottoman forces.

MEDICI, COSIMO I DE'. Grand Duke of Tuscany at the time of Lepanto.

MEHMET SCIROCCO or ŞULUŞ MEHMET PASHA. (Scirocco) Ottoman governor of Alexandria, he commanded the Ottoman right wing at Lepanto. Some chroniclers report that he died of wounds in captivity, others that his Venetian captor (Giovanni Contarino) beheaded him to spare him a long agony from his wounds.

MELES, RIVER. (Melas, fonte Melete) A river in Ionia situated in the Ottoman heartland of Anatolia.

MERöE. A kingdom of the upper Nile.

MESSINA. (Messsana, Mamertinos) The Sicilian port from which the Holy League fleet set out for Lepanto.

MONOECUS. (Portus Moneici) The Ligurian port of Monaco, named for Hercules Monoikos.

MOREA. The Peloponnese peninsula.

MORINI. The term is used to evoke the Ottoman sultan's diverse eastern forces, pulling it away from the standard usage, denoting the people of Belgic Gaul, as in *Aen* 8.727.

MUSTAFA. *See* Lala Mustafa Pasha.

MYGDONIA. Macedonia, viewed here as an area of Ottoman encroachment.

NASAMONES. A people of the Mediterranean coast of Libya (Cyrene), used to refer to the North African forces at Lepanto.

NAUPACTUS. *See* Lepanto.

NAXOS. One of the Cyclades Islands of the Aegean Sea.

NESIS. (cont. Nisida) A Campanian island just north of Naples.

NOVARIA. Novara in the Piedmont region.

NUMIDIA. North African region that corresponds to Algeria, stronghold of Uluj Ali.

OCCHIALUS/OCCIALI. *See* Uluj Ali.

OEBALIA. Taranto, a coastal city in southern Apulia.

ORSINI, PAOLO. Led Venetian infantry on the *Santa Maria Maddalena*, suffering a severe burn wound.

ORSINI, PAOLO GIORDANO. (Duke of Bracciano) The son-in-law of Cosimo I de' Medici, he fought on the Lomellino flagship.

PACYNO (PACHYNOS). A river and cape in southeast Sicily.

PANNONIA. Roman provinces (Superior and Inferior) south and west of the Danube, north of Dalmatia, coinciding in the sixteenth century with Austria and Styria in the north, Hungary in the south. Viewed here as inland Europe's bulwark against Ottoman expansion.

PANORMUS. Palermo (Sicily).

PAPHOS. (cont. Pafos or Baso) A city in Cyprus.

PARTHENOPE. The city of Naples, so named for the tomb of the eponymous siren.

PARTHIA/PARTHIANS. Ancient Parthia coincided with sixteenth-century Safavid Iran (Persia) and present-day Iran. Though it was not under Ottoman dominion, several poets associate the Parthians with the Muslim coalition that fought at Lepanto. In particular, the skilled archers who fought on Ottoman galleys are referred to as Parthians, drawing on classical sources that spoke of their mastery of the bow and arrow.

PASHA. (Turkish Paşa) Ottoman title for governors and ministers (viziers) with political and military authority. Often transliterated in Latin as *bassa* (cf. Du Cange).

PASHA, ALI. *See* Ali Pasha.

PATRAS. Peloponnese town, just south of the battle site, under Ottoman control at the time of the battle.

PAUSILYPUS. (Ren. Monte Pausilippo; cont. Posilipo) A mountain in Naples.

PELASGIA/THE PELASGI. A general term for Greeks of the northern Aegean.

PERTEV PASHA. Second in command of Ottoman forces at Lepanto, he had reportedly argued against confronting the Holy League fleet, alleging the forces were exhausted from the year's campaign. He was wounded in fighting.

PIYALE PASHA. Ottoman commander at Djerba and Malta, he was forced to retire after allowing the besieged Famagusta to hold out much longer than the invaders had anticipated.

PLACENTIA. Piacenza (Liguria).

PHILIP II OF SPAIN (r. 1556–98). Son of Charles V and half brother of Don Juan de Austria, he did not inherit his father's title of Holy Roman Emperor.

PHLEGIAN. The Phlegyae were a people of Thessaly, mentioned here in general terms as part of the Ottoman fleet.

PIUS V. (Michele Ghislieri; pope 1566–72; canonized 1712) Ghislieri's crusading zeal was pivotal in the Holy League's formation. His role as the primary architect of the alliance and his intense prayer vigil during the battle became centerpieces of biographies written shortly after the battle (see Catena, *Vita del gloriosissimo Papa Pio Quinto*; and Fuenmayor, *Vida y hechos de Pío V*), as well as in his canonization process.

PROCHYTES, PROCHYTA. (cont. Procida) An island near Naples.

PROPONTIS. *See* Marmara, Sea of.

PSYLLI. In classical sources, an African tribe with special medicinal powers. Some poets mention them as part of the "barbarous" realms allied with Ottoman forces.

PYRENE. The Pyrenees Mountains separating France and Spain; metonymically, Spain.

REQUESENS Y ZÚÑIGA, LUIS DE. (Comendador Mayor of Castile) A Catalan nobleman, he led a group of three advisors whom Philip II ordered to supervise John of Austria.

RHENUS. The Reno River of Italy, at Bologna.

RHETAEUM. The site of Troy, here the Ottoman heartland, not to be confused with the Rhetic Alps of Genoa (Liguria).

RHODES. The island conquered from the Knights of Saint John of Jerusalem by the sultan Suleiman's forces in 1522.

RIPAEUS MOUNTAINS. The mountain range in northern Europe (Scythia), mentioned in this context as the farthest reach of Ottoman dominion.

SAINT JOHN, KNIGHTS OF/HOSPITALLERS/KNIGHTS OF MALTA. The chivalric order of the Knights of the Hospital of Saint John of Jerusalem, also called Hospitallers, Knights of Rhodes, or Knights of Malta. Their contingent at Lepanto brought powerful religious symbolism, connecting the Holy League force to the Crusades as well as to the defenders of Rhodes (1522), Tripoli (1551), and Malta (1565). Their forces suffered the heaviest losses among the Holy League armies at Lepanto after a contingent led by Uluj Ali attacked them.

SALAMIS. Known as Famagusta in the sixteenth century, it was the last Venetian stronghold on Cyprus. After a long siege, its defenders surrendered to the Ottomans in August 1571.

SANTA CRUZ, MARQUIS OF. See Bazán, Álvaro de.

SCIROCCO. See Mehmet Scirocco.

SCYTHIA. The region north and northeast of the Black Sea, inhabited in antiquity by nomadic people, used to denote the farthest northern reaches of the Ottoman Empire.

SELIM II (r. 1566–74). Son of Suleiman the Magnificent, he often appears in European sources as tyrannical and dissolute, hence the epithet of "Selim the Sot"; Ottoman sources present a more nuanced view of his leadership (see Lesure, *Lépante: La crise de l'empire ottoman*).

SERMONETA, DUKE OF. *See* Caetani, Onorato.

SMYRNA. (Izmir) The Aegean port that served as the gateway to the Ottoman heartland of Anatolia.

STRYMONA, RIVER. (cont. Strymon or Struma [Bulgaria and Greece]) The river that separates Thracia from Macedonia.

SULEIMAN I. (the Magnificent) Sultan from 1520 to his death in 1566, immediately after besieging the Hungarian fortress of Szigetvár.

SYENE. (Ren. Gaguera; cont. Aswan area) An Egyptian city.

SYRTIS. (Ren. Barbary/Berberia) Sandy flats on the North African coast, between ancient Carthage and Cyrene, under control of the corsair governor of Tripoli.

TAGUS. (Tajo, Tejo) A river that runs through the middle of Iberia.

TANAIS. The Don River (Russia), named in this context to evoke remote places.

TARUS. (Taro) A river in Northern Italy flowing primarily through Parma, tributary of the Po.

TELEBOES. (Regna Teleboum) Refers to the people who inhabited the islands off the coast of Acarnania, associated with the colonization of Capri.

THRACE. (Thracia) The region south of the Balkan Mountains, north of the Aegean Sea, with eastern coasts on the Black Sea and Sea of Marmara, mentioned in general terms as a part of Europe under control of the Ottoman Empire.

THYSSAGETAE. In ancient geography, a people of Asian Sarmatia, used in this context to denote eastern people under the Ottomans.

TIRYNS. (Tiryntha) A Peloponnese town, associated with the early life of Hercules.

TREBIA. (Trebbia) A northern Italian river flowing in Liguria and Emilia Romagna.

TRIDENT(I)UM. (Ren. Trento, Trent) A northern Italian city.

TURGHUD REIS. (Dragut) Founder of the Tripoli corsair principality, he was one of the most feared and respected Muslim naval commanders, having captured Tripoli from the Knights of Saint John and led the victorious forces at Djerba. His death in the 1565 Siege of Malta was a major setback for the Ottomans.

ULUJ ALI. (Kiliç Ali Pasha, Lucciaili, Luchalí, Occhiali, Ucciali, and Ruzzalis) A renegade from Calabria, he was the most experienced Ottoman commander at Lepanto and the only member of the high command to escape the devastation. In the years after the battle, he supervised the rebuilding of the Ottoman navy.

VENIER, SEBASTIANO. Commander of the Venetian fleet in the Holy League left wing, he was seventy-five when he led the republic's fleet at Lepanto, after approximately fifty years in public service.

VENUSIA. (cont. Venosa) A town in southern Apulia.

ZACYNTHUS. (Ren. Zante) An Ionian island ruled by the Venetians in the sixteenth century.

Appendix II
Biographical Information
❧❧❧

Basic biographical information about individual poets is presented in alphabetical order by last name. Noted in parentheses are each author's Latinized name, poem number in this volume, and the title of the featured poem. Our annotations draw on the following sources:

ABI   *Archivio Biografico Italiano* (ABI I) and *Archivio Biografico Italiano Nuova Serie* (ABI II). For example: *ABI* I.403.83 = *ABI* fiche 403, frame 83; *ABI* II.13.247–51 = *ABI Nuova Serie* fiche 13, frames 247–51.

Dizionario   *Dizionario biografico degli italiani*. Rome: Istituto della Enciclopedia Italiana, 1960–. Cited as *Dizionario* (entry author), for example: *Dizionario* (A. Stella).

Edit 16   *Censimento nazionale delle edizioni italiane del XVI secolo* (Italy), of the Istituto Centrale per il Catalogo Unico delle biblioteche italiane e per le informazioni bibliografiche (ICCU). Online at http://edit16.iccu. sbn.it/web_iccu/ihome.htm.

ALLEGRI, ALESSANDRO. (Alexandrus Allegrus; VI, [*A city in mourning pays homage to Hector*]) This poet's identity cannot be established with certainty. Available sources record an Alessandro Allegri (Florence, 1560–1629), a Florentine priest known for his Bernesque poetry, as in his collection of *Rime piacevoli*, Verona 1605 (see Vicenzo Caputo, *I poeti italiani dall'antichità ad oggi*, 1960, 336 = *ABI* I.33.116–37 and *ABI* II.11, 265). The *Dizionario* (A. Asor-Rosa) records two Latin works on Lepanto, *De Actiaca victoria* and *De eadem victoria ad Maurium Textorem*. If in fact this Allegri is the same as the Alessandro Allegri featured by Gherardi, the poem we feature would have been a schoolboy's exercise.

Amalteo, Cornelio (Oderzo, ca. 1530–1603). (Cornelius Amalteus; III, *Proteus*) Younger brother of Girolamo and Giovanni Battista Amalteo. He studied medicine in Padua and then followed the path of Giovanni Battista to serve in the chancery of Ragusa. The poem we include here also was issued in a quarto edition by the print shop of Onofrio Farri (Venice, 1572). His Latin poetry was collected posthumously several times along with works by his brother (see Amalteo, Giovanni Battista). *Proteus* was reprinted in the 1608 *Delitiae* anthology, 76–79. See *Dizionario* (A. Buiatti); Francesco Di Manzano, *Cenni biografici dei letterati ed artisti friulani* 1885, 101 = *ABI* I.37.221–25; and Giammaria Mazzuchelli, *Gli scrittori d'Italia*, vol. 1.1 1753, 178 = *ABI* II.13.354.

Amalteo, Giovanni Battista (Oderzo, ca. 1525–Rome, 1573). (Ioannes Baptista Amaltheus; XIII, *To Sebastiano Venier, admiral of the Venetian fleet*) Epitomizes the intellectual breadth of Cinquecento humanism. From a family steeped in those currents (his father, Francesco, plus brothers Cornelio and Girolamo), he studied law in Padua. In Venice, he served as a tutor for the Lipomanni family. A long European sojourn took him as far as London (1556), where he presented an eclogue to Queen Mary in honor of her wedding to Philip II of Spain. Shortly after, he served as secretary to the Republic of Ragusa (ca. 1558) and ca. 1562, he relocated to Rome. Under the pseudonym "Sollecito," he participated in the founding and regular activities of the Accademia delle Notti Vaticane, which brought him into close contact with its sponsor, Carlo Borromeo, whom he followed to Milan in 1565. With Borromeo's support, he attained important benefices as canon in Aquileia, Mozzo, and Padua, though in 1568 he had to abandon the latter due to his absenteeism. The quest for steady material support may also have prompted him in 1568 to join the Cistercian monastery of San Salvatore in Lauro in Rome. His lifelong literary vocation led to friendships with Pietro Aretino, Paolo Manuzio, and Ludovico Dolce, the latter of whom praised Amalteo's eloquence in Latin, Greek, and Italian. He composed a number of Horatian epistles and epigrams in Latin. An unauthorized compilation of his *Carmina* appeared in Venice, 1550. Five eclogues and three elegiac poems appeared in the 1608 *Delitiae*. Another posthumous edition entitled *Trium fratrum Amaltheorum . . . carmina* appeared in 1627, with poetry by the three Amalteo brothers. This also served as the basis for *Fratrum Amaltheorum . . . carmina* published in *Acti Sineri Sannazzarii . . . opera* (Amsterdam 1718 and 1728). Five eclogues by G. B. Amalteo were added in the expanded edition of the *Carmina quinque illustrium poetarum* (Bergamo, 1753). Several Italian translations of his Latin poetry appeared subsequently, including a compilation of previously unpublished poetry by the brothers (*Versi editi ed inediti di Girol., Giamb., C. fratelli Amaltei tradotti da varii*, Venice, 1817). See *Dizionario* (A. Buiatti); *ABI* I.37.252–361, and *ABI* II.13.247–51.

ARCUCCI, GIOVANNI BAPTISTA. (Ioannes Baptista Arcutius; XX, *The Victory at Naupactus*) Jurist and theologian of Naples. His surviving publications include a book titled *Paraphrasis in XII fidei articula*, *Elegia* (Naples, 1564), pastoral odes (*Odarum libri duo*, Naples, 1568), and a collection of *Carmina* addressed to the king of Poland (Rome, 1567). In his *Neo-Latin Literature and the Pastoral*, W. Leonard Grant judges Arcucci harshly for his heavy-handed citations from such models as Theocritus, Ovid, Vergil, and Tibullus (153–54). His poem on Lepanto, *Naupactiaca Victoria*, was also published separately in 1572, with a dedication to the Archbishop of Naples, Marco Carafa, and later reprinted in the 1608 *Delitiae*. Arcucci also contributed the introduction to an oration in honor of Don John of Austria prepared for the Neapolitan celebrations of Lepanto (*Oratione militare di Giovanni Battista Attendolo Capuano*, Naples, 1573). See *Dizionario* (M. Quattrucci).

ARNOLFINI, POMPEO (?–1604). (Pompeus Arnolfinus; XIX, *A shining song for the victor, John of Austria*) Illegitimate son of Vicenzo Arnolfini, a prominent financier and diplomat from Lucca. Pompeo participated in a literary circle in that Tuscan city that gathered in the home of Cristoforo Guidiccioni, a member of the Accademia degli Oscuri from its foundation in 1584. A decade after this collection appeared, he served as secretary to Giovanni Andrea Doria from 1592 to 1596 (*ABI* I.73.403–5). From this Ligurian connection, one of his Italian poems appeared in the 1591 Genoese anthology *Scelta di Rime di diversi moderni autori* (Genoa, 1591, 91).

His Doria connection may have brought him into contact with representatives of the Spanish monarchy, a hypothesis supported by the pension awarded to his son Orazio by Philip III in recognition of his own service and that of Pompeo. See *Dizionario* (G. Miani, entry under Vicenzo Arnolfini).

CANEVARI, GIOVANNI. (Ioannes Canevarius; VIII, *On Mustafa*) *Edit* 16 lists him as a jurist, but no other sources consulted mention him. *ABI* does not offer a plausible identification.

FORTUNIO, AGOSTINO (?–1595). (Agostinus Fortunius; XII, *On the Actian victory over the depraved fleet of Turks*) Born in Fiesole and spent much of his life in the hilltop monastery of Camaldoli near Arezzo. He gained distinction as the author of hagiographies, religious chronicles, and devotional poetry, including a history of his order (*De origine Ordinis Camaldulensis*). See Giulio Negri, *Historia degli scrittori fiorentini* 1722, 200; and Vincenzo Caputo, *I poeti italiani dall'antichità ad oggi*, 1960, 336 (in *ABI* I.426.136–40, 665; *ABI* II.249.218).

GADALDINI, BELISARIO. (Belisarius Gadaldinus; II, *On the treaty struck between the Christian leaders*) Born in Modena but raised and educated in Venice, where his father, the noted doctor Agostino Gadaldini (1515–71), practiced medicine and participated in humanist circles. In addition to Latin poetry, Belisario compiled medical treatises and published a commentary on Galen's *De differentiis febrium* featured in the *Opere* of Vittori Trincavelli. See Giovanni Casati, *Dizionario degli scrittori d'Italia*, vol. 3, 55 (= *ABI* I.443.254–56). The poem anthologized here was reprinted in the 1608 *Delitiae*, along with another poem by him on the battle.

GALLADEI, MAFFEO. (Maffeus Galadeus; IX, [*I am the moon; the fear of war has surrounded me*]) Legal scholar and poet active in Venice in the later sixteenth century. In addition to the poem featured here, he published a tragedy in Italian verse, *Medea* (Venice, 1558). The dedicatory page offers it to Spain's Philip II, paying homage to Charles V's prestige as Holy Roman Emperor. See also Giovanni Casati, *Dizionario degli scrittori d'Italia* (vol. 3, 55 = *ABI* I.403.83).

GHERARDI, PIETRO (?–1580). (Petrus Gherardius; as editor of *In Foedus et Victoriam contra Turcas iuxta Sinum Corinthiacum*) Born in Borgo San Sepolcro (Tuscany) and, although information about him is scarce, evidence suggests he worked in medicine, history, philosophy, jurisprudence, and theology. Surviving publications include his collection of *Carmina* (Florence, 1571), the Lepanto anthology of 1572 — in which so many of the poems featured here appeared — and poems anthologized in the first volume (1608) of the *Delitiae Carmina Italorum poetarum* compiled by Jano Grutero. Gherardi also translated works of Aristotle into Latin. Most information available on him comes from studies focused on San Sepolcro, including Lancisi Annibale's *Storia di Borgo S. Sepolcro, Commentario delle cose di S. Sepolcro* by descendant Girolamo Gherardi; Abbot Pietro Fanelli's *Annali di S. Sepolcro*; and Ludovico Jaobilli's *Bibliotea dell'Umbria* (= *ABI* I.470.335–36). In a prologue directed to Tommaso Mermann for his *Carmina* (Florence, 1571), Gherardi refers to his activities as a bibliophile and curator. In this respect, Ugo Viviani gives evidence that Gherardi was in Rome from circa 1570 to 1573, in the service of Marco Antonio Colonna, where he also worked to compile a library for Cardinal Girlato [sic], which is likely an erroneous transposition of Guglielmo Sirlèto (1514–85). The latter, a noted bibliophile from Calabria, had been appointed by Pius V as custodian of the Vatican Library and is the dedicatee of Gherardi's *Poemata Varia*. This relationship suggests important lines for further inquiry about Gherardi and his anthology of Lepanto poems. Sirlèto was a founder of the Accademia delle Notti Vaticane (*Biografia degli uomini illustri del Regno di Napoli*, v. 8, 1822, 2 = *ABI* I.916.274–79), in which at least one other poet featured here participated (Giovanni Battista Amalteo). Viviani reports that Pius V commissioned the Lepanto anthology, an assertion supported by the Sirlèto connection, but which would require further research to corroborate. See Ugo Viviani, *Medici, fisici e cerusici della provincia aretina* (= *ABI* I.470.335–36).

LATINO, JUAN (ca. 1517–?). (Joannes Latinus; XXII, *The Song of John of Austria*) The longest poem in this volume draws renewed attention to this remarkable figure of the Spanish Renaissance. This black-African former slave parlayed a hard-earned humanist education to gain a position teaching Latin in the Andalusian city of Granada. Taking stock of his 1573 volume of Lepanto poetry, scholars of African-Diaspora literature celebrate him as the first poet from sub-Saharan Africa to publish a book of poems in a European language (see Gates, Jr., and Wolff, "Overview of Sources on the Life and Work of Juan Latino"; and Seo, "Identifying Authority") His only other surviving publication is a book of elegies written to commemorate the transfer of the bodies of four members of Spain's royal family from their original burial place in Granada's royal chapel to the newly built Escorial Palace (*De augusta et catholica regalium corporum translatione per Catholicum Phillipum*, Granada, Hugo de Mena, ca. 1576). Latino's Lepanto poem culminated a traumatic half-decade in Granada, in which the Morisco rebellion and the resulting repression dovetailed with dangerous faction politics emanating from the royal court. In this context, the embrace of Latin as a publication medium not only built on his vocation as a Latin teacher but also offered a safe harbor in the international Republic of Letters. Elizabeth Wright traces Latino's early years and teaching career in Granada in *The Epic of Juan Latino*, a monograph under preparation. Seventeenth-century Spanish writers obscured Juan Latino's accomplishments as a poet and educator, recalling him through the filter of comic racial stereotypes (see Fra-Molinero, "Juan Latino and His Racial Difference"). The presentation of his Lepanto epic here restores the poet to the international literary community in which he claimed affiliation.

MALATESTA, CARLO. (Carolus Malatesta; I, *Song of the Nereids to the most serene John of Austria, son of Charles V, Holy Roman Emperor*) We know little about him, save that he was from Rimini, possibly from the same Malatesta family that had controlled city government in the fifteenth century. His surviving works include an important collaborative project, the bilingual edition and commentary of Vergil's *Opera*, signed along with Giovanni Fabrini da Fighine and Filippo Venuti. The editors herald it as a reference work for students of both Latin and Italian (*L'Opere di Virgilio mantoano, cioè la Bucolica, la Georgica, e l'Eneide* [Venice, 1580]). Malatesta contributed the commentary on the *Eclogues* (fols. 5–33v) and a "Trattato del artificio poetico" (fols. 34r–36r). The latter uses Vergil's *Fama* to present the humanist ideal of transformative *imitatio*, citing Ovid's emulation of the allegory as an example for poets of his day to follow. In so doing, he highlights a motif, *Fama* as an allegory for publication, that inspired a number of the Lepanto poets. Malatesta's other occasional poetry suggests ties to the Spanish Habsburgs and their Italian client states. His other surviving works include a funeral oration marking the deaths of Philip II's wife (Isabel de Valois) and heir (Don Carlos) in 1568, which credits the Genoese naval commander Giovanni Andrea Doria as coauthor ("Lacrymae in funere divae Isabellae reginae ac divi Caroli principis" (Genoa, 1569); a poem in praise of Doria's home city ("Genuae urbis amplissimae encomium," Genoa, 1568); and a funeral oration in honor of John of Austria on his death in 1578 ("In obitu serenissimi Ioannis Austriaci," in Archivo General de Simancas, Estado, legajo 1501, document 209).

MANINI, OTTAVIANO. (Octavianus Meninus; XVIII, [*The long-desired day at last dispelled the fading shadows*]) Wealthy nobleman from Udine, he appears at a crucial nexus where poets, chroniclers, and cartographers converged at the time just before and after Lepanto. Of particular note is Manini's patronage of the historian and geographer Tomasso Porcacchi, whose revised and expanded *L'isole più famose del mondo* (expanded edition, 1575; original publication, 1572) embeds a brief chronicle and historical analysis of Lepanto into his depiction of the Curzolaris Islands. Porcacchi depicts Manini as the Maecenas who inspired his *isolario* and also sustained its creation by hosting him in the Manini Estate outside Friuli, la Villa della Colombara ("Prohemio," Book 2, 61–64). Porcacchi notes that after the untimely deaths of two brothers, Carlo and Lodovico Manini, Ottaviano pursued a contemplative life in his estate. Manini is also the dedicatee of Porcacchi's *Funerali antichi di diversi popoli et nationi; forma, ordine, et pompa di sepolture, di esequie, di consecrationi antiche et d'altro* (Venice, 1574). Moreover, Porcacchi sets a dialogue, "Le attioni d'Arrigo terzo re di Francia, et quarto di Polonia, descritte in dialogo" (Venice, 1574) in the Villa della Colombara (translated and transcribed in Mulryne, *Europa Triumphans*, 140–83). In dialogue with Giovanni Gherardeo of Udine, Manini appears as an urbane nobleman who is well versed in history and familiar with the intricacies of European ceremonial traditions. Jöcher catalogs an epistle in honor of the Knights of Malta (*Epistolam ad equites melitenses*; in G. Jöcher, *Allgemeines Gelehrten-Lexikon*, vol. 3, 1751, 156 = *ABI* I.602.237–38). He lists 1573 as a date of death, though the Porcacchi prologue to the 1574 *Funerali* (dated May 21, 1574) suggests this is incorrect.

MOIZIO, GUGLIELMO. (Gulielmus Modicius; XXI, *Song on the victory of the Christian fleet*) The indices we have about Moizio, a native of Montemagno in Monferrato, relate to his 1575 treatise in defense of Vergil, which appeared in conjunction with epigrams in honor of the Holy Year 1575 (*Virgilius a calumniis vindicatus autore Gulielmo Modicio Monteferratensi. Eiusdem autoris epigrammata, et in sacrum annum MDLXXV carmen* (Perugia, 1575). His *De victoria christianae classis* was also printed separately (Naples, 1572). Basic information about him appears in Giuseppe A. Morano, in his *Catalogo degli illustri scrittori di Casale*, 194 (= *ABI* I.663.252–53).

ODESCALCHI, GIOVANNI ANTONIO. (Ioannes Antonius Odescalcus; XVII, *To the most reverend Paolo Odescalchi, Bishop of Penne and Atri*) Served as an emissary to the Duke of Mantua in Rome, from circa 1574 to 1582 (Pastor, *History of the Popes*, vol. 19, 583). *Edit 16* catalogs a legal comment of 1584 related to a dispute between the Duke of Milan, the Duke of Parma, and the city of Cremona about the diversion of the River Po, in which Odescalchi acted at the behest of representatives of the Spanish king. He is not listed in the *ABI*.

OLIVA, GIOVANNI BATTISTA (Ioannes Baptista Olivus; X, *The council of the damned and Ali in despair*) Doctor from Cremona, he published an *Oratio* in honor of Carlo Borromeo (Venice, 1580). He is best remembered for his catalog of the renowned Veronese museum of Francesco Calzolari (*De reconditis et praecipuis collectaneis ab honestissimo et solertissimo*

Francisco Calceolari Veronensi in Musaeo adservatis, Venice, 1584), which is dedicated to Girolamo Mercuriale, who taught at the University of Padua. See Jöcher, *Allgemeines Gelehrten-Lexikon*, vol. 5, 1816, 156 (= *ABI* I.713.224–25).

PALADINO, NICOLÒ. (Nicolaus Paladinus; V, *To those who died in the Holy War*) The poem featured here is the only notice we have of him.

PODAVINI, DAVIDE. (Davidus Podavinus; VII, *Hymn to Saint Mark and Saint Justina*) Priest and historian from Brescia, he reportedly served as *mansionario* for the city's cathedral. Other publications that survive include an *Oratio* dedicated to his home city's bishop (Brescia, 1576), the *Egloga Pescatoria Faustas* (1581), and a history of the local nobility, *De nobilitate Brixiae* (Brescia, 1587). See Vincenzo Peroni, *Biblioteca bresciana*, vol. 3, 1818–1823, 222 (= *ABI* I.797.172).

TAGLIETTI, GIOVANNI ANTONIO. (Ioannes Antonius Taygetus; XVI, *Nautical Eclogue, or The naval contest of the Christians and Turks*) Poet and doctor from Brescia who participated in that city's Accademia degli Occulti under the pseudonym of Notturno (*Edit 16*). The composition of the nautical eclogue caps off a period of intense activity centered in his native city, as he published a work of Marian poetry ("Hymnus ad Virginem Dei matrem," Brescia, 1562), an elegy in honor of renowned doctor Girolamo Mercuriale (1572), and several anthologies of Latin poetry that highlight activities of the *Occulti* (*Carmina praestantium poetarum*, Brescia, 1565; and *Poemata*, Brescia, 1568).

TRITONIO, MARC ANTONIO (1541–72). (Marcus Antonius Tritonius; IV, [*When nurturing Venus beholds the tragic ruin*]) Native of Udine, Tritonio, studied at the University of Bologna. He served from 1561 to 1562 as secretary to the papal nuncio in Poland, Giovanni Francesco Cannobio, after which he gained a position as an apostolic secretary in Rome, serving, among others, Cardinal Cristoforo Madruzzi and Michele Ghislieri (future Pope Pius V) when he was bishop of Mondovi. This service led to positions as a canon in the Collegiata di Cividale del Friuli and then in Aquileia. He also reportedly excelled in mathematics. His varied literary works include tragedies, a comedy, a translation of Euripides into Italian, two courtesy manuals, and an epitome and commentary of Ovid's *Metamorphoses* published in 1560. At the time of his death, he was preparing a universal history (*Historie universali in lingua latina*). See Giovanni G. Capodagli, *Udine illustrata* 1665, 49 (= *ABI* I.964.20–23) and *Edit 16*.

Note on the Texts

The majority of the poems from Italian poets included in this volume were first anthologized by Pietro Gherardi, *In Foedus et Victoriam contra Turcas iuxta Sinum Corinthiacum* (Venice, Guerraea, 1572). Other anthologies that appeared in the same first year and include Latin poetry about Lepanto are *Raccolta di varii poemi Latini, Greci, e Volgari* (Venice, Sebastiano Ventura, 1572); and Luigi Groto's *Trofeo della vittoria sacra* (Venice, Sigismondo Bordogna and Francesco Patriani, 1572). Poems from both the Gherardi and the Groto anthologies are included here. There is evidence to suggest that the poems in these anthologies had been printed previously. Poems by Moizio and Galladei were also published separately. We have consulted these editions and include the pertinent bibliographic information with the notes on each individual poem. Giovanni Battista Amalteo's poem, which we consulted in manuscript (Harvard University, Houghton Library MS Riant 41, fols. 32–35), was anthologized, with the author listed as anonymous, in Mattheaeus Toscano's *Carmina Illustrium Poetarum Italorum* (Paris, Gilles Gourbin, 1575). This anthology was reprinted with new selections and editions well into the eighteenth century, in the manner of Palgrave's Golden Treasury. The anonymous poem from the Colonna archive in Subiaco, which we consulted in manuscript (Biblioteca del Monumento Nazionale de Santa Scolastica: MS II A 28/17, fols. 153r–164v), was never anthologized.

The *Austrias Carmen*, the only poem in this volume written by a poet from Spain, was published once during Juan Latino's life, as part of his volume of Lepanto poetry. We note pertinent bibliographic information with the notes to this poem.

The meter of all the poems is dactylic hexameter, with the exception of two works in elegiac couplets, by Maffeo Galladei (IX) and Pompeo Arnolfini (XIX).

We have edited the Latin to conform to spelling in the *Oxford Latin Dictionary* and to remove what we saw as distracting capitalizations in words such as Dux, Urbs, Heros, and Divus.

All translations were the result of collaboration among the three titled editors except Poem XV (Anonymous), which was transcribed from manuscript and translated by Andrew Lemons alone.

Notes to the Texts and Translations

ॐ॥ॐ॥

I. SONG OF THE NEREIDS

Author: Carlo Malatesta

Text: Gherardi (1572), 10–14

Title: *Nereidum Cantus ad Serenissimum Ioannem, Austriacum Caroli V. Imp. Aug. Filium* (Song of the Nereids to the most serene John of Austria, son of Charles V, Holy Roman Emperor)

Context: One of a group of prophetic poems about the battle. The song of the Nereids, admiring the heroes of the Argo as they sail to capture the Golden Fleece, is derived from Catullus 64. The reference is also topical: John of Austria was made a knight in the Order of the Golden Fleece in 1566.

16. *Argolicis . . . heroibus:* Jason and the Argonauts were the first heroes to cross the seas. See e.g., *Ecl.* 4.34–35.

42. *insignia:* John of Austria's standard was a gift from Pius V.

45. *heros:* Alessandro Farnese; see Appendix I.

55. *Eridani:* A mythical river located in northern or western Europe, later associated with the Po.

56. *Tarus:* A river in northern Italy that joins the Po near Parma.

57. *Umbria . . . ducem:* Ascanio della Corgna; see Appendix I.

66. *spectatus puer:* Identity unknown.

74. *heros:* Marco Antonio Colonna.

80. *cum:* Emended from *dum.*

83. *defunctum munere summi:* Pius V ultimately chose John of Austria over Marco Antonio Colonna as the commander in chief of the Holy League fleet, though the latter retained a major supporting role as commander of the contingent of papal galleys. See Bennassar, *Don Juan de Austria,* 101–2.

108–29. *heroumque chorus . . . Rodulfus . . . Triumphator . . . Federicus . . . Ferdinandus:* The Habsburg dynasty attributed its stewardship of the Holy Roman Empire to the religious merits of its ancestors, especially Rudolph of Habsburg (r. 1273–91), whose legacy of *pietas Austriaca* passed to Charles V (*Triumphator*) and Frederick III (1415–93, r. as Holy Roman Emperor, 1452–93). See Coreth, *Pietas Austriaca,* 1–36. On the Habsburg appropriation of the Roman triumph, see Mitchell, "Charles V as *Triumphator.*" The passage traces the Habsburg line from Frederick's son Maximilian I (r. Holy Roman Emperor, 1493–1519) and grandson Philip "The Fair" (r. Philip I of Castile, 1504–6) to the two brothers (*gemini fratres*) Charles V and Ferdinand I (r. Holy Roman Emperor, 1558–64).

II. ON THE TREATY STRUCK BETWEEN
THE CHRISTIAN LEADERS

Author: Belisario Gadaldini

Text: Gherardi (1572), 339–41

Title: *In foedus ictum inter principes Christianos* (On the treaty struck between the Christian leaders)

Context: The Ottoman threat to Venetian holdings was characterized as apocalyptic in a series of vernacular poems rooted in Revelations 12 (see Paul, "'And the Moon Has Started to Bleed'"). Latin poems emphasize instead the optimistic prophecies of *Ecl.* 4 and *Aen.* 1.

1–3. *natalibus undis . . . aevi:* Cf. Lucan, *BC* 7.389–91.

1–5. The signing of the Holy League treaty on May 20, 1571, was marked by a three-day celebration in Venice. See Fenlon, *The Ceremonial City,* 166–67.

2. *Cynthius:* Apollo, identified at *Aen.* 8.704 as the god responsible for Octavian's victory at Actium.

3. *venturique inscius aevi:* Replicates the metrical position at *Aen.* 8.627, *haud vatum ignarus venturique inscius aevi.*

5. *foedera . . . vulganda per urbem:* Cf. *Aen.* 8.554.

6. *manibus date lilia plenis:* Cf. *Aen.* 6.883, in reference to the death of Marcellus.

7. *spargite humum foliis:* Cf. *Ecl.* 5.40.

9. *fatidicae . . . Parcae:* Cf. *Ecl.* 4.46–47, '*talia saecla*' *suis dixerunt* '*currite*' *fusis / concordes stabili fatorum numine Parcae;* Catullus 64.327, *currite ducentes subtegmina, currite, fusi.*

10. *saecla aurea:* The golden age, a topos in Augustan poetry sometimes presented as the result of imperial activity. See also *Ecl.* 4.

14–15. *Rector Olympi . . . commisit habenas:* Cf. *Aen.* 1.60–63, where Jupiter is reported to have given Aeolus dominion over the winds: *pater omnipotens . . . regemque dedit, qui foedere certo / et premere et laxas sciret dare iussus habenas.* For "reins" as a metaphor for sovereignty, see also *Aen.* 1.156 and 7.600.

20–21. *animis ardentibus arma / arma fremat:* Cf. *Aen.* 2.314–16, Aeneas in Troy, and *Aen.* 7.460, Turnus enraged by Allecto.

21. *raucoque simul clangore tubarum:* Cf. *Aen.* 2.313, as the Greeks descend upon Troy.

22. *et nemora, et silvae reboent collesque supini:* Cf. *Aen.* 2.304–8 and 8.305. Both passages juxtapose the bucolic with the martial.

23. *innumerae:* Emended from *innumera*, following *corrigenda* in Gherardi.

24. *scindunt vada caerula:* A striking image with no direct parallels in Vergil. The pair *vada caerula* does occur at *Aen.* 7.198 with the less dramatic verb *vexit.*

26–28. *Quis tibi . . . aequor:* Cf. *Aen.* 4.408–11, where the narrator addresses Dido as she watches Aeneas preparing to leave Carthage.

28. *dehiscere classibus aequor:* Cf. *Aen.* 5.142–43.

35–37. *vastum . . . morti:* A loose echo of *Aen.* 1.118, where Aeneas and his men are almost destroyed in a storm off Sicily.

37. *scuta . . . morti:* Echoes *Aen.* 1.101 and 8.539.

38–40. Compare the description of Turnus and his helmet, bearing a fire-breathing Chimera at *Aen.* 7.785–86.

40. *sulcat . . . litora:* Cf. *Aen.* 5.158 and 10.197.

43–44. *Euphratem Gangem . . . Nili:* See *Aen.* 8.711 and 726 for references to the Nile and Euphrates Rivers on the shield of Aeneas. Also see Lucan, *BC* (particularly Book 3) *passim.*

61. *volventibus annis:* Cf. *Aen.* 1.234.

63–64. *manibus . . . foliis:* See notes on lines 6 and 7.

III. PROTEUS

Author: Cornelio Amalteo

Text: Gherardi (1572), 3–6

Title: *Proteus*

Subtitle: *Hoc poemate auctor multo ante pugnam navalem ad Echinadas, futuram victoriam vaticinatus est* (In this poem, written long before the naval battle with the Turks, the author predicted the coming victory)

Dedication: *Serenissimo Principi Ioanni Austrio, Divi Caroli U. Aug. F. et Christianae Classis Imperatori* (To the most serene prince, John of Austria, son of the divine Emperor Charles V, commander of the Christian fleet)

Context: The prediction of the birth of a miraculous child in the fourth eclogue caused Vergil to be seen as a Christian prophet; Amalteo's poem suggests that the fourth part of each of Vergil's major works — the *Eclogues, Georgics,* and *Aeneid* — contains keys to the success of the battle at Lepanto. See Grant, *Neo-Latin Literature and the Pastoral,* 343.

1–3. *Tithoni . . . Eoö:* The goddess of the dawn and her lover, Tithonus, who withered away until he became merely a voice, because Eos had asked Zeus to grant him immortality but neglected to request eternal youth as well.

2–3. *pronaque Puniceo velerat sidera vultu, / cum Sol Eoö tollens e gurgite currus:* Cf. Catullus 64.14.

3. *tollens e gurgite:* Cf. *Aen.* 3.564.

5. *Proteus sese extulit undis:* A minor god of the sea famed for his shape-shifting abilities; also the seer consulted by the beekeeper Aristaeus in *Geo.*4.

7. *Cymothoe:* Part of Neptune's retinue who assists Aeneas' fleet at *Aen.* 1.144–45. In Hesiod's *Theogony,* she calms the waves and wind.

Arethusa: Cf. Ovid *Met.* 5.572ff. for the full story of Arethusa's journey.

8. *atque aliae vatem Nereides admirantes:* Cf. Catullus 64.15 for a parallel description of the Nereids.

9–10. *vaccinia nigra / pallentesque legunt violas:* Cf. Ecl. 2.18 and 10.39.

12–13. *altum iubet aequora murmur / ponere:* Proteus echoes *Aen.* 1.124ff.

15–16. *nutu suspenderit orbem / rex superum:* Cf. *Aen.* 9.106 and 10.115.

19–21. *Tum memorat Phoebi cursus . . . quid desolatus Orion:* Cf. the song of Iopas at *Aen.* 1.740–46, especially the order of *luna* and *sol* in Vergil (*Aen.* 1.742), mirrored by that of Phoebus and Luna here.

22–23. *His addit Lapithum . . . Medusae:* These various subjects — the brawl between the Lapiths and centaurs, Cadmus, and Medusa — are drawn from Ovid *Met.* 12.210ff., 3.1ff., and 4.563ff.

25, 30. *infelix virgo:* Cf. *Ecl.* 6.47, 52.

31. *toties auras mugitibus imples:* Cf. *Ecl.* 6.48.

33. *finemque impone labori:* Cf. *Aen.* 2.619.

34–36. For the story of Tereus and Procne, see Ovid *Met.* 6.424ff., where the story of Pelops is also told. For *candentesque humeros,* see Hor. *Carm.* 1.2.31. For the tale of Nisus and the loss of his purple lock (at the hands of his daughter Scylla), see Ovid *Met.* 8.6ff.

37. *Bistonii:* A term for Thrace, after the Bistones, a tribe living near Lake Bistonis.

43. *Taenarii:* Taenarum, a town in Laconia, home to a temple of Neptune, which boasts an entrance to the underworld.

44. *respexit:* Cf. *Geo.* 4.491, Orpheus's fatal backward glance.

51. *caelo caput Austria tollit:* Cf. *Aen.* 1.127.

53. *genus alto e sanguine divum:* Cf. *Aen.* 5.45, the start of the funeral games for Anchises.

53–58. *princeps . . . vires:* John of Austria became the focus of fervent hopes for a naval coalition to stop Ottoman expansion in the Mediterranean in the course of the 1570–71 Holy League negotiations.

56. *e specula totum praetexere pontum:* Cf. *Aen.* 4.586–87.

62. *abscindet manibus crines atque unguibus ora:* Cf. *Aen.* 12.871.

69. *Saturnia saecula:* Cf. *Ecl.* 4.6 and 6.41.

71–72. *Sponte sua . . . uva:* Cf. *Ecl.* 4.42–45, where the ram and lamb alter the colors of their fleece *sponte sua.* The lines that follow likewise evoke the renewed golden age of the fourth eclogue.

79. *Scyllam . . . Charybdim:* Famed monster Scylla with twelve feet and six heads living on the cliff opposite Charybdis, the whirlpool. According to Vergil, the two reside at the straits of Messina.

86–88. *Heliadum lacrimas . . . fulmine vidit:* Clymenes, according to Ovid *Met.* 1.755–59, is Phaethon's mother; see also *Met.* 2.333–66. Also see *Ecl.* 6.62–63.

89. *Ismarus Orpheo:* Ismarus was a city on the coast of Thrace, the birthplace of Orpheus. Also see *Ecl.* 6.30.

IV. [WHEN NURTURING VENUS BEHOLDS THE TRAGIC RUIN]

Author: Marc Antonio Tritonio

Text: Gherardi (1572), 19–20

Title: [Untitled]

Context: Conversation between Venus and Jupiter, typological antecedents of Mary and God, over the fate of the West at the hands of the Ottomans. The identification of Jupiter with God is commonplace in these syncretic works; that of Venus with Mary is attested in Neoplatonic writings of the time and, perhaps most clearly, in Renaissance paintings such as Botticelli's *Primavera.* See Panofsky, *Renaissance and Renascences,* 196.

2. *lacrimis suffusa:* Cf. *Aen.* 1.228, signaling the main source for this poem, Venus's conversation with Jupiter about the fate of Aeneas and the Trojans in the first book of the *Aeneid.*

5. *parce:* Cf. *Aen.* 1.257.

Erycina: Venus's ancient affiliation with Mount Eryx in Sicily serves to remind the reader of her alignment with the Spanish forces, who ruled Sicily at the time.

7. *ter sunt conati aeterna depellere sede*: Siege of Cyprus (1570–71), Siege of Malta (1565), and Preveza (1538). See Introduction.

8. *in viscera matris*: Cf. Ovid, *Met.* 2.274.

10. *Cretaeam . . . Idam*: The mythic birthplace of Jupiter.

15. *aquilam*: The eagle is the bird of Jupiter and the symbol of the Habsburgs and, by metonymy, the Holy League.

27. *Gnossia tellus*: Crete.

28. *Paphon*: Paphos, city on Cyprus sacred to Venus.

29. *Samon*: Samos, island sacred to Juno; see Ovid, *Met.* 8.345.

Pindi iuga: The Pindus is a ridge of mountains in northern Greece sacred to Apollo.

Athenas: Athens, Pallas' toponym.

30. *posito . . . ferro*: Favorite wordplay in both Vergil and Ovid: the golden age will flourish again with the iron (and the sword) having been put aside.

31. *nutu*: Jupiter traditionally affirms his ruling with a nod.

V. TO THOSE WHO DIED IN THE HOLY WAR

Author: Nicolò Paladino

Text: Groto, *Trofeo* (1572), 14v–15r

Subtitle: *Ad eos, qui in sacra pugna obdormierunt* (to those who died in the Holy War)

Context: Poem honoring those on the Holy League side who died at Lepanto.

2–3. Cf. *Aen.* 1.94–101, Aeneas's first speech in the epic, which echoes that of Odysseus at *Od.* 5.306–10; both celebrate those who died at Troy. Note the shift from Vergil's *beati* (*Aen.* 1.94) to Paladino's *felices*, which comes to mean "blessed" in the context of these poems, as well as his learned allusion to the earlier Homeric text through the phrase *ad scopulos Ithacae*. See Introduction.

15. *immortales mortali lege creatos*: Possible reference to the Resurrection.

VI. [A CITY IN MOURNING PAYS HOMAGE TO HECTOR]

Author: Alessandro Allegri

Text: Gherardi (1572), 210–11

Title: [Untitled]

Context: The poem was most likely addressed to Ettore Spinola, commander of the Genoese flagship, who was killed by an arrow during the Battle of Lepanto. The coincidence between the fallen commander's name and that of Hector anchors the prophetic work, which builds on the Trojan hero's appearance to Aeneas in *Aen.* 2.270–97.

2. *Rhetico . . . iugo*: The Rhetic Alps, which rise behind Genoa.

6. *Hesperiae simulacrum ingens*: Reminiscent of Andromache at Hector's tomb in *Aen.* 3.304.

36. *per compita*: That is, as a captive trophy in the West's triumph.

38. *divino . . . odore*: Cf. *Aen.* 1.403.

VII. HYMN TO SAINT MARK AND SAINT JUSTINA

Author: Davide Podavini

Text: Gherardi (1572), 432–36

Title: *Hymnus*

Subtitle: *In D. Marcum, et D. Iustinam* (To Saint Mark and Saint Justina)

Context: The hymn addresses two saints whose feast days coincide with the October 7 battle date: Saint Mark, a fourth-century pope from Rome (not to be confused with Saint Mark the evangelist, patron saint of Venice) and Saint Justina, a martyr whose relics were held in a Benedictine monastery in Padua named for her. After Lepanto, Justina's devotion became a major Venetian cult (see Fenlon, *The Ceremonial City*, 273–76).

6. *spargite humum redolente thymo:* Cf. *Ecl.* 5.40, *spargite humum foliis.*

6–7. *suspendite . . . hederasque:* Cf. Horace, *Carm.* 1.5.13–16, in reference to an offering hung up for Neptune.

9–10. *nec non . . . preces:* Cf. *Aen.* 2.238–39, referring to the welcome of the Trojan horse; and cf. *Aen.* 6.306–7.

18. *stipata caterva:* Cf. *Aen.* 1.497, *iuvenum stipante caterva,* and *Aen.* 4.136, *magna stipante caterva,* both in reference to Dido's attendants.

20. *o vos magni duo lucida lumina mundi:* Cf. *Geo.* 1.5–6, *vos, o clarissima mundi / lumina.*

25. *volventibus annis:* Cf. *Aen.* 1.234.

33. *saevoque manus armata flagello:* Cf. *Aen.* 8.703, Bellona's appearance at Actium; cf. also Lucan, *BC* 7.568, *sanguineum veluti quatiens Bellona flagellum.*

53. *Threicias urbes . . . binominis Istri:* Cf. Ovid, *ex Ponto* 1.8.11, *ripae vicina binominis Histri.* The Ister River, more commonly known as the Danube in Renaissance cartography, refers to the inland locale where Catholic European powers clashed with the Ottoman forces.

55. *praesepe:* Catholic powers aspired to recapture the Holy Land and Christ's birthplace of Bethlehem.

58. *Tempus adest:* Cf. *Aen.* 12.96, *nunc tempus adest.*

60. *Militiae ardet amore piae:* Cf. Ovid, *Am.* 1.9.1, *militat omnis amans, et habet sua castra Cupido.*

74. *madeant hostili sanguine campi:* Cf. *Aen.* 12.690–91, *ubi plurima fuso / sanguine terra madet,* in reference to Turnus reaching the city walls amid intense bloodshed.

80. *consurgit ad aethera clamor:* Cf. *Aen.* 5.451, *it clamor caelo.*

81. *dant . . . gurgite vasto:* Cf. *Aen.* 1.118, 3.197, and 6.741.

99. *caelicolae Manes, quibus haec accesio tanta:* Cf. *Aen.* 10.6–7, *caelicolae magni, quianam sententia vobis / versa retro tantumque animis certatis iniquis.*

VIII. ON MUSTAFA

Author: Giovanni Canevari

Text: Gherardi (1572), 169–71

Title: *In Mustafam* (On Mustafa)

Context: Details the deeds of Lala Mustafa.

1. *lectos:* Emended from *lector.*

4. *Mustafa:* Lala Mustafa's cruelty toward Venetians captured during the fall of Cyprus was shocking even by the harsh standards of the era (see Capponi, *Victory of the West,* 231–36).

7–8. *Lycia . . . Bithynia . . . Syene . . . Idume:* Traces a map of the Ottoman Empire, from the Turkish heartland of Lycia (Anatolia) and Bithynia, to Egypt (Syene) and the Middle East (Idume).

10. *pessime servorum Thracis:* Lala Mustafa Pasha had close ties to Selim II, having served as his tutor (see Capponi, *Victory of the West,* xxxi).

11. *temerator:* Cf. Statius, *Thebaid* 11.12–13, *quantus Apollineae temerator matris Averno / tenditur.*

16. *hoc animo virus Stygia inspiravit Erynnis:* Cf. *Aen.* 7.350–51, *fallitque furentem, / viperam inspirans animam,* Allecto's serpent poisons Amata's mind.

17–18. *gloria facti / pectus et invidiae stimulis agitaret iniquis:* Cf. *Aen.* 11.336–37, *quem gloria Turni / obliqua invidia stimulisque agitabat amaris,* Drances's counsel enflames Turnus.

24. *expertus et armis:* Cf. *Aen.* 7.235.

45. *Salaminia litora:* Refers to the Ottoman siege and capture of Famagusta through the name of the Greek city-state located there.

61–63. *aeternae . . . sedes:* Honors slain Venetian defenders of Cyprus, particularly Venetian patrician Marcantonio Bragadino, the governor of Famagusta, who was flayed alive on the order of Lala Mustafa.

IX. [I AM THE MOON; THE FEAR OF WAR HAS SURROUNDED ME]

Author: Maffeo Galladei

Text: Biblioteca Marciana (Venice) Inventario SIN 46914; Collocazione MISC 2096.016. In *Canzone per la gloriosa vittoria contra il turco con due sonette et un epigramma latino.* Venetia: [Giorgio Angeleri] 1571; anthologized in Groto, *Trofeo* (1572), fols. 12v–13r. Text follows Groto. Discussed by Vaccaluzzo, "Dei poeti latini," 225.

Title: [Untitled]

Context: The poem imagines a conversation between an Ottoman— identified specifically as Selim II in the version published in the Groto anthology— and the author.

1. *Luna*: Refers to vanquished Ottomans.

3. *Leo*: Refers to the lion of Saint Mark, patron saint of Venice.

5. *Volucrum regina*: Refers to the eagle as a symbol of the Habsburg dynasty.

X. THE COUNCIL OF THE DAMNED AND ALI IN DESPAIR

Author: Giovanni Battista Oliva

Text: Gherardi (1572), 114–20

Title: *Inferorum Concilium Halysque Desperatus* (The council of the damned and Ali in despair)

Context: The poem offers an unusual adaptation of the classical catabasis: the Ottoman admiral Ali Pasha— killed at Lepanto by John of Austria— travels to Tartarus to try to enlist underworld forces on the Ottoman side.

1–2. *armatas . . . amens*: Cf. *Aen.* 2.314, *arma amens.*

4–5. *gurgite . . . obruitur*: Cf. *Aen.* 1.118 and 3.197.

12. *Stygio nunc gurgite*: Cf. *Aen.* 6.310–12, *gurgite ab alto*, in the simile that compares the dead reaching the underworld to migrating birds.

18. *Halym, Halymque*: Cf. *Ecl.* 6.44, *clamassent, ut litus 'Hyla, Hyla' omne sonaret*, there in reference to Hylas, Hercules's beloved abducted by nymphs. In historical terms, Halys refers to Ali Pasha.

32. *gaudet Stygias innare per undas*: Cf. *Aen.* 6.134, *bis Stygios innare lacus*, the Sibyl's warning that Aeneas must cross the river Styx twice.

40–41. *tergeminumque canem . . . trifauci*: Cerberus.

42. *referens horresco*: Cf. *Aen.* 2.204, *horresco referens*, there also as a paren-thetical exclamation, as Aeneas trembles to recall the sea serpents that slay Laocoön.

45–47. *vox haerens. Tardos nequicquam extendere cursus / velle videtur et me-diis conatibus aeger*: Cf. *Aen.* 12.909–10, *nocte quies, nequiquam avidos exten-dere cursus / velle videmur et in mediis conatibus aegri*, a simile that likens Turnus's flagging strength to the vain efforts to speak while dreaming.

48. *Rhadamanthi*: Cf. *Aen.* 6.566.

49. *Aeacus*: Son of Zeus and the hero of Aegina, he was the only one of the primeval mythological figures to retain the gods' favor. He became a judge in the underworld, and he is the ancestor of Achilles and Ajax.

53. *nigros implexae crinibus angues*: Cf. *Aen.* 7.450, refers to Allecto as she pulls two snakes from her head when she enflames Turnus; and cf. Ovid, *Met.*4.454, where the Furies comb snakes from their hair. The metrical position here parallels both.

60. *flammarumque globos volvens*: Cf. *Aen.* 3.574, *attollitque globos flam-marum*, Aetna belching molten earth.

85. *luctifica Allecto*: Cf. *Aen.* 7.324, *luctificam Allecto*.

90–95. *Luctus . . . Bellum*: Cf. *Aen.* 6.274–79, where Aeneas and the Sibyl encounter a similar retinue of negative personifications at the entrance to the underworld.

95. *Atae*: Refers to *Ate*, the Greek goddess of delusion. See Du Cange.

97. *Ulmus et annosa hic pallentes excitat umbras*: Cf. *Aen.* 6.282–83, *in medio ramos annosaque bracchia pandit / ulmus opaca, ingens*, the large shadowy elm which houses *Somnia* (personifications of dreams).

98–100. *His Briareus . . . sedibus orti*: Cf. *Aen.* 6.285–89, which offers a model for this catalog of monsters, with the poet here citing Vergil's *belua Lernae* and the *armata Chimaera* in the same metrical position.

102. *Tantalus, Ixion, Tytion, Sisyphusque*: Refers to the wrongdoers in the underworld, drawing in part on those mentioned in *Geo.* 4.481–84 and *Aen.* 6.595–601.

105. *sibilat hydris*: Replicates the metrical position of *Aen.* 7.447, there in reference to Allecto.

107. *concitat alis*: Cf. *Aen.* 7.408, *tollitur alis*, Allecto's wings, with the poet here replicating the metrical position.

111–13. *Ornaeo . . . Alastor*: Ornaeus, Ethon (Latin variants of the Greek names, Orphnaeus and Aethon), Nycteus, and Alastor were the four horses Hades drove in the abduction of Persephone; cf. Claudian, *De Raptu Proserpinae* 1.284–86.

111. *pernicibus alis*: Cf. *Aen.* 4.180, the wings of *Fama*, whose metrical positioning the poet replicates.

131. *omnis Arabs, omnes dominentur iura Sabaei*: Cf. *Aen.* 8.706, *omnis Arabs, omnes vertebant terga Sabaei*.

135. *sedibus*: Emended from *sedis*, following *corrigenda* in Gherardi.

142. *terribles visu formae*: Cf. *Aen.* 6.277.

168. *sileant umbrae*: Cf. *Aen.* 6.264–67, *umbraeque silentes*, there in the invocation that Vergil inserts just as Aeneas and the Sibyl enter the cave to the underworld.

169. *adventante Deo Christo*: The appearance of Christ in hell, the Harrowing of Hell, though not a part of the canonical Bible, was known through the apocryphal *Acta Pilati* (Acts of Pilate).

172. *obrutus . . . caeco carcere opacis*: Cf. *Aen.* 6.734.

XI. ON THE PAINTER PORTRAYING
THE SAME VICTORY

Author: Anonymous

Text: Gherardi (1572), 209–10

Title: *In pictorem eandem Victoriam fingentem* (On the painter portraying the same victory)

Context: Although it is conceivable that this poem describes an actual painting, such as the one Colonna commissioned for Paliano (see Capponi, *Victory of the West*, 295) or Tintoretto's painting of the battle displayed in the Doge's palace, destroyed in the fire of 1577, it is more likely an ekphrasis, comparable to the description of the Battle of Actium from *Aen.* 8.626–728 (Putnam, *Virgil's Epic Designs*, 119–88). The Battle of Lepanto was a favorite subject in painted works in Venice and Rome, including those by Vasari, *The Battle of Lepanto* in the Sala Regia of the Vatican palace; Veronese, *Allegory of the Battle of Lepanto* (ca. 1572) (Accademia); and Titian, *Allegory of Lepanto and Philip II* (Prado). See Strunck, "The Barbarous and Noble Enemy." The battle remains a subject today: see, e.g., Cy Twombly's twelve canvases in acrylic, crayon, and graphite, *Lepanto*, created for the Venice Biennale in 2001 (*Lepanto: A Painting in Twelve Parts*).

1. *Phlegrea:* Emended from *Plegma*, following *corrigenda* in Gherardi.

versat . . . pontum: Cf. *Aen.* 8.671–713.

3. *Endymion:* Mythical character beloved by the moon; in this instance, the Ottoman forces themselves.

4. *tonantis:* As a rule, the great Thunderer refers to Jupiter; here, as in Poem XX, the reference is instead to Selim and the Ottoman forces.

7. *tergeminam:* Cf. *Aen.* 4.511 and 8.202. Throughout these poems the adjective is adapted to describe the Holy League, possibly echoing the use in Livy, *AUC* 6.7.4.

7–8. *agmen . . . infandum:* Cf. Lucan, *BC* 4.259–60.

9. *Obstipuit . . . tonuit:* Cf. *Aen.* 8.529–30.

12. *pugnas e litore prospectantem*: Possibly reminiscent of Lucan, *BC* 8.579–81.

18. *pernicibus alis*: Vergil's *Fama*, though far more monstrous in the *Aeneid*, is also propelled by *pernicibus alis* (*Aen.* 4.180).

20. (*Fama*) *vulgabit in urbes*: Cf. *Aen.* 8.554. Throughout these poems, *Fama* is a positive force, seemingly associated with the print publication. See Introduction. For Renaissance adaptations of Vergil's *Fama*, see Hardie, *Rumour and Renown*, 78–125 and 411–38.

21. *supremo Marte cadentem*: Cf. *Aen.* 12.409–10.

XII. ON THE ACTIAN VICTORY OVER THE DEPRAVED FLEET OF TURKS

Author: Agostino Fortunio

Text: Gherardi (1572), 212–13; Toscano-Bottari (1719–26), 436–37; text from Gherardi

Title: *De Actiaca victoria ob profligatum Turcarum classem* (On the Actian victory over the depraved fleet of Turks)

Context: This short poem offers one of the most succinct depictions of the battle as well as dramatizing the moment when the Venetian galleasses fire the cannonade.

1. *Ut pelago incubuere rates*: Cf. *Aen.* 1.84 and 5.8.

4. *it clamor caelo*: Cf. *Aen.* 5.451, where Trojan shouts fill the air during the boxing match between Entellus and Dares.

6–7. *navale corona . . . adversi*: While the Turkish troops were arrayed in a crescent shape, the western ships amassed in a more linear fashion, here referred to as a crown (see Figure 1). See *Aen.* 8.683–84, *cui . . . tempora navali fulgent rostrata corona*, which refers to the crown worn by Agrippa during the Battle of Actium. This conflation of Actium and Lepanto becomes crucial in the poem's second half, especially in lines 22–23, where the poet describes the victory won at Lepanto an Actian victory (*Actiaca victoria*).

8. In the context of this poem the lion refers to the power of Venice, whose symbol was the lion of Saint Mark, and, by extension, to the Holy League in general.

10. *crebris ictibus ignes:* The poem's second allusion to the boxing match in *Aen.* 5.459–60.

11. The unusual series of hiatuses in these lines reflect the gunfire of the battle.

15. *fumi nebulas media agmina vastat:* Cf. *Aen.* 8.258.

17. *tanta . . . imagine mortis:* Cf. *Aen.* 2.369.

18. *rubeant ut caerula caede:* Cf. *Aen.* 8.695 for a similar image from the description of the Battle of Actium on Aeneas's shield.

20–23. Cf. *Aen.* 8.671–713 for a description of the Battle of Actium, and its importance to Augustus.

26. *Quirites:* Sons of Romulus and, by extension, the Holy League.

XIII. TO SEBASTIANO VENIER, ADMIRAL
OF THE VENETIAN FLEET

Author: Giovanni Battista Amalteo

Text: Houghton MS Riant 41, fols. 32–35. In-4; 4 pages. Copied in an unidentified hand in humanistic cursive book script. Dated ca. 1575. References: Germon and Polain, 1899, pt. 2, no. 41. De Ricci, 1004. Anthologized in Gherardi, 31–36, and Mattheo Toscano, *Carmina illustrium poetarum* (1575), fols. 71v–74. The manuscript was consulted; the edited print editions were used to establish the text. The manuscript and the Gherardi edition assert Giovanni Battista Amalteo as author; the Toscano edition lists the author as anonymous.

Dedication: *Ad Sebastianum Venerium, Venetae classis ducem* (To Sebastiano Venier, admiral of the Venetian fleet)

21. *Caystri:* Form of Caystros / Cayster, a river of Lydia, in the Turkish heartland, with powerful resonance as ancient Pergamum. See *Geo.* 1.384; Ovid, *Met.* 2.253.

35. *Ambracia:* A Corinthian colony on the river Arachthus, in eastern Greece.

36. *Achelous*: River near Naupactus.

39. *te*: Sebastiano Venier, the Venetian admiral.

42. *iuvenem*: John of Austria.

60. *Oebalias*: Castor and Pollux.

61. *Tyndaridae*: Agamemnon and Menelaus.

67. *et iam*: Emended from *etiam*, following the manuscript version.

83. *Euboicas*: The island of Euboia (Negroponte to Italians) was under Ottoman control.

93. *Propontidis*: Sea of Marmara.

97. *colubris hydram*: The Turks were often characterized as dragons in European propaganda.

100. *Rhetaeum*: Rhoeteum, the territory that included Troy.

103. *Mygdonia*: An ancient territory, including parts of Thrace; see *Aen.* 2.342.

104. *Taygeti*: A range of mountains in Laconia.

Tempe: A narrow gorge in northeastern Thessaly.

105. *Permessides undae*: River on Helicon sacred to the Muses.

112. *Solymorum*: Jerusalem. The lines that follow link the Battle of Lepanto with the Crusades, broadly understood. To many this was the final battle of that centuries-long campaign.

114. *Carmeli rupes*: The cliffs of Mount Carmel, supposed location of the biblical prophet Elijah's contest with the priests of Baal (1 Kings 18).

Idume: Alternate form of Idumaea, the hilly low country of southern Judaea.

116. *Libani valles*: The valleys of Lebanon, home to many of the oldest Christian monasteries.

palmifer Hermon: Mount Hermon; see Matthew 16:13, Mark 8:27.

131–32. *lactea . . . orbita*: Saints were said to reside in a cloudy, or milky, area of the ether. See Brown, *The Medieval Cult of Saints*, 72.

XIV. ONE HUNDRED VERSES: TO THE CITY

Author: Anonymous

Text: Gherardi (1572), 252–55

Title: *Centum carmina: ad Urbem* (One hundred verses: to the City)

Subtitle: *In M. Antonii Columnae Triumphum* (On the Triumph of Marco Antonio Colonna)

Context: The poem records the triumphal entry of Marco Antonio Colonna into Rome on December 4, 1571, an event widely reported in news bulletins (e.g., Albertoni, *L'entrata che fece l'eccellentissimo signor Marc'Antonio Colonna in Roma alli 4. di decembre 1571* (Viterbo, 1572?). On the lavish event and the political intrigue surrounding it, see Bazzano, *Marco Antonio Colonna*, 159–60.

9. *decus Italiae spoliis Orientis onustum:* Cf. *Aen.* 1.289.

11. *genus insuperabile bello:* Cf. *Aen.* 4.40, where the phrase refers to the Gaetulians who threaten Dido in Carthage. The tribal name is used throughout these poems to refer to the Ottomans.

13. *abiuratasque rapinas:* Cf. *Aen.* 8.263.

16. *manibus post terga revinctis:* Cf. *Aen.* 2.57, referring to Sinon.

18–19. *populantur tempora . . . nares:* Cf. *Aen.* 6.496–97, describing Deiphobus.

23. *viduarunt civibus urbes:* Evander in *Aen.* 8.571 describes the effect of Mezentius on his neighboring town.

24. *latos vastant cultoribus agros:* Cf. *Aen.* 8.8, detailing the forces gathered by Mezentius and Turnus to attack Aeneas and the Trojans.

32. *truncus arena:* Cf. Lucan, *BC* 1.685, on the death of Pompey at the hands of forces in the East.

34. *pascet sine nomine corpus:* Cf. *Aen.* 2.554–58, the death of Priam.

40. *omnia tuta vides:* Cf. *Aen.* 1.583, Achates to Aeneas in Carthage.

47. *Saturnia regna:* Cf. *Ecl.* 4.6.

61. *summo fundens de vertice lumen:* So the light is said to radiate around Iulus's head in *Aen.* 2.682–83.

72. *letum:* Emended from *laetum* in Gherardi.

73. *rursum caput obiectare periclis:* Echo of Aeneas returning into burning Troy to seek his wife, Creusa, *Aen.* 2.751.

76. *manibus date lilia plenis:* Cf. *Aen.* 6.883.

77. *Martis:* Allusion to Colonna's lineage through Romulus to Mars.

78–79. *sub Tartara misit / mille die, victor disiecit mille carinas: Aen.* 2.198, that Sinon was able to do what a thousand ships could not.

84. *saecla aurea:* The golden age sung of by Horace, Vergil, and other Augustan poets.

87. *Afforet Austriades utinam:* One of Pius V's hagiographers reported that the celebration was deliberately subdued out of deference to the absent John of Austria (Fuenmayor, *Vida y hechos de Pío V,* 234–35).

92–93. *Quas nunc te terras, et quanta per aequora vectum / accipimus? Quantis iactatum, magne, periclis:* Cf. *Aen.* 6.692–93, Anchises to Aeneas in the underworld.

98–100. *Felix . . . manebunt:* Echoes the poet's apostrophe to Nisus and Euryalus in *Aen.* 9.446–49.

XV. [I WILL NOW SING OF THE HAPPY DEEDS]

Author: Anonymous

Text: Biblioteca Statale Monumento Nazionale di Santa Scolastica di Subiaco: MS II A 28/17, fols. 153r–164v: from a collection of Latin and vernacular poetry about Lepanto, probably sent to Marco Antonio Colonna shortly after the battle.

Title: [Untitled]

Context: This poem appears in manuscript only, written or copied by two or possibly three scribes; there is alternation evident in the two hands starting at the caesura of line 399. The hand is late sixteenth century; internal dating suggests the poem was written before May 1, 1572, and, most probably, around the time of the triumphal entry of Marco Antonio Colonna into Rome on December 4, 1571. It does not appear in any of the early anthologies.

19. *pulchris . . . palmis:* Note ambiguity between victory palms and the hands mentioned in the preceding lines.

55–56. *mandata . . . clavigeri:* Pius V sent blessings, prophecies, and instructions to John of Austria through the Nuncio Paolo Odescalchi (summarized in Catena, *Vita del gloriosissimo Papa Pio Quinto,* 209–11).

65. *sequere Italiam ducentibus astris:* Cf. *Aen.* 4.381, *sequere Italiam ventis.*

69. *nulla . . . aevo:* Cf. *Aen.* 9.447, *nulla dies umquam memori vos eximet aevo,* Vergil's apostrophe on the deaths of Nisus and Euryalus.

71. *Lucifer:* In this context, Lucifer, as Hesperus, is identified with the West.

79. *Tiberinaque longe:* Cf. *Aen.* 1.13.

81. *moenia:* Emended from *Menia.*

84. *Fernandum:* Emended from Ernandum. Refers to Fernando de Mendoza, Philip II's emissary to Pius V (see Setton, *The Papacy and the Levant,* 1066).

93. *nec possunt expleri corda tuendo:* Cf. *Aen.* 8.265, in reference to Arcadians seeing Cacus strangled by Hercules.

98–99. *Phoebea . . . Phoebus:* Associates the two sides to the battle with Diana and Apollo, complicating the rivalry by asserting this sibling relationship.

100–104. *Messanam . . . Parthenopes:* Parthenope refers to Naples, which fielded the largest fleet and whose officials had close ties to John of Austria. Messina, for its part, was the first city to honor Lepanto's victor with a triumphal entry (see Bennassar, *Don Juan de Austria,* 142–44). Rivalry between these two major cities dates back to their vying roles in the Kingdom of the Two Sicilies.

137. *incumbunt remis:* Cf. *Aen.* 8.108, *incumbere remis.*

139–42. This epic simile, though patterned on those found in Vergil, is original to this poem.

144. *recidunt:* Emended from *ricidunt.*

167. *iustitiae:* Emended from *iustiae.*

172. *Pietas:* The personification of piety refers both to Christ and to Pope Pius V.

181–82. *volutans / secum corde:* Emended from *voluntas.* Cf. *Aen.* 1.50, *secum dea corde volutans.*

185. *vexillo sacro:* Refers to the standard the pope gave to John of Austria, which depicted the crucified Christ on one side.

188. *signum insuperabile bello:* Replicates the metrical positioning of *Aen.* 4.40, *genus insuperabile bello.*

202. *praevertere cursu:* Replicates the metrical position at *Aen.* 7.806–7, *praevertere ventos,* there in reference to Camilla.

213. *Germanae . . . Pannonia:* Refers to the 1566 land battle in central Europe (Austria and Hungary), when the sultan Suleiman crossed the Danube and besieged Szigetvár (see Capponi, *Victory of the West,* 98).

220. *aere cavo . . . ferit aethera:* Replicates the metrical position of *aere cavo* at *Aen.* 3.288, there in reference to the shield of Abas, which Aeneas leaves at Actium; likewise, *ferit aethera* replicates *Aen.* 5.140–41, there in reference to the start of the boat race.

223. *aethereas* is deleted from the end of the line as metrically superfluous, with the sense provided by the start of line 224.

232. *grandine nimbi:* Replicates the metrical position at *Aen.* 10.803–4.

251. *nilque:* Emended from *nilique* for reasons of scansion.

265. *Thraci:* Emended from *Traci.*

265–67. *occurrit Thraci Aly . . . prosternit:* Reports Ali Pasha's death in direct combat with John of Austria in a manner in line with the first report delivered to Venice (cited in Setton, *Papacy in the Levant,* 1060, n. 54).

269. *iam celsa in puppi fundunt cum sanguine vitam:* Cf. *Aen.* 8.680, *stans celsa in puppi,* in reference to Augustus at Actium; and cf. *Aen.* 4.621, *hanc vocem extremam cum sanguine fundo,* there as Dido's dying words.

270. *divina:* Emended from *divinae.*

326–28. *Caracossa . . . Honorati:* Onorato Caetani captured and killed Kara Hodja (Bicheno, *Crescent and Cross*, 313).

331–32. *Farnesi . . . matre Austrica:* Alessandro Farnese, son of Margaret of Austria, who was the daughter of Charles V and half sister of John of Austria and Philip II. His father was Ottavio Farnese, the Duke of Parma.

348. *Ipsae:* Emended from *Ipse.*

363. *tanti pars magna laboris:* Cf. *Aen.* 2.6, *quorum pars magna fui,* there as Aeneas prepares to recount the horrors he witnessed during Troy's destruction.

375. *gazam . . . in aequor:* Cf. *Aen.* 1.119, *gaza per undas.*

442. *intrantique urbem sanctam laeta omina pandet:* Suggests the poem was written for the triumphal entry of Marco Antonio Colonna into Rome on December 4, 1571. See notes to the preceding poem (XIV) for further detail on this event.

449. *amplexuque Pii Patris:* Supports the dating of the poem prior to Pope Pius V's death on May 1, 1572.

XVI. NAUTICAL ECLOGUE, OR THE NAVAL CONTEST OF THE CHRISTIANS AND TURKS

Author: Giovanni Antonio Taglietti

Text: Gherardi (1572), 173–87

Title: *Ecloga Nautica (seu Christianorum et Turcarum navale certamen)* (Nautical Eclogue, or the naval contest of the Christians and Turks)

Dedication: *Ludovico Federico Iurecon. Clariss. Patricio Brixiano D.* (To Ludovico Federico, Renowned Lawyer, Brescian Nobleman)

Context: A nautical eclogue that draws on many of the conventions established in Vergil's bucolic poems. This poem is a dialogue occasioned by a chance encounter, much like *Ecl.* 1; like that eclogue as well, this poem turns around issues of liberty. Notable here is the stance taken by Idmon, taken captive during the Ottoman raid on Cyprus and forced to row as a slave during the Battle of Lepanto. Eyewitness testimony of the battle is foregrounded, and the Vergilian identification with the underdog found in the *Austrias Carmen* of Juan Latino is here underscored. Note that the dialogue of this nautical eclogue is between sailors, not shepherds, and takes place at the edge of the water, rather than in either the mythical or land-based setting of the *Eclogues*, adjustments appropriate to the occasion. See Grant, *Neo-Latin Literature and the Pastoral*, 342.

1–6. *Dic age Pieridum . . . quae me graviora canentem:* Cf. Vergil, *Ecl.* 4.1, *Sicelides Musae, paulo maiora canamus.*

10. *Astraea . . . Chelas:* Astrological signs of Virgo and Libra, dating the action of the poem to early October, shortly after the battle on October 7.

14. *Federice: De Brixiana Literatura* (1739, 341–42) identifies the dedicatee as Ludovico Federico, a member of the Accademia degli Occulti and author of a number of Latin poems.

19. Euridamas is from Knossos, therefore Cretan.

20. *per vada salsa:* Cf. *Aen.* 5.158, where, during the boat race, the ships *Pristis* and *Centaur* vie for the lead, cutting across the foaming waters: *et longa sulcant vada salsa carina.*

21–22. *et soles . . . lunae:* For one possible source of these lines, cf. *Ecl.* 6.31–40, Silenus's cosmogony. See also the song of Iopas in *Aen.* 1, particularly line 742, *hic canit errantem lunam solisque labores.*

25. *gemina formosior arce:* For a similar construction see *Ecl.* 7.38, where Galatea is said to be more beautiful than pale ivy: *hedera formosior alba.*

26. *aequoreas . . . undas:* Cf. Ovid, *Met.* 12.580, where Neptune calms the seas with his trident: *at deus aequoreas qui cuspide temperat undas.*

27–28. *aquarum / agmina:* For this peculiar description of an autumn storm, see *Geo.* 1.322, *saepe etiam immensum caelo venit agmen aquarum.*

32. *Cyprius Idmon:* Idmon, the second speaker of the poem, is from Cyprus, where he was taken captive during the earlier raid by the Ottomans.

33. *quod vesceris aura:* So *Aen.* 1.546–47, *si vescitur aura / aetheria.*

36. *atque epulas et Bacchi dona ferentem*: Geo. 3.526–27, *atqui non Massica Bacchi / munera, non illis epulae nocuere repostae*. Also *Aen*. 2.49, *et dona ferentes*.

51–53. *nam . . . cohors*: A reminder of the importance of spoils at Lepanto as in other Mediterranean naval battles of the period. Many news bulletins finish with a tally of the slaves and other loot captured (e.g., Giovanni Pietro Contarini, *Historia*, fol. 55v).

54. *reddita libertas*: Cf. *Ecl*. 1.27.

59. *fama loquax*: For two classical epic sources see Ovid, *Met*. 9.137 and Lucan, *BC* 8.782, in addition to the primary description of Fama in *Aen*. 4.173–90.

61. *pendebimus*: Cf. *Aen*. 4.79, where Dido likewise hangs on every word of Aeneas's war story.

72–74. *Doriclo . . . Alcimede*: Identification of Ali Pasha's parents is unknown, except that his father was a müezzin who called the Muslim faithful to prayer. These names may be fictionalizations.

83. *Siroccus*: Sulus Mehmet Pasha, who fought on the right flank.

88. *per marmora ponti*: A stunning and highly unusual description with its roots in Ennius, adapted by Vergil in *Aen*. 7.28.

113–14. *Aurora . . . / lutea*: Cf. *Aen*. 7.25–26, *aethere ab alto / Aurora in roseis fulgebat lutea bigis*.

147. John is here referred to as the offspring of Augustus, understood as Charles V, who as Holy Roman Emperor was often called Caesar.

170. Note how Ali Pasha is likened to Aeneas as he addresses his comrades in Carthage and struggles to hide his own feelings: *Aen*. 1.208–9.

176. The banner of the crucified Christ given to John of Austria by the pope.

182. *caelumque remugit*: For a similar depiction of the din of battle, see *Aen*. 9.504, *sequitur clamor caelumque remugit*.

188. *aequoreis credas scopulis concurrere montes*: So the Battle of Actium is described on Aeneas's shield: *credas . . . montis concurrere montibus altos*, *Aen*. 8.691–92.

211–19. *Carcozza . . . Superantius:* Memorializes young Venetians from the rearguard killed in fierce combat with Kara Hodja's forces; available sources suggest the fighters would have served on the galleys of Giovanni Loredan, Catarino Malipiero, and Gian Battista Benedetti (Bicheno, *Crescent and Cross,* 269). *Superantius* is Benedetto Soranzo.

214–15. None of these figures can be identified from trusted sources, though all echo ancient names (e.g., Lausus, son of Mezentius; Atys, sixth king of Alba Longa and the descendant of Aeneas through Silvius; and Abas, the twelfth king of Argos, who fought alongside the Greeks in the Trojan War).

228. *Cenomanum genus:* Broadly speaking, Venetian forces.

229. *Pentheus:* Identity unknown. See above, note to lines 214–15.

234. *contorto aere:* Rifled cannons that allowed for better aim.

235. *cerebri in ventribus:* "Ventres cerebri," or cerebral ventricles, appear in contemporary medical treatises. See, e.g., Vesalius, *De humani corporis fabrica libri septem* (1543). Given Taglietti's medical training, it seems plausible that he would have known of this designation.

271. *Haemi:* Cf. Geo. 1.492.

283. *Melite:* The Maltese, or Knights of the Hospital of Saint John of Jerusalem (also Knights Hospitaller), had defended Rhodes until its 1522 fall, withstood the Siege of Malta (1565), and also linked this clash to the Crusades.

286. *Non mihi centenas . . . linguas:* Cf. Aen. 6.625 and Ovid, Met. 8.532.

290. *Ismarium . . . Acin:* Suggests a figure renowned for religious and literary learning, whether a soothsayer who spoke through verse (*kahin*), poet (*sha'ir*), or priest (*ulema*). Identity unknown.

293. *lampada:* The weapon used by Venier is most likely a firepot filled with greek fire, a chemical blend that could not be extinguished by water.

316. *Baeticolum:* Andalusian fighters, after the Roman colony Hispania Baetica.

327. *sulcant . . . puppes:* So Aen. 5.158, where, during the boat race, a ship likewise "plows" the sea: *et longa sulcant vada salsa carina.*

331. *auri . . . fames: Aen.* 3.56–57, where the death of Polydorus occasions an apostrophe against greed.

366. *validos impellite remos:* Cf. *Aen.* 4.594, *date tela, impellite remos.*

371–72. *aequor / verrit:* For the phrase, cf. *Aen.* 3.290, 5.778, *aequora verrunt.*

385. *expleri nequeunt:* Cf. *Aen.* 8.265, the Arcadians stare openly at the strangled monster, Cacus.

XVII. TO THE MOST REVEREND PAOLO ODESCALCHI, BISHOP OF PENNE AND ATRI

Author: Giovanni Antonio Odescalchi

Text: Gherardi (1572), 86–92

Dedication: *ad Reverendissimum D. Paulum Odescalcum Patruum Episcopum Atriensem* (To the most reverend Paolo Odescalchi, Bishop of Penne and Atri)

Context: The shortest of the epyllia about Lepanto. The opening reference to the fourth eclogue suggests its origins in the most succinct of Vergil's genres. See Rota, "View of the Battle of Lepanto" (Figure 2), for a parallel visualization of Jupiter watching the battle that pairs well with the one offered here.

1. *paulo maiora:* Cf. *Ecl.* 4. 1.

14. *bipatentis Olympi:* Cf. *Aen.* 10.5.

16. *triplex . . . clavis:* Views papal heraldry with Holy League numerology, evoking the crosses carved out of the bits of the two papal keys; with the bits pointing upward, each key would indeed appear to have three points — top, left, and right — emerging from the base of the crucifix. See Heim, *Coutumes et Drout Héraldiques de l'Eglise*, 65–66.

19. *praecipitare moras:* Cf. *Aen.* 8.443, Vulcan to the Cyclops.

23. *finem requiemque laborum:* Venus to Jupiter in *Aen.* 1.241, *quem das finem, rex magne, laborum?*, where Aeneas is contrasted with Antenor, a Trojan already settled in Venice.

28. *Omnibus unus amor pulchrae succedere pugnae:* So Nisus and Euryalus in *Aen.* 9.401.

30. *Qualis Massylum . . .:* See note to Poem XII, line 8.

51. *ferit aethera clamor:* Cf. *Aen.* 5.140, the noise of the boat race.

53–55. *Qualis si pelago evulsa ab radicibus imis / incedat silva:* Cf. *Aen.* 8.691–93 for a related simile.

65. *stans celsa in puppi:* Appears several times in the *Aeneid*, most notably at 8.680, where it occupies the same metrical position.

72. *gelidus subita formidine sanguis: Aen.* 3.259, *subita gelidus formidine sanguis,* after the false prophecy of the Harpies.

83. *ignivomis ardet galea horrida cristis:* Recalls Turnus's helmet at *Aen.* 7.785–88.

88. *Huic natam haud laetis sociaverat ante Tyrannus:* In fact, Ali Pasha was brother-in-law, not son-in-law, of Sultan Selim II.

101–2. Dramatizes the three charges John of Austria led in order to finally take the Ottoman flagship (*Scythian*).

105–8. *Quas vos hic fortia facta / editis o memoranda manus? Quot sternitis ense / corpora Medorum? Nil illos tela, vel arcus, / nil validae iuvere manus?* Comparable to scenes of *aristeia* in the *Aeneid*, e.g., 11.664ff.

112. *spoliis . . . opimis:* Spoils won in one-on-one combat between two opposing generals of an army; cf. Livy, *AUC* 1.10.

113–14. *Inde citi flectunt cursum, qua plurimus hostis / urget, et insani gliscunt incendia Martis:* In *Aen.* 12.9 Turnus is compared to a lion, and the verb used of his violence is "gliscit."

118. *pallida mortis imago: Aen.* 2.369.

134–35. *corpora volvit aquis, clypeos, galeasque micantes:* A variation of *Aen.* 1.101.

143. *manibus post terga revinctis:* So Sinon in *Aen.* 2.57.

150–53. *ceu quondam in montibus altis / conspecto cane cerva fugit praeruptaque saxa / et cautes superans silva se condit opaca / ille nemus late latratibus implet acutis.* Epic simile comparable to many in the *Aeneid,* esp. 10.724–29. No direct parallels in Vergil.

154. *Victores gaza innumera: Aen.* 1.119.

175–78. Death of Agostino Barbarigo; see Appendix I.

XVIII. [THE LONG-DESIRED DAY AT LAST DISPELLED THE FADING SHADOWS]

Author: Ottaviano Manini

Text: Gherardi (1572), nine unnumbered pages between 128 and 129; Bottari, 167–73.

Title: [Untitled]

Context: A poem remarkable for its synthesis of echoes from the major Augustan poets, which serve to reinforce the notion that the victory at Lepanto is a victory for Hesperia, broadly defined here as the western Mediterranean.

1. *At Latio:* Beginning the poem with *At* recalls the opening of *Aen.* 4: *At regina.* The mention of Latium, however, moves our attention to the second half of the *Aeneid* and the battle in Latium between the Trojans and Latins. Throughout this poem that struggle is invoked as the Battle of Lepanto is seen through the scrim of Aeneas's battle over land rights.

dispulit umbras: Cf. *Aen.* 5.839.

3. *Iam . . . iam:* Echoes both *Ecl.* 4 and Catullus 64; both speak to the beginning of a new era.

12. *vasto gurgite fractae: Aen.* 1.118.

16–17. *qualis ubi . . . complet:* Echoes simile of Laocoön, *Aen.* 2.223–24.

19. *Achaemeniae . . . tiarae:* Achaemenes, the founder of the Persian dynasty.

22–23. *quas condat . . . nivalem:* Cf. *Geo.* 4.517–18.

24. *Nomadum:* Cf. *Aen.* 4.535.

29. *bella, horrida bella:* Cf. *Aen.* 6.86, where the Sibyl warns Aeneas of the struggles that lie ahead in Latium.

41. *res stetit Itala:* Reading *res* with Gherardi (over *rex* in Bottari).

44–45. *Propriamque amens in viscera dextram / condidit:* Cf. Lucan, *BC* 1.3.

53. *Thraciam in Italiam portans et tristia fata:* An adaptation of *Aen.* 1.68, *Ilium in Italiam portans victosque penatis*, where Aeneas is portrayed by Juno as carrying Troy to Italy. Here it is the enemy who threatens the West.

54–60. *Qualis ubi hiberno consurgens . . . franget:* Echoes *Aen.* 10.803–8, Aeneas's *aristeia*, which, in turn, evokes an agricultural Georgic setting.

64. *Tu:* John of Austria.

91. *Quo ruitis:* Cf. *Aen.* 12.313, Aeneas to the gods; also Hor. *Carm.* 7; *pestes Dirae, Aen.* 12.845.

95. *cornua lunae:* The Ottoman tactic of arraying in a half-moon formation resonated sharply in symbolic terms given the crescent moon symbol of Islam. See Figure 1.

96. *geminae classes:* Conveys the view of a left and a right flank that branch off from the center, an effect also visible in Figure 1.

99. *Cum:* Reading *cum* with Gherardi (over *quam* in Bottari).

102. *Ferte faces:* Cf. *Aen.* 4.594, *ferte . . . flammas*, where Dido calls for flames and weapons in an effort to stop Aeneas from leaving Carthage.

104–5. *carinam / impulit: Aen.* 5.241–42, *pater . . . Portunus euntem / impulit.*

111. *Ismaren . . . Rhodopen . . . Olympo:* Modeled on the address to the reader in *Aen.* 8.691–93.

112–13. *fumidus ad caelum densa caligine nimbus: Aen.* 12.466–67, *solum densa in caligine Turnum / vestigat lustrans.*

113. *volvitur, ex oculisque diem eripuere tenebrae: Aen.* 1.88–89, *eripiunt . . . diemque . . . ex oculis.*

116. *Et fera Tisiphone, luctusque et mortis imago:* Cf. *Aen.* 6.571.

118. *fragmina remorum passim, fluitantia passim / transtra natant, proras demersis aequora rostris*: As Aeneas returns from meeting the Etruscans in Pallanteum to Latium via the Tiber River, he crashes his boats on the shore: *Aen.* 10.306–7, *fragmina remorum quos et fluitantia transtra / impediunt.*

127. *Fama*: Notice how abbreviated and positive the mention of *Fama* has become.

130. *advenisse diem*: Cf. *Aen.* 7.145 and 10.215.

136. *barbaricam nostra excussam cervice securim*: *Aen.* 2.223–24, simile describing Laocoön's death.

159. *vestri pars una fuissem*: Cf. *Aen.* 2.6.

167. *dona suprema ferunt*: A favorite phrase of Vergil's with its origin in *et dona ferentes* of *Aen.* 2.49. Underlying the use here is a reading based on the fortunate fall.

169. *Scipiadae . . . Camilli*: Famous Roman heroes. Scipio and Camillus are mentioned together in Propertius 3.11.67; the Scipios are mentioned in the same metrical position in *Aen.* 6.843.

179. *populi Aurorae . . . litora rubra*: So on Aeneas's shield at Actium, *Aen.* 8.686.

180–81. *haud hic vestigia plantae / figunt certa meae*: A reference to crusade literature, e.g., William of Tyre, *Chronicon*, where the fact that Christ walked on the land under dispute argues for Christian entitlement.

182–83. *Maius opus*: An echo of *Aen.* 7.44, *maior rerum mibi nascetur ordo, / maior opus moveo.*

187. *urbs antiqua*: Echoes *Aen.* 1.12, suggesting a link with Carthage.

189. *Quae mora*: Iterates widespread calls for an expedition to retake Constantinople in the post-Lepanto euphoria.

190. *surgamus*: Cf. *Ecl.* 10.75, marking the end of the last eclogue and the beginning of a new phase.

193. *caput*: In the context, this suggests Constantinople or the sultan (see l. 189 above).

195. *quam se perpetua solvant formidine terrae:* Cf. *Ecl.* 4.14, *inrita, perpetua solvent formidine terras.*

200. *Bactra:* Cf. *Aen.* 8.688, associated on Aeneas's shield with Cleopatra.

207. *Aut desolata cadat ingens truncus arena:* Lucan, *BC* 1.685; *Aen.* 2.557–59.

211–12. *O ne mors fuscis caput hoc circumvolet alis:* *Aen.* 7.408, describing Allecto in Latium, flying around on *fuscis alis.* Manini himself may indeed have been at an advanced age or ailing, though the 1573 date of death that Jöcher lists is too early (in *ABI* I.602.237–38). A Tommaso Porcacchi dedication to Manini, dated May 21, 1574, suggests he lived one year longer. See Introduction.

217. *Leminis:* Also called Lemine, the medieval toponym of a large territory in Lombardy in the vicinity of the River Brembo.

221. *Grimane heros:* Venetian Giovanni Grimani, *Patriarca* of Aquileia and noted antiquities collector, helped finance the Venetian fleets (see Giovanni Pietro Contarini, *Historia,* fol. 6r; *Dizionario,* G. Benzoni and L. Bortolotti). His connection with Elba (*tellus Ilvia*) is unknown.

229. *huc ades:* Cf. *Ecl.* 9.39, *Huc ades o Galatea: quis est nam ludus in undis?*

XIX. A SHINING SONG FOR THE VICTOR, JOHN OF AUSTRIA

Author: Pompeo Arnolfini

Text: Bologna, Ioannis Rosii, 1572 (Newberry Library, Case Y 682.A75)

Title: *Lucen. Carmen. Ioan. Austriaco Victori Dicatum* (Shining song for the victor, John of Austria)

Context: In a typically Ovidian gesture, the poem frames its subject matter against what it is not, by foiling the generic expectation implicit in its metrical form. Having banished the genre of love elegy but not its characteristic meter, the poem passes through a series of cosmological reflections strongly reminiscent of the beginning of Ovid's *Metamorphoses* before moving on to more Vergilian territory, imagining the reactions of divine entities to the mortals' preparations for battle. Near its end the poem returns again to the ironic Ovidian tone as the speaker invokes a series of contemporary poets each of whom, he claims, would be more suited to his own poetic task. This list brings to mind the similar catalog of poets in *Amores* 1.15.

3. *disiectasque rates . . . aequore*: See *Aen.* 1.43.

7. *Bella cano*: Cf. Ovid, *Am.* 2.18.12; also see Lucan, *BC* 1.1–2, for a possible echo.

11. *magni primordia concinat orbis*: So Ovid, *Met.* 15.67, where Pythagoras likewise reveals the world's origins; also cf. Lucretius, *DRN* 1.158–60.

12. *nec bene digestum . . . Chaos*: See esp. Ovid, *Met.* 1.7–9.

13. *Deus . . . molem*: The unnamed god that appears on the chaotic scene of *Met.* 1 is here supplanted by the Christian God, whose gathering of the embattled primordial elements is likened, by way of the significant term *miro . . . foedere*, to the "miraculous" Holy League of Europe's Catholic powers.

18. *bella parata Iovi*: This second refashioning of the opening line of the *Amores* furnishes a convenient transition from the *Met.* passage. Here again the poet self-consciously adapts Ovidian language to fit the Vergilian theme.

17–20. *Alter terrigenum . . . sepulta sinu*: Reference to a gigantomachy; in *Amores* 2.1.11–16 the poet declares that he was writing a poem of gigantomachy until his beloved interrupted him.

21–24. *Crudeles alius . . . signa viri*: The poet dismisses other epic topics, e.g., the Theban cycle (the war against Thebes as depicted in Statius's *Thebaid*, Oedipus's incest), and the sack of Troy and Aeneas's escape described in the *Aeneid*.

37. *atros fluctus Aquilone secabant*: Cf. *Aen.* 5.2, where Aeneas sails away from Carthage on a northern wind: *fluctusque atros Aquilone secabat*.

63. *Vulcania fortior arma*: Cf. *Aen.* 12.740, where Turnus's sword shatters like ice when it comes into contact with Aeneas's Vulcan-made armor: *arma dei ad Volcania ventum est*.

65. *Aurea caesaries humeris, atque aurea fulgent*: Echoes the description of the Gauls at *Aen.* 8.659, *aurea caesaries ollis atque aurea vestis.*

75. *video humano spumantem sanguine pontum*: Cf. *Aen.* 6.87, the river Tiber foaming with blood: *Thybrim multo spumantem sanguine cerno;* also the gruesome aftermath of a naval battle in Lucan, *BC* 3.572–73, *cruor altus in undis / spumat, et obducti concreto sanguine fluctus.*

86. For the land of the Phaeacians, see *Odyssey* 5–8.

89–91. *Et iam Leucadii nimbosa cacumina . . . rupes, ardua saxa, Ithacas . . . nemora alta Zacynthi*: For the general model, see *Aen.* 3.270–75, which refers to *nemorosa Zacynthos* (270), *Neritos ardua saxis* and *scopulos Ithacae* (271–72), and *Leucatae nimbosa cacumina montis* (274).

93–108. Note that much like the poet, who has traded his amorous subject for one of war, Venus too eschews her standard elegance in favor of a rugged and battle-ready appearance; cf. *Aen.* 7.803–17 for the description of the warrior Camilla; also see *Aen.* 1.315–20, where Venus appears to Aeneas in the guise of a huntress.

94. *capta . . . Papho*: Refers to the fall of Cyprus through Paphos, sacred to Venus, located in the southwest of the island.

113. *sine labe*: Through this phrase Venus is typologically related to Mary. See note on Context to Poem IV.

131. *Amathuntis onusta*: Ancient port city of Cyprus, known in the Renaissance as Limiso.

139. *Unius ob culpam Pallas evertere classem*: Cf. *Aen.* 1.39–41, where Juno mentions the punishment of Ajax as a justification for her treatment of Aeneas: *Pallasne exurere classem / Argivum atque ipsos potuit summergere ponto, / unius ob noxam et furias Aiacis Oilei?*

140. *et potuit Danaum mergere rostra mari*: A variation of *Aen.* 1.40.

151. *latrantem in gurgite Anubin*: Note the appearance of Anubis in the Battle of Actium ekphrasis at *Aen.* 8.698, *latrator Anubis.*

169–70. *Haec ubi dicta . . . locum*: Echoes *Aen.* 1.402–3, *Dixit et avertens rosea cervice refulsit, / ambrosiaeque comae divinum vertice odorem / spiravere,* as

Venus turns to leave Aeneas in Carthage, revealing her identity as she goes.

195. I.e., trees of Dodona, connected mythologically to Achelous.

213. *fulmineo caelum tonat omne fragore:* So *Aen.* 9.541, *caelum tonat omne fragore.*

221. *vasto . . . in gurgite:* The phrase (*in*) *gurgite vasto* occurs four times in the *Aeneid.*

233–34. *Vixque una . . . Ossialene manus:* In reality, Uluj Ali escaped with a small fleet of thirty galleys (Guilmartin, *Gunpowder and Galleys,* 262).

237–38. *Neptunus placidum summis caput extulit undis / spectansque:* Cf. Neptune, stirred by the storm's commotion, raising his head from the sea at *Aen.* 1.127, *prospiciens, summa placidum caput extulit unda.*

242. *Maeoniis:* Lydian mode, or the style of Greek epic.

245. *Capilupus:* Ippolito Capilupi, born in Mantua in 1511 and died at Rome in 1580. See Intra, "Di Ippolito Capilupi e del suo tempo," *Archivio storico lombardo* XX, 1893.

250. *Angelius:* Florentine poet Pietro Angeli (1517–69), who wrote of Cosimo I de' Medici and translated Sophocles, *Oedipus Tyrannos.*

254. *Carga:* Giovanni Carga, born ca. 1520. Bolognese poet who sang of the Bolognese cardinal Lorenzo Campeggio and published *Turcis ad Echinades superatis,* elegies on the Battle of Lepanto, in 1572.

255. *Felsinei . . . Rheni:* Evocation of Northern Italy (Emilia-Romagna) through Bologna (Felsina) and the Reno River (Rhenus).

XX. THE VICTORY AT NAUPACTUS

Author: Giovanni Baptista Arcucci

Text: Gherardi (1572), 136–52

Title: *Victoria Naupactiaca* (The Victory of Naupactus)

Context: In this epyllion, Arcucci makes use of the poetic and narrative possibilities suggested by the diverse names listed in reports of the Ottoman battle lines. See, for example, the chart of names provided in

Giovanni Pietro Contarini's *Historia* bulletin, fols. 43v–47v. Appendix I lists the most prominent of the enemy commanders mentioned in the poem who can be identified with reasonable certainty. In terms of the literary tradition, he draws enthusiastically on the events surrounding the boat race in *Aeneid* 5. Arcucci shows the strongest fictionalizing impulse as he envisions the hand-to-hand combat, conjuring enemy names and some biographical details.

1. *facta:* Emended from *fasta* in Gherardi.

3. *Clio:* Muse of history.

5. *terrarum:* Emended from *verrarum.*

8. *condita plectra:* Together with *dulcibus . . . numeris* of line 2, reference to the use of ancient genres and meters.

15. *Ponto . . . in medio:* Traditional introduction of a *locus amoenus*, which, in turn, highlights the violence of the Ottoman invasion.

Dione: Mother of Venus.

22. *foedera rumpit:* The 1570 Ottoman invasion of Cyprus came after four decades of peace with Venice, as Selim II broke with his father Suleiman's policy.

25. *belli reserat portas:* So Juno in *Aen.* 7.613.

29. The conversation that follows between Venus and Jupiter echoes that of *Aen.* 1.223–96.

37. *contemptor divumque:* So Mezentius, *Aen.* 7.648.

43. *Tonantis:* Traditionally Jupiter himself; here also God.

49–50. *Stygii per flumina fontis / obtestor:* So Juno to Jupiter in *Aen.* 12.816–20, *adiuro Stygii caput implacabile fontis . . . obtestor.*

58. *Hydaspes:* Tributary of the river Indus. See *Geo.* 4.211, where it is mentioned together with *populi Parthorum.*

64. *utraque et Hesperia, et Venetum Respublica dives:* Note the distinction between Venice and Hesperia, which includes both the Spanish contingent and that of the pope. This distinction is reinforced by the detailed account of Italian, particularly western, geography throughout the poem.

65. *Suada:* In place of the more common *Fama,* Baptista uses *Suada,* who appears in Ennius, *Ann.* 308.

70. *bella horrida: Aen.* 7.41.

83. *pater huc alto me misit Olympo:* Echoes Mercury's words to Aeneas in *Aen.* 4.268, *ipse deum tibi me claro demittit Olympo.*

91. *Alciden:* Hercules.

94–95. *urebat iam terga Leonis / Sol:* The back of the lion is the end of the zodiacal sign of Leo; i.e., the end of August, when the Holy League assembled in Messina.

95. *marmora ponti:* See *Aen.* 7.28, a phrase borrowed from Ennius. In this context, though, it evokes as well the Sea of Marmara, north of Turkey.

99. *alter . . . mundus . . . Antarctica:* Spain's American colonies, with Antarctica referencing today's Patagonia.

107. *pernotus:* In this context, a key Neapolitan official, possibly Álvaro de Bazán, Marquis of Santa Cruz, in his capacity as Captain General of the Naples Fleet.

115. *per tela, per hostes:* Cf. *Aen.* 2.358.

117–26. *Parthenopes . . . Pausilypus . . . Capreas:* Traces John of Austria's departure from Naples (August 20) for Messina.

127. *Non has . . .:* The nymph's prophecy echoes those given Aeneas throughout the epic, most notably by Creusa in *Aen.* 2.776–89 and by Apollo in *Aen.* 3.94–98.

139. *Xerxis cum Danais:* Battle at the straits of the Hellespont after 483 BCE, comparable to the straits at Lepanto.

140. *Cleopatrae:* The battle between Octavian and Antony and Cleopatra took place at Actium, just north of the location of the Battle of Lepanto. See Introduction.

144. *Tertia iamque dies aderat:* Aeneas's journey from Troy to Rome begins with a long sea journey comparable to this one. Vergil links Sicily with happiness at the start of the poem; perhaps the echo here is meant to remind the reader that this joy was also fleeting.

161. *Heraclidarum:* Reference to the ships built by descendants of Hercules at Naupactus, where they encountered the allied forces of Achaeans, Ionians, and Arcadians. See Euripides, *Heracleidae.*

163. *'Arma, arma o socii':* A possible conflation of the first word of the *Aeneid* with Aeneas's famous address to his comrades in Carthage, *o socii (neque enim ignari sumus ante malorum),* 1.198–207.

169–85. *Genitore Thoante / ortus Alys . . . dictis:* Reliable sources do not corroborate Ali Pasha's father's name. The ornate weapons Arcucci conveys do reflect the arms captured by Spaniards and still on display in the Royal Armory of the Palacio Real of Madrid.

169. *diva refer:* Cf. *Aen.* 7.641–46, a similar appeal to the Muses at the start of a battle.

173. *in curvae speciem lunae:* The Ottoman boats were arrayed in a crescent shape. See Introduction and Figure 1.

178. *Polyphemus:* The one-eyed monster blinded by Odysseus (*Od.* 9) and seen by Aeneas on Sicily (*Aen.* 3.641).

179. *Et latere a laevo pendebat maximus ensis, / effulgens cuius capulum decorabat iaspis:* So *Aen.* 4.261–62, where Aeneas in Carthage is described in similar terms, dressed in finery and weapons given him by Dido.

181. *clypeum gestabat Abantis:* Echoes the description of the trophy left by Aeneas at Actium, *clypeum, magni gestamen Abantis, Aen.* 3.286.

186. *'Gradivo quantum Geticis qui praesidet arvis . . .':* See *Aen.* 3.35, *Gradivumque patrem, Geticis qui praesidet arvis,* part of Aeneas's prayer at the first stop after Troy, identified with the Thracians.

187. *Tonanti:* As in Poem XI, the Thunderer here refers to Selim and the Ottoman forces.

191. *Damis:* Possible variant of Diana.

196. *Nireus:* A Greek warrior celebrated for his beauty in the Trojan War. *Phrygia vel raptus ab Ida:* Ganymede; so *Aen.* 5.252–55.

197–203. *Huic fabricata . . . clypeum:* So Venus supplies arms to Aeneas in *Aen.* 8.608–16.

199–200. *consertam . . . hamis*: *Aen.* 5.259–60, *levibus . . . hamis consetam auroque trilicem / loricam.*

208. *duo fulmina belli*: *Aen.* 6.842.

215. The conversation between Venus and Neptune may be modeled on *Aen.* 5.779–815.

219. *celsa ex puppi*: A variant of the phrase characterizing Aeneas and Augustus as naval leaders, esp. *Aen.* 8.680.

225. *sanctus . . . senex*: I.e., Pope Pius V.

231. Although in the context the word clearly translates as "brazen," the emphasis placed on it in the first foot suggests its homynym, the hero Aeneas.

233. *Quis . . .* : This series of rhetorical questions underscores the unspeakable enormity of the battle echoes, e.g., *Aen.* 11.664–65.

241–42. *Psylli, Garamantes, Aethiopes, Daci, Morini, Cilicesque, Getaeque*: Here, Turkish troops; in the *Aeneid*, Roman colonies on the edges of the empire. See *Aen.* 8.727–28.

245. *ut leo*: Similes comparing the Venetians to lions turn on the symbol emblazoned on their banners and enable the poet to draw on the many similes Vergil uses comparing the enemy to a lion; see, e.g., *Aen.* 9.339 and 12.1.

256–60. Dramatization of the fierce fighting that resulted in severe losses to Sicilian forces under Juan de Cardona.

259. *Barco*: Ali Pasha's helmsman, unattested elsewhere by name. In this context it may be Pertev Pasha, whom early Spanish accounts erroneously claimed had been thwarted by Cardona (Bicheno, *Crescent and Cross*, 250).

269. *clypeo septemplice*: So the shields of ancient heroes were often said to be composed of seven layers; see *Aen.* 8.448.

275–92. Exaggerates John of Austria's limited hand-to-hand fighting to catalog prominent Ottoman leaders killed that day. Sources suggest but do not confirm the following identifications: Aghadi Reis (Agat), Dardagan Pasha (Dadagus), Kara Hodja (Cara), Hassan Pasha (Casa), Mustafa Esdri Pasha (Mustafa), Giesman Ferat (Giafferrus), Osman Reis (Osman), Piri Reis (Perus), Aziz Agha (Assys), Previs Agha (Prouys), Mehmet Scirocco, Caur Ali (Caralys), Murat Reis (Morattus). Good sources do not allow for hypothesis for Ligerys (281) and Cappadocus of the *Periba* (288).

293–308. Sources do not allow for a reasonable identification of Gyalus and the captain of the *Laeana* (Nearchus), or the sons of Dragut (Turgut Reis).

296. *Pistrice:* The name of this boat is unattested, though, strikingly, it echoes the name of one of the boats in the ship race of *Aen.* 5.116.

314–16. *Monsorrem . . . Myrmillum:* Turks unattested elsewhere.

317–18. The line echoes the exploits of young Iulus in Carthage, *Aen.* 4.151–59, which may have been suggested by his name (*Andraleo*).

319–26. *Ligur Auria . . . veloce:* Renders the fighting on the seaward flank of the battle as a gigantomachy, though sources do not allow precise identification of *Corinaeus* and *Chelypus* with those in the Holy League right wing led by Doria (*Ligur Auria*), nor do they suggest plausible identifications for the Ottoman left (the galley *Tygris, Solymaeus,* and *Cloanthus*). This skirmish culminated in Uluj Ali's escape, which proved the most controversial in the historiography (see Guilmartin, *Gunpowder and Galleys,* 261–62).

324. *acremque Cloanthum / insequitur:* Replicates the name of one of the competitors in the boat race, *Aen.* 5.152.

327. *Militiaeque duces Melitensis:* The Maltese, whose participation in the battle provides the clearest link with the earlier Crusades.

340. *Brontis:* Etiological tales of this kind are common in Vergil. See, e.g., the backstory to Camilla in *Aen.* 11.535–94.

358. *Arcadiam:* Here, Greece, or even perhaps Turkey.

365–66. *Sangam . . . Phydrum:* Turks unattested elsewhere.

370–71. *Carrafia proles . . . Lirim:* Vincenzo Carrafa was a Knight of Malta whose Neapolitan family heritage is referenced through the River Liris; he was rewarded with the title of Gran Priore d'Ungheria after Lepanto (Argegni, "Condottieri, capitani, tribuni," in *Enciclopedia bio-bibliografica italiana*, vol. 1, 1936, 356 = *ABI* I.iii, 443).

384–87. Refers to major rivers of the Italian and Iberian peninsula. See Appendix I.

388–93. *Ursinae . . . Mammettumque:* Paulo Giordano Orsini, member of the famed Roman family who captured and killed Mahmud Bey.

396. *Cassanumque Halymumque . . . Stassyn.* Dramatizes fighting on the landward side (Holy League left wing against the Ottoman right flank). It is uncertain whether these names record specific Ottoman commanders killed here or plausible transliterations of common Turkish or Muslim names and honorifics (Hassan, Ali, Sinan, etc.).

400. *Scyroccus:* Sulus Mehmet Pasha.

404–5. *Gurgut . . . Smyrnae . . . Melete:* Evokes a leader from the Anatolian heartland of the Ottoman Empire in terms of Smyrna or Izmir and the River Meles, slain by the Duke of Urbino, who fought on the flagship of Savoy in the center flank. Again, the degree of transliteration and the overall context do not permit a precise identification.

416. *Qualis sub nocte:* Cf. *Aen.* 9.59–64, Turnus as wolf; see Moizio, XXI *ad* 545–47.

420–25. *Cardinei iuvenis . . . Barbarigus:* Records two of the most widely reported Holy League deaths, Bernardino Cárdenas, the son of a Spanish grandee, and Agostino Barbarigo, the Venetian leader. See Appendix I.

430. *Soranzus:* On the death of Benedetto Soranzo, a Venetian captain, see Giovanni Pietro Contarini, *Historia*, fol. 53v.

432. *Bisballus:* Bernardino Bisbal, a Neapolitan nobleman (count of Briatico) killed in battle (see Paruta, *Historia venetiana* II, 160).

434. *Musis Toraldus amicus:* Arcucci, like the Spanish poet-chronicler Fernando de Herrera, erroneously reports the death of the soldier-poet

Gaspare Toraldo (*Relación de la guerra de Cipre*), a confusion that may reflect the heavy casualties suffered by the unit he led in a charge to board an Ottoman galley, at which point Toraldo suffered an arm injury. A friend of Torquato Tasso, Toraldo himself published a 1572 oration in honor of John of Austria and a 1573 *Discorsi cavallerischi* (see Luigi Aliquò-Lenzi and Filippo Aliquò-Taveritti *Gli scrittori calabresi*, vol. 3, 1955, 26; in *ABI* II.626.384). The erroneous report of his death attests to how soon after the battle Arcucci wrote his poem.

437. *gens Melites:* The death of the Maltese sailors is detailed in Poem XXI, lines 497–531.

448. *Belli anceps fortuna:* A variation of the much-quoted line that originates in Cicero, *Marc.* 15, *anceps fortuna belli.*

448–52. God's decision to send Apollo to end the war echoes *Aen.* 8.704, where the appearance of Apollo decides the outcome of the battle.

458. *velut accipiter pavidas . . . columbas:* For a dove and hawk simile, see *Aen.* 11.721–24.

472–73. *Austriades . . . triumphum:* John of Austria returned to Messina (October 31), where city officials organized a triumphal entry (Bennassar, *Don Juan de Austria*, 143–44). A monument to him was built in Messina, engraved with the following verses by the Messinese polymath Francesco Maurolico. See Vaccaluzzo, ""Dei poeti latini," 198–99.

> Gesta fidem superant Zancle ne longa vetustas
>   deleat hic vultus finxit in aere tuos.
> Hostem horis binis superas datur aere colossus:
>   nunc eat et factis obstrepat invidia.
> Iam satis ostensum est quo sis genitore creatus
>   Africa regna parens ipse Asiana domas.
> Non satis unus erat victo tanto hoste triumphus esse
>   triumphator semper in aere potes.

473. *victor in Italiam:* A subtle reworking of *Aen.* 1.68, quoted above as the Ottomans threatened Italy, revised here to speak to John of Austria's ultimate victory for the Holy League.

XXI. SONG ON THE VICTORY OF
THE CHRISTIAN FLEET

Author: Guglielmo Moizio

Text: Gherardi (1572), 42–76. Also published separately in 1572 in Naples apud Josephum Cacchium. Dedicated to Alexander Farnese.

Title: *De victoria Christianae Classis Carmen* (Song on the victory of the Christian fleet)

Context: The Naples edition is preceded by a letter from the poet to Cardinal Alexander Farnese detailing the circumstances of the poem's creation. In this letter, Moizio, referencing Catullus, Horace, and Vergil, agrees to write this account of the battle if Cardinal Farnese would endorse it ("ut hos versus sub tuo nomine in vulgus exire patiare"). He also writes of being urged by the cardinal to write it quickly, before the public excitement had died down. His goal is to celebrate those *viros nobiles et fortes* from Rome who fought in the battle, leaving the accounting of the contribution of other cities to future poets. The letter is dated the Ides of November 1571.

2. *quae mulcens aethera cantu:* Cf. *Aen.* 7.34, where Aeneas sees birds singing in the seaside groves at the mouth of the Tiber.

11. *exarsere animis: inque aspera bella ruentes:* For the image of smoldering rage (specifically in a martial context), cf. *Aen.* 2.575. See also *Aen.* 9.182, where Nisus and Euryalus are described in similar terms, *pariterque in bella ruebant.*

13–14. *Neptuniaque . . . cruore:* For the striking image of Neptunian fields growing red with blood, see *Aen.* 8.695.

65. *quos primo flore iuventae:* A common expression for adolescence; cf. *Aen.* 7.162. John is characterized throughout these poems by his youth, contrasting him to Venier, on the one hand, and Ali Pasha, on the other, and likening him to Apollo.

70–71. *praefectus Iberae . . . classi:* Comendador Mayor of Castile, Luis de Requesens.

73–91. A narration of how the Spanish contingent under John of Austria joined forces with those of the Duke of Savoy and the Republic of Genoa (July 1571). The Duke of Urbino (Guidobaldo Della Rovere) is the Feltrian hero (75), given the proximity of Feltre to Rovere; he joined Alessandro Farnese on the flagship of Genoa.

89. *omnibus effundit fulgentes aere catervas:* Cf. *Aen.* 8.592–93.

91. *Calabri furibundi Martis alumni:* The Neapolitan fleet featured numerous Calabrian fighters, though the context does not allow for precise identification.

100. *Ut catulus fulvi Massyla per arva leonis / dura pati discit vento pulsatus et imbri:* See note to Poem XII, line 8.

103. *spectatus pridem:* Marco Antonio Colonna, then just twenty years old, had commanded troops in the Italian wars of the 1550s on behalf of Charles V of Spain and Cosimo I de' Medici.

105. *Allobrogum:* The population based in the Alpine region that roughly coincided with the Duchy of Savoy. The leader of the Allobroges is Emmanuel Philibert, Duke of Savoy.

108. *arce Monoeci:* The Ligurian harbor of Monaco, named for Hercules Monoikos.

109–10. *unde caput . . . Eridanus:* Po River. Cf. the appearance of Neptune at *Aen.* 1.125–27.

130. *altera sulcavit proris stridentibus aequor:* Cf. *Aen.* 5.158 and 10.197.

133. *saevi Martis amorem:* So *Aen.* 7.550, where the fury Allecto boasts to Juno that she has successfully stirred up war among the Trojans and Latins: *insani Martis amore.*

136–37. *Venerius in armis, / imperiis pridem:* Alludes to the Venetian commander's advanced age (seventy-five) and youthful military service in Candia, Friuli, and Brescia. See also Appendix I.

146. *summum ferit aethera clamor:* Cf. *Aen.* 5.140–41, *ferit aethera clamor / nauticus.*

155. *Corda pavore tremunt:* Cf. *Aen.* 5.137–38.

157. *disiectae ad terram ingentem traxere ruinam: Aen.* 8.191–92, describing the monster Cacus's home.

158. *Oppida tot pelago credas innare:* Cf. *Aen.* 8.691, describing the Battle of Actium.

160. *propugnacula:* Cf. *Aen.* 4.87, where the word occurs in the same metrical position.

170. *terrorem ancipitem Latiis incusserat arvis, / Hesperios temnens reges:* Note the emphasis on Vergilian Latium and Hesperia, in keeping with the author's stated goal (see "Context" above).

181. *Lyaeo:* Bacchus, metonymy for wine.

188. *Octobres nonas:* The Nones of October, or October 7.

194. *Stans celsa in puppi:* Phrase used most notably of Augustus at the Battle of Actium, *Aen.* 8.680.

197. *vastator Achilles:* Cf. Statius, *Achil.* 2.32, where Ulysses addresses Achilles in this manner: *magnae vastator debite Troiae.*

198. *Geticis Mavors bellator in arvis:* Cf. *Aen.* 3.35.

199–200. *Carolus . . . insignibus:* Proposes the analogy of the youthful John of Austria at Lepanto, in a de facto imperial command position, to the election of his father, Charles V, as Holy Roman Emperor in 1519 at age nineteen. See also Appendix I.

212. *pro laude in ferrum et pro libertate ruendum:* Cf. *Aen.* 8.648, on the shield.

216. See Figure 1.

229. *caligine caelum:* Cf. *Aen.* 11.187, where Aeneas, alongside King Tarchon, burns the bodies of the slain and smoke obscures the sky.

230. *et geminans longis resonat mugitibus aether:* Echo perhaps of Statius, *Achil.* 1. 524, *Tandem fessa tremens longis mugitibus.*

232. *Calydon, Naupactus . . . Corinthus:* See Figure 3.

233. *pecus omne sub undis:* For the description of fish in flocks, cf. Horace, *Carm.* 1.2.7–8.

260. *maximus . . . tribunus*: Renders Barbarigo's title of *proveditor generale di mare* and celebrates his role as emissary to John of Austria in key tactical discussions.

263–75. Details fighting closest to shore, between the Venetians in the Holy League left flank and forces on the Ottoman right. Barbarigo shifted his forces to better attack those of the Bey of Rhodes, before succumbing to Ottoman weapon fire. *Campsanus* transliterates the name of a fighter from Rhodes, though precise identification is not possible.

268. *fluctibus absorpti fundo voluntatur in imo*: Cf. the Titans and their punishment in the underworld at *Aen.* 6.581.

277. *et fluvidos trepidant siccare cruores*: Cf. *Aen.* 4.687, where Anna attempts to help the wounded Dido.

292. *ferreus imber*: See *Aen.* 12.284, where a mass of spears is twice likened to a storm.

293–326. Catalog of fallen Venetians.

293. *Landus*: Marc Antonio Lando.

298. *Caterinus*: Catarino Malipiero.

301. *Superantius*: Benedetto Soranzo.

309–10. *Hieronymus atque Marinus . . . Contarenae*: Gerolamo and Marino Contarini.

316. *Laurentanus bonus . . . Pascalius*: Giovanni Loredan, Marco Antonio Pasqualigo.

317. *Quirinus*: Vincenzo Quirini.

325–26. *Illustres . . . fratres . . . Cornelia*: Identities unknown. Appropriately, the grieving mother of four slain Italian fighters bears a name associated with Roman maternal devotion; cf. Cornelia, mother of the Gracchi.

329. *omnibus unus amor erat*: Cf. *Aen.* 9.182, *his amor unus erat.*

336–37. *Lacaena . . . mater*: See Plutarch, *Life of Agesilaus*, chap. 29 (612c–d) for a comparable tale.

385. *corpora dat leto*: So *Aen.* 12.328, where Turnus, seeing Aeneas in flight, rages across the battlefield, leveling all before him.

398. *informe solo pedibus calcare cadaver:* See Hercules's display of the corpse of Cacus at *Aen.* 8.264–65. The allusion grants Venier a Herculean valence.

399. *iunctis raptare quadrigis:* Possible evocation of Mettus on the shield of Aeneas, *Aen.* 8.642.

416–21. Two nephews of Pius V, Michele Bonelli (*puer . . . Michael*) and Paolo Ghislieri (*Paulus*).

437–97. The boarding of Ottoman galleys, hand-to-hand combat.

437. *proles Farnesia . . . Dacos:* Conveys how Alessandro Farnese attacked an Ottoman reserve galley, here referred to as Dacians.

441–42. *ingens / Iordanus:* Paolo Giordano Orsini carried the banner of the Order of Saint Stephen, founded by his father-in-law, Cosimo I de' Medici, to combat Turks and pirates in the Tyrrhenian Sea.

451. *Etrusca iuventus:* Paolo Giordano Orsini, Tuscan himself, was connected to the Grand Duke of Tuscany by marriage into the Medici family. See also Appendix I.

458. *Sfortia:* Paolo Sforza led an infantry contingent from Lombardy.

459. *Cilicas:* The inhabitants of Cilicia were notorious pirates.

476. *Ascanius:* Ascanio della Corgna; the *Chabrian* dukes are French knights of Saint John. The adjective, borrowed from French, is indeclinable in Latin.

479. Pompeo and Prospero are both Colonna.

480. *Paravicinus:* Sforza Pallavicini, a Venetian commander.

482. *Pyrrhus:* May be Martín Pirola of the Venetian forces.

484. Brescian poet Lorenzo Gambara published *Carmina . . . pro victoria christianae religionis contra Turcas* (Naples, 1571).

485. The *Gonzaga lords* refer to Sigismondo Gonzaga on the flagship of Gian Andrea Doria and Ottavio Gonzaga, who led a Savoy contingent.

490. *Gallus . . . Ramagusus* is the French Knight of Saint John (Malta), Mathurin d'Aux Lescout de Romegas.

496. *caelum omne remugit:* Cf. the terrible din as the Volscians attack at *Aen.* 9.504.

507. *truces Numidae:* The North African forces under Uluj Ali.

512. *quingenti ac mille prehensos:* Refers to how Uluj Ali initially captured the Maltese flagship and approximately twelve other galleys on the Holy League right wing; once the North African commander realized the Ottoman fleet had lost the battle, he abandoned his prisoners to flee, leaving behind the shattered Maltese command ship and hundreds of dead. See Guilmartin, *Gunpowder and Galleys,* 262; and Bicheno, *Crescent and Cross,* 275.

535. *Massylos:* Uluj Ali's North African forces.

541. *caligine caeca:* Vergil makes use of the phrase twice in the *Aeneid,* at 3.203 and 8.253.

543. *Victores:* Emended from *Vistores.*

545–47. *Ut lupus . . . condit opacis:* Cf. *Aen.* 9.59–64.

568–72. A clear description of the standards of the three admirals: the lion of Venice, the eagle of the Holy Roman Empire, and the crucified Christ, sign of Pope Pius V.

579. *spoliis . . . opimis:* See note on Poem XVII, line 112.

586. *carina carinam:* The first of many displays of polyptoton, which Vergil uses to great effect in the *Aeneid* to portray scenes of civil war.

590. *Fragmina remorum:* Cf. *Aen.* 10.306–7.

591. *clamor ferit aethera:* Cf. *Aen.* 5.140, the start of the boat race.

631. *Ursinae:* Paolo Giordano Orsini.

640. *Vicine:* Vicino Orsini (also called Pier Francesco), father of Paolo, severely burned in the battle.

641–77. This extraordinary passage condemning the violence of gunfire and lamenting the impotence of the poet to prevail under such circumstances resonates with the complex Vergilian tone of many of these verses.

670. *decurrentes humano sanguine rivos:* Cf. *Aen.* 9.450–56, as the Rutulians make their way across a bloody battlefield.

481

674. *Magno miscentur caerula luctu:* Cf. the cries that spread throughout Troy at *Aen.* 2.298.

685. The two teenaged sons of Ali Pasha, Saïd and Muhammad, were taken as prisoners.

687. *Partheus* (Parthians, roughly Safavid Iran of the era, not part of the Ottoman Empire); *Caracossius* is Kara Hodja; *Assis* is Aziz Agha. *Bassarei* signifies "pashas," from the medieval *Bassa.* See Du Cange.

701–4. *Parmae . . . Castri . . . Placentinam . . . Trebiam, Tarrum . . . Novaria:* The navy brought together fighters and commanders from diverse Italian cities. See Appendix I.

712–62. *Peribis* might refer to Previs Agha, but sources do not corroborate the mistress in the sultan's inner circle. Other actions do follow chronicles: John of Austria's capture of Ali Pasha's two sons (l. 741), Onorato Caetani's capture and execution of Kara Hodja (748–61); the latter was a convert to Islam, born in Italy.

758–60. *Praedonis caput . . . magnus:* With its depiction of a beheading and the adjective *magnus,* this short passage is reminiscent of the beheading of Pompey (Magnus) in Lucan, *BC* 8.663–75.

806. *apis per candida lilia:* Cf. *Aen.* 6.707–9, *ac veluti in pratis ubi apes aestate serena / floribus insidunt variis et candida circum / lilia funduntur, strepit omnis murmure campus.*

808. *magnanimum . . . hostem:* Ali Pasha was indeed viewed favorably in a number of sources, particularly for how freed Christian galley slaves praised his "humane treatment and kindness"; see Herrera, *Relación de la guerra de Cipre,* 363.

836. *iuvenis fortissimus:* John of Austria.

Halym: Emended from Haly.

840. *Arma viri, chlamydem pictam:* This near-quotation of the opening of the *Aeneid* suggests that the result of the Battle of Lepanto was the fulfillment of the promise of the *Aeneid.*

842. *spoliis . . . opimis:* See note on Poem XVII, line 112.

858. *Sanguine . . . rubescit*: Cf. *Aen.* 8.695, description of the Battle of Actium on Aeneas's shield.

889. *sedesque beatas*: See *Aen.* 6.639, where the line ends with this phrase.

909. *traiectum pectora ferro*: See *Aen.* 1.355, where the ghost of Sychaeus appears to Dido in a dream.

910. *Nasamones*: A nomadic tribe living in modern-day Libya.

914. *non enarrabile dictu*: This echo of *Aen.* 8.625, *non enarrabile textum*, is striking, since Moizio's quotations from Vergil are thoughtfully selective.

937. *culex*: Possible allusion to the short work by the same name thought to be by Vergil.

948. *pectora foedabant pugnis atque unguibus ora*: See *Aen.* 12.871, where Juturna sees the fateful omen sent for Turnus.

965. *arma viri*: See above, line 840.

971–72. *hymnum . . . cantant*: The *Te Deum*, an early Christian hymn of praise, was traditionally ascribed to Saint Ambrose, bishop of Milan (c. 340–397).

974–76. *Conversis . . . alto*: Echoes of the beginning of Book 1 and end of Book 2 of the *Aeneid*. In the first, the Trojans are characterized as *laeti*, as they believe they are at the end of their journey; in the second, the daystar rises as Aeneas and the Trojans leave Troy. Emphasis in both is placed on new beginnings.

XXII. THE SONG OF JOHN OF AUSTRIA

Author: Juan Latino (Joannes Latinus)

Text: *Ad catholicum pariter et invictissimum Philippum Dei gratia hispaniarum regem*, Granada, Hugo Mena, 1573. A royal secretary granted approval for the publication of the poem on October 30, 1572, which suggests that the poet completed his work in time for the battle's symbolically important first anniversary. The book comprises two sections bound together with separate gatherings and folio numbers. The first consists of epigrams and elegies addressed to Philip II; his newborn heir, Prince Ferdinand

(b. December 4, 1571); and Pope Pius V. The second section features the two books of the *Austrias Carmen* (fols. 1–35 of the second gathering; A4, B–E8), followed by an epilogue ("Peroratio," F4). We have followed the witness cataloged as R/28, 263 in the Biblioteca Nacional de España (Madrid) but have also examined a copy owned by the Biblioteca Histórica of the Universidad Complutense de Madrid (FLL 11, 641). A missing line in the latter witness (236) is corrected with a marginal note, attesting to at least two printings of the *princeps*. Marginal glosses on each folio attest to Juan Latino's vocation as a schoolmaster, in that they provide clarifications targeted to Latin apprentices. Space limitations prevent a complete transcription of them; the notes below refer to glosses that provide essential contextual information. Readers can examine the glosses in the digitized copy of the Universidad Complutense witness now on Google Books. There are no known reeditions from the author's lifetime. The *Austrias Carmen* was reprinted—minus some marginal notes and the last sixteen verses (ll. 1822–38)—in volume 5 of Juan Tamayo Salazar's *Anamnesis sive Commemorationis Sanctorum Hispanorum* (Lyon, 1658, 440–78), where it marks the October 7 feast of Our Lady of the Victory, a Marian devotion promoted in the wake of the battle. A facsimile edition of the *princeps* appeared in 1971 (Kraus reprints), though it does not include an introductory study or other explanatory annotations. A 1981 Castilian translation of the *Austrias Carmen* by José Sánchez Marín lacks annotations.

Title: *Austrias Carmen* (The Song of John of Austria)

Context: The poem presents Lepanto as the culmination of a conflict that began with Granada's Morisco revolt (1568–70; see Introduction). Yet even as the poem gives voice to militant Catholic propaganda—without which the poet would not have gained publication permission—the work stands out for its sympathetic portraits of Muslim adversaries at Lepanto. These include a rare portrait of a Muslim galley slave before the battle and a tribute to the skill and magnanimity of the Ottoman admiral Ali Pasha.

1. *pietate insignis:* Cf. *Aen.* 6.403, there signaling Aeneas's virtue. Pedro de Deza was King Philip II's highest ranking official in Andalusia (here *Baetis*). The opening lines record the intertwining institutions and offices that made him so powerful: he was a high-ranking Inquisition official, president of the royal court of first instance (*Audiencia Real*), and president of the royal chancery (*Chancillería Real*). The epilogue ("Peroratio") that follows the *Austrias Carmen* (second gathering, F1–F4) states that Deza commissioned the *Austrias Carmen:* "Deza hoc opus componi iussit" (Deza ordered this work be written, F1r, n.n.).

17–25. *Pervigil . . . tumultu:* Deza spearheaded the crown's controversial repression and expulsion of Granada's Moriscos. On the connections of this event with Lepanto, see Introduction.

27. *domus . . . fori:* John of Austria stayed in Granada's Royal Chancery when he led the campaign by crown troops to quell the Morisco revolt (see Mármol Carvajal, *Historia del rebelión y castigo de los moriscos del Reino de Granada*, 6.5, fol. 134v). The government palace included Deza's living quarters, as well as law courts, a jail, and the offices of prosecutors and judges (see Harris, *From Muslim to Christian Granada*, 14).

77. *Petrus Guerrero:* Pedro de Guerrero, archbishop of Granada from 1546–76, supported the expulsion of Granada's Moriscos, despite the fact that they were baptized Christians (see Coleman, *Creating Christian Granada*, 145–76).

80. *orandi . . . lege:* Archbishop Guerrero is described as protecting Granada with the "rule of prayer," echoing the early Christian liturgical principle that prayers express belief (*lex orandi, lex credendi*; cf. Stelten, *Dictionary of Ecclesiastical Latin*).

82. *saxo . . . vetusto:* City and church officials promoted narratives of a remote Christian past in an effort to obscure the city's Muslim roots (see Harris, *From Muslim to Christian Granada*).

85. *Nuntia fama:* Cf. *Aen.* 4.174–88.

97. *spumas salis aere secabat:* Repeats the metrical positioning of *Aen.* 1.35, *spumas salis aere ruebant*, there in reference to the first direct view of the Trojan fleet on the high sea.

III. *Mare . . . Siculum:* Refers to the Mediterranean Sea east of Sicily.

114–18. *cernunt . . . Salvator mundi:* The approaching Ottoman fleet sees the crucifixion depicted on John of Austria's standard, a gift from Pius V. For a photograph of the banner, now held in Spain's *Real Armería* (Madrid), see Rodríguez-Salgado, *Armada 1588–1988,* 65.

121. *Hebraice . . . Latine:* Cf. Latin Vulgate, John 19:19–21, *scripsit . . . Pilatus . . . hebraice graece et latine.*

141. *stans celsa in puppi:* Cf. *Aen.* 8.680, there in reference to Actium.

155. *Lunae curvantur:* Muslim navies employed a loose crescent formation, the tactical advantages of which Guilmartin explains in *Gunpowder and Galleys,* 216. The crescent moon's symbolic resonance followed from its appearance on the battle standards of Muslim armies since the era of the Crusades.

192. *ensem fulmineum:* Cf. *Aen.* 4.579–80, where Aeneas cuts loose his boat to leave Carthage.

209. *Nescia mens hominum:* Foreshadows Ali Pasha's doom, drawing on *Aen.* 10.501, where Turnus tears away Pallas's belt.

245. *Scipio:* Associations of John of Austria with Publius Cornelius Scipio — who took the cognomen Africanus after defeating Hannibal in the Battle of Zama (202 BCE; cf. Livy, *AUC* 26.18–19 and 30.45) — attest to the young Habsburg's well-known aspirations to be crowned king of Tunis (see Bennassar, *Don Juan de Austria,* 170–74).

284. *regni cupidis:* John of Austria had sought the privileges reserved for official members of the royal family, but his half brother Philip II had refused to grant them; see Bennassar, *Don Juan de Austria,* 27.

295. *Getulis Syrtibus:* The Mediterranean coast of North Africa was the site of Spain's devastating loss at Djerba in 1560. See Introduction.

326. *dicere . . . tentare:* A marginal gloss identifies the statement of caution as an aphorism from Scipio (source unknown).

340. *Alea iacta est . . . parati:* Pairs Caesar's proverbial declaration of resolve with a biblical exhortation, *estote parati* (cf. Latin Vulgate, Matthew 24:44, Luke 12:40).

425. *exultat:* With the Ottoman navy in view and the fleet poised for combat, John of Austria reportedly danced a galliard on the deck of his galley to display utter confidence. See Capponi, *Victory of the West,* 265–66.

431–32. *Caesar Iulus:* Cf. Suetonius, *Jul.* 63.

434–38. *Lenisiusque . . . Mariscallos:* Luis Fernández de Córdoba oversaw John of Austria's travels. *Mariscallos* (l. 438) refers to his inherited military title of *Alférez Mayor de Córdoba.*

439–41. *Gonsalvos . . . Suessas . . . Camillos:* Gonzalo Fernández de Córdoba, the third duke of Sessa, was Juan Latino's one-time master. By the time of Lepanto, the grandee had famously accumulated a heavy debt burden, an issue the poet connects to the story of Marcus Furius Camillus as told in Livy, *AUC* 5.49.7–8.

442. *Soto:* Don Juan de Soto was John of Austria's personal secretary.

443. *Augusta Philippus:* Philip II did not secure Charles V's title of Holy Roman Emperor, yet here as elsewhere, the poet ascribes imperial qualities by attaching the Roman honorific.

468. *commendatarium maiorem amplectitur:* Luis de Requesens was the *comendador mayor* of Castile; here, the poet shows the notoriously tense relationship between Requesens and John of Austria in a positive light (cf. Bicheno, *Crescent and Cross,* 232–34).

493–95. *scindere . . . saltu:* John of Austria ordered the rams removed from galley bows to lower the level for firing guns (see Capponi, *Victory of the West,* 255–56).

505–24. *pater . . . Quintini:* Refers to Habsburg victories of the past two generations: Charles V's 1547 defeat of Protestant princes in the Battle of Mühlberg (507); Suleiman's ultimately unsuccessful siege of Vienna in 1529 (515–16); Charles V's 1535 defeat of Khaireddin Barbarossa to capture Tunis (521–22); and Philip II's 1557 victory against the French at Saint Quentin (524).

551. *velivolum pontum:* Cf. *Aen.* 1.224, there in reference to Jupiter looking out over the sea.

567–86. *Venetos . . . subsunt:* Evokes Venice's storied civic rituals (cf. Gasparo Contarini, *De magistratibus et republica venetorum* 259–82). The *templa* (577) refer to the six Venetian galleons retrofitted with heavy artillery, which dwarfed traditional galleys. Their height and weight were unprecedented in Mediterranean warfare at sea.

621. *tendentes bracchia remis:* Replicates the metrical position at *Aen.* 5.136, there in reference to the young Trojans preparing for the starting signal in the boat race: *intentatque bracchia remis.*

654. *gemuit sub pondere puppis:* Replicates the metrical position of *Aen.* 6.413, *gemuit sub pondere cumba,* there in reference to Aeneas sailing into the underworld.

682–84. *Agrippinna . . . Colona:* Agrippina the Younger, for whom Colonia Agrippinae (Cologne) was named, was murdered by her son Nero after she had suffered a wound in a shipwreck he too had plotted (see Tacitus, *Ann.* 14.1–13).

711. *armiger . . . Iovis:* Cf. *Aen.* 5.255. Associations of John of Austria with Jupiter's eagle draw on the prominence of the double-headed eagle on Habsburg flags.

754. *Deceptus Maurus:* Refers to Uluj Ali in his capacity as governor of Algiers. Ottoman commanders initially interpreted the Holy League fleet's maneuver into formation as an effort to escape toward open sea (Capponi, *Victory of the West,* 257).

776–77. *si duo . . . benignus:* Cf. Matthew 18:20.

779. *Abel:* Abel here is genitive. Proper nouns derived from Hebrew are frequently indeclinable in Latin. This form for the genitive appears in the Latin Vulgate in Luke 11:51, Matthew 23:35, and Hebrews 12:24.

789. *imprimisque . . . Veneti:* For Spanish forces, the military alliance with Venice was strategically important and unusual in light of mutual mistrust and longstanding rivalry. See Capponi, *Victory of the West,* 164–72.

793. *Sternitur aequor aquis:* Cf. Neptune in *Aen.* 5.821 (*sternitur aequor aequis*) and the personified Tiber in *Aen.* 8.89 (*sterneret aequor aquis*), with metrical position replicated in both. The two Vergilian passages in which

maritime deities protect Aeneas offer fitting allusions through which to dramatize the sudden shift in winds and calming of waters that favored the Holy League on the morning of the battle.

803–5. *sacerdotem . . . suadet*: Priests and friars traveling with the Holy League fleets heard confessions and celebrated Catholic mass as forces readied for combat (Capponi, *Victory of the West*, 264). King Philip II had ordered soldiers and commanders to undergo regular confession, in an effort to counterbalance dissolute conduct on the galleys (see *CODOIN*, vol. 28, 62–65).

828–32. *Lenisius*: Luis Fernández de Córdoba (cf. l. 434 above).

836–38. *Neptunusque . . . Tethys*: Cf. *Aen.* 1.124–56, there in reference to Neptune calming the storm. Tethys, consort of Oceanus, is conflated with Thetis, mother of Achilles.

843. *abscindere Parcas*: Foretells Ali Pasha's death in battle, in keeping with the poem's narrative structure, which follows the Lepanto chronicle from the vantage point of the citizens of Granada reading the news bulletins as they first reached the city just over a month after the battle transpired (cf. l. 85 above).

869. *castasque puellas*: Replicates the metrical position of *innuptaeque puellae* at *Aen.* 2.238 and 6.307.

872. *Myrmidones, Dolopesve*: Cf. *Aen.* 2.785, there from Creusa's lament as she bids farewell to Aeneas.

875. *Inundis* from *princeps* (fol. 18r) resolved as *in undis*.

903–4. *harundine pisces . . . piscator visus*: See Ovid, *Met.* 14.651 (Vertumnus and Pomona).

910. *fuit ille moratus*: Before the Ottoman invasion of Cyprus.

921–24. *Epiri . . . Syrtibus*: Refers to Ottoman victories at Preveza (*Epirus*) and Djerba (*Getulis Syrtibus*), which had fomented belief in the invincibility of the sultan's fleets.

936. *Appellat . . . Hispanos*: A marginal gloss in the *princeps* (fol. 19r) directs readers to Livy *AUC* 1.2.4–5, offering a Roman imperial precedent for how the Spanish monarchy unites diverse nations.

948. *ardentes oculos*: Replicates the metrical positioning of *ardentis oculos* in Vergil, *Geo*. 4.451, there in reference to the blazing eyes of the sea god and prophet Proteus.

969. *nec poteris . . . Philippi*: The Ottoman admiral prays that his flagship never carry the Spanish standard, which displays the crucifixion (*Dominum*), nor bear John of Austria (in the event of capture).

976. *Quo diversus agis*: Adapts and replicates the metrical positioning of *Aen*. 5.166–77, *quo diversus abis*, there in reference to Gyas's anger at his pilot's tactical blunder in the Trojan boat race.

980. *Pandite nunc*: Cf. *Aen*. 7.641.

983. *magnanimosque duces . . . proelia, numquam*: The apostrophe to Pedro de Deza as patron echoes Vergil's promise of an epic poem to Maecenas in *Geo*. 4.4–5.

992–94. *signis aquilarum . . . fixus*: Another evocation of the standards identifying John of Austria's flagship, which included the Habsburg eagle (cf. 711 above) and the crucifixion (cf. 114–18).

999–1003. *grues . . . clangentes*: Cf. *Aen*. 10.263–66, there in reference to the Trojans poised for battle against the Rutulians; cf. Lucretius, *DRN* 4.181, where the cranes' clamor (*clamor in aetheriis dispersus nubibus austri*) is unfavorably compared with the swan's song. Cf. also Mart. 13.75, as well as Cicero's commentary on the "wonder" of this phenomenon (*ND* 2.49).

1014. *accipiunt undam*: Cf. *Aen*. 1.123, *accipiunt inimicum imbrem*, there in reference to the storm that batters the Trojan fleet.

1034–35. *tanta mole*: Cf. *Aen*. 1.33 and 8.693.

1033–35. *Mendozius heros*: In the Battle of the Island of Alborán (October 1, 1540), Bernardino de Mendoza defeated the Barbary corsairs Al Borani and Ali Hamet (transliterated as Caramano and Aliamat). See Herrera, *Relación de la guerra de Chipre*, 337.

1044. *excutitur . . . pronus in hostem*: Cf. *Aen*. 1.115, *excutitur pronusque magister*, another allusion to the storm that Juno unleashes on the Trojan fleet.

1054. *Byzantum*: Syncopated form of *Byzantium*.

1061. *comminus ense*: Cf. *Aen.* 9.347, with a replication of metrical positioning. The allusion is the first of a chain of references to the story of Nisus and Euryalus, here referring to the latter's slaughter of the Latin sentry Rhoetus.

1063. *custodes . . . obstant*: Philip II required John of Austria to submit tactical decisions to a trio of senior advisors. John openly chafed at the restrictions and ultimately disobeyed his brother's order not to engage in direct combat. See Capponi, *Victory of the West*, 223; and Bicheno, *Crescent and Cross*, 268.

1073. *delphinum similes*: Cf. *Aen.* 5.594, there in reference to the Trojan swimming contest.

1085. *pulchrum . . . in armis*: Cf. *Aen.* 2.317.

1090–91. *fulmen belli . . . Horia*: The Genoese commander Giovanni Andrea Doria appears here with reference to the Scipios in *Aen.* 6.842.

1093. *telorumque seges*: Cf. *Aen.* 3.46, there in reference to Thracian treachery in the story of Polydorus. A marginal gloss in the *princeps* expands the theme, noting "ne sagittis pugnes cum Parthis" (may you never battle Parthian archers), echoing the longstanding — often specious — European allegation that Muslim archers used poisoned arrows. See Fallows, "Against the Arabs."

1102. *Stuppea flamma*: Cf. *Aen.* 8.694, there in reference to Actium. Vulcan's art (*Vulcani ex arte*) refers to the complex, even esoteric skills that gunnery in Mediterranean galley warfare required (see Guilmartin, *Gunpowder and Galleys*, 182).

1105–7. *Commendatari . . . Faventini Barcino*: *Commendatari* draws more on the Catalan term for "the receptor or guardian of an order or instruction" (see Alcover, *Diccionari català–Valencià*, III, 319) than on the Medieval Latin term denoting ecclesiastical authority (cf. Du Cange). The celebration of Catalan forces at Lepanto draws on Barcelona's Roman name, Colonia Faventia Julia Augusta Pia Barcino. On the pivotal role of Catalans on the Spanish command ship, see Herrera, *Relación de la guerra de Chipre*, 320.

1115–17. *Parthenopes . . . Gens campana:* Marginal glosses in the *princeps* (fol. 22r) attest to the poet's pedagogical vocation, as they instruct the reader that Naples took its name from the siren Parthenope (cf. Plin. *Nat.* 3.28).

1131. *fluctus . . . caede rubescunt:* Cf. *Aen.* 8.695, there in reference to bloodshed at Actium.

1135. *pube tenus:* Cf. *Aen.* 3.426–27, the Trojan passage through Scylla and Charybdis.

1137. *innantes gurgite vasto:* Cf. *Aen.* 3.421 (Scylla and Charybdis) and 1.118 (opening storm).

1151. *candentes:* Refers to the crosses that adorned the clothing and armor of noblemen, signifying their membership in prestigious military orders.

1152. *commendatari:* See line 1105 above.

1158. *Turcas iam notos:* Holy League commanders slaughtered several hundred Ottoman officers without trying to take them prisoner (see *CODOIN,* vol. 3, 219) in addition to captives seized for ransom or slavery.

1170. *sanctam navem:* The flagship of the Knights of Saint John (Malta), which Uluj Ali captured.

1177. *inimica nomina gentis:* Cf. *Aen.* 11.84. Memories of how the Knights of Saint John broke the prolonged Ottoman Siege of Malta in 1565 remained a powerful inspiration for both sides at Lepanto (see Introduction).

1192. *Hannibalem referens:* Compares the Venetian commander Agostino Barbarigo's mortal eye injury to the eye Hannibal lost in the Second Punic War; cf. Livy, *AUC* 22.13.

1193. *Placida nunc morte quiescam:* Repeats the metrical positioning of *Aen.* 6.371, *placidis in morte quiescam,* there in reference to Palinurus's plea for Aeneas to take him across the River Styx.

1196. *magno clamore videntum:* Replicates the metrical positioning of *multo clamore sequuntur* in *Aen.* 9.466, there in reference to the doomed Nisus and Euryalus.

1198. *ora . . . fluentia tabo:* Echoes a chain of violent deaths; cf. *Aen.* 3.626 (the devoured companions of Achaemenides), 8.197 (the victims of Cacus), and 9.472 (impaled heads of Nisus and Euryalus). A marginal gloss in the *princeps* (fol. 23v) paraphrases Vergil's apostrophe from *Aen.* 9.446–49, "Eurali et Nisi sic capita Vergil cecinit."

1211. *Sunt . . . laudi:* Cf. *Aen.* 1.461, there in honor of Priam's lasting fame. On freed Christian galley slaves' praises for the Ottoman admiral, see Herrera, *Relación de la guerra de Chipre,* 363.

1216–17. *Augusta Philippo . . . victoria sancto:* Cf. 443 above for the symbolic "imperial" honor the poet confers on Philip II, a dimension to which the *princeps* adds typographical emphasis with *VICTORIA* capitalized in line 1217.

1221. *par nobile fratrum:* Cf. Horace, *Serm.* 2.3.243.

1222. *cuspide pili:* Cf. Lucan, *BC* 1.242.

1252. *convertite ferrum:* Cf. *Aen.* 9.427.

1274. *ullam sperare salutem:* Replicates the metrical positioning of *Aen.* 2.354, *nullam sperare salutem,* there from Aeneas's account of his rush to defend the burning Troy.

1279. *rapto . . . saepe videbat:* A subtle reference to the notorious looting of the Spanish forces who suppressed Granada's Morisco revolt. See Introduction.

1280. *cornua rauca:* Cf. *Aen.* 7.615 and Lucan, *BC* 1.238.

1282. *hoc . . . nomine:* Refers to the Turk's name or Allah, in implied contrast with the *nomine Christi* of the Holy League forces. Turkish battle standards were embroidered with Allah's name, as attested in a Spanish officer's description of the standard captured from the Ottoman flagship (see *CODOIN,* vol. 3, 270–73).

1283. *aere canoro:* Cf. *Aen.* 9.503.

1287. *subiectis more pepercit:* A marginal gloss in the *princeps* (fol. 25r) depicts John of Austria as a magnanimous victor, echoing the Vergilian prophecy of Roman imperial virtue in *Aen.* 6.853: *Parecere subiectis et debel-*

lare superbos. In reality, the first-line battle report sent from the Spanish command element at Lepanto offers a matter-of-fact account of how Spaniards summarily executed Ali Pasha and five hundred other high-ranking Ottoman fighters (see *CODOIN*, vol. 3, 219).

1291. *revomentes pectore fluctus:* Cf. *Aen.* 5.182, in which an angry Gyas throws Menoetes overboard in the boat race.

1302–10. *seditione . . . pectora mulcet:* Cf. *Aen.* 1.148–53, there in the simile that compares Neptune calming the opening storm to a statesman calming a riot. The judge Nabbas (1309) is Doctor Navas de Puebla; his mention attests to the poet's access to inside information, since his name does not appear in published bulletins (cf. Archivo General de Simancas, "Lepanto papers," documents 76 and 182).

1324–26. *seriem longam:* Cf. *Aen.* 1.641, *series longissima,* there in reference to Dido's banquet tables.

1352–53. *nuntia . . . Famaque:* Cf. *Aen.* 4.174–88. The Algerian *claustra* in line 1347 (*bagnios,* slave houses) did indeed connect to Mediterranean communications networks through merchants, corsairs, and captives (see Garcés, *Early Modern Dialogue,* 233 and 243).

1374–76. *Hispanosque duces . . . regale:* Conveys the Spanish monarchy's most powerful governing bodies through Roman terms (Council of State, Council of Castile, and the Council of War), noting the power of Cardinal Diego de Espinosa, president of the Council of Castile and inquisitor general. See Parker, *Felipe II,* 532.

1378. *non enarrabile fatum:* Repeats the metrical positioning of *Aen.* 8.625, *non enarrabile textum,* there in reference to Aeneas's shield.

1390. *cantaret in ora:* Cf. *Aen.* 4.195, *diffundit in ora,* there in reference to Fama.

1396–1403. *Pellebam . . . Philippi:* Pedro de Deza supervised the controversial expulsion of Moriscos from Granada to other locales under the jurisdiction of the Crown of Castile, the realm where the king lived, conveyed as *moenia . . . regis.* Cf. lines 17–25.

1434. *Crassum*: Marcus Licinius Crassus (115–53 BCE), Roman governor of the province of Syria, was defeated and then murdered by the Parthians (see Plutarch, *Crass.* 33).

1451–54. *Caroli . . . Saxoniumque*: Refers to Charles V's 1547 victory over the alliance of German-Protestant princes in the Battle of Mühlberg.

1467. *Bernardine vale*: Bernardino de Cárdenas. The identity of the second fallen fighter mentioned here is unknown. Cf. Horace, *Carm.* 2.16, *nihil ex omni parte beatum*, and *Aen.* 11.98, there in reference to Aeneas mourning Pallas.

1472. *victores . . . potiti*: Cf. *Aen.* 9.450, which reveals yet another echo of the doomed raid of Nisus and Euryalus: *victores praeda Rutuli spoliisque potiti*.

1479. *claustra Pelori*: Cf. *Aen.* 3.412, there in reference to the first Trojan view of Sicily.

1480. *Fama volans*: Cf. *Aen.* 4.174–88.

1508. *Petrum . . . undas*: See Latin Vulgate *Matthew* 14:28–33.

1509. *currus Pharaonis*: Cf. Latin Vulgate *Exodus* 14:15–21, the parting of the Red Sea.

1576–78. *Fama . . . implet*: Cf. *Aen.* 4.246–56, there in reference to Mercury crossing the Atlas Mountains.

1584–89. *Vasconesque . . . Cantaber . . . Astur*: Refers to the inhabitants of the northernmost peninsular lands ruled by the Spanish monarchy, drawing on notions of their ancestral resistance to outside conquerors. On the story of Basque cannibalism during a siege, a marginal note in the *princeps* (fol. 30v) refers to Plutarch, *De Esu.* 2, and Juvenal, *Sat.* 5.15. Metellus (l. 1584) is Caecilius Metellus, the Roman consul who campaigned to subdue the Celtiberians of northern Hispania but could not overcome the resistance of Numantia and Termantia in 143 BCE (cf. Appian, *Hisp.* 13.76).

1626. *Didacus . . . Spinosa*: On Cardinal Diego de Espinosa, see 1374–75 above.

1644–52. *fama . . . garrula . . . Indus:* Cf. Sen. *Her.* 194–95. The battle news reaches the Nile region and then spreads eastward to Asia. The "walls of Cadmus" conflates the Egyptian city of Thebai with the Greek city of Thebes. The passage refers to Philip II's well documented aspirations to universal monarchy, which intensified in the wake of Lepanto.

1691. *horisque simillima:* Cf. Fuenmayor, *Vida y hechos de Pío V,* 233. Pius V was reported to have miraculously sensed the victory on October 7.

1706–8. *ex conspectu Siculae . . . certamine:* Cf. *Aen.* 1.34–35.

1710. *sale tabentis artus:* Cf. *Aen.* 1.173, there in reference to the storm-ravaged Trojans landing on Libyan shores.

1727. *senique duces:* Identities unknown.

1738. *Expleri nequeunt:* Cf. *Aen.* 8.618.

1743. *officii sancti patres:* The Inquisition, known officially as the Holy Office of the Inquisition.

1745. *Marchio . . . Pescarae:* The viceroy of Sicily, Francesco Fernando Avalos, Marquis of Pescara, had died before Lepanto (July 31, 1571); however, the family — with retainers and relatives — would have been prominent in Messina's triumphal parade after the battle, since Philip II had not yet named a replacement.

1748. *in numerumque:* Refers to the Habsburg ceremonial practice of appearing in processions according to rank.

1757–58. *expugnetque . . . sepulchrum:* Advisors to Philip II devised plans for reconquering Constantinople and Jerusalem, with some urging the king to revive the imperial title of Byzantine emperors (see Parker, *The Grand Strategy,* 101).

1788. *ne sumere:* Pius V threatened excommunication to any fighters who retained war spoils without authorization, though foot soldiers and officers alike flouted the order with near impunity (see Capponi, *Victory of the West,* 288).

1795. *pueri, castaeque puellae:* Replicates the metrical positioning of *Aen.* 2.238 and 6.307.

1803. *aemula virtus:* Cf. Lucan, *BC* 1.120, there in reference to the rivalry between Pompey and Caesar.

1822–23. *rumor . . . moenia complet . . . natum:* Crown Prince Ferdinand was born on December 4, 1571. The spreading news in Granada (*moenia complet*) parallels Lucan, *BC* 1.468, there in reference to rumors of an imminent civil war.

Bibliography

Alcover, Antoni María. *Diccionari Català–Valencià–Balear*. Palma de Mallorca, 1954.

Barbarics, Zsuzsa, and Renate Pieper. "Handwritten Newsletters as Means of Communication in Early Modern Europe." In *Correspondence and Cultural Exchange in Europe, 1400–1700*, edited by Francisco Bethencourt and Florike Egmond, 53–79. Vol 3 of 4 of *Cultural Exchange in Early Modern Europe*. Cambridge, 2007.

Barbero, Alessandro. *Lepanto: La battaglia dei tre imperi*. Bari, 2010.

Barsi, Silvio. *La battaglia di Lepanto e il De bello turcico di Bernardino Leo*. Milan, 2008.

Bazzano, Nicoletta. *Marco Antonio Colonna*. Rome, 2003.

Bennassar, Bartolomé. *Don Juan de Austria: Un héroe para un imperio*. Madrid, 2000.

Benzoni, Gino, ed. *Il Mediterraneo nella seconda metà del 500 alla luce di Lepanto*. Florence, 1974.

Bicheno, Hugh. *Crescent and Cross: The Battle of Lepanto 1571*. London, 2003.

Brown, Peter. *The Medieval Cult of Saints: Its Rise and Function in Western Christianity*. Chicago, 1982.

Caetani, Onorato, and Gerolamo Diedo. *La battaglia di Lepanto (1571)*. Edited by Salvatore Mazzarella. Palermo, 1995.

Capponi, Niccolò. *Victory of the West: The Story of the Battle of Lepanto*. London, 2006.

Casale, Giancarlo. "The Ethnic Composition of Ottoman Ship Crews and the 'Rumi Challenge' to Portuguese Identity." *Medieval Encounters* 13 (2007): 122–44.

Catena, Girolamo. *Vita del gloriosissimo Papa Pio Quinto*. Rev. ed. Rome, 1587.

CODOIN (*Colección de documentos inéditos para la historia de España*). Edited by Martín Fernández de Navarrete et al. Vol. 3 (Lepanto Documents), Vol. 21 (Herrera Account of Lepanto), Vol. 28 (Morisco Revolt of Granada). Madrid, 1843–56.

Coleman, David. *Creating Christian Granada: Society and Religious Culture in an Old-World Frontier City, 1492–1600*. Ithaca, 2003.

Contarini, Gasparo. *De magistratibus et republica venetorum*. In *Opera omnia*. Paris, 1571.

Contarini, Giovanni Pietro. *Historia delle cose successe dal principio della guerra mossa da Selim ottomano a venetiani fino al dì della gran giornata vittoriosa contra turchi*. Venice, 1572.

Coreth, Anna. *Pietas Austriaca* (1959, rev. ed. 1982). Translated by William D. Bowman and Anna Maria Leitgeb. West Lafayette, IN, 2004.

Crowley, Roger. *Empires of the Sea: The Siege of Malta, the Battle of Lepanto, and the Contest for the Center of the World*. New York, 2009.

Database of Latin Dictionaries. Online ed. Brepols Publishers.

Diedo, Gerolamo. "La Battaglia di Lepanto descritta da Gerolamo Diedo." In Caetani and Diedo, *La battaglia di Lepanto (1571)*, 177–224.

Dionisotti, Carlo. "Lepanto nella cultura italiana del tempo." In Benzoni, *Il Mediterraneo nella seconda metà del 500 alla luce di Lepanto*, 127–51.

Discorso sopra due grandi e memorabili battaglie navali fatte nel mondo, l'una di Cesare Augusto con M. Antonio, altra delli sig. Venetiani, e della Santissima Lega con Sultan Selim, signor di Turchi. Bologna, 1572.

Dizionario biografico degli italiani (abbrev. as *Dizionario*). Rome, 1960–.

Elliott, J. H. *Imperial Spain: 1469–1716*. London, 1990. First published London, 1963.

Fallows, Noel. "Against the Arabs: Propaganda and Paradox in Medieval Castile." In *Medieval Iberia: Changing Societies and Cultures in Contact and Transition*, edited by Ivy A. Corfis and Ray Harris-Northall, 57–69. London, 2007.

Fenlon, Iain. *The Ceremonial City: History, Memory and Myth in Renaissance Venice*. New Haven, 2007.

Fra-Molinero, Baltasar. "Juan Latino and his Racial Difference." In *Black Africans in Renaissance Europe*, edited by T. F. Earle and K. J. P. Lowe, 326–44. Cambridge, 2005.

Fuchs, Barbara. *Exotic Nation: Maurophilia and the Construction of Early Modern Spain*. Philadelphia, 2008.

Fuenmayor, Antonio de. *Vida y hechos de Pío V* (1595). Edited by Lorenzo Riber. Madrid, 1953.

Garcés, María Antonia, ed. *An Early Modern Dialogue with Islam: Antonio de Sosa's* Topography of Algiers (1612). Translated by Diana de Armas Wilson. Notre Dame, IN, 2011.

Gates, Henry Louis, Jr., and Maria Wolff. "An Overview of Sources on the Life and Work of Juan Latino, the 'Ethiopian' Humanist." *Research in African Literatures: The African Diaspora and its Origins* 29.4 (1998): 14–51.

Göllner, Carl von. *Turcica: Die europäischen Türkendurcke des CVI. Jahrhunderts.* Vol. 2 of 3 (1551 to 1600). Bibliotheca Bibliographica Aureliana 23. Bucharest, 1968.

Grant, W. Leonard. *Neo-Latin Literature and the Pastoral.* Chapel Hill, 1965.

Guilmartin, John Francis Jr. *Gunpowder and Galleys: Changing Technology and Mediterranean Warfare at Sea in the 16th Century.* 1974. Rev. ed. London, 2003.

Hankins, James. "Renaissance Crusaders: Humanist Crusade Literature in the Age of Mehmed II." *Dumbarton Oaks Papers* 49, Symposium on Byzantium and the Italians, 13th–15th Centuries (1995): 111–207.

Hardie, Philip R. *Rumour and Renown: Representations of* Fama *in Western Literature.* Cambridge, 2012.

Harper, James, ed. *The Turk and Islam in the Western Eye, 1450–1750.* Farnham, Surrey, UK, 2011.

Harris, A. Katie. *From Muslim to Christian Granada: Inventing a City's Past in Early Modern Spain.* Baltimore, 2007.

Heim, Bruno Bernard. *Coutumes et droit héraldiques de l'Église.* Paris, 1949.

Herrera, Fernando de. *Relación de la guerra de Chipre y suceso de la Batalla Naval de Lepanto.* In *CODOIN*, vol. 21, 243–382.

Hess, Andrew C. "The Battle of Lepanto and Its Place in Mediterranean History." *Past and Present* 57 (1972): 53–73.

——— . "The Moriscos: An Ottoman Fifth Column in Sixteenth-Century Spain." *American Historical Review* 74.1 (1968): 125.

Inalcik, Halil. "Lepanto in the Ottoman Documents." In Benzoni, *Il Mediterraneo nella seconda metà del 500 alla luce di Lepanto,* 185–92.

Jordan, Jenny. *Imagined Lepanto: Turks, Mapbooks, Intrigue, and Spectacular in the Sixteenth Century Construction of 1571.* PhD diss., UCLA, 2004.

Kallendorf, Craig. *Virgil and the Myth of Venice: Books and Readers in the Italian Renaissance.* Oxford, 1999.

Lesure, Michel. *Lépante: La crise de l'empire ottoman.* Paris, 1972.

López de Toro, José. *Los poetas de Lepanto.* Madrid, 1950.

Mammana, Simona. *Lèpanto: Rime per la vittoria sul Turco. Regesto (1571–1573) e studio critico.* Rome, 2007.

Mármol Carvajal, Luis del. *Historia de la rebelión y castigo de los moriscos del Reino de Granada.* Málaga, 1600.

Mitchell, Bonner. "Charles V as *Triumphator.*" In *Carolvs V, Imperator,* English supplement 4752. Edited by Pedro Navascués Palacio. Barcelona, 1999.

Mulryne, J. R., et al. *Europa Triumphans: Court and Civic Festivals in Early Modern Europe.* Vol. 1 of 2. Aldershot, 2004.

Nebrija, Elio Antonio de. *Dictionarium Latinohispanicum, et vice versa Hispanicolatinum: Ad haec Dictionarium propriorum nominum* (abbrev. Nebrija). Antwerp, 1560.

Ortelius, Abraham. *Synonymia Geographica.* Antwerp, 1578.

Panofsky, Erwin. *Renaissance and Renascences in Western Art.* Stockholm, 1960.

Parker, Geoffrey. *Felipe II: La biografía definitiva.* Translated by Victoria Eugenia Gordo. Edited by Santiago Martínez Hernández. Barcelona, 2010.

——. *The Grand Strategy of Philip II.* New Haven, 1998.

Paruta, Paolo. *Historia vinetiana.* Venice, 1645.

Pastor, Ludwig. *The History of the Popes from the Close of the Middle Ages: Drawn from the Secret Archives of the Vatican and Other Original Sources.* Vol. 19 of 40, edited by Ralph Francis Kerr. London, 1938–61.

Paul, Benjamin. "'And the Moon Has Started to Bleed': Apocalypticism and Religious Reform in Venetian Art at the Time of the Battle of Lepanto." In Harper, *The Turk and Islam in the Western Eye, 1450–1750,* 67–94.

Porcacchi, Thomaso. *L'isole più famose del mondo.* Venice, 1572; expanded ed., 1576.

Putnam, Michael C. J. *Virgil's Epic Designs: Ekphrasis in the Aeneid.* New Haven, 1998.

Quint, David. *Epic and Empire: Politics and Generic Form from Virgil to Milton.* Princeton, 1993.

Randel, Mary Gaylord. *The Historical Prose of Fernando de Herrera.* London, 1971.

Rodríguez-Salgado, M. J., ed. *Armada 1588–1988: An International Exhibition to Commemorate the Spanish Armada.* Exhibition catalog, National Maritime Museum, London, 1988.

Seo, J. Mira. "Identifying Authority: Juan Latino, an African Ex-Slave, Professor, and Poet in Sixteenth-Century Granada." In *African Athena: New Agendas,* edited by Daniel Orrells, Gurminder K. Bhambra, and Tessa Roynon, 258–276. New York, 2011.

Setton, Kenneth M. *The Papacy and the Levant (1204–1571): The Sixteenth Century from Julius III to Pius V.* Vol. 4 of 4. Philadelphia, 1984.

Spence, Sarah, and Michèle Lowrie, eds. *The Aesthetics of Empire and the Reception of Vergil.* Special Issue, *Literary Imagination* 8.3 (2006).

Strunck, Christina. "The Barbarous and Noble Enemy: Pictorial Representations of the Battle of Lepanto." In Harper, *The Turk and Islam in the Western Eye,* 1450–1750, 217–42.

Talbert, Richard J. A., ed. *Barrington Atlas of the Greek and Roman World* (abbrev. *Barrington Atlas*). Princeton, 2000.

Twombly, Cy, with Richard Howard and Kirk Varnedoe. *Lepanto: A Painting in Twelve Parts.* New York, 2002.

Vaccaluzzo, Nunzio. "Dei poeti latini della battaglia di Lepanto." *Archivio Storico per la Sicilia Orientale.* 6.2–3 (1909): 197–226.

Wright, Elizabeth R. "Narrating the Ineffable Lepanto: The *Austrias Carmen* of Joannes Latinus (Juan Latino)." *Hispanic Review* 77.1 (2009): 71–91.

Wu Ming, *Altai.* Turin, 2009.

LIST OF ARCHIVAL SOURCES

Archivio Biografico Italiano (abbrev. ABI I) and Archivio Biografico Italiano Nuova Serie (abbrev, ABI II). Munich: K. G. Saur.

Archivo General de Simancas (Estado, legajo 1134). "Lepanto papers."

Index of First Lines

❦

Index

❧❧

Notes in this volume are numbered according to line numbers of the Latin text. Notes covering multiple lines are here referenced by the first line number; thus 436n108 refers to the note on page 436 to lines 108–29 of Poem I, Malatesta's *Song of the Nereids*. References to unnumbered notes are given as page number plus n; thus 435n refers to the unnumbered note to Poem I, appearing on page 435.

Doria, Giovanni Andrea, xi, xiii–xiv,
101, 129, 141–43, 157, 207, 215, 231,
245, 251, 311, 357, 373, 379, 409,
412, 425, 429, 473n319, 480n485,
491n1090
Doriclus, 123
Doris, 171, 189, 205, 223, 412
Drances, 444n17
Dryads, 189
Drymo, 203

Ebro (river), 219, 231, 413
Echinades (Curzolaris Islands), 75,
149, 189, 408, 412
Egypt/Egyptians, 75, 193, 311, 383,
393, 403, 414
Elba, 175, 465n221, 414
Elbe (river), 321
Elijah (prophet), 451n1114
Elis, 211
Elysian grove, 171
Endymion, 65, 448n3
Ennius, 458n88, 470n95; *Annals*,
470n65
Entellus, 449n4
Eos, 438n1
Epirus, Isthmus of, 295, 347, 412
Erebus, 21, 57, 131, 211; daughters of,
59
Eridanus, 233, 412, 435n55
Erinys, 15
Erycina, 27
Eryx (mount), 441n5
Espinosa, Cardinal Diego de, 375,
391, 494n1374, 495n1626
Ethiopians, 209, 393, 403
Ethon, 59, 447n1111
Etruscans, 464n118

Euboeans, 75, 245
Euboia island (Negroponte), 412,
451n83
Eumenides, 51, 55, 119. *See also* Furies
Euphrates (river), 15, 437n43
Euridamas (speaker in Poem XVI),
119–45, 457n19
Euripides, *Heraclids*, 471n1161
Europe, xiv, 31, 39, 55, 157, 163, 165,
169, 195, 205, 221, 309
Euryalus, 453n98, 454n69, 461n28,
476n11, 491n1061, 492n1196,
493n1198, 495n1472
Eurydice, 21, 57
Evander, 452n23
Evening (personification), 169
Evenus (river), 179, 412

Fabaris, 133
Fama (personification), xx, 65, 75,
123, 125, 169, 283, 293–95, 345,
373, 381–83, 387–89, 391–95,
447n111, 449n18, 449n20, 458n59,
464n127, 470n65, 494n1390
Famagusta, xii–xiii, 418, 419,
444n45, 444n61
Farnese, Alessandro, x, 5, 109, 219,
231, 253, 269–73, 435n45, 456n331,
476n, 477n73, 480n437
Farnese, Ottavio (duke of Parma),
109, 456n331
Fates, 9, 13, 23, 43, 77, 79, 91, 93, 113,
173, 175, 197, 297, 303, 309, 319,
341, 345, 347
Faunus, 217
Favii, 171
Fear (personification), 55, 59, 61, 63

§§§§

§

Scylla, 23, 203, 341, 345, 439n34, 440n79, 492n1135, 492n1137

Scythia/Scythians, 15, 39, 41, 91, 95, 101, 107, 147, 153, 179, 187, 191, 199, 205, 211, 219, 223, 413, 419, 461n101

Second Punic War, 492n1192

Second Revolt of the Alpujarras (Morisco Revolt of Granada), xii, xxiii, 414, 484, 485n27, 493n1279

Selim II (sultan; Tyrant, Thracian Tyrant, etc.), xii, 15, 23, 33, 35, 45, 47, 57, 61, 63, 69, 83, 99, 107, 123, 153, 161–63, 173, 185, 195–99, 223, 227, 229, 251, 261, 271, 283–85, 295, 297, 299, 301, 303, 319, 321, 335, 339, 341, 345, 347, 355, 367, 371, 377, 379, 385, 387, 391, 393, 397, 401, 403, 408, 419, 444n10, 445n, 448n4, 461n88, 469n22, 471n187

Seneca the Younger (Lucius Annaeus Seneca the Younger), *Madness of Hercules*, 496n1644

Sessa, dukes of, 315–17, 487n439

Seville, 261, 413

Sforza, Paolo, 255, 480n458

Sibyl, 446n32, 446n90, 447n168, 463n29

Sicily, Sea of, 199, 295

Sicily/Sicilians, 53, 147, 203, 205, 211, 231, 233, 255, 381, 397–99, 417, 437n35, 441n5, 470n144, 471n178, 472n256, 486n111, 495n1479, 496n1745

Sinon, 452n16, 453n78, 461n143

Sirens, 203

Sisyphus, 59

Sleep (personification), 59

Smyrna, 219, 420, 474n404

Socrates, 267

Solymaeus, 215, 473n319

Solymites, 255

Somnia, 446n97

Sophocles, *Oedipus the King*, 468n250

Soranzo, Benedetto, 133, 221, 245, 459n211, 474n430, 479n301

Soto, Don Juan de, 317, 487n442

Spain/Spanish, ix, xi, xiii–xv, xx, xxiii n7, 3, 13, 21, 53, 75, 93, 97, 107, 125, 135, 137, 139, 165, 177, 199, 201, 205, 207, 221, 231, 261, 271, 273, 277, 283, 291, 293, 295, 297, 299, 305, 307, 309, 311, 317, 319, 321, 323, 329, 333, 335, 337, 343, 345, 347, 349, 351, 353, 355–57, 359, 367, 369, 373–75, 377, 379, 389, 391, 393, 397, 399, 401, 403, 405, 418, 441n5, 469n64, 470n99, 471n169, 472n259, 477n73, 486n295, 488n789, 489n936, 490n969, 491n1105, 493n1279, 494n1287, 494n1374, 495n1584

Spartans, 247

Spinola, Ettore, 442n

Stassyn, 219

Statius, Publius Papinius: *Achilleid*, 478n197, 478n230; *Thebaid*, 444n11, 466n21

Stephen, Saint, Order of, 255, 480n441

Publication of this volume has been made possible by

The Myron and Sheila Gilmore Publication Fund at I Tatti
The Robert Lehman Endowment Fund
The Jean-François Malle Scholarly Programs and Publications Fund
The Andrew W. Mellon Scholarly Publications Fund
The Craig and Barbara Smyth Fund
for Scholarly Programs and Publications
The Lila Wallace–Reader's Digest Endowment Fund
The Malcolm Wiener Fund for Scholarly Programs and Publications